SHERWOOD ANDERSON

KIM TOWNSEND

SHERWOOD ANDERSON

A *Richard Todd Book*

HOUGHTON MIFFLIN COMPANY   BOSTON   1987

Library of Congress Cataloging-in-Publication Data

Townsend, Kim.
Sherwood Anderson.
   "A Richard Todd book."
   Bibliography: p.
   Includes index.
   1. Anderson, Sherwood, 1876–1941 — Biography.
   2. Authors, American — 20th century — Biography.
   I. Title.
PS3501.N4Z87   1987   813'.52   [B]   87-12580
ISBN 0-395-36533-3

Printed in the United States of America

P 10 9 8 7 6 5 4 3 2 1

The author is grateful for permission to quote from the following works:

Winesburg, Ohio by Sherwood Anderson. Copyright 1919 by B. W. Huebsch. Copyright
renewed 1947 by Eleanor Copenhaver Anderson. Reprinted by permission of Viking Penguin,
Inc.

Sherwood Anderson: Selected Letters, edited by Charles E. Modlin. Copyright © 1984 by The
University of Tennessee Press/Knoxville. The Sherwood Anderson letters in this volume
copyright © 1984 by Eleanor C. Anderson.

The Torrents of Spring by Ernest Hemingway. Copyright 1926 by Charles Scribner's Sons;
copyright renewed 1954 by Ernest Hemingway. Reprinted with the permission of Charles
Scribner's Sons.

Every effort has been made to locate the authors of unpublished letters to Sherwood Anderson
to obtain permission to reprint them. Any errors or omissions are unintentional, and
corrections will be made in any future editions if necessary.

To
Marty

Contents

	List of Illustrations	*ix*
	Preface	*xi*
1	"Jobby": 1876–1896	*1*
2	"The Undeveloped Man": 1896–1906	*31*
3	Breakdown: 1906–1912	*58*
4	Becoming a Writer: 1912–1915	*83*
5	"Emerging Greatness": 1915–1917	*109*
6	Unrest: 1917–1919	*135*
7	Alabama and Paris: 1920–1921	*162*
8	Another Flight: 1921–1922	*184*
9	Tutoring Faulkner and Hemingway: 1922–1926	*203*
10	Withdrawal: 1926–1929	*233*
11	The Political Years: 1929–1933	*253*
12	Finally at Ease: 1933–1940	*287*
13	Starting Out Again: 1941	*316*
	Notes	*327*
	Selected Bibliography	*356*
	Index	*358*

Illustrations

Following page 114

Emma Smith Anderson (By permission of the Newberry Library)
Irwin McLain Anderson (By permission of the Newberry Library)
The Anderson children, ca. 1886 (By permission of the Newberry Library)
"Jobby" (Courtesy of Marion Anderson Spear)
Bicycle factory, Clyde (By permission of the Newberry Library)
The Anderson children, ca. 1896 (By permission of the Newberry Library)
Members of Company I (By permission of the Newberry Library)
"The Undeveloped Man," 1904 (By permission of the Newberry Library)
Cornelia Platt Lane (Courtesy of Marion Anderson Spear)
The Anderson family, 1909 (Courtesy of Marion Anderson Spear)
The Anderson Manufacturing Company (By permission of the Newberry Library)

Following page 242

The Andersons in the Ozarks, 1913–1914 (Courtesy of Marion Anderson Spear)
Anderson back at Taylor-Critchfield, 1914 (Courtesy of Marion Anderson Spear)
Tennessee Claflin Mitchell (By permission of the Newberry Library)
Members of the Fifty-seventh Street colony, 1914 (Courtesy of Marion Anderson Spear)
Marietta ("Bab") Finley (By permission of the University of Illinois Press)
Anderson on Lake Chateaugay, 1917 (By permission of the Newberry Library)
Anderson, by Alfred Stieglitz, 1923 (© The Art Institute of Chicago. All rights reserved.)
Elizabeth Norman Prall and Anderson, by Imogen Cunningham, 1923 (By permission of The Imogen Cunningham Trust)
Anderson caricatured, 1926 (By permission of the University of Texas Press. Caricature by William Spratling © 1966 from *Sherwood Anderson and Other Creoles* by William Spratling and William Faulkner.)
"He left his factory" (By permission of the Newberry Library)
Ripshin (Courtesy of Marion Anderson Spear)
Eleanor Copenhaver (By permission of the Newberry Library)
Eleanor Copenhaver and Anderson, 1937 (By permission of the Newberry Library)
Anderson and Thornton Wilder, 1941 (Wide World Photos)

Preface

SHERWOOD ANDERSON was an advertising man and a businessman —
president, at one time, of the Anderson Manufacturing Company. He
was also a writer, the author of *Winesburg, Ohio* and of seven novels,
including *Poor White, Many Marriages,* and *Dark Laughter.* In the
twenties, H. L. Mencken called him "America's Most Distinctive
Novelist." He was a poet and a playwright, a newspaper editor and
a political journalist as well.

So taken was Anderson by the variety and the drama of his own
life that he went further and dared — as he put it — to proclaim
himself the American Man. He was astute enough to appreciate how
inflated his claim was; on the other hand, in his sixty-four years, he
tried to do whatever was expected of an American man, and he usually succeeded. Growing up in Ohio in the 1880s, he was told that
"money made the mare go," so he set out to make it. When the
country went to war or into business, he went too. If it needed to
worship higher deities, he would lead it in prayer. When the country
had to go to its people for inspiration, he was among them celebrating their virtues.

He was representative in his efforts to realize the American
dream — but even more representative in his failures. In fact, out of
his emotional breakdown in 1912, out of his gradual move from the
business world to the world of letters, he and others created proof of
what America had to do to fulfill its promise as a nation. He was
seen as pointing the way, showing how men might come together
rather than make fortunes for themselves. He himself seemed to be

what America needed — no longer a self-made man, but one whose writings called for a recognition of the worth of others.

"With Anderson," Elizabeth Hardwick once wrote, "'the man' is overwhelmingly important." As a writer, he remains in Dreiser's shadow (which is exactly where he thought he belonged), obscured further by the generation that followed him, by Hemingway and Faulkner especially, both of whom he helped get started (and both of whom then turned on him). But as a man, "as *a case*," Hardwick went on to say, he is "unfailingly interesting." Anderson was a man who was, among other things, a writer.

We do a disservice to many authors by always looking for what is possibly autobiographical in their work. Reading Anderson we must be cautious. He was a teller of tales, and we need to be sensitive to the fact that he let many of them get out of hand. But Anderson saved his life both *by* and *in* writing, and we should expect to find him there. In the many changes he went through, in his several careers, in his three failed marriages, he found his material as a writer. In turn, his writings continually direct our attention back to the story of his life. In this book I have tried to tell that story.

In doing so, I have incurred many debts, and it is a pleasure to acknowledge them.

My indebtedness to Anderson scholars is clear from my notes, but I should like to single out William A. Sutton, whose long labors in the field have preserved materials that are invaluable to anyone interested in Anderson's life. I have drawn extensively on his findings about Anderson's parents and about Anderson's years in Clyde, the Army, Cleveland, and Elyria. Sutton also allowed me to see Anderson's letters to Marietta Finley before he published them and to reproduce her picture. Also, I have always admired Irving Howe's judicious study of Anderson, and I have been saved many steps by Ray Lewis White's reference guide.

Hilbert H. Campbell showed me his edition of *The Sherwood Anderson Diaries, 1936–1941* before its publication. Charles E. Modlin's reading of an early version of my manuscript was only one of his many kind and helpful gestures. I owe thanks to them both (as trustees of Anderson's literary estate), to Harold Ober Associates, and to the Newberry Library for permission to quote from Anderson's published and unpublished writings.

Among the people who talked with me or provided me with materials about Anderson are: John Anderson (Sherwood's son), Malcolm Cowley, Sarah Greenough, Irving Howe, Thaddeus Hurd, George Kimball, Margaret Lyon, Stephen Oates, Rhea Radin, Helen Rogers, Rose Schulman, Mark Sturgill, and Welford Taylor.

Marion Anderson Spear (Sherwood's daughter) has been most helpful, offering insights about her father, allowing me to see her letters from him (and to quote from them), and providing me with photographs.

I also had the pleasure of meeting with Anderson's widow, Eleanor Copenhaver. Like every Anderson scholar, I am indebted to her for establishing the collection of Anderson materials at the Newberry Library. I am grateful to the Library itself for making me a fellow in 1984, and to the Curator of Modern Manuscripts, Diana Haskell, for her invaluable assistance throughout. Ada and Whitney Addington made Chicago home for me while I was there.

Richard Fink and Peter Pouncey, and through them the Trustees of Amherst College, have been generous in their support of my work, as has the staff of the Robert Frost Library, particularly those in the Reference Department.

Among the colleagues and friends who have kindly heard or read me on Anderson are: Sacvan Bercovitch, John Cameron, Benjamin DeMott, George Kateb, Barry O'Connell, Andrew Parker, William Pritchard, and Catharine Stimpson. William McFeely was the first to say that I would undertake this project. A suggestion of Neal Bruss's enabled me to understand what happened to Anderson on November 28, 1912. I am especially grateful to Robert May and Dale Peterson for reading a draft of my manuscript and for their encouragement and companionship along the way.

Madeline Casey, Stephanie Pasternak, and Meg Worcester helped in the preparation of *Sherwood Anderson,* as did Helena Bentz, Sarah Flynn, Robert Overholtzer, and Louise Noble at Houghton Mifflin. Margo Shearman's editing improved it in countless ways. I owe special thanks to Gabriel Cooney and Betty Steele.

Working with Dick Todd was a continual pleasure. I cannot imagine a better editor.

I've dedicated this book to my wife, with whom it all began.

Of all the writers of his day, he was least ashamed
of a loving nature.
— *Josephine Herbst on Sherwood Anderson*

ONE

"Jobby"

1876-1896

SHERWOOD ANDERSON was born in southwestern Ohio, in the town of Camden, on September 13, 1876. In his sixty-four years he would live in countless places, but none could compare with Camden. It was his favorite, and for a very simple reason: he did not remember a thing about it. He was free to make of it what he would.

His Camden was, he later wrote, "a place of mystery — the home of romance." It was a pristine town, "a little white town," tucked in among the hills, so cut off from the modern world that it might have been in ancient Judea. Its citizens were honest, hard-working people, who planted their corn by hand and harvested wheat with scythes. They were people Anderson felt he could understand, people, in turn, who always understood him. It was a place where he had never cheated anyone, owed no one any money, never been unfair to any woman.

He could retreat to "Camden" whenever he wanted, when he was successful in business, or as a writer, and was staying at some big-city hotel. After what might have been a disagreement, or just too much talk too late into the night, he could go up to his room, close his eyes, and once again he would be walking the hills above his fancied town, making his way down through its fields, and then wandering back among the houses of the people he felt he knew, and who had the good grace never to disappoint him. The man he thought was brave and kind was still brave and kind; the girl he thought would grow up to be a beautiful woman had done so.

"Camden" had no basis in reality, but still, like so much of what he imagined, it embodied ideals that he celebrated and strove for as a writer and as a man. It was inhabited by men and women who worked with their hands, who recognized not financial but human worth. It was a community. In his later years, when Anderson allowed himself to become political, in the life of "Camden" he would envision democracy at work.

To Anderson's father, Irwin McLain Anderson, Camden was one more Ohio town in which he tried to establish himself in the harness-making business to support his growing family. He had grown up near West Union, Ohio, one of eleven children in a devout and prosperous farming family. In 1863 he enlisted in the Ohio Voluntary Infantry and a year later in the Seventh Ohio Cavalry, and in his sixteen months of service he saw action in Kentucky and Tennessee and Alabama. In the fall of 1865 his father sent him and one of his sisters to the Xenia Female College, a United Presbyterian school dedicated to instilling "Health, Energy, Promptness, Industry and Earnest Systematic Application" in its students. Like the other fifty or so "gentlemen" enrolled, Irwin lived in town, but even that felt like constraint, so after a year he went west to seek his fortune. He did not find it, but by 1872, he was the owner of his own saddlery and harness business in the town of Morning Sun, Ohio, and a member of the nearby Hopewell United Presbyterian Church. It is probably there that he met Emma Smith.

Anderson always liked to think that Emma was a "bound girl," but though she went to live on the Faris farm at eight or nine, when she was old enough to work, she did so only because her mother, the mother of three, abandoned by one husband and widowed by another, could not take as good care of her as the Farises could. When Emma met Irwin ten years later, it must have seemed that he too could take care of her. He was an attractive man — lean, dark-eyed, handsome. He seemed to be headed somewhere. He was also a veteran and he taught Sunday school. Emma herself had what Anderson later called "a strange kind of dark beauty."

A diary that she kept during 1872 shows her to be a hard-working and a lively young woman, happy to do her chores, to churn, to clean up the yard, to wash and iron, delighted to go on the social rounds that school and church and the rituals of courtship prescribed. A diary that Irwin kept shows him to be industrious, pious, and a lover of women. In the beginning of that year, his desire for one named Linda was ardent enough to prompt Emma to bet her ten cents that

Linda would marry him. But in April Linda left for California. "This morning they say I am / a widower," Irwin wrote on the twenty-ninth. After a month without a letter, he was undone: "The world is lonely to me so *lonely* / Oh Lin why don't you write," and then two days later, "Oh what misery / come ruin come death come forgetfulness / come anything." The next day he received a letter and he was "the happiest man living." The lovers corresponded, and in August he could still feel the pain of separation; but then in the fall it began to disappear, and he turned his attention to Emma. On the twelfth of September he went to play croquet at the Farises'; a week later Emma noted: "Anderson was to come and play / croquoa but called / on me."

By the end of the year, his numerous visits inspired Emma to write:

> *Bless me and my man*
> *Alice and her man*
> *Us four and no more.*

Irwin summed things up with less enthusiasm, less assurance:

> *This is the last day of* 72
> *Have known great joys and*
> *great sorrows but I feel the*
> *Lord has been with me through*
> *all nuntheless I would not*
> *like to live it over*
> *May the next year be happy.*
> *"Praestare Fidem Morti."*

Henceforth — until death — he would perform his duty faithfully. In March of 1873, in Hopewell Church, Emma Smith and Irwin Anderson were married. The following January they had a son they named Karl, and later that year they moved a few miles east, to Camden.

During their three years in Camden they had a daughter, Stella, and their second son, Sherwood. In 1877, when Sherwood was a year old, the family moved north, to Mansfield, where another son, Irwin junior, was born, and then in 1879, they moved to Caledonia, Ohio, where they had yet another son, Ray. They stayed in Caledonia for four years.

Anderson's memories of Caledonia are for the first time "real," but they are mostly archetypal. He remembered flood waters that seemed to have rushed past their house, and a fire that seemed to have burned down half the town. He remembered a sow, lying in a field, giving birth. Only one memory sounds particular to the young Sherwood. It is of the pungent smell of leather in his father's harness shop and of clouds of steam going up when his father lowered a great piece of hot iron — of the sort used for coupling freight cars — into a tub. His father might have been a man a young boy could look up to, but Anderson also remembered wondering: his father had never had a thing to do with the railroads; had he stolen that piece of iron? Certainly by the time Irwin Anderson had moved his family to Caledonia he could have been tempted. The decline of his fortunes was well under way.

In 1883 the Andersons moved to Clyde, Ohio. There a fifth son, Earl, was born and, five years later, another daughter, Fern, who died just before what would have been her second birthday.

As Irwin's responsibilities increased, his ability to meet them lessened. He may have been negligent in paying his bills, or just too generous to stop giving credit, but whatever his business practices, he was doomed. The market for individually crafted harnesses was shrinking. In the never-never land of "Camden" that was all people used. They didn't have any desire — or money — for anything more. But by the 1880s, Ohio farmers were welcoming products turned out by factories specializing in agricultural implements, and they could afford them. In Clyde, Sherwood's father went to work for the Ervin brothers, themselves harness manufacturers, but soon he lost that job and went into business for himself once more, this time as an itinerant house painter and paperhanger. In Clyde, Irwin's hold on his position as head of his family would slip altogether; but it was there that his son Sherwood's life began.

When the Andersons arrived, Clyde was a town of about 2,500, destined, it seemed, to become another Columbus or Toledo, both of which would be cities of more than 80,000 by 1890. The railroads had put the town on the map about thirty years earlier. Before that, it was only corners — Hamer's Corners — eighteen miles south of Lake Erie and about eight miles west of the old Connecticut Western Reserve. For two decades the Maumee and Western Reserve Turnpike had crossed a former Indian trail there, carrying settlers and traders out to Indiana and Michigan, and a little trading center had sprung up. There were a few stores, William McPherson's blacksmith shop, a church, a cemetery, and two taverns, the larger one, a log building perched on a sand dune, being William Hamer's tavern. It was a trading center, and a resting place for travelers, too. In the spring and during much of the winter the roads leading in to town were a sea of mud, and going west they were no better. The Pike cut through forests and the great Black Swamp. Felled logs laid side by side barely distinguished it from the surrounding muck. People said it was the worst road in America.

Then in the summer of 1852 the railroads came, and crossed. The Mad River line, which ran south from Sandusky to Dayton and Cincinnati, laid its tracks right past Hamer's tavern; the Toledo and Norwalk, running on to Cleveland, went just south of the tavern (and, having arrived at the intersection first, ever after had the right of way). Where the lines met, a Junction House Hotel was built, and then two more hotels, and more stores, and Main Street came into being. An elegant Victorian Gothic depot, built in the shape of an L to serve both lines, became the hub of the village. No one recalled any great center of commerce that had a corner in its name, so the citizens met at Hamer's tavern to find another name. Centerville was the obvious choice, but among those who had come from or who had stopped over for a generation in New York State on their way from New England was a persuasive man from Clyde, New York. So Anderson's town became Clyde, Ohio.

In 1883, trains went through day and night (two years before, a third line, carrying coal from West Virginia to Lake Erie, had opened up), and in the years that followed, one light industry after another arrived. Northwestern Ohio was farming country. There was corn, of course, and wheat; Clyde specialized in vegetables, especially cabbages, and berries. But in Anderson's day there were two steam-powered flour mills and a company that packed enough fermented cabbage to give the town the nickname "Sauerkrautville." The tool works of two other brothers became the Clyde Cutlery Company, and someone built a factory for making organs. The organ factory was badly timed — the piano was just coming into vogue — but in the late 1880s and early 1890s the country went wild over bicycles, and a bicycle manufacturer moved into the same building. In 1886 the Clyde Natural Gas Company bought rights to drill on the edge of town. The gas well idea literally went up in smoke, and, as the local paper reluctantly reported, "Management muffed generally," but the failure seemed only a minor setback at the time.

Clyde's first settlers were from New England. After them came the

Irish, to work on the railroads — working twelve-hour days for a dollar a day, as Anderson recalls it — and to settle in "small cheaply constructed wooden affairs with a garden at the back" in the south-eastern part of town. After the Irish came the Germans, to clear and farm the swampland to the north and west. "Drummers," or traveling salesmen, passed through continually. A respectable class of businessmen and their families emerged, and with it respectable institutions and associations, an elementary and a high school, debating societies, fraternal organizations, theatrical groups. Among the many churches that went up was one in the Gothic style, made out of brick. By the time the Andersons arrived, Clyde's social calendar was full. The town offered everything from Episcopal ladies' entertainments or a concert by the Slave Cabin Jubilee Singers at Terry's Opera Hall, to a meeting of the Clyde Political Senate or a reunion of Civil War veterans at the Armory; the curious could find anything from a performance by a troupe from the Madison Square Theater of New York, to a meeting of the Chautauqua Literary and Scientific Circle that featured Mrs. Everett's reading a long poem she had written to celebrate the life of Clyde's Civil War hero, General James Birdseye McPherson.

Yet the town still betrayed traces of the unsettled West. A generation earlier, in Martin's Ferry, in the eastern part of the state, the young William Dean Howells could still gawk at Indians in the street. There were none in Clyde, but for most of Anderson's years there, the streets were dirt, and at night they were only dimly lit. They "were lighted by kerosene lamps set on posts," he wrote in *Tar: A Midwest Childhood.* "They were far apart, at the street corners mostly, and between the lamps was darkness." He did not see paved streets until he went to Cleveland; and riding the rails a few miles west to Fremont, he saw his first electric street lights. Clyde was still a frontier town. There were seventeen saloons catering to its 2,500 citizens, and at least two houses of ill repute. The quality of life, as it was represented by the goings-on at Hamer's tavern, earned Clyde another nickname: "Bang-All."

Irwin had brought his family from town to town in search of work. In Clyde, he still had them on the move — from Race Street to Vine to Mechanic to Duane Street, and then to the Piety Hill section on the southern side of town, to the end of a street that had started as Main Street but trailed away into dirt by the time it reached the Andersons. They began in what Anderson described only as "a tiny brick house" and ended on the edge of town "in an old rented frame house, the cornfields coming down to our kitchen door." They probably moved each time because they could not pay the rent. When they moved, they sometimes carried their belongings on their backs because they could not afford a wagon. If anything distinguished the Andersons' house from the other frame houses on and around Piety Hill, it was the fact that the Andersons didn't own theirs, or that it was extraordinarily small for a family of eight or nine.

Anderson's family was among Clyde's poorest, but one of the things that he always appreciated about the town, and about small towns like it in America, was that no one was forgotten, that finally no one could be lost. In older civilizations one could find hopeless poverty, he once observed, but little communities like Clyde saw to it that everyone was somehow taken care of. Anderson would worry about having enough money all his life, but as he was growing up, there was food all around him and, if need be, people to take him in.

There were, for example, the Hurds, who lived less than a mile away, across from the Presbyterian church in the center of town. Owning a grocery store and, what more clearly symbolized wealth in Clyde, a carriage, they were among Clyde's prosperous. Their house was spacious. Their table, it seemed, was always set for twelve or so. The son, Herman, just a few months younger than Sherwood, was his best friend, so close that Herman thought Sherwood probably ate more meals at the Hurds' home than at his own. And next door to the Hurds were the Padens, the mayor's family. Their son Clifton was two years older than Anderson; he took music lessons and would go on to college, but he too was a good boyhood friend.

Anderson would not starve, but still, he registered the fact that his family could never open up its home to others the way the Hurds and others did to him. He knew that people thought the Anderson family had "some class" but that they were "ruined." And his sense of impoverishment went deeper: his family ties were so fragile.

Christmas was the hardest time. Not to be a family on that holiday — worse, to be beholden to other, more cohesive and prosperous families — was a humiliation that Anderson experienced several times. He never forgot going to the homes of other children with his brother Karl, seeing all their presents, and then hearing Karl begin to curse what he saw. Karl took the presents as a sign that their friends were loved. They themselves had gotten few presents, or none.

At home, with so many children coming so fast, there was little time for feeling. "No one had time to breathe, to look out," Anderson once said. Among so many children one child got lost. Nor were the children close. "I was raised, you see, in a family of five strong-jawed boys, and always among us there was a philosophy of blows," he later wrote. "We aimed to hit to hurt. When one got an idea, he had to fight for it." If there was even that much communication — for brothers, he often said, were not likely to share much with each other.

Karl, with whom he would have been most likely to sympathize and with whom he had the most contact, told him little, "because I am his brother and brothers so seldom tell the real adventures of their lives to one another," he recalled. "Karl is in a strange way a shadow," he wrote his youngest brother, Earl, in 1926. Earl was much more of one. He was the last, and he felt it. In midlife he dropped out of sight for more than a decade and reappeared only when he was discovered collapsed on a street in New York City. In his pocket was a draft of a letter to Sherwood, describing life in Clyde from his perspective. These were the first words anyone had had from him in years:

> I think Karl had 100% parental OK upon his birth, I think each succeeding birth received less with less favors. I myself got a parental OK upon my birth close to zero. I turned to mother for affection and got a cold shoulder. Probably she was so worn out with the effort of living that she had nothing left to give. I turned to each of the rest of the family in succession and got a view of their backs.

To his brother Irve (Irwin), almost two years his junior, it was Sherwood who was the shadow, and Irve who could stand up to an older boy who had thrown a stone at him, Irve — not Sherwood — who could stare down his father, who was about to beat him with a stick when he was not at fault. As for Ray, when in the 1940s an Anderson scholar met him in a grocery store where he was a clerk, he said only that he couldn't understand why anyone would want to do research on his brother.

In the 1920s, Anderson watched a set of his in-laws rise to the defense of a young daughter who had been unjustly accused of stealing, and he was astonished. "He had never before known anything like this kind of family loyalty," his wife reflected. "He had lived a lonely life and his family had been so hardworking and scattered that they had never had any time for this kind of unity." So far as he was concerned, as Anderson wrote in 1922, it was "characteristic of the American race that no one knows as little about one as one's own family."

If Anderson wanted anyone to blame for his having so little sense of family, there was — clearly — his father. Irwin never did quite live up to his vows. He was happier swapping tales about the Civil War or playing the alto horn than he was fulfilling the obligations of a husband and a father. When Irwin was about to move his family to Caledonia, his own father wrote him: "For the sake of those little ones remember that time is money and you will never be able to get a home by blowing the horn and spending your time with the band." By the time he reached Clyde, it was obvious that Irwin had not heeded his father's warning. He was almost all show. He went around town with a cart that had "I. M. Anderson" painted on it, and he built up something of a business, painting a house here, paperhanging there, painting advertisements on board fences along the highways when he obtained farmers' permission — and by stealth when he didn't. But he was not one to persevere. When he took his oldest boys along to help in the work, he would stop everything to tell them stories about the Civil War. On one occasion Sherwood got so impatient that he threw down his brush and walked away. When on his own, Irwin might just walk off the job himself or, supposedly scouring the countryside for work, disappear for days on end.

The most Anderson could say about his father's loyalty to his mother was that he was devoted "in his own way." Once when his father took him to a camp in the country for a night, the young boy discovered that his father was having an affair with another woman. And in Caledonia Irwin had begun to drink. He became less and less of a support to his family, more and more of a spectral figure at home. In a particularly stunning version of this story that Anderson published when he was fifty, he still thinks of his father as a man lurching home drunk, his return, after however many days, "a kind of assault upon the spirit of the house." He might try to act his part, to make it to the table and begin dishing out the meal, but after two or three unsuccessful stabs at the potatoes, the mother would go over, take the plate away, and serve her children. Or he would roar around the room, ranting at the stove about the people who hadn't paid him and then about the impossible demands of manhood: "I have tried being a man but I cannot make it. . . . I made a mistake when I married. I love my wife but I have been able to do nothing for her." All the while the children would eat in terrified silence, their mother withdrawing into a silence that was still more terrifying:

> When something happened she did not approve she went about the house with a strange lost look in her eyes. The eyes frightened. . . . All became self-conscious, afraid. It was as though she had been struck a blow and when you looked at her you felt at once that your hand had delivered the blow.

Somehow it seemed the children's fault that their father was such a curse upon the house.

Anderson was furious at his father, not only because he did not provide, but because he left Anderson to face his mother's pain alone. At home Irwin was as frightened as his children. Yet once out of the house he could perform. He loved parades: he was an officer of the guard, a member of the band, and in 1895 he was chairman of the committee in charge of Memorial Day celebrations. He helped amateur theatrical groups put on patriotic entertainments during the Spanish-American War, and Anderson remembers his going out on the road with a friend with his own magic lantern and song-and-dance routine, their stage "a broken-down horse and a spring wagon." And always he could gather a group around him and tell stories about the Civil War. But to his son, all his performances were at best pathetic. Anderson's disappointment and bitterness surface in his writings continually. Irwin was one of what Anderson called "The Sad Horn Blowers," unable symbolically to have any influence over others, to make anything happen. In his son's first published novel, *Windy McPherson's Son,* he is "the blustering, pretending, inefficient old one," "the boasting, incompetent father," who had talked his way up to the head of the Fourth of July parade and then as it was about to start, only then, when "a thin piercing shriek followed by a squawk" came out of his bugle, learned for himself that he could not play. He is Tom Willard in *Winesburg, Ohio:* "Nothing he had ever done had turned out successfully. However, when he was out of sight . . . and had no fear of coming upon his wife, he swaggered and began to dramatize himself as one of the chief men of the town."

Disappointed, feeling almost bereft, Anderson wondered if maybe Irwin was not his father after all. Perhaps some rich man was his father, some rich man who suddenly had had to flee the country, or perhaps just the grocer, Mr. Hurd, who clearly had enough food to go around. But no, his father was this man who flitted in and out of his life — and into anyone's who came along:

> He was like this, let's say an Irishman came to our house. Right away father would say he was Irish. He'd tell what county in Ireland he was born in. He'd tell things that happened to him in Ireland when he was a boy. He'd make it seem so real, telling little details of his life as a boy in Ireland, that, if I hadn't known where he was born, in a county down in southern Ohio, I'd have believed him myself.
>
> If he was a Scotchman the same thing happened. He became a Scotchman. He'd get a burr into his speech. Or he was a German or a Swede.
>
> He'd be anything the other man was. He seemed anything but a father.

But once he had vented his anger, Anderson could admit to feeling some pride in his father, and he could recall his mother's sharing some of this feeling. "Don't you worry," he remembers her telling a woman who had stopped her along the road. "He isn't ever dull like most of the men in this street. Life is never dull when my man is about." Though Irwin did not provide enough for his family, and though he might seem an ineffectual buffoon in public, he could be entertaining at home. The Andersons owned only the few books one would expect — *Pilgrim's Progress, Robinson Crusoe,* Tennyson's *Poems* — but Irwin would read from them, and of course he also had his own stories to tell. There may have been no butter in the house, but Irwin could disarm criticism: "Well, heavens and earth," he would say, "you've got the bread haven't you?"

And he could be a presence after all, and there was something lovable about him. Sherwood discovered it one rainy summer night when his father returned home after an absence of two or three weeks. Sherwood's mother was not at home; he was reading in the kitchen. His father came in, seemingly beaten down by the weather and by what the boy recognized as his deep sadness, sat down, and looked at his son without saying a word. For some reason, this time Sherwood wasn't afraid. Even when his father made the surprising suggestion that they go for a swim, he did not hesitate. After they reached a pond about a mile out of town and his father told him to take off his clothes, he still did not hesitate. His father led him down to the water, and once in, he had Sherwood hold on to his shoulder as he struck out for the opposite shore and had him hold on for the return trip as well. It was a summer night and the rain was warm, so rather than dress, the two lay on the bank, the son looking at his father, seeing still the sadness in his face, the father going on about how the colors in the sky and water were really not black but deep purple. "In me there was a feeling I had never known before that night," he wrote in his *Memoirs*:

> It was a feeling of closeness. It was something strange. It was as though there were only we two in the world. It was as though I had been jerked suddenly out of myself, out of a world of the school boy, out of a world in which I had been ashamed of my father, out of a place where I had been judging my father.

By the time they got back, Emma had returned. Addressing them as "boys," she smiled and asked them where they had been. As if to say he was not a boy but a man and a father, Irwin said nothing, looked at his son, and with "a new and strange dignity" went upstairs to change.

But insofar as the Andersons were a family, it was Emma's doing. Though in his adoration and his gratitude, Anderson surely exaggerated the hardships and the measures she took to meet them, there is no doubt that his mother deserves all the credit he gives her for keeping the family as much of a unit as it was. You could have thrown a cat through the walls of their house, he says in *Tar*. It was Emma who went around with him and his older brother nailing strips of wood and cloth on the walls to keep the weather out.

The story he was particularly fond of telling about his mother involved cabbages. On Halloween the local boys liked to go out into the fields to collect and pile cabbages on their wagons, stalks and all, ride around to houses, and, swinging the cabbages over their heads, hurl them at people's doors. The boys would wait until dark so as not to get caught and in order to terrify those who supposedly had gone to sleep. At the Andersons' house, Emma had turned out the kerosene lamp and, with her children, was lying in wait. When the first cabbages landed she would rush out into the night, seemingly outraged, but really to invite more. And they would come, and she would rage, and more would come. (In one version of the story Anderson got the number up to "two or three hundred.") After each "sally from the fort," Emma would bring back the spoils. When the attacks were over, the children would go out with lanterns to retrieve any she had missed, and later they would all carefully bury the cabbages in a trench, the stalks sticking out of the ground — their store of food for the spring, "something at our backs."

If not always in precisely this way, Emma was continually providing. On cold nights the Anderson boys would vie for the middle, warmer positions in the bed they shared, the oldest usually winning; after they were settled in, Emma would come with warm animal fat and put it on their hands to help them fall asleep. And she worked for the family in less dramatic ways: she took in other people's wash.

Anderson dedicated his most famous book, *Winesburg, Ohio,* to Emma Smith Anderson, crediting her "keen observations on the life about her" with awakening in him "the hunger to see beneath the surface of lives." Almost twenty years after that Anderson wrote that he thought of her as the inspiration behind his inquiries into the lives of working women:

> I have seen my own mother stand all day over a washtub, washing the dirty linen of pretentious middle-class women not fit to tie her shoelaces, this just to get her sons enough food to keep them alive, and I presume I shall never in my life see a working woman without identifying her with my mother.

When you have such a mother, he said in *Tar,* and she dies when you are young, "what you do all your life afterwards is to use her as material for dreams."

For example, at one point a five-year-old Clyde boy drowned in a freak accident while playing in an old Indian spring near one of the Andersons' houses. Emma found the boy, but rather than try to revive him, she had fled in panic; when the boy's mother found him it was too late. In Anderson's *Memoirs,* however, it is Emma who discovers the dead boy and carries him in her arms to his mother. In his dreams, Emma was an abiding, saintly presence.

Emma died when Sherwood was eighteen years old. He had never been able to draw near enough to her. As he said quite freely of himself, "he was in love with her all his life." To him she *was* a "bound girl." She was oppressed, stifled, long-suffering. She was kept, kept from living life fully by the burden of her many children. For her he made up Italian ancestry, because it was "so wonderfully comforting to think of one's mother as a dark, beautiful and somewhat mysterious woman," and into her silence he read her power. He would always think of her as Woman, a figure who inspired him to do good, to write. If he could not approach her when she was alive, he would approach her through his works. He would try to address the world the way he imagined she had — with tolerance and extraordinary insight.

In actuality, to ease his mother's burden, so that perhaps she herself would not have to work, so she could be cared for when she was sick, and, more generally, to offset his family's poverty, the young Sherwood Anderson worked. He worked with the energy and the intensity that would characterize him all his life. He took advantage of every chance to make a dollar and to make more dollars as he qualified for harder or more demanding jobs. He would do anything and everything. He worked in town: mowing lawns, sweeping out stores, bringing water to the men who were putting in the sewers and paving the streets; he worked in the fields: cutting corn, reaping, planting cabbages. He drove Mr. Hurd's grocery carriage, and he hung around the tracks at the fairgrounds and helped the "swipes." He worked at the printer's, he went out with his father to paint signs, he worked in the bicycle factory, and at the end of his stay in Clyde he worked in a livery stable. He was known for his ability to scramble, to get ahead. Everyone in Clyde knew him as "Jobby."

Anderson worked out of love and out of necessity. He did it too because the townsfolk and the age encouraged him. The town elders gave him their versions of "Poor Richard" as advice — "Money makes the mare go," "Take care of the pennies and the dollars will take care of themselves" — and he took them for his mottoes. He grew as the town grew and shared its values, its obsession. And so he fell in love with money. "I wanted passionately to rise in the world, to make money," he wrote in the foreword to his *Memoirs*. "I loved money, loved the feel of it, was hungry for it. It seemed to in some way warm me, comfort me. Money would buy warm clothes, food, safety."

He hawked the weekend edition of the *Cincinnati Enquirer* in the streets and in saloons, and developed and perfected an ability to put things over on people that he would both use to advantage and deplore throughout his life. As a boy, Anderson could convince a tired farmer in a saloon to buy more than one copy of the *Enquirer;* he also knew how to watch a man's eyes to tell whether he could get the man to forget about the change. Sherwood would be down at the station when the Cleveland *Plain Dealer* and the Toledo *News-Bee* arrived on the five o'clock train, and he would deliver them in the streets of Clyde well past dark; or he could be seen jumping on the train just as it arrived and then jumping off just as it pulled out, having raced through every car making sales. In the first pages of the first version of himself that he offers us in print (in *Windy McPherson's Son*), he is

Sam McPherson, bribing the Irish baggage man with a cigar to hide his rival's stock of papers, then working the whole train himself and dropping off the last car, "his pocket jingling with coins," amidst the cheers and laughter of the passengers on board and the idlers on the platform.

Anderson's rise in the world would be accomplished by his moving up from job to job, not up from one school grade to another. His education was rudimentary, spotty. Having just arrived in Clyde, he started "C Primary" (the equivalent of second grade) in October 1884. Apparently he skipped fourth grade, but then the next year he missed so many days doing odd jobs that he had to stay in fifth. Beginning in the fall of 1891, Anderson put in a total of about nine months in high school, leaving in the winter of 1893 at the age of seventeen.

Americans had not yet learned that they had to go to school to get ahead. Anderson's sister Stella lent the family the one bit of distinction it seems to have enjoyed by staying in school, becoming valedictorian of her class, and then going on to teach, but her brothers were not interested. Sherwood had no trouble getting by in his classes, but neither did he win any honors. Karl would complete only one more year of school than he did. The principal, "the one man in town who owned books," Karl recalled, invited the two of them to his house one day. He seemed particularly interested in Sherwood and said that he could get the boy a scholarship to college if he would like to go, but Sherwood simply "shrugged the idea off." There was work to do.

And there, representing achievement in the world, was the principal's son, Hal Ginn. He was a bit older, he was Karl's friend, but Sherwood never forgot him. He wrote about him in *Tar* thirty years later. In 1938, when Karl told him that Hal Ginn had died, Sherwood remembered the winter day when Hal and some others were skating on the Waterworks Pond, not far from the Andersons' house on the edge of town. While Anderson was watching them, standing by a small fire that the boys had built, Hal came over and asked him to hold his overcoat. When Hal came to get it later, he gave Anderson fifty cents and this lasting impression:

> I still remember what seemed to me the extraordinary fineness of the cloth and the lining of the coat and with what sharp pleasure I caressed the fabric so that I think that forever afterwards Hal has remained in my mind in connection with the incident and with the whole idea of elegance.

At the time, the incident was a reminder that his family was among the poorer families of Clyde and an incentive for him to do something about it. "If Tar's mother had such a coat," he mused.

A reminder that came to Sherwood from boys closer to his own age was likely not to inspire but to enrage. There was the time, for example, when he was with a group of them at the home of the Whiteheads, a family so well-off as to have a stable of race horses of their own. It was Easter, and the boys were all dressed up. Relatively slightly built, wide-eyed, and thin-skinned, it seemed, in every sense, Anderson cannot have been an imposing presence under the best of circumstances. Here, at the Whiteheads', he was certainly not at home. But like the others, he sported a straw hat. He mingled with them, kept up, until someone teased him and then knocked off his hat, whereupon, as his friend Herman Hurd reported it, Anderson fell apart: "He went all to pieces." He was enraged, but then, rather than go after the boy who had teased him, he jumped up and down, crushing his own hat. It was as if he had been told that for all his efforts he would never live up to the standards of fashion of his peers. So in response, in his fury, he destroyed every trace of ever having tried.

The incident suggests that there was another side to the boy. "Jobby" was not just going about his various businesses trying to be accepted, trying to get rich; he was doing so under enormous pressure. He knew his way around town, he knew how to get ahead. But he was driven to do so. More specifically, he was driven to produce results that his father never could. He would be as gregarious and resourceful as his father, but he would be a man himself, he would be there for his Emma. But he was only a boy, and Emma was his mother.

There are stretches in his writings in which Anderson runs down and through the various rituals and activities of the town as if to suggest that he had joined in with ease. There was swimming where Coon Creek was dammed up, sleigh and surrey rides; there were dances and songfests, and ever so complicated negotiations to see who would walk home with whom after church. Though he was no athlete ("He couldn't have caught a ball to save his life," Hurd later said), for a time he played right field on the Clyde Stars, and then he became their manager. Later he joined the ranks of the National Guard.

We can imagine Anderson in the Clyde of the Historical Society or, in what is even more popular and influential, the idealized Small

Town, the American version of the pastoral, the organic community, that was soon to be overshadowed, shattered, replaced by the impersonal, mechanized life led in the cities. We can imagine him in *A Boy's Town*, William Dean Howells's Hamilton, Ohio, which was written halfway through Anderson's stay in Clyde, about life thirty or forty years before, to show any boy "who read *Harper's Young People*" that what he had in common with his fellows was God-given and that what "seems quite your own . . . is from your silly self, and is a sort of perversion of what came to you from the Creator." We can make Anderson appear on that common and alluring site, but finally, he was no more at home there than Howells. From between the lines Howells tells us that he himself was a priggish and a friendless boy; openly and at great length, Anderson tells us that however hard he tried, and however much he seemed to have succeeded, he was often scared, alone, and sometimes, even, afraid he would lose control of himself altogether. He had no social or economic or educational advantages. He was the typical American boy, trying to gain those advantages, trying to *be* typical. But there was another side to him that was atypical, only barely known. There was a place — unknown territory as yet — where he stood and watched "Jobby" work away. He was of another mind. As a boy he knew very little about that mind, but already it was at work, doubting, challenging, occasionally upsetting "Jobby's" plans. Already it had begun to imagine another life for him.

From his earliest days, like his father, Sherwood performed. He was "Little Jimmy" in a five-act "Military Comedy Drama" put on to benefit the local National Guard unit, but he was forever playing parts. He played, he dramatized himself especially. He was not just "Jobby," but other, almost antithetical figures that brought out his sense of himself as less powerful, less acceptable, always more sensitive than those he lived among. Once he cast himself as a kind of Tom Sawyer, gathering a gang in a "pirate's cave" behind the Spring Avenue house and having each boy sign a pledge of allegiance with his own blood, but usually he projected himself into the roles of the defeated and the outcast. Emerging from the gang's reading of *The Last of the Mohicans* Sherwood was Hawkeye, the scout, "La Longue Carabine," to his brother Irve's Uncas, "Le Cerf Agile," and thus he was "the despised white, the paleface." Whereas Irve could fight, stick even to a lie until death, there was in himself, he thought in retrospect, "something of the doglike, the squaw man." Still imagining his brother as Uncas, he watched him confront his father, watched his father back down, and then admitted to himself that he too was "one of the weak ones of the world." When the trains pulled into Clyde, he tried to earn nickels and dimes by putting on a little Wild West show, a showdown, for passengers waiting to switch trains. On the small strip of lawn beside the platform, he and another boy would advance toward each other with wooden knives, he would disarm his foe, but then, having retrieved his weapon, he would offer the other boy his choice of either and another chance, at which point he himself would be ceremoniously run through, "the victim of too much nobility."

Though no model schoolboy, nor as a boy a great reader, Anderson could lose himself in books — and emerge a version of them. He was an indiscriminate reader, as we can see from the list he gives in *A Story Teller's Tale* of authors and books he read up through his early twenties:

> Laura Jean Libbey, Walter Scott, Harriet Beecher Stowe, Henry Fielding, Shakespeare, Jules Verne, Balzac, the Bible, Stephen Crane, dime novels, Cooper, Stevenson, our own Mark Twain and Howells and later Whitman.

They were, "like life itself," he says, "only useful to me in as much as they feed my own dreams or give me a background upon which I can construct new dreams." More specifically, they tended to be adventure stories, stories like *Robinson Crusoe,* that he remembers his father's reading to him, that held out the promise that it was possible to start all over again, to construct a world elsewhere in a language that was not so relentlessly materialistic as Clyde's.

In this he had the help of a man who was a more nearly genuine artist than his father, a man named John Tichenor. Tichenor had inherited a little money, married a prosperous milliner, and he painted and gave lessons. (Karl was one of his pupils, Mrs. Hurd another.) It was the Tichenors who put on the "Military Comedy Drama" that Anderson acted in. In *Windy McPherson's Son* Tichenor is John Telfer, the person who instills a sense of beauty in "the quiet, industrious, money-making boy." In his white flannels and white shoes, his jaunty cap and swinging cane, he belonged on promenades at summer resorts; on the streets of Anderson's Iowa Clyde, he is just a character. "I do not paint pictures; I do not write books; yet am I an artist," he proudly declaims. "I am an artist practising the most difficult of all arts — the art of living." Seeing evidence of the creative spirit in the boy, even as he cheats his rival in an attempt to monopolize the newspaper trade, Telfer lends the boy novels, introduces him to Whitman, and thereby introduces him to his own body, and starts him yearning for a grander life than was possible in their little town.

He also cautions the boy at great length about women:

> "My foolishness is more than half earnest," he said. "I think that a man or boy who has set for himself a task had better let women and girls alone. If he be a man of genius, he has a purpose independent of all the world, and should cut and slash and pound his way toward his mark, forgetting every one, particularly the woman that would come to grips with him. She also has a mark toward which she goes. She is at war with him and has a purpose that is not his purpose. She believes that the pursuit of women is an end for a life."

It is a comic portrait, all energy and exaggeration, Anderson's creation of a figure who had stirred up inspiring and anxious thoughts and feelings in him twenty years before. But the sources of those feelings were all within. They were himself, his desire to make money and to please, his fear of women, and (Whitman or no Whitman) his fear of his own body. He never mentioned Tichenor/Telfer other than in the pages of *Windy McPherson's Son.* His writings are, in large measure, his own explorations of his own dissatisfaction with his ardent pursuit of money and success, and about the troubles he would have with women.

Anderson's difficulties in defining his sexuality were perhaps no greater than anyone else's, but few can rival the sensitivity with which he wrote about them. Others have been more explicit, others have been more defiant, but one turns to Anderson to appreciate the tension a boy experiences as he moves toward what the culture calls manhood.

What Anderson tells us about his own emergence into manhood is almost always tentative. There was, for example, his first boyhood friend, Jim Moore, who lived near him on Piety Hill. The two of them would go out into the cornfields, find Coon Creek, and follow it until they reached a little valley. There they would undress, play in the creek, and run naked among the trees, trying sometimes to swing from them like monkeys. Then they would lie down on the grass beside the creek, watch the clouds move through the sky, watch raccoons approach the berry bushes nearby and eat. And "in the quiet of that place something began." In the *Memoirs* Anderson says it is a questioning of what the other was like, what he was thinking. In *Tar* he describes it this way:

> Sometimes when Tar and Jim were lying like that, on the creek bank, one of them touched the other's body. It was a queer feeling. When it happened they both sprang up and began to run about.

One time a man saw them, and they hid in the bushes. "They were in a close place and had to lie close together. After the man passed they went at once to get their clothes, both feeling strange." After that, the talk shifts to a boy they knew "who had the nerve to do anything," which means he had taken a girl into a barn and later bragged, "It isn't the first time." It was a safe move, a move away from his attraction to his friend. They talked about what it would be like with girls much more than they wanted to, Anderson says. It made them uncomfortable, but they couldn't help it. Whether the source of their discomfort is a sense of betraying their own intimacy or fear upon entering new territory, Anderson does not say, but it was a necessary move. Under the cultural circumstances, a young boy could not linger over his feelings for another boy. He had to go out and prove he could be a man.

Anderson must have been about twelve when he first entered that territory. He did so by following in the footsteps of a girl named Lula, whose father was a carnival man. She had told the butcher's son that she wanted Anderson, and then one night she took his hand and walked him out past the baseball field, to the edge of town. On the way he tried to imagine he was no longer under his mother's watchful eye ("Perhaps she had gone to church," he said to himself. "She did occasionally. She would be sitting there, with the people, in her dress, the proud silent mother I knew."), but he was still not safe, for another boy had followed them. Anderson and Lula walked along the railroad tracks and found a grassy spot. She took off her "panties," he his short pants, when out of the darkness came gravel, stinging his buttocks. Impulsively he ran, but not without crying out repeatedly, "Get your pants, Lula. Get your pants, Lula." It was a cry the locals did not let him easily forget. In reflecting on the incident in his *Memoirs,* Anderson tries to bring out not only its amusing side but also its economic implications. It was Lula's "panties" that he thought of as he ran: "Perhaps I did not want her to lose them," he says. "There is this sense of property we all have. It is bred into us early in life."

The resonances of other encounters are more unnerving, deeper.
He was shocked, for instance, by one of the ways Karl tried to help
the family out. It had its economic side, but what was horrifying was
the way it involved sex and deformity, the way it seemed to deform
sex. Karl tried to make money by taking care of a man who had the
body of a baby and the head of a man. Usually he wheeled the man
around in a baby carriage for twenty-five cents a day. The little man
swore and whined and begged; he sold pencils and needles, and lived
in perpetual fear of being robbed of the nickels and dimes he earned.
Sometimes Karl took him to a neighboring town (the man was allowed to ride free on the train) where there was a "house" and in it
women who, feeling sorry for him, would give him money and let
him fondle their breasts. Anderson later wondered if the women
didn't see a fellow outcast in the man: "If it was vile they felt themselves vile." More immediately, the sight of his older brother's charge
was shocking to Anderson, the thought of what his brother went
through at that "house" sickening.

Whatever the circumstances, as a youth Anderson approached
women cautiously, sometimes in terror. He was bewildered by every
encounter. Early on, when he was eleven or twelve, a young girl came
to town to live with her aunt and uncle. Anderson delivered papers
to their house, and once the girl asked him around to the back door
to give him some cookies her aunt had baked. It was enough to start
him dreaming about her: "I had thought about her at night when I
was in bed with one of my brothers. She had become increasingly
beautiful to me." The following winter, one of those boys with
"nerve" took him around to the girl's house after dark to "show him
something" and had him wait in a hiding place behind a bush until
the girl appeared. She had come to undress and warm herself in front
of the stove before going to bed. And so Anderson saw what he had
long thought he wanted to see more than anything else in the world:
"a naked woman." One might almost say it was what every boy
would like to see, but Anderson's reaction was extraordinary:

> And then suddenly, for some obscure reason, I turned and struck
> my boy friend as hard as I could in the face with my fist.
> I knocked him into the snow. The young girl was still warming
> her slender body by the glowing stove. She was turning her young
> body slowly around before the stove.
> I struck him in the face with all my might and then I ran. I
> kept running and for a long time couldn't go home. I just walked
> about alone in the winter streets of the town.

It wasn't that he was angry with the other boy. In his *Memoirs,* trying to explain himself, he associates the experience with one he had many years later, when in an effort to gather material for a story, he was about to watch a surgeon perform an appendectomy on a young girl, was about to until he saw the girl lying "quite nude" on the operating table. "I wanted to grab the surgeon's arm," he says in retrospect. "'Don't. It's too beautiful. Don't cut it.'" But he fled from the room instead.

And that experience, in turn, reminds him of a story that he told and retold many times until it became "Death in the Woods." It is about an old woman, once a "bound girl," who devotes her life to feeding animals — "horses, cows, pigs, dogs, men." One winter day the old woman goes to town for provisions and on her way home sits down, exhausted, by a tree. It gets late, snow begins to fall, and she loses consciousness. As she dies, dogs circle her and then devour the food that she was carrying on her back. A day or two later, a hunter finds her, and Anderson is one of the crowd that comes out from town to see. The dogs had torn her dress, so what he sees is "everything." To him the woman's body seems "the body of some charming young girl," and he adores it. In its presence, his own trembles "with some strange mystical feeling."

In the winter of 1916, Anderson wrote a friend a long letter from Clyde. The occasion was his first visit to his hometown in twenty years. He told of the isolation and the preindustrial innocence of the town as he remembered it, of carrying papers at night, and of carpenters who might meet on the street in the evening and talk "for hours concerning the best way to cut a window frame or build a door." "Romance dwelt about these corners then," he said. But he devotes much of the letter to two incidents involving women. In one of the incidents, Anderson is once again a newsboy, invited in to eat, this time by a woman who had once run a whorehouse in Sandusky but who had come to Clyde to run a hotel with her husband, "to settle down and be quite respectable people." Things were not going to go the way they usually did with girls in the dining room of a country hotel, not in Maria Welling's hotel. What she said to them, she said to Anderson:

> "You stay away. It's rotten," she cried. "You're a clean boy and I want you to stay away from girls. Just mind this. Don't you pay and don't you have anything to do with them as takes pay. . . ."

Her voice broke and she drew me down until my head lay on her breast. "I'd rather been a slut on the street because I was just naturally bad and wanted loving than to have been what I was for money," she said brokenly.

In the other incident, the admonition in fact comes from his mother. In this case, a girl far more experienced than he accosts him in the street, leads him "down into this dark place," takes off her cloak, and invites him to kiss her. "That was a night for me," he writes. "I was full of pride and shamed too. I remember with what a strange mixed feeling I later went home to my mother."

We need not insist on the connection between the girls to whom Anderson was drawn and the "bound" girl who was his mother, but in the presence of women young and old, confronted with their sexuality, Anderson heard a voice within him say: Don't. Too beautiful. And behind that voice he heard another one, a voice that sounded very much like his mother's, that added: Men are brutish beings. Don't you be one of them.

Perhaps because of his own experiences, some of Anderson's best writings are renderings of this sensitive boy's responses to his sexual awakenings. There is, for example, the tale of George Willard, "Nobody Knows," in *Winesburg, Ohio,* a tale of a boy coming through the culture's rite of initiation into manhood. Once again a girl approaches him — with a note saying, "I'm yours if you want me." George sees his chance, but Anderson knows he cannot approach it without fear:

> George Willard found Louise Trunnion in the kitchen of her father's house. She was washing dishes by the light of a kerosene lamp. There she stood behind the screen door in the little shedlike kitchen at the back of the house. George Willard stopped by a picket fence and tried to control the shaking of his body. Only a narrow potato patch separated him from the adventure. Five minutes passed before he felt sure enough of himself to call to her. "Louise! Oh Louise!" he called. The cry stuck in his throat. His voice became a hoarse whisper.

When she comes out he trembles "more violently than ever"; he notices she is "not particularly comely," notices a black smudge on her nose where she must have rubbed after handling some kitchen pots. She "quibbles"; she says, "You think you're better than I am. Don't tell me, I guess I know," and draws closer. And then he acts. He remembers a look she had given him, remembers the note, and:

Doubt left him. The whispered tales concerning her that had gone about town had given him confidence. He became wholly the male, bold and aggressive. In his heart there was no sympathy for her. "Ah, come on, it'll be all right. There won't be anyone know anything. How can they know?" he urged.

It is past ten when George comes back into town. "He wanted more than anything to talk to some man." The drugstore is still open, so he talks to the clerk for a while and then, feeling better, starts for home. On the way he stops, stands "perfectly still in the darkness, attentive, listening as though for a voice calling his name." But he is determined not to hear it, and in the tale's last words he tries to drown it out with the tones of his newly won manhood: "Then again he laughed nervously. 'She hasn't got anything on me. Nobody knows,' he muttered doggedly and went on his way."

One of the things that makes Anderson most attractive as a writer is his inability, his unwillingness, ever to succeed in silencing that voice. "A man, if he is any good," he wrote in *Tar*, "never gets over being a boy." Not that a boy should not mature, not that he should never be a man. What Anderson saw was that any man who did not question the manhood that he achieved, did not keep alive the possibility or the expectation of something better, would be less than a man. He would be only that churlish, dogged figure that had no sympathy for others, least of all anything "other" in himself.

One of Anderson's more famous stories, "I Want to Know Why," is told from the point of view of a fifteen-year-old whose love for a horse trainer is shattered when he overhears the way the trainer talks to whores. In Jerry Tilford's handling of his horse the boy sees an image of ideal manhood, he sees power tempered and enhanced by grace and tenderness. The day that horse wins the boy feels he likes Jerry "even more than he ever liked his own father." That night he follows Jerry out to a "rummy looking farm house," and once again from a perch among the bushes, he sees Jerry and others sit on women's laps and hears their "rotten talk." It is enough to make him hate the man. "What did he do it for? I want to know why," he says. Why did his father, why do men in general, think that such behavior proves that they are men?

It seemed ever the same: human sexual relations were always debased. As a newsboy, Anderson noticed a man come into town in his buggy, wait in a side street, curtains drawn, and soon he saw a woman get in, and the two of them drive off. He knew who they

were, and the man knew he knew — and gave him the unheard-of
sum of five dollars to be quiet. One evening he also saw the drugstore
clerk and his new wife roaring around their house without any clothes
on. They had forgotten to draw the blinds. He watched them dart in
and out of rooms, saw the clerk vault over the couch; and then they
disappeared. He knew the clerk had to work after supper, so later he
went by the drugstore to marvel at the man's standing there behind
the counter, greeting customers as usual.

When he was too old to sell newspapers Anderson went to work
at a livery stable and spent the nights there as another way of helping
out his family. There was again much talk about impossible sexual
conquests, and this time it fired Anderson's imagination. But when
the sexual ways of men and women assaulted him more directly, he
recoiled. He was afraid, acted like a frightened girl. (Many years
later, referring to one of his "first jobs," he said he had been a "chambermaid in a livery stable.") One night a man brought a woman back
with him, they drank, they made embarrassing noises; revolted, Anderson got up to dress and as he did so, he heard them laughing at
him, and then the man called out: "Ah what's the matter with you,
kid? Wait. Maybe I'll share with you. What do you say, Kate?" Hearing the woman's laughter, he raced outside and walked the streets for
an hour or two, thinking with shame about his own lust, before
going back to finish out the night in the bed he shared with his
brothers.

When he went to work at the bicycle factory at the age of about
seventeen, Anderson encountered more crudeness, but now it seemed
one of the costs of progress, one of the effects of industrialization.
The work there seemed so threatening to men's sense of their own
manhood that they had to boast of their sexual exploits, real or imagined, as a way of retrieving or securing it. There were forty men
working in the factory by December 1894, perhaps as many as a
hundred a month later. Anderson worked with a crew of ten or
twelve, assembling parts and putting bicycles together, and he listened to the talk:

> The men seemed everlastingly anxious to assert their manhood, to
> make it clear to their fellows that they were potent men able to do
> great deeds in the realms of the flesh and all day I stood beside a
> little stand-like bench, on which the frame of the bicycle was stuck
> upside down, tightening nuts and screws and listening to the men,
> the while I looked from their faces out the window to the factory

walls and the rubbish heap. . . . There were days as I worked in that place when I became physically ill and other days when I cursed all the gods of my age that had made men — who in another age might have been farmers, shepherds or craftsmen — these futile fellows, ever more and more loudly proclaiming their potency as they felt the age of impotency asserting itself in their bodies.

The actor in him tried to gain relief. He would complain of headaches, go over to the window for fresh air. Feeling sorry for him, his fellow workers would fill in; they would even bring him remedies from the drugstore or their homes. But soon he felt he had "worked the sick headache racket to the limit." He really had to escape, so after only a few months of factory work he quit.

As a boy, in Clyde, Anderson was trying to be a sexual man. But all the while he balked. He would come to "know" women, but a voice in him would persist in calling that knowledge forbidden, dirty. It was as if he were no better than his father. It was as if Woman were being defiled. As a boy, in Clyde, Anderson was also trying to make money, and in those efforts too he balked. Earning money was a way of making up to his mother, but still a voice in him persisted in calling any success he had suspect, cheap. But it was the culture — not just his family — that set the terms on which a young man might succeed. He would not be the ne'er-do-well his father was, treating his mother the way his father did, failing to provide, but neither would he be a simple product of the industrial age, treating women the way the age required. Fearing women, revolted by men's behavior toward them and their talk about them, he often seems a prig, but at the same time he was reacting against the cultural imperative that turned men into adolescent braggarts, the women — for all the men knew, or wanted to know — mindless whores, and in doing that he showed a kind of courage.

Neither as a son, nor as "Jobby," bouncing from one exploit and activity to another in his up-and-coming town, did Sherwood Anderson appear to have the makings of much of a man. As one resident put it, "To most folks around here, Sherwood Anderson was just a poor boy who lived in Clyde for a while." It would be years before the conflicts in him would become the subjects of his writing, years before he would be able to clarify and even resolve them in his writings. In Clyde, he lived with tension he could not then have described — and occasionally he snapped. At Easter, when they taunted him, he had a tantrum. He had hit the boy who showed him a naked girl warming herself before a stove.

The tension Anderson lived with revealed itself in another important incident. Shortly after the family's move to Piety Hill, when Anderson was swimming with a gang of young men and boys at the Coon Creek pond, one boy had an epileptic fit, and Anderson fled in terror, leaving the others to rescue the boy; when Anderson emerged they danced around him, pelting him with mud and stones. Sobbing, and furious with himself for sobbing, he struck out at them but had only the miserable satisfaction of pushing a pale and sickly boy into the water — a boy who could not swim. "So there it was," Anderson wrote in retrospect, "the innocent one made to suffer and come near losing his life because of the boyish cruelty of the others, myself thus tortured striking not one of my persecutors but an innocent bystander." True, he seems to forget his cowardice too easily, but that is exactly the price, he seems to suggest, that boys pay to become one of the boys: "Presently," he says, "I would grow older and bigger and would join the others in pelting some other new boy."

During one period of his youth the tension almost totally overwhelmed him. That part of him that could no longer tolerate the strain seemed simply to take leave of him, or it could no longer make connections with the world and the world seemed to float off. Anderson wrote about it several times. In one version his hands seemed to leave his arms and soar out over the trees; in another, the tree itself — and voices that he heard — would drift away, and then suddenly return. His summary version in the *Memoirs* goes like this:

> I sat under the tree and it seemed to me that I held my own life in my hand. I became faint and weak. I had my own life in my hand and it slipped out of my grasp.
> It became like a bird. This was on a clear day in the lovely fall and there were no clouds in the sky.
> My life was flying away from me. It was going, going, going. It got very small, far out there in the clear blue sky. It was a very speck in the distance. . . .
> There was my own life, going away from me, far away. I had the definite feeling that, if it went quite out of sight, out there, I would be dead. My eyes clung, with desperate intensity, to the little dark spark against the blue out there.
> Then it came back, slowly at first, and then, suddenly, with a rush. It flew back to me.

He associates the feeling with an illness, but he knows too that it is "something of the mind." It could come upon him out of doors or at the table, when he was mowing lawns or selling papers, or when he was with his friend Herman Hurd — poor Herman Hurd, shouting at him, "What's the matter with you?" and concluding, "You're a nut."

One scholar calls these "mystic episodes," but Anderson himself gives them no such reading. Psychological wisdom would have it that they are "fugue" states. Occurring in "preadolescent and adolescent phases of development," as Henry Stack Sullivan describes them, they are prolonged spells of "dreaming-while-awake," in which "the relationship with circumambient reality and with the meanings to which things attach from one's past is, to a certain extent, fundamentally and as absolutely suspended as it is when one is asleep." (Sullivan also relates them to epileptic seizures, which could help explain why Anderson fled from Coon Creek pond: in that boy he perhaps saw an uncontrollable version of himself.) All Anderson knew — or thought he knew — was that these episodes stopped when he was about sixteen. He never did know just what had happened to him. Nor did he ever make the connection, but they had stopped only to recur, more intensely, more dramatically, twenty years later when he was a seemingly successful business- and family man in another Ohio community.

The one event that was sure to sever his ties to Clyde occurred just a few years later, when he was eighteen: his mother died. The family had already begun to drift apart. Karl had gone on to Mansfield and then to Cleveland to take a job designing gravestones. Sherwood was living at the livery stable. Emma was only forty-two, but she had little strength left with which to fight consumption, "hasty consumption," her niece called it. She died on May 10, 1895.

In its obituary, the Clyde *Enterprise* described her as "a most estimable lady" who had left many friends, and in the same issue, a note from "I. M. Anderson and Family" thanked those friends for their help during and after her illness.

Stella was now the woman of the house. She had already taught school for two years; with her mother's death, she took on the responsibility of her brothers instead. And another woman, Anderson's maternal grandmother, might have helped. She was a pious German woman who had been married and unmarried twice, a difficult person, to be sure, but Anderson transformed her into an Italian woman who had buried four husbands. She was "the dark evil old woman with the broad hips and the great breasts of a peasant and with . . . glowing hate shining out of her one eye." In his wildest story about her, when a tramp tried to rob her, she beat him into submission with her fists, after which the two got drunk on hard cider and then went singing down the road together.

Stella told stories about her too. She also thought their grandmother was Italian, and though it is not clear just when the older woman arrived in Clyde, Stella thought it was after Emma's death. She said her grandmother came and told her to get back to teaching, and then came after her with a knife. Part of *that* story is told by Anderson, who describes his sister's coming to him and her brother Irve with her savings, saying they had to get their grandmother on the five o'clock train if they wanted *her,* Stella, to stay — it was one or the other. All of which tells us not that Anderson was a liar, or that his sister was as unreliable as he, but that the two of them — Sherwood especially — were devastated when their mother died, that nobody could take her place, that anyone who tried was hateful.

In Anderson's imaginings, nobody could possibly do enough to make up for the loss, least of all his father. From a long, May 17 *Enterprise* article on preparations for Memorial Day celebrations, signed by Irwin and two other men, and from the report on the event itself, it is tempting to infer that Irwin was not overwhelmed by his wife's death. "Never was Memorial Day more fittingly or elaborately observed in Clyde than it was yesterday," the article said. "The committee of arrangements in charge of the affair are to be congratulated." Only a week had gone by since Emma had died. It seems the widower had better things to do than mourn. From two fictional versions of Anderson's response to his father, one in *Windy McPherson's Son,* the other in the unpublished *Talbot Whittingham,* one may be on surer ground: he wanted to kill the man. In the former story, Sam McPherson comes around the table to his father, takes him by the throat, and says to himself: "I could repay all of the years mother has spent over the dreary washtub by just one long, hard grip at this lean throat. I could kill him with so little extra pressure." His father's eyes begin to stare, his tongue protrudes, "across the forehead ran a streak of mud picked up somewhere in the long afternoon of drunken carousing," but Sam stops short of killing his father lest he see that face for the rest of his life.

In any event, a few years later Irwin left town, married again, and had another son. In 1914 he was admitted to the soldiers' home in Dayton and died there in May 1919 as the result of a fall from a ladder (he had been helping paint the soldiers' home). And he was an entertainer as well as a painter right up to the end. It is reported that during his stay at the home he coached schoolchildren for their parts in Memorial Day exercises. After Irwin left Clyde, Anderson never laid eyes on him again.

Sherwood remained in Clyde a few more months, but with his mother gone there was no more reason to stay. And besides, for all his doubts and reservations, at nineteen, Sherwood Anderson had one goal in life — to make something of himself, which is to say, to make money. It was the only way he knew about in 1895, and in America, at the time, Chicago was the place in which to do it. So about a year after his mother died, Anderson boarded the train for Toledo, connecting there with the train for Chicago.

The words with which he concludes *Winesburg, Ohio* are as close as we can come to imagining how he felt. George Willard's father is there to see him off, sounding to the very end like an American Polonius: "Be a sharp one. Keep your eyes on your money. Be awake. That's the ticket. Don't let anyone think you're a greenhorn." As for himself:

> The young man, going out of his town to meet the adventure of life, began to think but he did not think of anything very big or dramatic. Things like his mother's death, his departure from Winesburg, the uncertainty of his future life in the city, the serious and larger aspects of his life did not come into his mind.

He thought instead of little things, a man carrying boards down the main street, a lovely woman who had once stayed overnight at a hotel in town, the lamplighter going about his rounds, the girl whom he has come closest to (in the text) at the post office, putting a stamp on an envelope. "One looking at him," he says, "would not have thought him particularly sharp." He leans back, closes his eyes. When he opens them again, his town is gone and "his life there had become but a background on which to paint the dreams of his manhood."

TWO

"The Undeveloped Man"

1896-1906

B Y THE TIME Chicago was incorporated in 1837, 4,000 people had made their way there, by stagecoach or along canals. In midcentury, the railroads began to take over. They all led to Chicago; not a train passed through without stopping, and Chicago's population soared. In 1850 it was 30,000; in 1870, almost 300,000. By 1890, it was over a million. When Sherwood Anderson arrived, in 1896, it was about a million and half. Tens of thousands who came were like him, taking the train from farm country, tens of thousands more were from abroad. Three-quarters of them were either immigrants or the children of immigrants. In seventy years, the architect Louis Sullivan said in 1901, Chicago went from a mudhole to a human swamp.

But out of it arose the greatest industrial city of the West. Beginning in 1865, those men who came to Chicago made the rails that people rode. Two years later they began to make the cars. They worked steel furnaces that by the end of the century would have the largest capacity in the country. They helped make Chicago the greatest slaughtering and meat-packing center in the country, first in the production of farm implements, and second only to New York in printing. They helped establish the mail-order business in America — Montgomery Ward in 1872, Sears in 1886. All of them, no matter who they were or what they did, kept alive the dream that like Armour and Swift, McCormick and Deering, Ryerson and Pullman, Marshall Field and Potter Palmer — any American man could make a fortune.

To Harriet Monroe, Chicago's was "a birth sublime." "New thoughts are thine: new visions rise / Before thy clear prophetic eyes," she wrote in 1899. "On to the future . . ." One could actually see it coming into being: Richardson's Marshall Field warehouse in 1887, Burnham and Root's twenty-two-story Masonic temple in 1892, Sullivan and Adler's combination hotel, auditorium, and office building along Congress Street in 1899. On the South Side, the University of Chicago rose up from the edges of the swamps after John D. Rockefeller gave $35 million in 1890. ("An expensive ornament worn on the soiled hand of a street urchin," Anderson later called it.) The Art Institute opened in 1892, the Newberry Library in 1893, the Stock Exchange in 1894. The "Loop" was completed in 1897. The future was most grandly symbolized, of course, by the Columbian Exposition of 1893. "All at once and out of nothing," Theodore Dreiser wrote, "in this dingy city . . . [that] but a few years before had been a wilderness of wet grass and mud flats . . . had now been reared this vast and harmonious collection of perfectly constructed and showy buildings, containing in their delightful interiors, the artistic, mechanical and scientific achievements of the world."

No matter that Chicago was what Sullivan called a city of "vacant, sullen materialism." No matter, even, that men's most basic material needs were not always fulfilled. No matter that the Exposition opened its doors on the worst depression of the century, that in 1893 twenty-four local banks failed, that business failures increased by 50 percent, that mills and factories and furnaces closed down, and that the suffering continued for at least five years. As Sullivan himself went on, Chicago was young — "and where youth is, there is always hope." There could be no new New York. The damage — architectural and otherwise — had been done, that city's aesthetic and social descent irreversible, its soul irredeemable. Chicago might burn for its sins, but even Sullivan detected sparks in its ashes and imagined that fate might yet fan them into "a flame of democratic fire."

What with its new libraries and universities, art schools and galleries, the city's tone was lifting too. "The city is passing to a higher and maturer stage of civic existence," the editor of the *Dial* wrote:

> Centres of social activity are thus forming, in which artists and scholars and educators will gather, at which ideas and ideals will prevail, and which, as an informal "Academy," will set standards that shall mitigate and transform the grossness of our hitherto material life.

There was the Civic Federation, formed in 1893 to rid the city of Charles Tyson Yerkes and the men he had placed in City Hall. It promoted causes that would clean up and order the city in other ways as well: a civil service law, relief for the poor, the closing of gambling houses, and, in the first decade of the new century, Daniel Burnhams's comprehensive plan for the city. There were Henry Fuller, Hamlin Garland, Robert Herrick, and other writers, protesting against spiritual and political corruption in the name of ethical standards inherited from the East, in novels that took their shape from what fictions were admired there. There was the group associated with "The Little Room" that gathered in studios in the Fine Arts Building for tea and conversation on Friday afternoons after the symphony concerts. Novelists, architects, publishers, artists, arbiters of literary taste — they were part of what in 1897 Henry Fuller called "The Upward Movement in Chicago," a way of fighting "for those desirable, those indispensable things, that older, more fortunate, more practiced communities possess and enjoy as a matter of course."

In 1896, Anderson was one of the thousands of people these artists and social critics were worried about. He had come for no other reason than to make money.

When he arrived, he may have shivered with what he described in *Poor White* as "the nameless fear of multitudes, common to country boys in the city," but unlike many of them, he had a place to go. Having moved to Chicago in 1893, Clyde's former mayor and his family, the Padens, ran a boardinghouse on the West Side. What was even more comforting, Sherwood's brother Karl had come from Cleveland two years before to study at the newly opened Art Institute, and he was staying at the Padens'. For the time being, Sherwood could share his room. For as long as it took him to get his feet under him, Sherwood had support. What with these reminders of Clyde surrounding him and his talent for getting on in the world, if he was at all afraid, he did not betray the fact. He was still "Jobby," fair-complexioned, dark-eyed, dark-haired — grown now to almost five feet nine — eager as ever to succeed.

The day he arrived he told everyone he would start out as a grocery clerk and work his way up from there. It was familiar territory, a good place to start. The following evening he appeared at the dinner table and announced that he had been offered ten such jobs and that he would flip a coin to "see which fellow is to have my services." "A callow youth," his brother called him. But a girl who happened to be visiting the house that night was more impressed. She told her father about this ambitious newcomer, and he introduced Anderson to a different kind of job: he put the young man to work in his cold-storage plant, hauling frozen meat and handling barrels of apples and crates of eggs.

If Anderson made any financial headway during his months in Chicago, it was only by moving to another warehouse. In *A Story Teller's Tale* he describes "rolling kegs of nails out of a great sheet-iron warehouse." Whether it was frozen meat or barrels or kegs that he moved, his labors were hard and led nowhere. If anything, he seemed likely to lose ground, for he could not concentrate just on himself. Their parents gone, his siblings too were the more susceptible to Chicago's lure, and though he himself may not have been so inclined, they were the more likely to want to band together. Soon his sister Stella came to town, bringing their brothers Earl and Ray with her, and he did what he could to help them. He took two rooms in a tenement building where they could stay with him, he in one room, soot coming down on his bed from the stovepipe overhead, his sister and brothers in the two beds in the other.

Clifton Paden's sister later said that while he was in Chicago Anderson "talked about his dissatisfaction and unhappiness all the time." It was Clyde, only worse. Anderson had never felt entirely at home back in Ohio, but he knew his way around, and the house on Spring Avenue was at least a refuge. In Chicago the traces of community and family life grew dim. Most important, the jobs he held did not lead to success after all. He was making about two dollars a day for ten hours' work. Karl sent a little money each month, but Anderson still looked at the fragments of his family that surrounded him and asked, "Why should I be saddled with them?" He also cried, as he had cried before, "Money. Money. God damn money."

For guidance and support he looked to Clifton Paden, the former mayor's son, more than he did to his brother Karl. Paden was slightly older, he was socially superior, and he showed by his example how a man could get ahead. If he wanted a job, Paden went after it with cold determination. He learned the prejudices of his man, rehearsed his speeches to the fellow the night before, and the next day was employed. He set about becoming choirmaster in a large Chicago church; once in place, he created an excellent boys' choir by making each boy, the rowdiest as well as the most docile, feel that *he* was worthless, that the choir was all. "People like to be commanded," he told Anderson. "They want someone to tell them what to do, how to feel." He knew his women too and got his way: he just asked. In many women, he said, he sensed "vulgarity," and "they like his casual way with them. It in some queer way left them free." He knew how to play on people's weaknesses. His young friend's problem, he told him, was that he was too serious: "You want them to be in love with you," he told Anderson. "You are always falling in love. It means too much to you.

But Paden was a loyal friend and would remain one. Though neither ever knew of Sherwood's father's fate, to Paden, Anderson was always affectionately known as "Swatty," the name for a veteran so poor he ends up in a soldiers' home. Anderson always feared ending up poor, and Paden did a great deal to ease his fears. In Chicago, when Anderson was sick, Paden split his wages with him. When Paden later in fact became a success as a movie producer, marrying Anita Loos (and changing his name to John Emerson), he gave Anderson a token job in the industry. He was forever giving Anderson money without a thought of being paid back. Paden was not just being charitable, though. He saw that not all of Anderson's heart was set on getting to the top, that he was not that tough; in his young friend's presence Paden could assure himself that *he* was not just an ambitious man. He went so far as to wonder if Anderson was the only man he could ever love. In his later years, when he himself was fairly miserable, Paden seemed to switch roles with Anderson. Looking back, he saw that Anderson had lived each passing hour, whereas he "always had to be looking ahead." "Fear has been my curse," he wrote Anderson in the midtwenties, "of failure, of inferiority, of missing what was best in life; above all of poverty and old age in the poor house."

For all his admiration and dependence, Anderson saw Paden as a classier version of the men back in Clyde at the bicycle factory and at the livery stable. Paden's ways with women offended him. On the other hand, the alternatives were bewildering. Anderson knew about "sissies," but in the warehouse district there were men that no behavior, no name calling, nothing in Clyde had prepared him for. There were men who actually painted their cheeks and lips. His fellow workers mocked and taunted them. The big German next to Anderson said if one ever made a pass at him he'd "knock his goddam block off," but Anderson did not join in. In retrospect, these men seemed to Anderson to emerge from "a kind of dark pit, a place of monstrous shapes, a world of strange unhealth"; but when one of "them" said he had noticed that Anderson had not insulted them and then invited Anderson to stop by anytime, he was not angry. He was revolted, he was scared, he felt sorry for these men, he did not know what to think.

His confusion stemmed from his even greater confusion about women. He wondered about the prostitutes he saw, saved his money, tempted himself, and then withdrew in fear. Once he followed through. He went with a woman to her room, but then lost heart when he saw that in order to go about her business she had to put her two sleeping children in an alcove. Here, just take the money, he said. But she refused, not wanting to be an object of pity. Afterward, in the street, he cried, as he had when he had shoved an innocent boy into the pond, out of shame for all of them, he told himself, locked in such a culture.

In Chicago he did establish some kind of continuity. There was one woman who helped him solve what he called in his *Memoirs* "a problem that had, for weeks, been keeping me in a kind of fever." Just what the "problem" was he does not say, but it is fitting that the woman was much older, as much as fifteen years older. She made Anderson feel at home but only intermittently. He came to her only in the night, and he came wrapped in lies about a bad marriage and an invalid wife. He did so because he felt obligated to marry her.

It is possible he did intend to marry another woman, a Miss Mabel Harper, but all we can be sure of is the intensity of his concerns. It was his way, as Paden saw. After thirty years and three failed marriages he would still be the same. "Most men . . . almost all men," he wrote his daughter in 1932, "experiment with several women. I have married them."

Meanwhile, in assessing his material conditions, he saw that they would not improve as long as he was a day laborer, so beginning in September of 1897 he went nights to what was then the Lewis Institute (now part of the Illinois Institute of Technology) to take a course on "New Business Arithmetic." He tried to learn about bookkeeping and accounting, and he did earn the grade of ninety, but his strongest memory is of the classroom's warmth after a day's work in the cold, of putting his head down on the desk, and then, before he knew it, falling asleep.

Education had not worked for him in Clyde. It was not working in Chicago either. But even if it had, at the outset of what might have been a second term, it could not possibly compete with what was then and has always been a seductive call to young men wondering how they are ever going to succeed, wondering if they are man enough: the call to war. Not education, nothing could compete. In fact, Anderson did not even wait for the call to come. The *Maine* was sunk on February 15, 1898, signaling the beginning of the Spanish-American War; in a few weeks, he wrote to the captain of his National Guard unit:

> Captain Gillette:
> Dear Sir: if by any chance this war scare amounts to anything, and the company is called please telegraph me 708 Michigan Boulevard and I will be with you.

If there was any chance of doing so, he was going off to war. Stella had interrupted her teaching career to take care of her brothers; the plan was for her to return to it once Anderson could assume the burden of support. But he was going to give up trying. It was, he later said, "a shabby trick."

Three years before, in Clyde, Anderson had enlisted in Company I of the Sixteenth Regiment of the Ohio National Guard. In the not so distant past the regiment had had to put down a labor riot in Wheeling Creek and on another occasion to collect food and provisions for miners and their families in the Hocking Valley. Possibly Sherwood went to Tiffen, Ohio, in November 1895, when the regiment was called out to deal with a labor disturbance. But there is no indication that he was troubled by conflicts of interest or sympathy. For the time being, he was content to be one of about fifty men in Company I, perhaps going out on a maneuver, going to camp for a week the summer after he enlisted and then again the next summer, and marching in an occasional parade. After he went off to Chicago in 1896, nobody bothered him about any military obligations.

A month before Anderson enlisted, the revolution in Cuba against Spain began, under José Martí; a year later, the U.S. Senate passed a resolution elevating the rebels to the status of "belligerents," and the United States enthusiastically prepared itself for a fight. In the prospect of war, politicians and their backers saw chances to broaden avenues of trade, to divert attention from a depressed economy, and to become themselves not only officeholders but heroes. Even Peter Altgeld, the governor of Illinois, who had distinguished himself (and later lost his office) by pardoning the men wrongly accused of murder in the riot in Haymarket Square ten years before, joined in, writing in William Randolph Hearst's New York *Journal* that slave trade and cannibalism were "innocent amusements" compared with what Spain had been doing for over a century in Cuba.

Anderson was only too happy to take part, as dashing a part as he could get. On the freight train he rode back to join his regiment he invited and enjoyed the hoboes' admiration. Before reaching his hometown he prepared himself to face a more important audience. He got off at a stop or two before Clyde, bought a new suit of clothes, a new hat, and even a walking stick so that the townsfolk would think he had given up a good job in Chicago in order to defend his country's honor. The Clyde *Enterprise* had said as much. It had also printed his letter to Captain Gillette as evidence of how local boys would acquit themselves should war be declared against Spain. After it was (on April 24), the paper cited him again, along with a boy who had offered to come from Shreveport, Louisiana, boasting: "That's the sort of material Clyde boys are made of."

After "the boys" were given their orders, the ladies of Clyde produced a banquet with more than 150 settings, and the men formed an honor guard that escorted Company I through cheering crowds to its train. But Clyde did not let them get very far out of sight. The Clyde Ladies' Society began to collect funds to provide each member of Company I with a medal, and Sergeant Robinson sent regular reports back to the Clyde *Enterprise*. What Carl Sandburg said of his unit from Galesburg, Illinois, was true of Company I: it was a "living part" of the town. That made it difficult for the U.S. Army, or rather for anyone, to think of there being such a thing as the nation's army. Watching over promotions with a jealous eye, following their unit, even ministering to its sick wherever possible, the towns would not let go. Nor were the volunteers about to cut their ties to home. The captain of Anderson's company had been a janitor in one of the town's public buildings, one lieutenant raised celery, another ground knives in the cutlery factory. They were first known and they would be known again as fellow townsmen. They had only so much authority.

Amidst more cheering the company went in and out of Toledo, then on to Columbus, where it became part of the federal service; newly defined, it spent several months camping and decamping, marching and countermarching through the South. During that time Anderson bartered stolen uniform buttons for food and kisses, and — the essential loneliness of his life surfacing — tried to prolong relationships with girls he met along the way with exchanges of pictures and letters. But for the time being, he was a man among men and terribly happy. He did not have to worry about earning a living. He forgot about his past. He was never in danger. His company did not embark for Cuba until four months after the armistice was signed.

Once there, Anderson heard a disturbing story about the gang rape of a Cuban woman, and he knew that the "natives" who celebrated with the soldiers were anxious to be rid of them, but he did not think too much about such things. Often he withdrew to read, adventure stories, mostly, but also Edgar Howe's *The Story of a Country Town* on the recommendation of a young German man. Otherwise, he let himself be swept along with all the others, let his body do all his work for him. He became intoxicated with physical exhaustion. There was, he said, a "physical hardening process" that he "instinctively liked." Even if he had to drop out for a moment, to stop by the wayside for the stone in his shoe, he felt the others' strength:

> I was, in myself, something huge, terrible and at the same time noble. I remember that I sat, for a long time, while the army passed, opening and closing my eyes.
> Tears were running down my cheeks.
> "I am myself and I am something else too," I whispered to myself.

Once back at camp, his appetite for food and company gone, he threw himself down on his cot like a man in love, "in love with the thought of the possibilities of myself combined with others."

The process, the bonding, was exhilarating. Around the warehouse, no real man could admit to imagining any possible "combination" with other men. One joined others only in revulsion. The Army, however, not only endorsed but also encouraged men's allegiance to one another, to the Army itself, and allegiance could take many forms. In the Army a real man could lose himself in other men and have no fear. If there was anything to be afraid of it was men's scorn for any sign of reluctance. At Columbus, faced with the decision whether to join the federal ranks with his company, Anderson thought once more of his siblings. Two or three men were going back; the father of one had been kicked by a horse, and the parents of all of them needed the money they could earn. The other soldiers had no sympathy for them. They were quitters. "Let's get 'em. The skunks," the cry arose. Anderson thought for a moment of Stella and their younger brothers, and then he joined in the mob that formed. The men retired into their tents, he later wrote,

> but we dragged them forth into the company street. We beat them. There were four of us who grabbed one of the smaller of the men and ran him away to a place of trees. We took, each man, an arm or a leg. We beat his buttocks against the tree. He screamed with pain. It went on thus, for a time, none of the men who were going home resisting much, none of our officers interfering, their clothes torn and their bodies bruised and then we gave it up. Our victims had crawled back into their tents and again we others gathered in groups.

Life in the Army turned common men into heroes, Anderson said. More evidently it corralled them into groups and afforded pleasures that none of them need try to name.

Anderson remained fascinated by his short experience in the Army and would draw on it many times. (Late in life he would welcome a pension for his services — first twenty dollars, and then thirty-five dollars a month.) But starting in 1914, the glamour of it faded fast. The Army had learned to split its men up and train them among strangers. And there were the realities, realities Anderson had never had to face during the Spanish-American War. In February 1915 he told a friend that he had had dreams of men "marching shoulder to shoulder and doing big deeds." "Instead," he went on, "as you know men have gone into the ground and there is only the horrible, mechanical guns and the deafness and the stench of decaying bodies." (Ten years later he was surprised to learn that men were told to attack dummy figures with bayonets and were "even told to grunt as they plunged the bayonet into the figure.") In the 1930s he associated the bonding and the bullying he had once enjoyed with lynching. He also realized, "It is the strength of fascism."

In retrospect, the Spanish-American War seemed to Anderson "a glorious national picnic," "rather a joke as everyone knows." Worse, it was "like taking pennies from a child, like robbing an old gypsy woman in a vacant lot at night after a fair," but he had picked what he called "the right war." Clyde had never seemed so much a town as when some of its young men were joined together hundreds of miles away, faced with a common enemy they never saw. Men had never seemed so fine and so democratically bound one to another as when they had lost their individuality under their commander. Anderson himself had never felt so pure, so much a man, as when he had all but lost consciousness of himself.

Company I left Cuba on April 21, 1899, having spent four months there, and returned to Clyde to one more patriotic orgy. The *Enterprise* said the scene at the depot was "beyond description," "such kissing and handshaking has not been witnessed for many a day," and then the town closed *its* ranks: "Dinner was waiting in dozens of homes and travel stained soldiers were soon enjoying a square meal at mother's table." Anderson's father could have been there, his brother Ray almost certainly was, but his brother Irve was in Chicago, having taken Sherwood's job at the warehouse, and Karl and Stella were in Springfield, Ohio, where both worked for the Crowell Publishing Company.

Anderson went to Springfield for a month and then returned to Clyde to work with Frank Wertel's threshing crew while staying on Wallace Ballard's farm. He did well, feeding and cutting, but now no amount of exhaustion could enable him to forget about the future. The occasional walk into town to see the remnants of his family and the Hurds was not enough to make him think he had a home. He had talked to Karl and Stella about going back to school, to Wittenberg Academy right there in Springfield. The money he was earning, added to the hundred dollars he received on mustering out of the Army, would make it possible, so in September he went back.

He enrolled a few days after turning twenty-three, in what amounted to a senior year of high school, and he raced to catch up. To his fellow students he seemed attractive but retiring — and thin. The Army had left him leaner than ever, "all skin and bones," Karl said. But he seemed full of energy. He was the one who kept the physics class after the bell with his questions. By the end of the year he had taken fourteen courses, done very well (A's in almost everything), and impressed everyone with his eagerness and intelligence. He also joined the Athenian Literary Society.

The year 1899–1900 was productive academically for Anderson. He wasted no time, but if his novel *Marching Men* is any indication of his feelings, the teachers at Wittenberg did not have the answers he was looking for. His hero, Beaut McGregor, interrupts a class discussion of global unrest by shouting at the professor: "Why do not you, who have trained brains, strive to find the secret of order in the midst of this disorder?" He then turns to the class: "Why do not men lead their lives like men?" But they are just students, and "among the students at the University," Anderson says bluntly, "McGregor had seemed very old."

He found more of what he wanted among more mature men and women, at "The Oaks," where he lived. The Oaks was a twenty-one-room boardinghouse, an old square brick house on the edge of town, owned and run by a widow named Louisa Folger. She was, Anderson said, "a sort of second mother" to him. She let him earn his keep mowing the grass, shoveling snow, tending the stoves, and filling the kerosene lamps. She also helped him with his schoolwork. Karl, now resident artist for Crowell's *Woman's Home Companion,* was staying there too. Harry Simmons, the advertising manager of the magazine, took his meals there. Edward Steiner, pastor of the First Congregational Church and later author of twenty-seven books, and Karl Hochdoerfer, who taught German at Wittenberg College, lived there, as did two schoolteachers. By 1899 Marco Morrow had married and moved out, and soon after he would leave his job as managing editor of the Hosterman publications, which included the Springfield *Republican Times,* for an advertising job in Chicago, but while he was still in Springfield he established a friendship with Anderson that would be lifelong. So too would George Daugherty, like Morrow a Springfield native and a newspaperman, who with his wife lived across the street but who often ate at The Oaks. It was the most interesting and supportive group of men and women Anderson had yet known. At table there were not just fellow townspeople, but people who in one way or another worked with words, and Anderson did not feel left out.

The person to whom he was the closest was Trillena White, a high school teacher who lived and worked nearby. Ten years older, she was a tall, broad-shouldered, athletic woman ("a big-legged, big-breasted German woman," as he put it), the more effective and influential for never having had Anderson in class. The two walked out at night enough to cause people at The Oaks to talk and to cause Louisa Folger to warn him against being "taken in." She had seen it happen before: there had been another boy, another boarder, who had married a woman almost twenty years older than himself, and that woman too had been a schoolteacher. Trillena must have been a passionate soul like Kate Swift, whose portrait in *Winesburg, Ohio* she seems to have inspired, and she may, like Kate, have made her passion known, but the deepest impression that she left was literary. "She was a great woman to me," Anderson wrote in 1939, when she was dying of cancer, "and the one who first introduced me to fine literature."

Here, in and around The Oaks, were family and school, work and fellowship, men and women, in harmonies he had never heard. And here, finally, as the century turned, Anderson heard his calling.

Though he might easily have gone on from Wittenberg Academy to the College, once again and for the last time Anderson left school. At his graduation on the evening of June 4, 1900, after some music and prayers and eight other speakers, he gave an oration on "Zionism." He had spoken to the Athenian Literary Society about England's rights in its war with the Boers in Transvaal, about the Dreyfus case, and about the Mormons. Clearly he was interested in social justice and in the ways people organized. But what was most impressive was his manner. He was a good talker, obviously persuasive. The advertising manager of the *Woman's Home Companion*, Harry Simmons, was so impressed that right there and then he offered Anderson a job in Chicago with his company, and right there and then Anderson accepted. He could not go on being "Jobby," the country boy who could do just about anything. He was getting on, and the Age of Professionalism had begun. Here was another chance for him to make a success of himself in Chicago, this time starting not as a common laborer, but as an advertising solicitor for the Crowell Publishing Company. What was more, his friend Morrow would be there (and before long, as it turned out, Daugherty would join them both). Advertising — it was a likely profession for the recent graduate.

Not surprisingly, a short time after he returned to Chicago, Anderson had established himself as a good advertising solicitor, turning even his own and others' ineptitude to his advantage. His first assignment was to collect on an order for two thousand lines — what the stenographer had mistakenly written down as two hundred lines instead. Anderson was new at the job and not all that welcome, as it turned out. (His job had been intended for someone else.) When he went out on his assignment he said nothing. He just watched his customer make the change to two thousand; then he reported back, not to people in the Chicago office but to their superiors in Springfield, that his client had increased his order tenfold; and then he said nothing again, when Springfield wired on its commendations of the new man. On another occasion he was sent to convince a particularly tough customer to take out a thousand lines, but he came back with five thousand because he had appeared nervous to just the right degree. He brought in business simply because he was a good salesman; when he seemed not to be, he brought in business too.

But the atmosphere was tense; or what was worse, the routine was "staid and monotonous." Anderson needed to be doing more, and he had to communicate with the world in a style more imaginative than that of "Yours of the 5th inst. at hand and contents noted." His chance came in a matter of months: Marco Morrow persuaded his company, the Frank B. White Advertising Agency, to take on Anderson as a copywriter as well as a solicitor. And so began a long association with White's Agency, and with the Long-Critchfield Agency, which absorbed it in 1903. What with an office on Wabash Avenue, in the heart of the Loop, Anderson felt that he had gotten somewhere. For the first time in his life, he could imagine being financially secure. He was only in his midtwenties, in a position "Jobby" could be proud of.

In 1905, five years after his return to Chicago, Anderson gave another speech, and again it climaxed the proceedings. Eleven speakers preceded him this time. The occasion was the Long-Critchfield Corporation dinner, held at the Palmer House, just a few blocks away from his office, on May 1. Thirty-six relatively young men were present, Anderson one of five representing the Copy and Promotion Department. In the photograph that was taken "promptly at six o'clock," we can see them there, sober, confident, proud, and we can see Anderson in good position, seated on the horizontal near the center, to the right of Mr. Long, looking down on the two rows of men in front of him. Mr. Critchfield introduced the evening. Mr. Sawin spoke on Getting Business, Mr. Ridgway on What the Art Department Needs, Mr. Haswell on Helping the Order Department, Mr. Thain on Creating Advertisers, and then, after several more, Mr. Anderson on Making Good.

. And so he was, and did. During his career, by his various recountings, Anderson wrote copy about everything from ditch-digging machines to canned tomatoes, from patent medicines for loose bowels and thinning hair, toothpaste and washtubs and kitchen cabinets, to a remedy for diseases for hogs. Looking back, one of his colleagues, Don Wright, said, "I'd give my account to Anderson sight unseen. . . . I wouldn't bother him or tell him what to do. How he got the story and turned it into advertising would be strictly his business. And it would be good business." Anderson became so confident of his success as a mail-order advertising man that he boasted to the young women in the office that he could get them husbands through the mails.

Anderson's move into copywriting was obviously a happy one, and from copywriting he branched out again. "Anderson was both a producer (of everything from layouts to sales policies) *and* a salesman," Wright went on. "During his early years in the business he was even a high pressure salesman, though he later developed into a *subtle* salesman, disguised as copy-writer." He developed with the business of advertising itself, first as a solicitor, then, when agencies began to hire men to fill the spaces that they sold, as copywriter, and finally, when advertising agencies evolved into something like their present form in the first decade of this century, as adviser or would-be policymaker. It is there, in that role, that we find him a month before his speech at the Palmer House, writing on "The Sales Master and the Selling Organization": "The relation of the advertising agency man and the organization man is also changing," he says, as if pointing to the flow chart before him. "There is a growing demand for the advertising man of a quick sympathy and appreciation of the ends sought by the sales manager."

Word traveled beyond the agency, and no less a figure than Cyrus H. K. Curtis, the publisher of the *Ladies' Home Journal* and the *Saturday Evening Post,* came looking for Anderson. ("Advertising," Curtis once said, "that's what made me whatever I am. . . . I use up my days trying to find men who can write an effective advertisement.") But Anderson was out of town. The organization continued to pursue him. The editor of the *Post* invited him to submit an article, but the match missed again, this time, Anderson felt, because what he wrote was not flattering enough to business. But, persisting, the Curtis Company summoned him to Philadelphia, and there negotiations finally broke down. As Anderson weighed matters, the Curtis Company seemed too big, too much. He had come very far, very fast; there were limits to how much success he wanted or could handle. He decided he was doing just fine at Long-Critchfield.

He was prospering in other ways as well. He was moving around Chicago with ease this time, walking confidently along Michigan Avenue, passing all those new skyscrapers, rather than confining himself to the West Side. His salary increased, he built up something of a wardrobe (he began to wear spats and even bought a dinner coat), he went to parties. He established business contacts, and prospective buyers took him home to dinner. He had a few old friends and made new ones fast, more friends than customers, it seemed at first, but not just because he was intent upon getting on in the world. He was curious about people. He liked them, and they liked him. "His charm, interest and sympathy made friends and enabled him to draw out more deep down inside thinking and hidden experiences than a father confessor of Holy Church," Daugherty said. What was most important, Anderson was writing.

Our inclination is to imagine the future famous author going about his business, tolerating it, enduring it, but all the while knowing better and gaining confidence in that knowledge as he prepares to share with us what is *really* on his mind. Perhaps he is like Dr. William Carlos Williams, his writing the more passionate and tender for his work with patients, or like Wallace Stevens or T. S. Eliot, something of a mystery to everyone at the office, or like Hart Crane, clear and vocal in his desire to escape the business world altogether. We want our literary heroes to be literary, better still, romantic, in the world but not of it, and indeed one day Anderson would try to put the devilish adman behind him. But at the same time, as that adman, he was learning and practicing the art of writing. "The advertising business is one that lends itself peculiarly to what I wanted to do in life," he wrote in 1918 in a publicity essay, an advertisement for himself:

> I do not understand why more novelists do not go into it. It is all quite simple. You are to write advertisements for one who puts tomatoes in cans. You imagine yourself a canner of tomatoes. You become enthusiastic about the tomato. You are an actor given a role to play and you play it.

Division, tension there was. It had been there from the earliest days in Clyde, and it would increase as time went on, but the advertising profession gave Anderson the chance to heal divisions and ease the tension. Advertising gave him the chance to write, and in writing the chance to come to terms with the conflicts in his life. In turn, as he later came to express his thoughts and feelings in fictions that had nothing to do with advertising, he did so in prose that would always show traces of its origins in the work he did for Long-Critchfield.

By 1918 he could no longer bear to write just advertisements (though he had been drawing pay from Long-Critchfield for almost two decades). By 1918, as he put it in the publicity essay and in many other places, he was saved: "The impulse that led me to write novels was the impulse for my own salvation. I did not want to become in reality the canner of tomatoes." But fifteen years earlier, ten years earlier, all along, he was finding out that he could write, finding what he wanted to write about, and beginning to develop the seemingly simple style by which readers would always recognize him.

When did Sherwood Anderson start to write? The simple answer is 1902, the year his first publication appeared in *Agricultural Advertising,* a monthly journal "pertaining to agricultural newspaper advertising," put out by Long-Critchfield and edited by Marco Morrow. For the next few years, mostly in the same publication, Anderson produced a steady stream: aphorisms and fillers (which are probably but not certainly his), seven or eight miscellaneous articles, and two series of articles that ran through 1903 and 1904, titled "Rot and Reason" and "Business Types." In all of it, as to varying degrees would be the case throughout his writing life, one can hear Sherwood Anderson discovering and exploring what it was that mattered to him — which is to say, himself, an American man, discovering himself in writing.

There are nice, personal, reflective touches: "A Vacation Story," which draws on Anderson's knowledge of the workings of a bicycle factory, "The Solicitor," about one of his first experiences on the job, or this appreciation of the life he had left behind:

> There was an old fellow at home that hoed corn. He was grim, grey and silent, but because he pleased my boyish heart I was glad to hoe beside him for the dignity of his presence. One hot day when we had hoed to the end of a particularly long and weedy row and were resting in the shade by the fence he put his big hand on my shoulder and said, "Don't the corn make you ashamed, Sherwood, it's so straight?"

And in the same issue, these "Chicago Inspirations":

> The morning sun shining on the Field Columbian museum.
> The lake front at night with the lights of the trains and the lake ahead, and the roar of the city behind.
> The front platform of an elevated train going around the Union Loop.

The view on Upper State Street at night.

The new offices of Agricultural Advertising in the Powers Building.

The young man from farm country recalls the idealized world he has left behind; he also registers the creative force that he imagines is alive and at work in the not-so-straight and tranquil life of the great city. He tells of both in simple terms, terms that would serve to alert potential customers, but terms that would also later bear the weight of his complex feelings about young men trying to find themselves in the modern world.

Certainly "making it" still mattered. First on a list he made of "Men That Are Wanted" was: "Men that sleep and eat and live with the desire to get on in the world tingling through their whole beings." Anderson seems to have no doubt about the value of trying to make it on a grand scale and achieving manliness in the effort. The question was how best to do it. The economic system was coming of age. It needed not pioneers, not roughshod self-made men, but men who could organize and maintain its expanding empire. Anderson saw such men around him and pointed to what was a familiar array of heroes for comparison: Julius Caesar, Napoleon, Lincoln, and Carlyle's Victorian savior, the industrial hero. We may think that "the Napoleons are dead and the world has settled down to mere buying and selling and the eating of three meals a day," Anderson wrote in an article on "Silent Men," but that is a pessimistic view of life not held with much favor among advertising men:

> And as it was the silent, earnest men who gripped a mad world then and turned the fierce energies of a people to the orderly carrying of muskets, so now it is the silent man of the business firm who moves it with orderly force along the lines of success.

We have to wait twenty years for Bruce Barton to reveal that Jesus was in the advertising business, but in his enthusiasm, Anderson thought Abraham Lincoln would have done well in the profession, and William Gladstone, and Davy Crockett. Long before Albert Lasker declined Teddy Roosevelt's offer of the title "America's greatest advertising man," saying "no man can claim that distinction so long as you live," Anderson was celebrating Roosevelt in the pages of *Agricultural Advertising* for "Advertising a Nation." In the same pages he said every good advertisement is a nail in the social structure, and he pounded away.

That was his job. When he expressed concern about his job (and he did so repeatedly), he did it in writing. His speech at the corporation dinner, or all we have of it, is an example. Not "Making It," but "Making Good." Anderson knew that the successful man could not be merely prosperous; he had to be upright and decent as well. The country had had its fill of claims for patent medicine; the advertising business was beginning to reform itself. Anderson was, as ever, a man of his times. If he was exceptional in 1905, it was because of the intensity of his concern.

He had explored what it meant to "make good" at some length the year before, for example, in an article about "The Man of Affairs." Two-thirds of the material of it is, as Anderson knows, typical: Peter Macveagh (like Hugh McVey, the hero of his novel *Poor White*, like Anderson himself) is yet another self-made man. He leaves the farm for Chicago, stays in a boardinghouse, works as a solicitor, and performs "the simplest task there is to do: that is to say, about the simplest task for men like Peter." He gets very rich. All the stories, Anderson says, "go just as far with their man as I have gone with my Peter Macveagh, and then they drop him." Anderson would write the sequel for the rest of his life, the writing would *be* the rest of his life, but now, in 1904, he would just deplore what the system could make of a man. "Peter, grown in power, is not the Peter of old days." Like the bullies back home, like Anderson's friend Paden, "he has learned the weaknesses of humanity now and is busy playing upon these weaknesses, and the blood that hurries through his brain draws warmth from his once big heart." The loss is everyone's, his for being despised, ours in having allowed such "Business Types" to thrive.

In a piece called "The Lightweight," in which Anderson sounds a little like Huck Finn feeling sorry for the clown while all the others laugh, he is concerned about the man who loses out to the likes of Peter. "Did you ever go to school with a fellow that could hit harder, jump higher and steal more melons than you? And didn't you most handsomely hate that fellow?" Anderson asks. Out of that "you" evolves the type around the office who, seeing others beat him out, confesses only to the stenographer or else just radiates discontent: "He's on a fair way to the horror column unless he meets a man who sees and knows." We have to help this man; we have to "make a winner out of a possible suicide." Here, in the pages of a two-bit trade journal, Anderson was beginning his lifelong career of warning us of the dangers of a society of crude individuals, and in doing so was presenting himself as one of its more tortured and vulnerable members.

In "The Boyish Man," Anderson asks, "When you were a little boy did you ever pretend you were two people?" He himself had done more than pretend. He had been both the braggart and the boy who wondered why men bragged, the ambitious one and the one who seemed to retire to another world. Splitting himself in two was a habit, as he said, that he had never gotten over. Now he was one of those men who saw life "painted in the colors of boyhood," men with unbounded hope, the kind of man the profession needed. And he was still two people in other ways as well: both "Jobby" and "Swatty," "The Man of Affairs" and "The Lightweight," a man who was succeeding and at the same time worrying about success. In sum, he was what he titled another piece — "The Undeveloped Man."

In the text, what distinguishes this "type" is his ability, his "undeveloped" talent, with words. The subject is a brakeman, so inventive in his cursing, so delighting in his powers of utterance, as to prompt the advertising man who hears him to wish the man were in his business. "He's a word man, that brakeman is," he says, "and words are the greatest thing ever invented." In ten years Anderson would discover Gertrude Stein and credit her with having taught him to treasure words for their own sake, and ten years after that he would strike up a lasting friendship with her, but he was already learning for himself. In describing all these "types," he was learning to see himself in others and to see the world through others' eyes — which is to say he was learning to be a writer. But he would not have put it that way. He had no desire, as yet, to be a writer. He was at most a copywriter, authoritative about only his work. "Men sometimes seem to forget that they are themselves the more easily convinced by well written, plain, excellent stuff that tells the story in an earnest, convincing way and then stops," he would observe, or, equally heavy-handedly: "The man who can beat the old plan of telling the truth in a plain, simple, direct way was around yesterday looking for a job."

"The Undeveloped Man" is the one piece that Marco Morrow chose to illustrate with the author's picture. As we read the text, our eyes move down the page and come to "Jobby," but "Jobby" now having "made good" in the world. His head is thrown back, there is a touch of hauteur in his glance, his mouth is slightly drawn, his hair slicked down. He will be the last speaker at the banquet in the spring, the one from the Copy and Promotion Department. Anderson is doing well, but he is still "The Undeveloped Man."

In offering tips to fellow copywriters he was describing just the kind of advertising that was coming into fashion as he was writing. It was called "Reason Why" advertising because its purpose was to tell customers why they should buy a particular product. That and no more. It sought to say what a good salesman would say face to face. No pictures, no displays, no frills. He was also describing the style he aspired to in his handling of words all his life. Ten years later, he wrote a short piece in *Agricultural Advertising* titled "Making It Clear," and in it pointed to Henry Fielding and Jonathan Swift as writers from whom a copywriter could learn: "Either of these worthies would have made crackerjack writers of advertisements because they had a sense of the fact that good copy isn't good copy unless it gets across, unless it is perfectly clear to the most simple minded." Detouring through the eighteenth century is no way to arrive at an appreciation of Anderson's own writing, but taking the short route from contemporary advertising is a good approach. One can see how both try to convey the truth, in language that is relatively simple: plain, excellent "stuff" that convinces with its earnestness.

In these early articles Anderson questioned his profession, but only in order to make it more respectable. If he asked, implicitly, what he was doing in it, it was primarily to enhance his position. In 1903 or 1904 he could conclude that both he and his profession were "making good." So it seemed only natural that he should establish himself even more firmly — get married, raise a family. It was time, we might say, to drive one more nail into the social structure.

Anderson met Cornelia Platt Lane in 1903, through a woman who once lived in Clyde and had become a neighbor of hers in the stately "Old West End" of Toledo. Just a few months younger than Anderson, Cornelia was an attractive woman, attractively situated in life. Her father was head of R. H. Lane and Company, a wholesale firm that had been in business for half a century, and was an upstanding member of his community, a deacon of the city's First Baptist Church and for a time its treasurer. Cornelia finished high school and a year at the local Baptist college; and then in June of 1900, while Anderson graduated from Wittenberg Academy, she received her degree from the College for Women of Western Reserve University. After that she traveled; while abroad, she attended the Sorbonne. To the man who courted her she was, as Karl Anderson put it, a woman "of much erudition." She was a handsome woman. A childhood illness had left her mouth slightly paralyzed on one side, but the effect was only to make her eyes seem the more alert, her smile the more knowing. She was gregarious and sociable, at the College for Women a sorority girl, a member of the Present Day Club, organized to discuss current events, and of the Browning Club, the prom committee, and the Student Association (of which she was president her senior year). She was well aware that the young man from Chicago was of humble origins and that her father did not approve of him, but he was handsome, charming, and clearly had a future.

A year after meeting Cornelia, Anderson married her. Karl was getting married that spring too, and in March Anderson wrote Karl's fiancée, Miss Helen Buell, to say that the event raised his hopes of some of the family's being together once again: "We at home have seen but little of Karl for many years and I have almost grown old in the wish that I might some day live near him." He could even imagine following his brother to the East, where Karl had moved, to do so. And then from age he bounced back to announce jauntily that "Miss Cornelia Lane of Toledo Ohio is venturing the voyage with me," and to say he hoped that Miss Buell and Karl would be there for the ceremony in May. Miss Buell did not come; Karl and Stella did. But Marco Morrow, and not Karl, was Anderson's best man. Margaret Lane was her sister's bridesmaid. It was a small ceremony, held at the Lanes' home on Robinwood Avenue.

Soon the Andersons were in Chicago, in an apartment on a small street, Rosalie Court, on the South Side, not far from Lake Michigan. The traveling solicitor and copywriter was in his own home for the first time in almost ten years.

In February of the previous year Anderson had written a piece in the *Agricultural Advertiser* celebrating the replacement of the kind of man who "went forth with his soap, his cigars and his ladies' underwear" by "the new business man, the new manufacturer, the new buyer — clean, well-read, clever men." These new men, he said, preferred to buy from "men who can be quiet, earnest and decent, even when away from home and with eyes of high school girls and waitresses upon them." The month before he married, his article on the type of "The Traveling Man" was a little less righteous. The old travelers were "hungry, lonely, story telling, hustling wanderers, outriders in the march of commerce," but still, it was a good thing that this man, "commonly called 'one of the boys,'" was being swept aside by "modern methods, rapid transit, mails, electricity and advertising." It was good for business, good for advertising itself, "finest of all for the wives and babes, who will then be able to keep tab on the goings and comings of daddy," and "who knows," he ended, "perhaps they can keep him straight."

Such must have been at first the case. Anderson settled into a modest, pleasant way of life. Though the occasions at which she presided were far from sumptuous, Cornelia was a good hostess. A favorite activity was reading aloud by the light of the fire, at the "good fireplace at Rosalie Court," as Cornelia would remember it forty years later. And reading became more and more important to Anderson himself; he became more careful selecting it, because of the pressures of his work and the guidance of his friend from Springfield, Trillena White. In 1903, he wrote two articles for *The Reader,* a publication put out by Bobbs-Merrill, one on "A Business Man's Reading," the other on "The Man and the Book." In the latter he described what must have been very like his own situation:

> The man in the street, — he who knows the unravelled tale in the sound of music from lighted houses at night, from lovers walking arm in arm in the park, and from wan, tired faces in the drift of the sidewalks, — the man, in short, who having much work to do in a short time, has learned the value of the hours given to reading and how to apply the good gleaned to the militant game of life as he plays it, — this man, believing that the salvation of his soul can be worked out in the shoe business or the hardware business, is apt to demand the kind of reading that will make him a better man in his work, and often falls into a habit of depending upon a few close friends among books.

In both articles Anderson defended the practical use, the immediate application of reading.

The businessmen he knew thought that the best place to test their mental strength and to acquire knowledge was in the *real* world or in argument with him, but they would be well advised, he said, to try to shake Robert Browning's faith instead, or to take on Carlyle, or Tennyson, or Emerson, who was "shrewder and clearer-headed than Jay Gould." Seek *them* out, he urged. "You will be a better man in the market place," and, what is more, you will thereby leave me alone with *my* reading: "We shall smoke our pipes in peace."

His reading was no longer aimed at raising the spirit of adventure that was always in him. The spirit of a kind of rebellion, yes. In discussions of the reading circle, Cornelia said, Anderson always leaped to the defense of Bernard Shaw, for example. But mostly, at this early stage, the reading he recommended served to elevate and discipline a man. He cited the case of the salesman for a wholesale grocery house who always took Macaulay's essays along with him on his trips in order to have a strong presence near him when he set out to sell sugar or, more generally, in his hours of weakness. There was the young commercial artist whose restlessness, whose desire to seek out the landlady's daughter, was calmed by Robert Louis Stevenson. We do not know how seriously Anderson suffered from the artist's malady, but the medicine was his. "When I first knew him, he was reading Stevenson," Cornelia said. "Stevenson was his god. He bought every book. Then he went to Carlyle and read every word of Carlyle." "You know how a fellow loves to linger over the sentences," Anderson has the artist's friend say. "It's like kissing a sweetheart."

And then there was another "friend" Anderson wrote about, a man who came from a family "whose men had for generations burned the oil of life at a fierce blaze and gone to their deaths loved of women." Anderson knew, he says, how hard he fought, "how grimly went the fight, and how in desperation he cast about for an outlet for the fierceness inside him." He went out with him one night, he says, and walked the two miles home with him, the last half mile in a storm, marveling all the while at the man's energy, the excitement in his eyes: "Full of the old blood, I thought to myself and shuddered." But once back home, in front of the fire, his fears turned to admiration as he learned just "how the battle went with him":

> He had made a game fight, that is all we need to know, and when the lust of his fathers was strong on him and he was near to the sin he fought against, he would go into his room alone, and over and over repeat King Henry's cry to the English at Harfleur, "Once more unto the breach, dear friends!" He told me that at such times he forgot even the meaning of the words on his lips, but that the rolling music of them soothed him and at last made him sleep unbeaten.

In these early years of marriage, it seems that reading helped keep him at home by the fireside.

But sex had always been and would always be an issue for Anderson. He was, by his own estimation, "very strongly sexed." He was attractive to women (with no need of soap or cigars or ladies' underwear as lures), and he responded to their eyeing. But as had been the case on his first trip to Chicago, and before that in Clyde, men's ways with women confused and disgusted him — his own most of all.

For all his and his profession's attempts to take the high moral line, it was good business practice to take clients out on the town, to show them a good time. One man he knew kept a mistress and convinced himself he was faithful to his wife because he had never kissed his mistress. But Anderson knew he was no better than his clients. He would slip away from them, into an alley, for his own quick good time, or check into a hotel under an assumed name.

Once he took a woman to a cheap hotel. After making love, as they lay in bed together, she had tried to make him see a white spot, a small white cloud, say, floating on the ceiling, some sign that he could share something beyond satisfaction of the flesh with her. He tried. He told her how on hot summer nights he and his brother Earl used to lie together, too, and imagine that they were floating out of their house in Clyde and off into space. And she was satisfied. But after they left the hotel, after he had assured her that something beautiful remained, that he would not forget, and put her in a cab, he admitted to himself that it had been just another sordid night, and that he was just like other men. "A lie," he said to himself. "There was no beauty."

Anderson was as compelled to flee from women as to approach them. He feared as much as loved them (or loathed them, another analyst might quickly add). "Most women simply frighten me," he later wrote. "I feel hunger within them. It is as though they wished to feed upon me." Was he fearful lest, like his father, he not be man enough to meet his responsibilities, or ashamed of having misbehaved and fearful of the consequences? Was he scared of the power with which he had endowed women, and angry at them for thereby holding sway over him? Was he appalled at what he might do to them, or wish on them? He would look for answers to such questions throughout all his writing life, in countless characters he would set forth in pursuit of answers for themselves. As a rising young advertising man — still not yet thirty — at the Long-Critchfield Agency he went about his business and performed well; at Rosalie Court he read and talked and wished that he were a better husband than he was.

Just how unfaithful he was we do not know. The stories he told span many years. But it is certain that almost from the beginning of his life with Cornelia he was restless. What happened one night soon after the Andersons were married makes that clear. They had a visitor for dinner, a young woman named Marian. The evening began pleasantly enough. After the meal, as the three of them were having coffee, Anderson offered their guest a cigarette, and she accepted. He had never seen a woman smoke before. But what was more startling was her conversation. At one point she said that always on such an occasion as the one they were enjoying, she was glad to see it end, glad to see people go, and she explained, "When it is over I stand like a child in a strange place fronting new and wonderful possibilities." The remark, the figure of a woman smoking, perhaps Marian herself — another woman — signified to Anderson that he was in an all too familiar place, cut off from who knew what possibilities, and his thoughts leaped to another life. He too imagined an end to the situation he was in. He was so excited by what Marian said about being glad to see people go that he leaned forward and added, "And death too. I would feel that way about the death of anyone I know, except a child."

Twelve years later he still remembered that moment — Cornelia's shock especially. He knew he had hurt her, and that he would go on to hurt her more. Looking back he imagined her thinking he wanted her dead, and added, "and I dare say I did."

Anderson could not stay for long at Rosalie Court, but he did not flee to some strange place. In the fall of 1906, he and Cornelia moved to other, even more conventional surroundings. He took a new job, one that offered more money, more perquisites. A mail-order house in Cleveland with which he had done business was in trouble and needed someone to rescue it. His move made very simple, practical sense. "Reason Why" advertising lent itself admirably to the mail-order business. There being no middlemen, copywriters spoke directly to the customer. Anderson had become adept at writing that kind of copy. He was eminently qualified.

More would be riding on his writing, and he would be more appreciated. Switching his allegiances with his change of jobs, Anderson had already begun to bridle as a copywriter at the fact that "contact men," solicitors, took all the credit and the plusher offices for work done by copywriters. They even took 10 percent commissions from publishers whose space the copywriters filled. In his new position, these would no longer be concerns. From now on his word would carry extraordinary weight, not only because he was going into the mail-order business, but because he would be speaking with extraordinary authority. He was going forth to lead a company. He would be president.

THREE

Breakdown

1906-1912

SHERWOOD ANDERSON'S MAJOR PUBLICATION for the
United Factories Company of Cleveland, Ohio, was a
roofing catalogue. It came out in October 1906, the month after he
assumed his new responsibilities. On its cover was a picture of its
sizable headquarters and the company motto, "Straight to You." After a few pages of explanation and assurances, Anderson introduced
himself, first with the picture that Marco Morrow had run of him as
"The Undeveloped Man" and then, underneath it, with "My Word
to You." "I promise as a decent man," he vowed,

> trying to be square that every man, rich or poor, small or large,
> shall have a square deal from my company.
>
> Every word of this book is written under my personal supervi-
> sion, and for it I am responsible to you.
>
> As you and I may never meet face to face I give you my
> word now that what is written in this book is true in spirit and in
> fact.
>
> I stand ready to do what is right by you, the buyer, and if you
> at any time buy anything of the factories whose goods are sold
> through my catalogues, and if you are not satisfied, you can feel
> free about taking the matter up with me personally, and I prom-
> ise you that I will not delegate the matter to a clerk or pile up
> words to confuse you, but will satisfy you with what you have
> bought or return every penny of your money no matter what we
> lose by it.
>
> SHERWOOD ANDERSON
> President

It is the word of a writer trying to create a voice that makes you feel he is talking directly to you, in words that you can trust. It is the word of the president, imagining himself addressing a society of equals. He is trying so hard to "make good." He will go on trying, trying harder and for six more years — until finally he will crumble under the pressure.

In 1902 several farm implement manufacturers consolidated their operations and became International Harvester; the next year Armour, Morris, and Swift became the National Packing Company. United Factories was a dream of yet another conglomerate, the dream of a financial backer named Edward Cray, a general manager named George Bottger, and Sherwood Anderson, the adman, who would speak for them. Anderson was "president," but in effect he was still a solicitor and copywriter. He had worked on the United Factories account while he was at Long-Critchfield; in his new job he was still trying to promote the company and get it business through his catalogues. With Cray, Anderson called on manufacturers, manufacturers of stoves and incubators, buggy tops and farm tools and paints, hoping to convince them to enter into their factory combine. Turning to his potential customers, he went to great lengths in his catalogues to explain how many middlemen were cut out if one did business with him, resulting in savings of how much, and to assure his readers that he would deal with them personally if they had any complaints.

None of his efforts was successful. The manufacturers were reluctant to relinquish their power to make decisions concerning their own operations. Customers did indeed complain, and Anderson did not enjoy his efforts to make good on his promises to be responsive. He actively disliked having to fire the people he thought were responsible, and in general, he turned out not to be very good at managing an office. What sealed his doom was six hundred incubators, made, incidentally, by another company with whom he had done business while working for Long-Critchfield. Of the more than three thousand that he sold, six hundred were returned as defective. United Factories lost thousands of dollars and was involved in a lawsuit.

Anderson had been hired with the understanding that his position at United Factories would be reviewed and, if necessary, redefined, after he had worked one year. When the time came to consider their future together, no one could have argued very convincingly that they had one.

Anderson's failure was a setback, but within weeks he was more rather than less committed as a businessman. In September 1907, he went twenty miles southwest of Cleveland to Elyria, Ohio, to become head of another company — and this time he was president in fact, not just title. He was also committed as a family man: in August, two weeks before their move, Cornelia gave birth to a son, whom they named Robert Lane after Cornelia's father.

Elyria was a town of fewer than ten thousand when the Andersons lived there. Anderson might have compared it to Clyde, another relatively small Ohio town that was not on the map, but he could see that it had advantages that Clyde did not have: not only railroads but also the Black River ran through it, to help power its factories; it was near a big city; and more important, having been the county seat since the 1820s, it was a central settlement in its own right. Long before Anderson arrived, it was a town that was solidly in business. The Elyria Iron and Steel Company, the Columbia Steel Works, the Fox Furnace Company, and the Weller Manufacturing Company were already firmly established there. So too were the Western Automatic Machine Screw Company, the Federal Manufacturing Company, makers of bike saddles and tool bags, the Worthington Manufacturing Company, makers of golf balls, the Fay Stocking Company, and others. And there was an institution of higher learning in town: the Elyria Business College. It had opened its doors in 1895; by 1906 it was graduating (and placing) more than 150 students a year.

Elyria presented a challenge to a young man taking over a company at the age of thirty, and Anderson rose to it eagerly. He began by selling a compound he called "Roof-Fix" through the mails, and guaranteeing, as an early advertisement had it, "to put any old leaky, worn-out, rusty, tin, iron, steel, paper, felt, gravel or shingle roof in perfect condition." His factory was situated along the river, across from the Lake Shore and Michigan Southern railroad depot. The following year he expanded his business, teaming up with a paint manufacturer who had a factory in Lorain. In the process he devised a scheme he called "Commercial Democracy," whereby hardware dealers could buy stock in his company. "Let Me Start You In Business," his ad for "Commercial Democracy" proclaimed:

I will furnish the capital and advertising. I want one sincere, earnest man in every town and township. Farmers, Mechanics, Builders, Small Business men, any one anxious to improve his condition.

He was making good in a town that specialized in making good, and as he envisioned it, everyone could share in his prosperity.

In 1911 his company expanded to where it could claim to manufacture and sell anything relating to the roofing and painting business (and some things not — ironing board springs, for example). As a corporation it attracted not just hardware retailers but Elyria's business- and professional men as investors. "We thought we had a world-beater," a local doctor said. "We were going to put Sherwin-Williams out of business." In order to prepare it for this role, Anderson changed the name of his business from the Anderson Manufacturing Company to the American Merchants Company.

He spent five years building this house of cards. It is not clear what monies got him started, perhaps Clifton Paden's, perhaps the man's whose factory space he first rented, perhaps his own, or rather the impression he managed to convey that he had ample backing. But soon enough he was making real money. He was, he said, "a salesman who had got control of a factory," and it took him no time to find what H. G. Wells called the key to success in business: namely, selling cheap products in expensive containers. The markup on his Roof-Fix was 500 percent, and Anderson was not above substituting cheaper ingredients as they came along.

But he was not just a schemer. He still had in mind "innumerable tales of men who had begun with nothing and had become great leaders, owners of railroads, governors of states, foreign ambassadors, generals of armies, presidents of great modern republics," Jay Gould and Cornelius Vanderbilt, Abraham Lincoln and Ulysses S. Grant. Anderson still wanted material success for everyone. "Commercial Democracy" was to be both, a successful business venture and a society of equals, and he published a magazine, or more likely pamphlets (no copies survive), to explain what he called his "idea of altruism in manufacturing and retailing." He often made the dubious claim that he had written a long book called *Why I Am a Socialist* — "afterward fortunately destroyed" — while still running his factory. "There would be a great factory," he imagined, "with walls going up and up and a little open place for a lawn at the front, shower baths for the workers with perhaps a fountain playing on a lawn, and up before the door of this place I would drive in a large automobile." Whether or not he committed them to print, his hopes were that he could be at the head of the company (financially or socially) and, wholly selfless, be both very rich and very pure. What drove him was his ambition, his idealism, and his enthusiasm, as Cornelia pointed out: "He was an enthusiast and believed in his own ideas," she said years later, "and his enthusiasm was contagious." What drove him too was the burden of supporting an increasingly large family. After Robert Lane came John Sherwood, born on New Year's Eve, 1908, and a daughter, Marion, born October 29, 1911.

All the while, the Andersons gradually ascended Elyria's social ladder. For the president of the Anderson Manufacturing Company, little houses with gravelly yards at the end of streets were things of the past. He first housed his family a few blocks from the town square, almost within sight of its imposing, classical courthouse, a short walk from his factory; then he moved them seven or eight blocks south to a quieter, residential area. It was not the "older" section of town — no mansions, no great lawns — but the Anderson house on Seventh Street stood out from among its neighbors. It was slightly larger, and with its bay window on the second floor, it was a bit more elegant. So too was Anderson himself. As his prosperity increased, he began to indulge his taste for expensive clothes, for the fine fabrics that appealed, he said, to the sensualist in him.

The Andersons became joiners. Anderson frequented the Elks Club, where he liked to play pool. Two years before he came, several men affiliated with the Worthington Manufacturing Company had founded the Elyria Country Club. In 1907, the Andersons were given one of its 150 family memberships. At the club Anderson developed a respectable game of golf — Class B, his caddy recalls. One of the directors, Starr Faxon, an executive at Worthington, was his regular partner. Cornelia had an old college friend who brought her into a literary club called the Fortnightly. In 1910 the Andersons joined others in the young married set to form a discussion group, more formal than the one that had come to Rosalie Court in Chicago, called the Round Table Club. At the former, Cornelia presented an occasional paper; at the latter, Anderson tried out his ideas about "Commercial Democracy."

In Elyria, Anderson found what he had set out looking for when he left Clyde. By the standards of most men, he had arrived. But he was not settled. He was far from comfortable, and a part of him rebelled. He sometimes shocked the members of the Round Table Club with his doubts about the country's business ethic, or with his attempts to reconcile that ethic with his vaguely socialistic views. When talk turned to books, he defended Arnold Bennett because Bennett had the good sense to want to meet Theodore Dreiser when he came to the United States. But "his *Sister Carrie*," they said, "it is so crude." Finally, though he was only a social drinker, by his own standards, he began to indulge too much.

Gradually, people in Elyria began to realize that Anderson was simply not one of them. One man thought that he was "an eccentric, a dreamer, an agnostic." He "didn't seem to live in the same world with us," he said. "He had some very rabid views about various matters." Another thought that he was "erratic," that his opinions were "modernistic." He seemed to believe in free love, for example. Not everyone felt that way. Others found him quite sociable, a good conversationalist, a "kidder" — "a fine, upstanding man." But his banker considered him rather self-contained and "strange over-all." Perhaps it was the subject of their conversations. On the other hand, the druggist had the same impression: Anderson was "very moody," he said, "not a mixer. He had few close friends."

Golf was a diversion. Cornelia thought it did him good; it helped relieve the pressures he was under. But the men at the club were not his friends. They were just business associates, yet more versions of the men in the bicycle factory, this time even less tolerable because by now Anderson was more obviously one of them. He drank with them at the club bar or in the locker room, but as he listened to their conversation he thought more and more about the emptiness of success. On one memorable occasion he sliced his ball far into a neighboring cornfield and, ignoring his partner's advice to let it go, climbed over a barbed wire fence and walked out across the fields to find it. And then suddenly he started to mutter to himself, "You go to hell, you bastard," and repeated the same thing under his breath to the one of the foursome who came after him. When the man was within earshot, Anderson managed to come up with the excuse of a headache, saying he was sorry but he had to go back to the clubhouse, and then, faking his return, made for the woods instead.

He could get away with tricks like that just once. If he was to survive in Elyria, he would have to make a more lasting refuge for himself. And he did: he set aside a room for himself upstairs, in a wing at the back of the house. It was no den, no lair where trophies hung, no reminder of his conquests in the world of men. It was just the opposite, a barely furnished room: a cot, two chairs, a flat-topped desk, his books. He had a lock put on the door and kept the key himself. It was a place where he could escape all responsibility and be totally alone.

As he wrote his daughter many years later, he "never did domes-

ticate well." Bob was difficult, John the easy one, Mimi (as they
called Marion) somewhere in between, but when they were little they
all seemed trouble. Soon, he confessed, he became "hardened to the
smell of baby manure, diapers about, etc.," and he fled to his room,
"shut the door softly and often prayed." Once there, alone, he tried
to make some sense out of his life.

He took strange measures. In his room, he tried to make the metaphor "come clean" a fact, literally tried to wash away all traces of
what he thought were the sins of his business practices and of his
flesh. When his wife and children went out, he had the maid bring
him a pail of water, soap, and cloths, and then he would take off his
clothes and proceed to scrub the woodwork and the floor. When he
had finished, he would run down the hall, take a bath, and then
scurry back. The stage set, he would try to regain control over his
life by trying out, acting out versions of it. He had bought some toy
soldiers for his boys on a trip to Cleveland and they were still there
in his room, in their box on a shelf. They could serve as props. He
would take them down and arrange them all in ranks, little redcoats
on foot or riding black horses, other soldiers in blue coats mounted
on white horses; he would then take out his walking stick and proceed to march up and down in front of them, shouting out com-
mands. That was one version of his life: he was a triumphant leader
of a company — "some great figure, little Corsican corporal, little
Ohio paint maker too," he later said sardonically. At other times he
would sit, gazing out the window, or pace the floor, trying to imagine a better version of himself.

Always he was trying to reach what he imagined to be himself,
but his efforts did nothing but confuse him. Marching up and down
his room, he both played the role of president of the American Merchants Company to the hilt and showed, with his insane parody, that
it did not suit him. Trying to prove that he was really not that man,
trying to start all over as only a naked man in a bare room, all he did
was strike another pose. He knew his Carlyle, especially *Sartor Resartus* ("the tailor retailored"), too well to be able to deceive himself: his
lack of clothing was just another cover.

The pressures of his business were real and increased as the business
expanded; the pressure to provide for his family mounted too. More
intense than both, though, was the pressure Anderson put on himself
as he saw himself becoming more and more corrupt, more and more
the little cheat, the seller of his self and soul. He was beside himself,

and as yet he had little idea of who *he* was. But he knew the way to find himself, and there, in his little room, he beat his final retreat toward that self. He did so in writing, in spelling out the many selves he was, in the very act of writing itself.

Anderson had been writing for years, and about himself, but a few years after he arrived in Elyria, he began to do so in order to bring himself into being. In his pieces for *Agricultural Advertising* and *The Reader* and in his reading, especially as it had been disciplined in recent years, he had explored the possibilities that the world of words opened up to him. Now he entered into that world. Other writers draw on their experience, compose, so as to recreate, illuminate their lives, but always, apart from the perfection, or imperfection, of the work, there is the life. In the case of Sherwood Anderson one is never sure, one never knows which is which, or rather one knows that Anderson was never sure himself.

Beginning in Elyria, he wrote in order to put one life aside and to discover another. Writing, he later said, was "curative"; it helped him face himself, to talk to himself. Reaching others with his writing, even the writing itself, these things were secondary. What mattered was that putting words down on paper enabled him to live. He would give up anything to be able to do it, lose all — his business, his family, what was left of his sanity if need be. Nor would he pause to consider others' feelings. Decades later he told his daughter that he hoped some of what he had written was "good and lasting": "It is the only justification I shall ever be able to find for the inconvenience and suffering I have brought on others as well as myself." But in Elyria he had no choice, he gave the matter little thought: writing was his only salvation.

Writing was the one "place" where Anderson felt he need not, could not lie. In writing he could talk straight to himself; that was why he was writing. If he hedged, if he missed, he could tell immediately, and would work until he got it right. Neither he nor his words would have it otherwise. When he succeeded, he felt clean and pure — no longer a "smooth son of a bitch" — as if for the first and only time in his life. When he felt he could steal the time, he wrote at the office. In his room at home he acted out his life and sat in silence, but he spent most of his time there — often most of the night — writing. He wrote versions of two novels, perhaps drafts of two others, and incalculable amounts — pages, reflections, dialogues, descriptions, notes — that cannot be categorized or retrieved.

In one winter he wrote *Windy McPherson's Son,* his first attempt to come to terms with the life that he had lived so far. Into its first and longest section he pressed his memories of growing up, and added one Mary Underwood, the familiar figure of the older woman, the teacher, who sees in Sam McPherson a son and dreams of making him "a man at work upon the things of the mind." So grateful is he for all that she has done for him that he tells her they must marry, but she sets him straight. She is his "new mother," she says, and she knows what would be best for him: it is time for him to leave town.

In the second section Anderson traced and combined the ways he had tried to make money in Chicago and in Ohio, starting with his stay with an "ex-Caxton family named Pergrin," going through his times as a traveling buyer for a commission firm specializing in groceries, as an advertising man, an investor, right on to where he once imagined he was heading, his name written "in the industrial history of the city as one of the first of the western giants of finance." He marries his boss's daughter and then takes over the company. The marriage feels something like the Andersons', beginning in idealism about devotion to children rather than to success, featuring social occasions at which Sam startles those present with his "modern" opinions, and ending in silence. "He began feeling that he must keep a check upon his tongue," Anderson writes. "It was, he thought, like trying to hold free and open communion with the people of an orthodox family, and he fell into a habit of prolonged silences, a habit that later, he found, once formed, unbelievably hard to break."

Mary Underwood's role is taken over by Janet Eberly, a crippled and dying — and totally dedicated — woman who points the moral, not exactly of the tale, but of what were Anderson's thoughts in writing it. What his prose lacks in subtlety is made up for by the intensity of his challenge to himself. "Books are not full of pretense and lies; you business men are," he has Janet say to Sam.

> What do you know of books? They are the most wonderful things in the world. Men sit writing them and forget to lie, but you business men never forget. You and books! You haven't read books, not real ones. Didn't my father know; didn't he save himself from insanity through books? Do I not, sitting here, get the real feel of the movement of the world through the books that men write? . . . You think you're doing things, you Chicago men of money and action and growth. You are blind, all blind.

Anderson's hero does not commit his efforts to writing, but after taking over his father-in-law's company (and thereby driving him to suicide), he leaves his wife, vowing "to spend his life seeking truth" — which he does, in attempts at everything from physical labor to philanthropy, from bartending to labor organizing.

It was not a goal Anderson knew how to reach. If he was imagining flight, perhaps even imagining an end to the pressure that might have come from his father-in-law, he was still, in fact, the head of a family and president of the American Merchants Company in Elyria, Ohio. He hated his life, but he was still trying to make it work.

In *Windy McPherson's Son,* he has his hero come upon a woman with three unwanted children, two boys and their younger sister, and because his own wife had miscarried as many before he left, he takes the children east with him to where she is living. As he returns to her, Sam imagines himself finding "a basis for love and understanding," immersing himself in life with her and the children. "There was the house darkly seen before him," Anderson says. "It was a symbol. Within the house was the woman, Sue, ready and willing to begin the task of rebuilding their lives together." But there is another, more ominous way of reading the house and the wife's readiness: "A place was being prepared for him inside there, a shut-in place in which he was to live what was left of his life," Anderson writes. From that, something in him recoils, what in a revised — and darker — version of 1922 he called "another personality, a quite different being altogether, buried away within him, long neglected, often forgotten, a timid, shy destructive Sam who had never really breathed or lived or walked before men." It was that in a boy that might lead him to smash his hat in rage, or something in the retiring type around the office that might one day let him kill himself. It is what tore Sam "out of his place in life, made of him a homeless wanderer."

In the end, Sam enters, "to sit again with Sue at his own table to try to force himself back into the ranks of life," or, as Anderson's revised version has it: "With his hand before him, as though trying to push aside some dark blinding mass, he moved out of the grove and thus moving stumbled up the steps and into the house." In either case, as Anderson put it with more irony than he intended: "The home-coming was not in itself a completely happy event."

Anderson's own assessment of his early writings was that they were too much the product of his reading, that he had "come to novel writing through novel reading"; and indeed, though one cannot always be sure how much of them he read, one thinks of other "realists" while reading *Windy McPherson's Son*. One thinks of William Dean Howells, whom Anderson did not like because he found him flat (and like himself, fearful), of Arnold Bennett and Thomas Hardy, whom he defended at the Round Table Club, perhaps of Henry Fuller or Frank Norris. Certainly Anderson was thinking of Theodore Dreiser, whose novels seemed so nearly what he himself wanted to accomplish, so much a challenge, that Anderson was as capable of slandering him as defending him before the members of the Round Table Club. On one occasion, when Dreiser's name came up, Anderson cried out, "What 'Dreiser,' the heavy Germanic son of a bitch?" and stormed out of the room.

By his own lights, though, it was none of these, but rather George Borrow, the eccentric Victorian traveler and writer, who most influenced him. Every lover of words has "some other and older writer who is to him the great master," he said in 1934:

> I remember how and when I found mine.
> George Borrow — to me the great writer.

Part picaresque fiction, part dream, part autobiographical account of Borrow's wanderings, *Lavengro* and its sequel, *The Romany Rye*, turned Anderson's attention to the people he had grown up with, people who had lived on and by the land. (He would dedicate *Windy* to "The Living Men and Women of My Own Middle Western Home Town.") These novels also gave Anderson license to indulge his view of himself as a bohemian, a vagabond, and they inspired him to come out and say what was on his mind. Borrow was the "hater of sham respectability," "the pure one" who "cared for nothing but the beauty and glory of writing" that Anderson himself was trying to be. Though one cannot believe it, one can understand Anderson's claim that he had read "all of [Borrow's] books 25 times."

It was probably Trillena White, disguised rather than misremembered in 1934 as a "dark and slender" schoolteacher, who introduced Anderson to Borrow in Elyria. And she probably sat for his portraits of both Mary Underwood and Janet Eberly, for not only did she visit the Andersons in Elyria, but she also seems to have taken up residence there, sharing some though not all the secrets of Anderson's life. Years later she recalled his getting up at four o'clock in the morning to have some time to write and then coming to have morning coffee with her. "Those were the days of the travail of your soul," she later wrote, but "none of us knew of it."

Anderson wrote as though some force within commanded him, but in retrospect he wondered whether perhaps there had not been one man who had suggested the idea of his being a writer. This man had a shop where he printed up form letters and circulars for Anderson. Reading them, he could tell that Anderson's heart was not in such writing, that he wrote sentences with passion in them but that what he was really trying to do was get in touch with the man he imagined he was addressing as he wrote. "You have a kind of talent in the use of simple words. Occasionally, when you try, you can make a sentence," Anderson has him say in the *Memoirs*. "It's rather a shame, really, Sherwood, for you to be in the racket you are in." The printer is a lonely man, a man who constantly pursues women, but whom women cannot satisfy. "'There is something should be built up between men,'" he tells Anderson. The two spend countless evenings together, the printer inspiring Anderson to such a need for the ability to appreciate artistic beauty that Anderson begins to keep a scrapbook of drawings cut out of magazines which he takes to the printer for occasional criticism. "The man interested me," Anderson said, "and I am not sure but that he became the first friend I ever had."

Another would-be muse was Anderson's younger brother Earl. He had stayed on in Chicago, eventually ending up as cashier in a cheap South State Street restaurant, making little money and ruining his health on its fare. Anderson brought him to Elyria and gave him a job as shipping clerk in his factory. Given his performance, Anderson said, it would have been cheaper to have kept him in unemployed luxury, but Earl was proud, he felt unwanted as it was, and Anderson dreaded losing him. There were so few men with whom he had anything in common. Earl was a companion on his walks. Earl opened up, talked about the beauties of the countryside, about a desire for women so passionate that he feared he might assault them in an effort to get some of their beauty for himself, about his ambition to be a painter like their older brother, and about his knowledge that he was doomed to fail. To Anderson his brother always symbolized the sensitive, lonely, vulnerable people of America, the kind of people who stood in stark contrast to any "business type" he knew or could imagine, the kind of person he would write about. Specifically, Earl's presence comes through Anderson's portrait of Enoch Robinson in "Loneliness" and makes that one of the most moving of the *Winesburg, Ohio* tales. In time Earl left to be with their brother Irve, who had become a manufacturer in New Orleans, and then in 1913 he disappeared altogether, until he was found thirteen years later on a street in New York City, having suffered a paralytic stroke.

Cornelia did not inspire Anderson. She did not oppose his writing, but what Anderson imagined and assumed to be her doubts, even the kind of support she offered him, he felt as more, and more subtle and intense, pressure. She seemed to him to be all too concerned with what she (and he) knew to be his untutored mind, and to try to exercise all too much control over his writing. In Cleveland, on Sunday mornings, Cornelia had tried to teach her husband and George Bottger, his general manager, some rudimentary French; there, and in Chicago and Elyria, she helped Anderson with his ads. The French lessons were unusual and, besides, would not go on for long; the help with the ads was absolutely necessary, for Anderson was, and would remain, a wretched speller and grammarian.

But Cornelia's feelings about her husband's writing were also infuriating. She thought he was not at all the kind of man who could end up as a man of letters. And she would know. As he readily admitted, "You see the woman I had married had been to college and had a degree. She had travelled in Europe while I, to tell the truth, I could at that time just spell the simplest words." Moreover, her reservations made practical sense. Even if he had the makings of a writer, Anderson would not be able to go on supporting his family in a way of life that was becoming increasingly comfortable and habitual. Finally, her opinions were unbearable — because they might be right. And for that, for maybe being right, he hated her, and insofar as she seemed to control his life generally, he hated being married to her.

Cornelia was only trying to point out what was best for him. As he knew full well, she intended only to be kind. She knew that though he was making something of a success of his business, he was still wondering what to do with his life. But whatever was going on in his mind, or up there in his room, or on his walks, it would pass. She thought it was good that he had his golf, but she had very little sense of what he was going through — because he told her very little. "She had always considered me a little twisted in the head and who can blame her?" he later said.

It was her fate to live with me in my terrible time and to know nothing of what went on in my soul and I could not understand

what went on in her either. In the house we looked at each other
with unseeing eyes. Now and then tenderness swept over us and
we sat in the darkness of the house late at night and wept.

But they said nothing.

Increasingly, what Anderson was thinking was unspeakable.
Again, in retrospect:

> Just because I was married to her when I did not want to be I
> imagined terrible things about her. It did not seem to me possible
> to escape out of marriage into life. I pictured her as my jailer
> and terrible hate woke in me. At night I even dreamed of killing
> her.

He kept up appearances, went about his business. If he talked at all
about his marriage, it was only to himself, in his room or on long
night walks.

One night, tired of sitting alone in his room, he walked the streets
until just before dawn. On his return, as he approached his house,
he saw Cornelia pacing back and forth in their back yard, obviously
distraught. But rather than go to her, he crept behind the hedge that
framed the yard and watched, saw the fluttering of her hands, and
heard her little cries — and steeled himself. "No you don't," he said
to himself. It was not only Cornelia that he saw, but also all that she
had come to represent: the business world, middle-class respectability, the idea that he could never be a writer, the idea, in sum, that
his life would never change. That image, that prospect he coldly
contemplated and to it said, "No you don't, goddamn you. You don't
get me in that way." And he just waited, waited until Cornelia went
back into their house and then, instead of following her, walked into
town for breakfast and then to his office.

The only place where Anderson could feel free was in his scrubbed-
down room; the only person he could bear to be with was the self he
made appear on the white pages in front of him. *Windy McPherson's
Son* may seem bookish, but it is also, as Anderson said, the history
of his own revolt "against money-making as an end in life." Its final
section, he went on, represented not his dependence on others' per-
ceptions and formulations but simply his own "floundering about in
life." *Marching Men,* the next novel that he wrote, is even more the
raw product of his own turmoil and desperation as he sat up in his
room on Seventh Street. In its pages Anderson flounders, but what
is more, he gives freer rein to those dark forces, takes a longer look

at that "dark blinding mass," that he had managed to set to one side for Sam McPherson.

There is much in *Marching Men* that can be traced back to Anderson's own life, a few recollections of Clyde, many more of Chicago, of his work life there, of his brief attempts to learn in school (there and at Wittenberg), of his explorations into the mysteries of sex and of women's lives. But it is the release of that "other personality," the being who is at once both shy and destructive, idealistic and cruel, that makes *Marching Men* a moving, a disturbing book.

The book is about a charismatic leader who organizes the masses, who makes them march. It is filled with rage. When its hero, Beaut McGregor, watched the National Guard come into his hometown to disperse striking miners when he was young, he was contemptuous of the miners because of their brutish and pathetic lives, admiring of the troops because of their efficiency. In Chicago, workers again seem aimless and stupid: "Losing step with one another, men lose a sense of their own individuality so that a thousand of them may be driven in a disorderly mass in at the door of a Chicago factory morning after morning, and year after year." And again McGregor rages: "It seemed to him right and natural that he should hate men." Everywhere he goes, among the workers, through the streets, into homes, up the social ladder, everyone and everything seems cheap, disheveled, ugly.

But all the while McGregor develops an idea that comes upon him when he returns to Coal Creek for his mother's funeral. Watching miners march behind the carriage that bears her body, he has a change of heart:

> He knew that he who had hated the miners had hated them no more. . . . "Someday a man will come who will swing all of the workers of the world into step like that," he thought. "He will make them conquer, not one another, but the terrifying disorder of life. . . . Someone must teach them the big lesson just for their own sakes, that they also must know. They must march fear and disorder and purposelessness away."

And of course that someone is to be Beaut himself. He has no program for them, no platform. "Suppose they could just learn to march, nothing else," he says. And that is exactly what he teaches them to do. His efforts succeed; hundreds of thousands of workers simply march; they need do no more. "In all of the time of The Marching Men," Anderson says, "there was but one bit of written matter from

the leader McGregor. It had a circulation running into the millions."
It begins thus:

> *"They ask us what we mean.*
> *Well, here is our answer.*
> *We mean to go on marching.*
> *We mean to march in the morning and in the evening when*
> *the sun goes down."*

It ends twelve lines later:

> *"We do not think and banter words.*
> *We march.*
> *Our faces are coarse and there is dust in our hair and beards.*
> *See, the inner parts of our hands are rough.*
> *And still we march — we the workers."*

No doubt the idea of "The Marching Men" was inspired by the sight
of his fellow guardsmen during the Spanish-American War, but the
idea appealed to Anderson then and there as he wrote in Elyria. However bizarre, it was his idea of order, of some refuge from the chaos
he was in.

In 1917, Anderson said of the theme of *Marching Men* that it "appealed strongly to my rather primitive nature." "The beat and
rhythm of the thing would come and go," he went on, "a thousand
outside things would flow in. I worked madly and then I threw the
book away. Again and again I came back to it." Sex flew into it: "A
new element assisted itself in the life of McGregor," as Anderson puts
it awkwardly. "One of the hundreds of disintegrating forces that attack strong natures, striving to scatter their force in the back currents
of life, attacked him. His big body began to feel with enervating
persistency the call of sex." Anderson's impatience with politics and
politicians flew into it too. He dedicated *Marching Men* to "American
Workingmen" and in it expressed nothing but contempt for those
who tried to organize them along party lines.

When *Marching Men* was published, Anderson wrote that "in a way
the whole big message of my life is bound into that volume" and,
looking back to the time when he wrote it, went on:

> It was all a great song to me then, a big terrible song. I was not
> strong enough to hold it. Sometimes I was not strong enough to
> hold it. I walked at night praying. My mind from too much wea-

riness stopped working once and I was for a time a wreck, wandering as aimlessly as society is aimless.

The human need for social organization and the artist's need for form crossed. Frequently Anderson draws analogies between creators in the realms of finance and of art, but his rage for order is mostly rage. *Marching Men* is not a book that tries to define and realize some sexual or social or artistic utopia. "We do not think and banter words," the marchers' flyer said. If any word were to spring to mind, as Anderson later had to admit, it would be *fascism*. But *Marching Men* is essentially a book that just cries out against things as they are.

The sight of Beaut McGregor arriving in Chicago, filled with hatred for Coal Creek, Anderson says, was enough to make the city tremble: "In his very frame there was the possibility of something, a blow, a shock, a thrust out of the lean soul of strength into the jelly-like fleshiness of weakness." At one point he has Beaut contemplate a fat spider and compare it to "the sloth of the world," its mating habits to those of men:

> "Ugly crawling things that look at the floor," he muttered. "If they have children it is without order or orderly purpose. It is an accident like the accidents of the fly that falls into the net built by the insect here. The coming of the children is like the coming of flies, it feeds a kind of cowardice in men."

In about ten pages that he inserted in (or perhaps later added to) *Marching Men,* Anderson tells about a barber who wanted to make violins, to emulate the Italian masters, and who left his wife and four children in Ohio because he could not do so while being reminded of family responsibilities. Try to let a woman live her life, ask her to let you live yours, the barber says. "'You try it. She won't. She will die first.'" It was easier to pay money for women's services than to try to be open and frank with one. His wife once told him it didn't matter whether or not violins were made, and that night the barber dreamed of choking her: "'I woke up and lay there beside her,'" he tells Beaut, "'thinking of it with something like real satisfaction in just the thought that one long hard grip of my fingers would get her out of my way for good.'" Again and again Anderson says that men have to establish order in their lives before they can go on and do anything else. They had to clean the slate.

For the time being, all Anderson's energy went into putting the past behind him. What followed, he did not know. He never did like plots. It was people, the real drama of their lives, that interested him. He felt that "shoving imagined people around" to fit a plot betrayed them. Thinking about form, "'form' as form," was a waste of time, he said. Form *was* content, it would take care of itself. Under what Anderson called the "rather trying circumstances" in which he wrote *Windy McPherson's Son,* it was especially hard to know how to end. He revised *Marching Men* incessantly. The text as we now have it ends with a woman Beaut courted being won away from him by her father, "the master of a plow trust." Sam McPherson may or may not commit himself to one (in an earlier ending, Beaut does marry and take to farming). The endings are as weak as Anderson's resolution at the time.

The strength of the texts lies elsewhere, or throughout, in their very arbitrariness, in the struggle that one senses Anderson experiencing in writing them. They tell us that Anderson is determined to set his life down in writing, to be strong there at least, and they suggest that eventually he would find some answers in his quest for truth. They also give us the feeling, though, that the immediate answer was not going to be a happy one.

Nowhere is that feeling stronger than halfway through *Marching Men,* where Anderson introduces a man who owns a factory in Ohio, "a man of the better sort, quiet, efficient, kindly," who has come to Chicago on business. In what follows, Anderson stunningly confronts himself. He stresses that this businessman is a thoughtful man, pleased with his station in life, but by the same token one of those Americans "with the disease of comfort and prosperity in his blood." On his first visit to the city, this man witnesses a barroom brawl and then sees Beaut McGregor, huge and redheaded, raising his fist into the air. Walking on, he imagines "the strange looking red man with the huge face" peering over his garden wall at his two boys feeding their tame rabbit there, intent upon destroying their future. At night, as he falls asleep, he sees Beaut again, this time glaring at him from his factory door. Beaut has just walked off his job in an apple warehouse, taken one as night cashier in a South State Street restaurant, and made preparations to go to law school, his way paid by a devoted milliner. In this way, he thinks, he can fulfill his dream of organizing men, "forcing men to do the simple thing full of meaning rather than the disorganized ineffective things"; in this way he can articulate his purpose and "sweep the people before him, starting

them on the long, purposeful march that was to be the beginning of
the rebirth of the world, filling with meaning the lives of men." He
looks at his own upraised fist and thinks: "I'll get ready to use that
intelligently . . . a man wants trained brains backed up by a big fist
in the struggle I am going into." When he, in turn, sees the Ohioan,
he seethes.

> It was then that the man from Ohio walked past, with his hands
> in his pockets, and attracted his attention. To McGregor's nostrils
> came the odor of rich, fragrant tobacco. He turned and stood,
> staring at the intruder on his thoughts. "That's what I'm going to
> fight," he growled, "the comfortable, well-to-do acceptance of a
> disorderly world, the smug men who see nothing wrong with a
> world like this. I should like to frighten them so that they would
> throw their cigars away and run about like ants when you kick
> over ant hills in the fields."

Anderson could accept much of what he had experienced in Chicago,
but *Marching Men* suggests that he was ready to reject everything he
had achieved thereafter. It suggests he was ready to destroy the self
that he presented to the world. In fact, he was about to bring down
the house and scatter the family of the nameless businessman from
Ohio.

By the end of November 1912, the psychological stress that Anderson was under was more than he could bear. On Thursday the
twenty-eighth he went to his office as usual and, as usual, his secretary, Frances Shute, was there. She had been working for him for
more than four years. She was "strong," he once said, "full of virility
and honest." She was a grown-up tomboy, apt to go out and wrestle
with the younger workers during the lunch break. Above all, she was
loyal, dedicated. She was the kind of secretary Anderson had described in an *Agricultural Advertising* piece: the defeated could confide
in her. She had watched him with "motherly solicitude" as his business ventures spread so thin he feared that others who had invested
in him might fall through. She knew better than Cornelia how much
of himself he put into his writing: she had often stayed late into the
night to type the stories he had written; she had typed the drafts of
Windy and *Marching Men*. When he too stayed on past quitting time,
they might walk out together and down along the tracks that ran
beside his office. Once she put her hand on his arm and said almost tearfully, "It would be wonderful if you could get clear of all
this."

Eight years later, in one of what he called his "New Testaments," Anderson fantasized about making love to his secretary at such a fateful time as this. He wrote of his urge to "return to the seeking of truth" and of walking with her out into the country:

> It was quiet in the field when I went there with the woman. "We are brothers and sisters," I said, "let us make love."
> My arms grew very hot and the white arms of the woman grew hot. . . .

Perhaps. But what the "testament" surely highlights is Anderson's confusion at the time. Although he wanted her, again he questioned his impulses. Were they "wholesome"? Certainly he had learned that he did not want a life or family with anyone. Was there really anything that he wanted to share? All he knew was, as he put it, "I cannot keep my footing on the side of the bowl of life." He was trapped in it, crawling up its sides, trying to get out, but with what desire he did not know.

When Anderson came into the office Thursday morning, he tried to work. He opened some mail, he started to dictate a business letter, but looking out his office window at the Black River and at the railroad tracks, he wrote a short note to Cornelia instead:

> Cornelia:
> There is a bridge over a river with cross-ties before it. When I come to that I'll be all right. I'll write all day in the sun and the wind will blow through my hair.
> Sherwood

Then he said something related to that to Frances, something about his feet being wet from having been wading in a river for so long. And then he left.

Four days later, on Sunday, Anderson walked into a drugstore on East 152d Street in Cleveland. He was still in his business suit, his trousers splattered with mud up to his knees. He was unshaven, seemingly dazed. He came in, sat down, asked where he was, and then got out his address book and gave it to the druggist in the hope that the druggist could help clear things up. Perhaps he could help Anderson find out who and where he was, or how to get ahold of his wife. The first name the druggist recognized was under the letter *B*. It was the name of an officer of the Chamber of Commerce, Edwin Baxter. He called Baxter, who came and of course recognized Anderson. Baxter also saw that something was amiss and arranged to have Anderson admitted to the hospital on Huron Road in downtown Cleveland.

On Thursday, Frances had called Cornelia to ask if her husband had been acting strangely. So far as we know, Cornelia said and did nothing, neither in response to Frances's inquiry, nor to the note that she soon delivered. If Anderson seemed to be acting strangely, it was not for the first time. If he stayed away from home, that would not be for the first time either. Although he did not return that day or the next, nobody notified the police. On Sunday Erwin Baxter called.

From a few notes that Anderson dictated at the hospital, we can get some sense of what he had been going through.

> *Went into an orchard &*
> *gathered corn & apples —*
> *Ate   "   &   "*
> *Brought away corn to*
> *show Robert & many apples*

they begin. They mention roads he walked along, streetcar tracks he must have ridden along to get so far east in so short a time, a store where he had bought a loaf of bread, a bridge where he had rested, a lumber yard, a fire he had tried to build — "but head hurt & couldnt." Far more revealing, though, is a set of notes he kept himself, notes that he kept on Thursday and Friday, and mailed to Cornelia on Saturday afternoon.

On the envelope he had written: Cornelia L. Anderson, President, American Striving Co. It was a sharp cut — or slip. His business was only endless, straining work, something in him was saying. She was at the head of it, determining all his efforts, driving him. Here were the results.

Years later, when Cornelia came across those notes and newspaper accounts of what had happened, Anderson told her he did not want to see them. When she asked again, just before he died, he asked to have them forwarded but said nothing more. His only comment on them comes to us indirectly: on the envelope his fourth wife wrote that he had said the whole episode was his way of getting rid of Cornelia. The notes themselves tell us quite precisely what was going on in Anderson's mind from the time he walked out of his office on Thursday until at least Saturday afternoon. His exodus from Elyria had in fact begun. He would soon be rid of Cornelia. But, tracing

the pattern of his movements and his thoughts, we can see that nothing that he did was coolly calculated.

There are more physical details. Anderson passed a "Mrs. Leonard"
(or one of his two Elyria neighbors named Leonard), he saw dogs,
children, a man chewing tobacco, another with his mouth "full of
dry crackers," he tried to drink a beer. But these were not just sights
along the way. All of these figures were conspiring to assault him.
The children were crying and in the way:

> *Among*
> *them ran yellow dogs with brown*
> *dirt stuck on their backs. . . .*
> *There*
> *are so many children and*
> *so many dogs and so*
> *many long streets filled*
> *with dirty houses. . . .*
> *Mrs. Leonard*
> *had a book in her hand*
> *and tried to hit me*
> *with it. . . .*
> *I tried to drink*
> *some beer but it was*
> *bitter and the room was*
> *full of men who would*
> *have hit me but I*
> *ran. . . .*
> *Tell Robert I saw a*
> *man chewing tobacco. It*
> *made his mouth nasty.*

What was driving Anderson to distraction was what had been driving
him to distraction all along: mess, filth, disorder, men's physical and
moral brutishness, overpowering women. His fear that others would
do him in is but the mask for his desire to obliterate them all.

He had wanted to contact Cornelia, but he had not been able to:

> *If one does ask he*
> *could find Cornelia but if*
> *you ask the people they*
> *will hit you.*

He wanted to get a message to his son Robert. As he said later, at the hospital, it was about the corn:

> *Give Robert*
> *Piece of corn — tell*
> *him how it grows.*
> *Dont let them hit*
> *him.*

There was, as he had often said, a straighter way. Right now, the best that he could do was to keep going, not talk to anyone, be still, and keep in mind the one safe way, the way that would get him over the river, the river that went by the factory, the river in his note to Cornelia, the river that divided one life from another. There was one more thing to remember:

> *Writing don't hurt your*
> *head.*

And then, throughout the notes, constantly recurring, one constant theme: think of Elsinore, going to Elsinore, get to Elsinore:

> *Elsinore — Elsinore*
> *Elsinore — Elsinore.*
> *Get to Elsinore.*
> *River at Elsinore.*
> *Bridge at Elsinore.*
> *Elsinore Water Works.*
> *T Powers head hurt*
> *also. went to Elsinore.*
> *They hit T Powers. One*
> *after another they hit*
> *him. like you.*
> *They put his name*
> *on a wall — near*
> *Elsinore.*

No T. Powers has turned up — none but Anderson himself, the man whom others seemed to be after, whose head hurt, but the man who would regain his power when he reached Elsinore. That is where this would-be literary man wanted to be, Hamlet the man he wanted to be. We do not know that Anderson knew the play especially well, but like Hamlet he was a mystery to himself and others, "mad north-

northwest," or "mad in craft," and like him he was confused by Woman. And *as* Hamlet he knew where he belonged. He belonged at Elsinore. Heading for Elsinore he was on his way to becoming a literary figure. He might still be lost, confused, but as Hamlet he would be lost and confused heroically. He could imagine he was a literary hero in his own right. Once he reached Elsinore, he would live in literature. At least he would have the power to write.

Anderson was looking for the terms that would make sense of himself to himself. The figure of the ascendant prince was one he often later used. He used it in writing to a friend, for example, who was moving from a career as an analyst to writing out versions of "Our Common Consciousness." "You are, to my mind, a man coming into his kingdom," he wrote to this friend. "No man in America ever really becomes anything until after forty, as the rest of his life is spent working his way through a fog. . . . In the morning now you can get out of bed facing yourself. You can breathe. You are really a prince come to his kingdom." That November 1912, Anderson was thirty-six years old, not knowing who or where he was, but, if only symbolically, he knew where he was going.

If we are to find a name for Anderson's condition during these three or four days, it is not "nervous breakdown," or "midlife crisis," terms so vaguely accurate as to be of little help. Nor is it really "amnesia." Anderson may have forgotten who he was, but he remembered Cornelia and the children, and what is most important, at one level he knew all about his life. His notes summed it up perfectly.

The term that comes closest to describing Anderson's condition is "fugue state," a state of flight, something like those Anderson had experienced as a youth when parts of his body, or the landscape, or his very life, seemed to float away. But this time Anderson's state of mind was organized or composed in such a way as to make uncanny sense. Strictly speaking, a person in such a state knows nothing of his previous life, does not realize that he does not know, and does not even appear conspicuous to people who did not know him in his former state. Anderson knew enough to send his notes to Cornelia; his muddy suit and unshaven stubble must have raised suspicions, but no one who did not know him need have been alarmed by the man who went about doing what he described himself as doing in his notes and in the notes he dictated on Sunday at the hospital. What is most significant about the "fugue state" is that a person enters it when too many "strivings, affects, and attitudes . . . become

contradictory to each other and become replaced by a single striving."
In an example cited in the literature, a man is found walking up and
down along the Hudson River, his head aching, wanting to end it
all, but harping on getting a new job, a course of action that ex-
presses, in condensed and acceptable fashion, his desire to escape
"many guilt-laden and so forbidden strivings." Coming out of such
a state, being made aware of it, "Mr. X" suffers from amnesia, wondering and then gradually remembering who he is. But *in* that state,
he had lost his old identity and had no awareness of that fact. He was
just a man who wanted to get out of a precarious financial situation
and to be rid of the responsibility of his wife and children. Wandering to Cleveland, Anderson was a man who wanted to get out of
business, to leave — if not destroy — his wife, but in his imagination, all he wanted to do was live in writing, be a writer.

From Thursday until Saturday, or early Sunday, Anderson was a
man who felt he had to avoid everyone, with the possible exception
of his older son. If he were to live he would have to be alone and be
a writer. Only later, by the time he walked into the drugstore and
handed over his address book, did he begin to remember details about
the other life that he had forgotten. "After several days of wandering," as he later put it, "my mind came into my body."

Cornelia came to the hospital Sunday evening, but in his recollec-
tion of the scene, not until he saw Frances Shute did Anderson feel
he had emerged from his tortured state. Looking back six years later,
imagining himself as a kind of Sleeping Beauty or nineteenth-century
novelistic heroine/hero, the fever having passed, he said:

> The touch of [Frances's] honest, broad hand awakened me. I sat
> up in bed ready to cry out, eager to express to her my joy at being
> back among the living but only the blank white walls of a new
> strange place confronted me. I had begun a new life.

Not entirely, for he still had to earn a living, and not for the first
time, because he already had his washed-down room on Seventh
Street. But after his ordeal, he was irrevocably committed to writing.

FOUR

Becoming a Writer

1912-1915

O N MONDAY, December 2, 1912, the Elyria *Evening Tel-*
egram reported that "Sherwood Anderson, head of the
Anderson Manufacturing Co., and well known as 'the roof-fix man,'"
had been found in Cleveland the night before, dazed and unable to
remember his name and address, suffering from what the doctors said
was "nervous exhaustion." "Overwork," his friends had called it, the
result of his trying to run a business by day and trying to write novels
and short stories all through the night. But his condition was not
critical, the *Telegram* said. A few days' rest would be enough to restore
his memory. On December 3, the paper went on to say that Anderson
had improved so much that he would probably be back home by the
end of the week.

He returned to Elyria, but for only a few days. In mid-December
the Andersons went to Toledo, to visit Cornelia's family. It would be
a change of scenery, something of an escape from all that the young
couple had just been through. No one in the Lane household would
press them about what had happened, or dwell on what might have
happened had Cornelia not married Anderson. As Cornelia later said
with some relief, her father was not one to say "I told you so."

Shortly before Christmas the family was back in Elyria, and then
in early February 1913 Anderson left for Chicago once again. What
was now the Taylor-Critchfield advertising company had agreed to
have him back. Though he had walked out on his company and on
those who had invested in him only three months before, his financial
affairs were in order; or rather, Waldo Purcell, the man who had

joined his paint business with Anderson's mail-order operation four years before, put them in order for him. It was he who arranged to have the American Merchants Company's debts paid off; the Roof-Fix business was sold to a company in Cleveland. There were never any repercussions from Anderson's failure as a businessman. Elyria did not need to — and did not — give Sherwood Anderson much more thought.

Cornelia and the children stayed behind, but just for a month or so, long enough to close the house on Seventh Street and wrap up the family's affairs, while Anderson was getting settled in Chicago. In April or May, when the weather was warmer, they would go up to Little Point Sable, Michigan, where Anderson's sister Stella had a cottage and where Anderson could visit them on the weekends, and then, probably in the fall, they would all regroup in Chicago. It seemed a sensible arrangement. The Andersons were not living together, but there was no talk of separation or divorce. Neither was there any talk of just when and how they would be united again, but they would be — in time.

From Cornelia's point of view, it might have seemed that Anderson had not turned his back on the business world over that late November weekend at all; he had never even intended to. He had crossed no symbolic river, he had had no world elsewhere in mind. He had simply turned his back on her and the children, deposited them somewhere in the country, and then returned to the business world without them. But although he may have imagined that reading of his behavior, Anderson would not have thought it fair. There was no one explanation. He had no specific plans. He did not know exactly what he meant to do — either back there in Elyria or now that he was in Chicago. All he knew was that he had to write and that he had to continue to earn a living for himself and others. Somehow it would all work out.

He was surest about the writing. That he *had* to do. What's more, sometime during this painful period, he got undeniable proof that he *could* write, that the world would accept him as a writer: he had his first story, "The Rabbit-Pen," accepted for publication. Though it did not appear until a year and a half later, in June 1914, perhaps the news was delivered to him in his room at the Huron Road Hospital, as he later claimed. (Certainly "The Rabbit-Pen" was written before he entered.) That itself makes a good story — Anderson ends his flight and emerges from his fugue state to confirmation that his new life has begun — but the text of "The Rabbit-Pen" tells a different one. Like almost everything else that he did at the time, the story suggests a confusion that could not be cleared up in a matter of months.

"The Rabbit-Pen" grew out of an argument Anderson had had with Trillena White over the virtues of William Dean Howells. They were seated in the Andersons' back yard on Seventh Street. Anderson was drinking. Howells was afraid, Anderson had maintained. He left too much out of his writing; he left out sex, for example. He wrote "poison plots" instead, just the kind of conventional and tricky things that you would expect to come from the "Editor's Easy Chair" from which Howells wrote in the pages of *Harper's*. As they were arguing, a buck rabbit killed some baby rabbits in a rabbit pen with blows of its hind feet. There, Anderson said to Trillena, there was an incident that could be made to stand for "life." Howells could not, he said, but *he* could do it justice. His confidence raised by drink, he vowed to prove his point: he would write a story about what had happened that *Harper's* itself would buy and print. And he was right.

The protagonist of Anderson's story is a writer who is drawn to a woman who in turn is strong enough to contain the kind of energy and destructive force that is represented by that buck rabbit. Like Anderson, he is working on his third novel, like him he is always "romancing" about women. In his fantasies, the woman he comes closest to is the German housekeeper of a friend, a version of Trillena White herself. It is she who keeps his friend's house in order, she who disciplines his children while his rich wife Ruth withdraws; it is she who symbolically saves the rabbit mother and her family from the killer buck, penning him up after he has killed one of their young and disposing of his victim. "Gretchen was complete," Anderson says. "She was a Brunnhilde."

"The Rabbit-Pen" is about Anderson's frustration with Cornelia — "dear patient woman," he once called her — and what must have been his attraction to Trillena. It is about that incompatible passion, but also about his more radically divided life, about the two men, the suburban host and the wandering writer, who lived inside him. So far as he was concerned, that was "life." And in its midst was a killer, caged for now, caged in the story with the help of a strong female presence, and caged in Anderson as long as he could find expressions for it in his writing, but it was by no means tamed.

The other, more respectable Anderson went back to Taylor-Critchfield, which was easy because Bayard Barton was now president of the firm. In the old days Barton had been a fellow copywriter (at the corporation dinner in 1905 he had spoken on "Learning the Business"). and there had been another side to him, as there had been to Anderson: he had been known to write a little poetry. On long walks the two of them had often put agency business in perspective or delighted in ignoring it altogether; they were determined to remain honest, not to believe themselves when they wrote "bunk." While Anderson was in Ohio, Barton had come to believe in what he said about Firestone tires, had acquired the Firestone account, and had risen to the top; when Anderson returned, he no longer heard much joy in his old friend's laughter, but what was of more immediate importance, that friend was in a position to give Anderson a job, and he had accepted gladly.

Anderson picked up right where he had left off in the fall of 1906. In the month of his return, a little piece of his titled "Making It Clear" appeared in the *Agricultural Advertiser*. In it he contrasted boys' inability to talk in front of their mothers with their powers of utterance amongst themselves. "That's where the advertising man comes in," he said. "If he is a good one he takes those fellows out into the other room and tells them to spread around and enthuse and tell the facts about themselves and what they are making." It is doubtful that Anderson could have appreciated the irony. Of course he had not made himself clear to Cornelia, or to anyone else. He couldn't have had he tried. But anyway, that was another matter. In the old days, he had expressed himself in his *Agricultural Advertising* articles; that was the only writing that he did. Now he was just doing a job.

So he went to work — uptown, to Taylor-Critchfield's new quarters in the Brooks Building on West Jackson Street, a few blocks south and west of the old office on Wabash Avenue. It was where respectable culture had taken root. The "New Chicago," Hamlin Garland called it that very year. Whereas Michigan Avenue was but rough pavement and a row of livery barns and shabby four-story buildings, lit by antiquated gas lamps in 1900, now, Garland said, it was a wide and handsomely lighted avenue, over which towered the New University Club, the Illinois Athletic Club, the new gas building, and "other examples of up-to-date commercial architecture." And the clubs in the city, Garland reported, from the City Club on the one hand, to his own Cliff Dwellers on the other, shared in "the spirit of uplift."

Six or seven years before, Anderson would have shared in it too. He would have walked among these buildings on his way to and from work with pride in the city's accomplishments and with confidence in his own eventual success, but on this, his third pilgrimage to Chicago, he only earned a living in one of them. He lived on the South Side in an apartment near Rosalie Court, where he and Cornelia had begun their married life, and he sought entrance into the counterculture that had sprung up in the area.

While Chicago was becoming the "New Chicago," an artists' colony had come into being along Fifty-seventh Street and Stoney Island Avenue in quarters that had once served as souvenir stores and popcorn stands during the Exposition. Painters, sculptors, actors, and aspiring students moved into these abandoned structures, covered up their storefront windows with curtains, made faucets serve as showers, kept the one big room warm by making fires, and imagined worlds less dependent on "assets" than did their counterparts uptown. The most magnetic attractions among them were Floyd Dell, the young editor of the Chicago *Evening Post*'s "Friday Literary Review," and his wife, Margery Currey, a schoolteacher and sometime reporter, who in April had moved from their apartment in the more fashionable Near North Side and rented studios around the corner from each other — hers the more distinctive because its previous occupant had been Thorstein Veblen and because it had a bathtub. Bior Norfeldt, a teacher at the Art Institute, who lived in the corner studio between the two, had established Dell as the Representative Bohemian with his portrait of him in high collar and black cravat. Martha Baker, a miniaturist, contributed to the legend with her painting of Dell and Currey in the nude.

The colonists were only a few blocks from the University of Chicago to the southwest, and they bordered the embankment of the Illinois Central, whose trains could easily run them north into the Loop, but mostly people came to them. Among the visitors were: Dell's old friends from Davenport, Iowa, George Cram Cook and Susan Glaspell; Lucian Cary and Llewellyn Jones, who would both succeed Dell as editor of the "Friday Literary Review"; Michael Carmichael Carr, an art teacher from the University of Missouri; Tennessee Mitchell, an independent spirit, a piano tuner and teacher, and former mistress of Edgar Lee Masters; Ben Hecht; and Carl Sandburg. One evening Arthur Davison Ficke, a lawyer (also from Davenport), might chant his verse by candlelight, while everyone sat in respectful silence on the floor; on another, clad in her Japanese robe, the poet Eunice Tietjens might go through the motions of a No dance that she had learned during her years in the East; on one occasion, Margaret Anderson, then working in a bookstore in the Fine Arts Building and reviewing for Dell, announced her plan to start the *Little Review*.

"There is no Middle West," Glenway Westcott has written, only "a certain climate, a certain landscape; and beyond that, a state of mind of people born where they do not like to live." And so they end up in Chicago, or New York, trying to create a sense of community that may or may not have existed in Clyde or Davenport or Galesburg, but which they did not feel themselves. No one among these colonists had any final answers as to how he or she was going to live after the escape, but the questionings of them were innocent and full of promise. It was Dell who best summed up their efforts: "We were in love with life," he later wrote, "and willing to believe almost any modern theory which gave us a chance to live our lives more fully. We were incredibly well meaning. We were confused, miserable, gay, and robustly happy all at once." Anderson had read about their kind (George Moore's *Confessions of a Young Man* had become a favorite of his), but they were a far cry from anyone he had ever known in Clyde, or in the Army, or in Springfield, a very far cry from the members of the Elyria Country Club. These people were bound to attract him.

Anderson was introduced to Dell and his friends in the late spring of 1913 through his brother Karl, who had become something of a figure in the art world. Karl had come on to Chicago that year because he had a show there and also because he was helping bring a portion of the famous Armory Show to the Art Institute. This time it was Karl who found temporary quarters with his brother Sherwood. While Margery Currey was reporting on his show Karl told her about his brother — he was new in town, he talked of becoming a writer — and she asked Karl to have him come to one of her Sunday evenings. And of course Anderson came. He had fled from factories and golf games and business in general; now here was what he had been fleeing toward. But when he arrived, he could not bring himself to enter.

It was a late spring night. The colonists were gathered as usual, seated in small groups on the floor, deep in conversation. Margery Currey was moving among them, occasionally serving drinks. Through the door that they had left ajar to catch the night air, while remaining safely out of sight, Anderson saw a dozen or so people, heard the tenor of their voices, and wondered if this weren't, after all, yet another place where he did not belong. This time the problem was that everyone seemed more or less wholly committed to the artistic life, while he was still, undeniably, just an advertising man. He had written stories and at least two novels, but although "The Rabbit-Pen" had been accepted, who was to say that his major efforts, his novels, were any good? How was he to know that they were not just more "slick" writing or bad imitations of the "realists"? And he could see that he was so much older. He would be thirty-seven at the end of the summer. Dell and Hecht, the two in the group he would come to know best, were twenty-six and nineteen. However good he or they might think his writing was, there was so much catching up to do.

He did not knock. Instead, he crossed Stoney Island Avenue to gather his thoughts in Jackson Park. In a little while the group emerged, seeking relief from the steamy air of Currey's studio in a walk by the lake. And again Anderson avoided them. But in doing so, he came upon a woman seated on a bench, a factory worker, he soon found out, and slightly crippled, and through her he regained his confidence. They talked, and initially he sympathized; but pity for her turned into pity for himself, and that into lust. He tried to embrace her, and she said no but he knew she did not mean it. He felt her loneliness, felt that she would have trouble attracting men, felt that he could easily become her lover, and he exacted a promise from her that they meet again. But as he watched her run, with her "curious little limp," back to where she lived, shame set in, and he knew he would never keep the date.

Two Sundays passed, and Anderson went to wait outside Margery Currey's studio once again, this time in order to stop her and introduce himself. More his age, perhaps even a little older, she turned out not to be threatening after all, and she too had a story to tell. The separate apartments that she and Dell maintained were not so much the result of advanced thinking about the institution of marriage as of the simple fact that their marriage was dissolving. She was someone to whom Anderson could confess his doubts about being a writer, someone, like Frances Shute back in Elyria, who would encourage him. In the course of their talk, Currey said that Anderson's brother had mentioned his writing, and she promised to show some of it to her husband.

Anderson was drawn to Dell and Currey not only because theirs were the most influential voices among the colonists, but because of the particular "modern theory" that they represented. They were leading the group in its exploration of the meanings of "freedom" and "love" and of the relations between these ideas. Whether or not their marriage would last did not matter (in fact it could prove more instructive if it didn't). What they read and wrote and did helped Anderson define his dissatisfaction with his marriage and enabled him to justify his recent flight from it.

Once drawn into their circle, he sat and listened, Currey later wrote, "with black eyes shining, taking things in." He wanted to know more. Soon he borrowed her copies of "that priceless periodical, *The Freewoman*," which was published in England between 1910 and 1912. He listened intently to Dell, but he could also read about what Dell thought in articles published in his "Friday Literary Review." There, in one piece, Anderson read that men were tired of subservient women. He read about Dell's hopes for the women's movement, about how it was going to inaugurate "a great human renaissance," and saw how he dismissed women who lived for love "as belonging to the courtesan type." Dell said that women had to find their work and *then* they might find their love. Anderson also read Dell's articles about women like Charlotte Perkins Gilman, and Olive Schreiner, and Jane Addams, not exceptional women, Dell claimed, but figures through whose example one could see "the essential nature of women" and what might be expected from "a future in which women will have a larger freedom and a larger influence" — articles that at the end of the year were collected and published as *Women as World Builders: Studies in Modern Feminism*.

In the late spring, Anderson had approached the Fifty-seventh Street circle cautiously, but before the summer was over, he was very near the center of it. It was where he always wanted to be. In the past he had had to fight his way, outsmarting other boys in town, or arguing past all the others sitting by the fire or gathered in a reading group; and once there he was not comfortable. What good was it if he had succeeded only in putting everyone on the defensive? In Elyria, the Round Table Club had listened intently enough while he tried out his radical theories, but what satisfaction was there in only proving once again that he was a little odd? Now there was no opposition. In fact, Margery Currey's friends would give him much more than the benefit of the doubt. The only barriers were those in his own mind; once over them, he was at his ease.

Currey was not his only sponsor. When Ernestine Evans, a recent graduate of the University of Chicago, then working for the *Tribune*, heard that Anderson had written a novel and that he liked to read from it, she planned an occasion for the colonists and their visitors to meet him. Robert Morss Lovett must have been wrong when he later said that Anderson appeared in house painter's clothes, but he was right about everyone's expectations. Anderson seemed, he said, "the proletarian writer for whom we were already on the lookout." He represented an alternative to the "New Chicago," to the almost pervasive evidence of Mammon's power. And in turn, Anderson was delighted to get a sympathetic hearing. In Elyria, he might trap a few people into listening to him read from *Windy McPherson's Son,* but the result was only a warning that the public would not tolerate what he wrote. On Fifty-seventh Street, his rendering of a business-man's searchings for higher truths and his encouraging (and oversim-plified) version of how he himself had resisted the culture's corrupting influence were just what his audience was looking for.

And he was attractive — simply attractive. The dress of men in the business world was, he later said, "all of a pattern." He had made efforts to enliven it with a little color here, an unusual texture there, but he had always looked the part of the up-and-coming man of that world. At this time and in this new company, though, he began to break out. Gradually he replaced his ties with brightly colored cloth that he passed through a heavy silver finger ring. In the photographs taken for *Agricultural Advertising* and in those taken later in Elyria, Anderson seemed to hold back his head and squint a bit, as if to ward off blows. Now everyone noticed the liveliness of his eyes. No longer did he neatly comb and part his hair; he let it grow. He was in fact of medium height (5 feet, 8¾ inches, his Army papers said), but those who saw him that summer thought he loomed large. "An ex-tremely handsome and attractive figure," Floyd Dell recalled, "a tall, keen, robust, laughing man, black-haired and blazing-black-eyed." To Ben Hecht, "he looked like an Italian barber but he exuded ego like a royalist."

Hearing him, Hecht went on, his voice seemed "full of caress and the smack of infinite superiority."

To what? To everyone who wasn't Sherwood Anderson. He held out a hand as he talked and fluttered it as if he were patting an infant on the head, the infant being his listener or, possibly, the world.

He loved to talk, he loved talk for its own sake. Now he was free to indulge himself. He was like Floyd Dell, Margaret Anderson wrote: he would talk to chairs if he had no other audience. He sat in "in a certain amazement (resembling fear)," she said, when she and Dell discussed Walter Pater and "living like the hard gem-like flame. . . . Nothing would induce him into such fancy realms"; but he delighted in talking about writers he had once had to defend, and delighted in learning about the Russians from Dell and Hecht and, a year later, about Gertrude Stein from his brother Karl. He picked up smatterings of Nietzsche and of Freud; like so many enthusiasts of the day, he ingested Whitman. What he liked most, though, was stories, his own, or others' that he could convert into his own: "He didn't talk ideas," Margaret Anderson said, "he told stories."

He told them well, but what mattered most that summer was that Dell liked *Windy McPherson's Son,* the story Margery Currey had passed on. At first it seemed just another manuscript, one among so many that Dell had had to read. If anything, it held out less promise than the others: a first novel by an almost middle-aged advertising man? But as he turned its opening pages, his excitement grew. The man wrote like "a great novelist," his was a powerful mind, Dell later said, "a mind vivid, profound, apparently inexhaustible in its energy. A mind full of beautiful, intense, and perilous emotion." In September Dell summed up his response in the *Evening Post,* saying that he had "seen in MS. recently an unfinished novel by a yet unpublished writer which if finished as begun will overtop the work of any living American writer." Nothing could have meant more to Anderson.

And then, at the end of the summer, people began to vacate their little dwellings on Fifty-seventh Street. Dell and Currey parted ways. In October, Dell resigned from the *Post* and went to New York to edit the *Masses,* and Currey accepted a job at the *Chicago Daily News.* Cook and Ficke and Glaspell had already moved East. "The robin's egg renaissance," as Anderson later called it, was over. Still, it had been a glorious few months, "a gay happy time," he wrote in his *Memoirs,* "the gayest and happiest I have ever known, a feeling of brotherhood and sisterhood with men and women whose interests were my own."

No one had been more important to him than Dell. In spite of the difference in their ages, they were very much alike, so much alike that they were bound to fall out as completely as they came together. Dell too had come from a small midwestern town, dropped out of high school, and, spurning college, worked for a time in a factory. He too lived, as he put it in his autobiography, under "the overwhelming domination of a good mother's love" and was cared for by older women. There had been the Davenport librarian who urged him to become a poet, and then Margery Currey, who had in effect created a salon for him on Fifty-seventh Street. He too was in the habit of falling in love with other women and agonizing over what that said about his marriage. But whereas Anderson had just recently started his explorations of the damage in his own case and of the possibilities of a more liberating life, Dell was already something of an authority on the subject.

Dell was, in the Oedipal terms that both would later throw around, Anderson's "literary father." His most memorable paternal gesture was to help make his predictions for his elderly son's writing come true by taking Anderson's manuscript with him to New York in the fall and trying to get it published. Anderson had already interested Alfred Harcourt of Henry Holt and Company in *Windy McPherson's Son*. Were it to be redone by a professional editor, Harcourt had said, his firm would publish it; but when Anderson saw the revisions, he balked. Though Dell himself later altered the ending, just lopping off a page and with it, several of the children Sam McPherson was bringing back to his wife, Dell thought he could sell it as it stood. After several unsuccessful attempts in New York, he sent the manuscript to the John Lane Company of London. It had published two of Dreiser's novels, so Anderson wrote Dreiser, asking him if he might take a look at Anderson's first novel and put in a word on his behalf. He asked H. L. Mencken too, but before either man did anything, Lane agreed to publish the novel through its American branch.

When Anderson came to visit Dell late that fall, or early the next year (on what was his first visit to New York), and stayed on a couch in Dell's Washington Square apartment, it was evident that the two had already begun to drift apart — to exchange roles, really. Dell had settled in at the *Masses* and had turned in his black cravat and walking stick for the blue flannel shirt that was, as he said, more suitable to a "socialist editor." On his next visit, it was Anderson who wore the black stock and high collar that befitted "the high priest of literary art."

Their ages, the literal distances between them, and then finally their completely different needs as writers drew them farther and farther apart. As Dell retreated from the realms of art, Anderson lost his fears of them. Dell later told Anderson that he had to guard himself against flights into "the fantastic, the super-normal," shun them "as the drunkard shuns the bottle." You might have to punish the poet in you, Anderson wrote back, but I have to let the poet in me breathe. It was his way of discovering his reality. He had begun this process even before he met Dell. The kind of writing he did had proved "curative." It was not even the writing itself that was so important; *what* he wrote down or how he touched others was secondary. It was the very process of writing. It helped him face himself, he told Dell, it "helped me tell myself things. I did and do find writing helped me to live."

Dell's example, Dell's company and conversation, Dell's enthusiasm for Anderson's writing and his willingness to act on it — these helped launch Anderson in the summer of 1913. Even had anything more like friendship been possible, there had not been time for more.

Meanwhile, that summer Anderson went out on occasion to Little Point Sable, and on occasion Cornelia came into the city and met the people with whom her husband was beginning his life anew. She was, as ever, reserved, by no means happy there in bohemia, but on the other hand not unnerved by what was going on. She did not quite belong, she did not fit in, but neither did she seem wholly out of place. She was well educated, she had spoken to the Round Table Club. Dell remembered her from one of his wife's parties as "a slender, delicate, self-contained, warm and understanding person." She wore a Dante wreath around her hair, what someone at the gathering called "her sole recognition of evening dress," and she talked to Dell about her children. A presence from another time and place in Anderson's life, she watched and waited as he began to sail off into a new orbit.

But he was not yet in it all the way. Dell went to New York, leaving Margery Currey behind, but right after Thanksgiving, Anderson took a leave from Taylor-Critchfield and went off with his family to a small Missouri settlement by the name of Hooker, in the Ozark Mountains. A friend knew someone with a hunting lodge. There the Andersons could determine whether there was anything left of their marriage.

They prepared for a more rugged existence than either had ever known. They found their landlord, a month after their arrival, who charged them ten dollars for as long as they wanted to stay. Michael Carr came down from the University of Missouri at Christmas time, bearing big juicy steaks that they broiled over a fire. Otherwise the

Andersons spent four or five months in virtual isolation, an isolation that was unquestionably deeper for Cornelia than it was for her husband.

In front of their house was the Little Piney River, and to the side, a branch of it that one crossed on stepping stones; on the other side of it was another house, which the landlord used during hunting season. They had the key; so there Anderson withdrew, to write. His son John remembered his mother's having to go to a neighboring farmer for help milking a cow and his father's riding in on a white horse — perhaps a vision of a presence that was never really there. Mother and father had very little to do with each other. In Anderson's words, "I lived in a separate cabin on a hillside, and together the woman and I went through poverty, hatred of each other, and all the terrible things which come from such a situation."

The only thing they shared was a misunderstanding, and it saw them through their stay. After what had happened in Elyria and from what she gathered from his behavior since then, Cornelia concluded that her husband was mentally unsound, and that, Anderson said, "awoke the mother instinct in her." With her wanting to care for him, they got along better. But while she cared for him or, caring, left him alone, he hardened in his resolve.

More specifically, like the hero of his first novel, he determined to acknowledge the destructive as well as the charming side of his character. In Hooker he thought he gained "the ability to be brutal with women," which was to say, he arrived at the conclusion that

> for me there must always be my own place, some hole in the wall into which I could crawl to pray and be alone and to catch and hold my own note out of the jar and jangle of noises.

On the surface of it, nothing new. He had had his room in Elyria. But this time, in his "own place," he would really be alone. For the first time in his life, he had to embrace failure, "utterly and finally." Thinking of both his culture's immaturity and of all that he had put his family through, Anderson said that to admit to the failure of his marriage was the hardest thing, "the one terrible, hard thing," for him, for an American man to do, but now, in order to grow up, he had to accept the fact: he did not want to be married to his wife.

Anderson later said that he had written a novel in his cabin there in Hooker and had thrown it out the window on his way back to Chicago. What he did was continue on with writings he had begun in Elyria, possibly *Windy McPherson's Son* (though it must have been revised enough by then), possibly *Marching Men,* and most certainly a third novel he called *Mary Cochran.* He would never publish *Mary Cochran,* but far from discarding it, he would hold on to it until 1921, when he published two stories out of it. Then he finally let it drop. Whatever the exact dates, the clearest and most interesting imprints on it are of those ideas and people he had met since coming back to Chicago the year before.

Anderson himself appears in *Mary Cochran* as one Sylvester Hunnicut, age thirty-five, a businessman, but one who carried a pad in his pocket "and went through busy city streets with a queer, glazed look in his eyes, as fervent writers sometimes do." He is another Sam McPherson, searching after truth, dreaming of "writing truly, living truly, making love truly." He wants not the truths of Robert Browning and Thackeray, not the freedom of "having a job or a love affair, smoking cigarettes or voting for a city alderman," but what "the Ibsens, the Tolstoys, the Whitmans" sought in looking past the state to individuals, to free men and women in a free world. That is the visionary Anderson. The more prosaic one is the Sylvester who is confused in his relations with women.

In his attempt to clear up his hero's confusion, Anderson goes right to Dell's *Women as World Builders.* Sylvester finds happiness with Mary Cochran (who is initially — and predictably — his stenographer) because she goes out and finds her work. As an American woman she is tempted to be a courtesan, to sell herself for a place in a home, and in turn Sylvester is tempted to settle for the short-lived satisfaction of such a deal, but tutored by two sisters who started their own printing business, Mary determines to be "the kind of woman who stood for something in her own person." Married, they live in separate apartments, and Sylvester sets about writing a book proclaiming that "the hope of the world lay in its quiet, obscure working women of the Mary Cochran type," that one day, "an indefinable unity, a sisterhood, an organization would spring up something akin to the 'Order of the Samari,' conceived by the novelist Wells." A few years later, Anderson considered revising his manuscript and putting his own stamp on it by refusing Mary love and marriage because she had not "been able to realize beauty in herself" and had not "that daring fling at life that belongs to the artist," but in 1913–14, Anderson sees Dell's simpler theory through to its conclusion: because Mary is willing to accept a life without love, because she can refuse the domestic courtesan's life, she can (and does) love without fear.

The manic and the doctrinaire Anderson looked to the distant future in the pages of *Mary Cochran*. He was imagining the kind of woman he would be happy with. The Anderson who had just decided to end his marriage looked to a more immediate future. Much of the novel was indeed stylistically unpresentable, made up of Anderson's notes to himself, with sentences falling all over themselves; but in rendering Sylvester's breakup with his wife, he does not miss a beat. They were, he says,

> like two strange animals condemned by some freak of nature to occupy the same hole in a hillside. They walked about glaring at each other. When they laid down to sleep at night they could not sleep and their eyes shining in the darkness, stared at each other or at the walls of the room. Gertrude was filled with a sort of blind fury and Sylvester was afraid.

Sylvester escapes from the company of a culture-seeker from Toledo too, but he has "a vision of becoming a friend to the woman to whom he had been a lover, of renewing old ties on a new basis, of seeing his son and perhaps talking with him." He also hopes she will take a new lover, and so fixated is Anderson on his own situation that he names the prime candidate "Doubtful Harcourt," after the man who was at that very moment having second thoughts about publishing *Windy McPherson's Son*. Redefining and thereby maintaining his relationship with Cornelia is precisely what Anderson saw as his task before leaving Hooker: "I had to undertake the delicate and difficult task of breaking up that marriage," he explained four years later, "and of trying to win the real love of that woman out of marriage and outside the difficulties and complications of sex." And he succeeded.

The Andersons agreed that they would never again live together as man and wife but that they need not divorce because neither wanted to remarry. "He did the right thing," Cornelia wrote many years later. "He wouldn't have been free to develop otherwise." With a touch of bitterness she said she agreed with the idea that a genius needed a mother rather than a wife, but all told, she concluded, she was "a much better person for having known him so well." He was, she told her daughter, a remarkable man.

After leaving Hooker in March 1914, Cornelia took a house in Union Pier, a lakeside town within commuting distance of Chicago. At the end of the year she began to leave her children with a family there in order to commute to Chicago to prepare herself for what she hoped would be a career in social work; that failing, she taught school, first in Union Pier, and then, from 1917 until she retired in 1943, in Michigan City, Indiana.

Anderson returned to Taylor-Critchfield and was less than enthusiastically received, but his friend Barton took him back. Anderson also rejoined what was left of the artists' colony and on weekends, when the weather warmed, went out with them to Union Pier. This group included, by one report, "Anderson, Ben Hecht, Alexander Kaun, Michael Carr, Tennessee Mitchell, Cloyd Head, Robert Titus, Fedya Ramsey, Margaret Allen, Margery Currey — ever so many more." Anderson spent the nights not with Cornelia, but with them, by a bonfire or in the little shack, perched on the edge of a sand cliff, that they made their headquarters. He still hung on their words when they talked books, but he joined in freely now as they all took walks or went bathing in the nude or sang on the beach at night. What private moments he had with another woman were with Margery Currey.

There on September 13, 1914, Anderson celebrated his thirty-eighth birthday. He wrapped himself in the oriental hangings that served as curtains for their shack and presided while his friends performed an arty, pagan rite, dancing around in costumes made out of bits of clothes, of bedding, and of the surrounding vegetation, and finally burying a sacrificial victim in the sand. "Such a wonderful feeling in us," he later wrote, "of leading a new free bold life, defying what seemed to us the terribly stodgy life out of which we had all come." On this occasion, the happiest reveler was the one who had come the farthest.

By the end of the year, Anderson had established himself as the most colorful man at Taylor-Critchfield, the best storyteller, the one who had in fact published a story; and he had no reason to feel out of place among the colonists. For a season he kept a beard that he had grown in Hooker — suitably trimmed, as if to symbolize his position between two worlds. He might once have been put off by Margaret Anderson's talk about Pater, but by now he had proved himself as something of an artist in his own right, and by now she had asked him to contribute to her new magazine, the *Little Review*. Life during this "epoch" was "just one ecstasy after another," she said, what with people stopping her in the streets of Chicago to encourage her in her new venture, what with Vachel Lindsay donating his *Poetry* prize money, Frank Lloyd Wright a hundred dollars, and Eunice Tietjens pawning her engagement ring for the cause. It was Sherwood

Anderson who struck the "New Note" for her in her first issue, published at about the time he and Cornelia returned from the Ozarks. The "new note," Anderson wrote, "is as old as the world." It is

> a cry for the reinjection of truth and honesty into the craft; it is an appeal from the standards set up by money-making magazine and book publishers in Europe and America to the older, sweeter standards of the craft itself; it is the voice of the new man, come into a new world, proclaiming his right to speak out of the body and soul of youth, rather than through the bodies and souls of the master craftsmen who are gone.

No modish cry for "the new," his was a call, not unlike that of the more famous modernists whom the *Little Review* would soon publish, for what he called "craft love."

In "More About the 'New Note,'" which he wrote for the April issue, Anderson went on to elaborate in his own characteristic way. There was nothing about the artist's impersonality, no godlike figure paring his nails. Quite the opposite. Neither Pound, nor Eliot, nor Joyce would have approved:

> Given this note of craft love all the rest must follow, as the spirit of self-revelation, which is also a part of the new note, will follow any true present-day love of craft.

In almost embarrassingly elementary terms, Anderson said he was tempted to pass on a formula he had just worked out: "It lies here before me, and if you will accept it in the comradely spirit in which it is offered I shall be glad." It was similar to the one Hemingway worked out seven or eight years later, watching bullfights. The first, "the most delicate and the most unbelievably difficult task" was, he said, "to catch, understand, and record your own mood." When a man learned to do that, when he could look at himself and record what he really thought, then he could go on to record the thoughts of others, or as Anderson would also have it, the lives of the dozens of men and women who live in the mind of the imaginative writer himself. He ended by saying: "I would like to scold every one who writes, or who has to do with writing, into adopting this practice, which has been such a help and such a delight to me." It was the lesson for the day; it was what he had been trying to do in writing all along.

Later that same year he discovered Gertrude Stein, whom he would always credit with freeing him from the influence of the realists, of Howells in particular, with teaching him that there was "a second person" in himself, and with showing him how he would go about discovering and releasing that self — "the poet-writing person," he called it — in writing. When his brother Karl showed him a copy of the recently published *Tender Buttons,* Anderson thought he had been given a whole new set of tools, a whole new familiarity with his own words. He later said that Stein had done the most important pioneering work in the field of letters in his lifetime, "a rebuilding," he called it, "an entire new recasting of life, in the city of words." He saw that she was experimenting with words "separated from sense — in the ordinary meaning of the word sense," and learned from her that writing did not make ordinary sense, did not simply refer to life or tell us about the things of this world. The small pieces in *Tender Buttons* were not *about* a carafe or a feather, about mutton or breakfast. They were not representations, but re-presentations of them in the medium of words, "not ordinary," as the first piece, on "A Carafe, That Is A Blind Glass," has it, but "not unordered in not resembling." Writing was what she called "intellectual recreation."

Stein was not a storyteller, perhaps not even an artist, Anderson wrote in 1926 — "An artist in phrase making, word combinations, something like that. She is a sort of tool maker" — but, he said, "She has given me a lot." It was not that she taught him specific skills, or "influenced" his writing in any *particular* way. It was that she had introduced him to his medium, as if for the first time, given him the sense that he could do anything he wanted to with it. And so she added to what was already his large measure of excitement and enjoyment that year. He learned not only that writing was the means by which he could discover and record the truth about himself, but also that it was fun. Quite simply, as Stein said, writing was recreation.

In the months that followed, Anderson wrote several stories that honored and defended the position of the craftsman, even if they did not immediately reflect what Anderson himself was learning. "Sister" is a short fantasy in which Anderson casts himself as "the world," or "the worker in the world," and his sister as "the young artist in the world," for whom he fears, because of what the world does to artists and, more to the heart of the story, because of his own mad love for her. He based "Blackfoot's Masterpiece" on the fate of Ralph Blakelock, a painter who actually did go mad because the public failed to appreciate or buy his work. In "The Story Writers" he mocked two men who, like himself, retired to a room to write, and complained of the dullness of their surroundings while missing all the richness of the life around them. In "The Novelist" he tells of a clerk in a Chicago dry-goods store on Wabash Avenue who writes furiously every night after work about a woman who had failed in life and about their imagined marriage. The point is that the woman people knew was a caricature of the one who lived in the clerk's mind, just as he is "but a shadow of something very real." "You see the novelist wants to explain himself also," Anderson concluded.

> He is a lover and so vividly does he love that he has the courage to love even himself. And so it is the lover that sits writing and the madness of the writer is the madness of the lover. As he writes he is making love. Surely all can understand that!

If nothing else, one understands that he is enthusiastic and sincere.

Anderson took his work at Taylor-Critchfield less and less seriously. He was "wholly uncommercial," a colleague said. He wrote copy for his clients, the Owensboro Grader and Ditcher Company, the M. W. Savage Company, a manure spreader manufacturer, and a few others, but did so as quickly as he could and often with mistakes that others had to correct. When he finished writing the ad copy, he would cast it aside with a dismissive flourish and turn to the huge pad on which he *really* wrote.

In 1914 and 1915, though his first novel was as yet unpublished, Anderson turned to his fourth, one that never would be published, called *Talbot Whittingham*. Like so much else that he wrote, it trumpeted his newfound life. "I am telling you the story of the growth and development of a master artist," he says halfway through — which is to say, this artistic version of the tale of Dick Whittington too is relentlessly autobiographical. It is about Anderson, his days in Clyde (or Mirage, and then, in another draft, Winesburg), in Springfield, in Chicago (working for an advertising agency called Lester and Leach). Most emphatically it is about his vision of himself as the greatest artist of them all, not just a great artist but one who was willing to give up the world for his art.

Whitman had said that Christ was the one true artist because only his was the word made flesh, and there were many who saw the great gray poet as a Christly figure. But Anderson used the comparison to Christ to justify his own belated emergence into manhood and to point him on his way as a writer. "I understand, dear woman, our love for the figure of Jesus," he wrote a friend in 1917. "He alone is the master artist." "How strong and true and virile that figure," he goes on. "He only dared to let his soul grow, asking no reward, seeking none of our silly modern goals, money, comfort, fame, an established place in a distorted world." Anderson's artist is a man who does not know the truths of existence but knows that truths exist and tries to record them. The hero of his novel haunts the streets, lectures a bewildered prostitute on "the new woman," and talks "of movement and marching men and life," determined to alert the people of the world to what they cannot understand by themselves. When he listens to people, he seems to hear them crying out to him: "'Help us that we may make ourselves understood, that all men and all women may make themselves understood.'"

Anderson would soon fulfill something very like these dreams of mutual sympathy in chastened and memorable prose, but here they are only wild (and indeed unpublishable) ravings. Some of his writings are cruel as well. Ben Hecht has told of Anderson's actually walking out on a woman, leaving her bewildered and distraught, and of his then explaining to Hecht that he was trying to find out what it was like to pretend to love a woman whose ugliness repelled and whose conversation bored him. Tiring of his lies, his experiment over, he just left, Hecht says. Whether or not that happened, in *Talbot Whittingham* Anderson nursed still more destructive fantasies.

He creates another cultured female parasite whose self-assurance his hero would like to see destroyed. "I should like to see her broken and sobbing," he says. "That would do her soul good." Another dedicated woman, an Indiana schoolteacher, Anderson has shot by a crazed admirer as she is walking along with Whittingham. Whittingham's response is very odd. In retrospect, he is not sure he registered the fact that she was dying from her wound, but decides he must have: "his exultation was due to that." They keep walking, they get back to her room, and there, as she is dying, he says to himself, "'It is her part, her thing to do.'" And then: "As though in a dream he saw the purpose of his life in a new aspect. A keen, almost overpowering sense of the hidden beauty came over him. And he knew that the quest of beauty was to be for him the end of life." This is not so much Edgar Allan Poe as Anderson recasting, rejustifying, glorifying his break with Cornelia, almost enjoying her suffering. Ten years later, he reworked the material of this ending into "The Man's

Story," his favorite story, he often claimed. He needed it even more at the time: his *second* marriage was ending. In 1915, though, what he felt would really justify him would be some indication that he could reach Talbot Whittingham's goal. Having committed himself to writing, having sacrificed so much for and to it, what Anderson finally required of himself was not moral exoneration but better prose, and in the fall it started to come.

For a year Anderson had been renting a room on the top floor of a boarding house at 735 Cass Street (what is now Wabash Avenue), in midtown, near the offices of the *Little Review* and *Poetry* (where he would also begin to publish), and also near the quite different offices that still defined a portion of his being, those of Taylor-Critchfield. The house itself was something of another artists' colony, filled with young writers, musicians, and actors, and again Anderson was surrounded and looked up to. But this time he wanted to set himself apart. Though he was gradually being accepted as one, he was by no means sure of himself as a writer; and living alone, working at Taylor-Critchfield, he had been patching together a sorry version of himself as a man. He knew that he had yet to come into his kingdom.

The excitement of life at the colony and of life at Union Pier had died down. The realities of his "new life" emerged. What with her own salary, and perhaps help from her family, Cornelia did not ask that Anderson help support her and the children, but he had to make a living. He made nothing like what he had made in Elyria; in his own mind he was never even sure, from one week to the next, that he had a job. He knew of two or three businessmen and one woman, another advertising writer, who had committed suicide. He drank a lot, played poker, womanized, and boasted about it. It was his way of pretending he was free; but it was all too much like behavior he had been revolted by in the past. He knew he had to be alone in order to reconstitute himself as a man. So on Cass Street he withdrew to another room on another top floor, which, again, was sparsely furnished — this time with a bed, which he had raised so that he could look out over the movement in the Loop, and the desk at which he wrote.

Across Cass Street there was a church and a church school called the "Little Children of Mercy." Looking around at his fellow boarders, Anderson called them the "Little Children of the Arts." At The Oaks, in Springfield, he had been grateful for being included as a member of Mrs. Folger's "family"; on Fifty-seventh Street, he was elated at being the center of attention; now, when he descended from his heights at all, it was just to sit contentedly on the edges of a conversation or because the "little children" came to him. They told him about their work, they asked him for advice. One evening, as he was going back up to his room, he came upon a woman, a large woman, dressed in men's clothes, crying on the stairs. Sitting down next to her, he heard her out as she told of her unrequited love for another woman.

Entering 735 Cass Street, Anderson was amazed by the separation of these people's lives from the other lives he knew; he felt he was coming out of the world in which he lived. He saw in these artists "a great delicacy" that he had never seen before. They seemed so gentle with each other. Partly it was, he thought, an absence, a near-absence of lust; partly it was the "terrible seriousness" with which they viewed their art. They went about their work, seemingly not in competition with each other, and about their lives without destroying things. In their presence he imagined himself possessing new confidence, new stature. In these younger artists he saw a pleasing image of himself. As he put it haltingly in his *Memoirs,* "These new people, in some way a bit hard to explain, emphasized in me, shall I say, my maleness."

The writing he did that fall confirmed him in that image: finding his style, he established himself as his own man. More specifically, as he would often say, in writing one particular story — "Hands" — he knew, now without a doubt, that he could be a writer and a different kind of man.

"Hands" is about Wing Biddlebaum, a born teacher, "one of those rare, little understood men who rule by a power so gentle that it passes as a lovable weakness," Anderson writes, one of those who, "in their feeling for the boys under their charge . . . are not unlike the finer sort of women in their love of men." And "Hands" is about Wing's hands, which "made more grotesque an already grotesque and elusive individuality." Twenty years before, in a Pennsylvania town, when he was Adolph Myers, Wing had almost been lynched by men who interpreted his affectionate and encouraging gestures toward his students as homosexual advances. Terrified, never quite understanding what had happened, Wing fled town, changed his name (to one he had seen on a box of goods at a freight station), and ended up in Winesburg, Ohio, his hands a source of another kind of fame: "With them Wing Biddlebaum had picked as high as a hundred and forty

quarts of strawberries in a day." Forty years old but looking sixty-
five, Wing lived alone on the edge of town, seeing no one, except
occasionally George Willard, the young reporter for the *Winesburg
Eagle*. With George, he would come to life again, his voice would
rise, his figure straighten, and

> the slender expressive fingers, forever active, forever striving to
> conceal themselves in his pockets or behind his back, came forth
> and became the piston rods of his machinery of expression.

His own life forever stunted, he tries to reach out to save George
from what he sees could be a similar fate, to encourage him to be the
writer he wants to be:

> "You are destroying yourself," he cried. "You have an inclination
> to be alone and to dream and you are afraid of dreams. You want
> to be like others in town here. You hear them talk and you try to
> imitate them. . . . You must try to forget all you have learned,"
> said the old man. "You must begin to dream. From this time on
> you must shut your ears to the roaring of the voices."

When he tries to reach out in fact, raises "the hands to caress the
boy," a look of horror comes over his face, and he flees again, "down
the hillside and across a meadow, leaving George Willard perplexed
and frightened upon the grassy slope." Our last images of him are as
a bird, quickly picking up crumbs off the floor by lamplight after his
dinner, and as a priest (perhaps suggested by Anderson's neighbors
across Cass Street), his fingers "flashing in and out of the light," like
those of one "going swiftly through decade after decade of his rosary."

Two years before, at Dell's instigation, the colony had discovered
Freud and the excitement of "psyching" each other. Anderson did not
do much of the reading, and he thought it slightly absurd when one
of the crowd took his snapping a twig to mean he really wanted to
be a woman, but he did bring up the subject of homosexuality and
told everybody about the transvestites who lived near the warehouse
where he had once worked. The subject had come up again at Taylor-
Critchfield. Now it was the copywriters, taunting themselves for not
doing something more dignified, something more manly than writing ads. They would go barhopping together, Anderson among
them, often ending up in the tougher parts of town. There, in their
banter, they would call each other names — "Little Eva," "Mabel"
— while the locals leered. It gave them "a kind of satisfaction,"

Anderson said, to be taken for "fairies" and ogled at. Defiant in, even titillated by their self-imposed degradation, they enjoyed themselves. It was "a kind of mutual recognition of our common whoredom." There was a question as to whether they were dominating men or servile women. And back at Cass Street, there had been that woman in men's clothes, crying on the stairs. The sexes and the genders were confused.

What "Hands" questioned were common understandings of what made men men and women women. "What the devil is a man and what is a woman," Anderson wrote the next year. "Of course you have put on skirts or trousers. You have arranged the conventions of your life and most people live by conventions. The artist tears them away." What "Hands" said was that there was something sad and even lovely about men like Wing (or any man, or woman) whom society had used and stunted in the process of establishing its own working definitions of manhood and womanhood, that there was something destructive in the roar of voices in town, and that a man, especially an old young man who fancied himself a writer, ought to have the courage to ignore those voices and to listen instead to one that came from a more complex and richer kind of maleness. It was not that he himself was homosexual (or that Wing was, or the woman on the stairs). Indeed, it was against such labeling that "Hands" protested. Affixing such labels to a person was like lynching. Or as Stein put it, less dramatically, naming was all right if you wanted to call a roll, but "is it any good for anything else?" And besides, what did Anderson (or any of his friends, for that matter) know about homosexuality, or even sexuality? What other than that sexuality was a new and fascinating subject? Anderson did know the damage that was done by people who thought they knew, or in their insecurity about their sexuality thought they had to know. His own was something of a mystery to him, a mystery that neither his marriage to Cornelia nor his encounters with nameless other women had done anything to clear up, but he did not set out to *solve* that mystery. What he wanted to do was give the silenced people of America a chance to speak, to hear their voices. And in doing that, in "Hands," he released his own.

Anderson wrote of Wing: "He was one of those men in whom the force that creates life is diffused, not centralized." We can say as much for Anderson's narrative, not focused, not building to a climax, not phallic, as it were, but weaving gracefully back and forth between past and present, between its business and digressions. We can say as much for Anderson's narrative voice, which begins with ease:

> Upon the half decayed veranda of a small frame house that stood near the edge of a ravine near the town of Winesburg, Ohio, a fat little old man walked nervously up and down.

This beginning ends in careful search of just the right image of Wing, and throughout, the narrative voice interrupts itself in order to explain or to efface itself:

> The story of Wing Biddlebaum's hands is worth a book in itself. Sympathetically set forth it would tap many strange, beautiful qualities in obscure men. It is a job for a poet.

Here is Anderson on Wing's manner, in a style that is very much like it:

> With the boys of his school, Adolph Myers had walked in the evening or had sat talking until dusk upon the schoolhouse steps lost in a kind of dream. Here and there went his hands, caressing the shoulders of the boys, playing about the tousled heads. As he talked his voice became soft and musical. There was a caress in that also. In a way the voice and the hands, the stroking of the shoulders and the touching of the hair were a part of the school-master's effort to carry a dream into the young minds. By the caress that was in his fingers he expressed himself.

No "poison plot," no more manic or childish voices in search of authority, "Hands" is a fine story by an accomplished storyteller, or, more precisely, by a teller of tales, whose power is so gentle it might seem to the inattentive only a "lovable weakness." It is the tale of and by a man whose love is not unlike that of "the finer sort of woman."

He wrote the story in one sitting, sometime in the fall of 1915. He wrote it on the reverse sides of the manuscript pages of *Talbot Whittingham* and later revised it. He toned down Wing's attraction to George considerably. He wrote "he still hungered for the presence of the boy" instead of "he still hungered for the boy"; he said that Wing's hands "stole forth and lay upon George Willard's shoulders" instead of just "stole to George Willard's shoulders." But it was as if the story had come from another world, perfect as it stood. "I think the most absorbing interesting and exciting moment in any writer's life must come at the moment when he for the first time, knows that he is a real writer," he later wrote.

> You read, read, read. You live in the world of books. It is only after a long time that you know that this is a special world, fed out of the world of reality, but not of the world of reality.
>
> You have yourself not yet brought anything up out of the real world into this special world, to make it live there.
>
> And then, if you are ever to be a real writer, your moment comes.

This was his.

When he saw what he had written, Anderson got up from his desk, in his excitement began to pace the floor, and then went out into the streets. Bursting with energy, he wanted to hug the passers-by, to shout: "I've done it. At last, after all those years I've done something." He went into a bar instead and stood people to drinks, and stayed until he had mustered up enough courage to return to his room to read "Hands" once more — to see if it was true. After an hour or so, he went back and sat down at his desk again. When he had finished reading, he saw that what he had written was good, and he began to cry. It was sound, it was solid, like a rock. "It is there," he told himself. "It is put down." So satisfied was he with what he had written, that night he thought that whatever happened to him "personally" did not matter. What mattered was the writing. "Hands" proved that he could be a writer, it proved him right. It was there, so finally he existed.

FIVE

"Emerging Greatness"
1915-1917

AFTER THE ACHIEVEMENT of "Hands," other tales soon
followed, some in quick succession, some separated by a
gap of a week or two. Anderson wrote many of them — as he had
written "Hands" — in what was essentially one sitting. When he
gathered them together as *Winesburg, Ohio* four years later, they would
number twenty-four. He probably wrote most of them in the fall of
1915 and the winter of 1915–16. He wrote in the evenings, sometimes during the day at Taylor-Critchfield or, because he could not
wait and took the day off, in his room, the curtains drawn to make
it seem like night, a candle on his desk. He felt "like a harp the wind
blew through," he told Cornelia. He said he felt "like a woman,
having my babies, one after another, but without pain," and (not
limiting himself to one sex) like a Rabelaisian man too, the stories
having "fairly gushed from his pen."

They were all about people like Wing Biddlebaum, Anderson said
in 1932, people who had not succeeded in life, but decent people
nevertheless. A "burlesque," a Methodist minister had called *Winesburg, Ohio,* and Anderson had leapt to its defense: "The book is, of
course, in no sense a burlesque, but it is an effort to treat the lives of
simple ordinary people in an American middle western town with
sympathy and understanding." "Certainly, I did not write to make
fun of these people or to make them ridiculous or ugly," he said; they
were "people I personally would be glad to spend my life with." And
of course he had. They came from Clyde, they came from Springfield,
they came from the boardinghouse on Cass Street in which he wrote

about them. He had retrieved them from his past, he could "see the glimmer of stars in the eyes of his neighbors" of his early days, he told a friend; he had escaped from business and from the Fifty-seventh Street colony to find them among his present neighbors. He loved them all, and in lovingly recreating them he envisioned how decent *he* could be now that he was no longer trying to be just a materially successful man.

Anderson had written several pages he called "The Book of the Grotesque" just before he wrote "Hands." He thought the piece might provide the title for his collection, but in the event it serves only to introduce the collection very well. The word *grotesque* was in the air. He might have come across it reading Poe, who had titled his satirical stories "Tales of the Grotesque and Arabesque." More immediately, Arthur Davison Ficke had published ten short poems in that first March issue of the *Little Review,* "Ten Grotesques," in which a woman who listened to poetry all night, a disturbed gentleman, the devilish author himself, and others spoke their piece. In November, at Chicago's Little Theatre, Lloyd Head produced *Grotesque: A Decoration in Black and White,* a free-verse play in which marionettes were used to explore levels of consciousness. Edgar Lee Masters's *Spoon River Anthology* had been published in April, and in the fall one of the "little children," a musician named Max Wald, lent Anderson his copy, and Anderson stayed up all night reading it. By the next morning, if not before, the idea of bringing together figures who had led buried lives and allowing them their say had certainly crystallized.

Anderson was clear on what made *his* figures "grotesque." "In the beginning when the world was young," he wrote, "there were a great many thoughts but no such thing as a truth." Out of those thoughts, man made his truths, "the truth of virginity and the truth of passion, the truth of wealth and of poverty, of thrift and of profligacy, of carelessness and abandon," and they were all beautiful. But when anyone took one of these truths, took one of them to himself, "called it his truth, and tried to live his life by it, he became a grotesque and the truth he embraced became a falsehood."

In this formulation Anderson placed himself in the tradition of Emerson and Whitman, urging his fellow men to look past the standards, the goals, society seemed to set for them, to recreate themselves in their own language, or to refuse to acknowledge language's limitations altogether — to surpass themselves. "Our friends early appear to us as representations of certain ideas which they never pass or exceed," Emerson had written in "Experience." Before long, we know what they stand for, and what they stand for never changes. By contrast, he proclaimed, "Everything good is on the highway."

It is true of all men and women, for example, that they are drawn, in greatly varying degrees, to members of their own sex. They become grotesque when they or others take attraction to be the truth about them. Wing Biddlebaum is not ugly, but misshapen, without and within, misinformed, his form wrongly taken (and taken in) from those who label him "homosexual." Don't take others' words for anything, he tells George; dream, imagine endlessly for yourself.

At thirty-nine, Sherwood Anderson was still young, practically newborn if we apply the rule he was happy to borrow from Joseph Conrad, "who said that the writer only lived after he began writing." The only truth he clung to was that he was a writer, and that freed him further, for it meant that he could take any form. In "The Book of the Grotesque," he introduces himself as an old man, lying in a bed just like Anderson's, one that has been raised to the level of his window. He is a man who imagines he might die suddenly, unexpectedly, but who takes pleasure in the thought because he has been saved by something young inside himself, not a baby but a youth, not a youth either, but "a woman, young, and wearing a coat of mail like a knight." Not Joan of Arc. The point is not to name: "It is absurd, you see, to try to tell what was inside the old writer as he lay on his high bed and listened to the fluttering of his heart. The thing to get at is what the writer, or the young thing within the writer, was thinking about." One must be true to the variousness of life, to the "long procession of figures" that went before the writer's eyes, "all the men and women the writer had ever known." Anderson was himself both the old writer who was the more alive for contemplating his death and for having the valiant woman/knight within him, and the young reporter who would go on dreaming and someday be a writer. He was the man who might have been "grotesque" at almost forty but for the fact that he had listened to his own advice and had stayed young. He was the man who at midlife found himself just born, come of age, because he was writing well.

Winesburg, Ohio is best known as a book about a small Ohio town during the years just before the coming of industry. It is a town almost entirely without religious or political associations. The minister never meets his congregation; most of his story takes place in a bell tower where he fights the temptations of the flesh that he can see next door through a hole in a stained glass window. George Willard's father is a Democrat whose political hopes vanished when the town went Republican, his one swipe at the "friendship" of McKinley and Hanna being all the talk of politics we hear. There are a few unhappy marriages, entered into as a relief from or atonements for the confusion created by lust, and soon regretted; the relations between parents and children are tenuous at best. The people of Winesburg are almost completely isolated one from another. They talk to no one. If their passions and dreams are not dead, they make one last, startling, pathetic appearance, usually before George Willard. They tell him what has been on their minds and never before expressed. Thus the tales.

After years of waiting for a lover who has no thought of returning, after trying "the devices common to lonely people" — whispered prayers to her lover, attachment to the very furniture of her room, watching the interest in her savings book mount up — one rainy night Alice Hindman runs through the streets of Winesburg without any clothes on, calling out to and for a passer-by, who turns out to be old and deaf. It is the last expression of her loneliness, her last resort, her "Adventure" (as the title has it). Coming to her senses, she crawls through the grass to her home, bolts the door of her room, and begins to try to make herself face the fact (Anderson says, wryly) "that many people must live and die alone, even in Winesburg." Wash Williams foams with misogynistic rage against the wife who betrayed him and the mother-in-law who tried to win him back by having her daughter appear before him naked. "I didn't get the mother killed," Wash tells George. "I struck her once with a chair and then the neighbors came in and took it away. She screamed so loud you see. I won't ever have the chance to kill her now. She died of a fever a month after that happened." One winter night, "The Teacher," Kate Swift, comes to the print shop of the *Eagle,* where George is working late. Thinking she'd seen a spark of genius in the boy, the summer before she had come to counsel him on how to be a writer. This night passion also urges her on, passion for a man, and a passionate desire that this young man know life — and he responds, only to feel her body stiffen, and her "two sharp little fists . . . beat on his face," before she runs away.

At the time, of course, because it insisted on portraying how men and women express their loneliness sexually, or rather, how futile such expression was, *Winesburg, Ohio* was considered unfit for some library shelves. Subsequently, it has been placed among those books debunking small-town life, somewhere between E. W. Howe's *The Story of a Country Town* or Masters's *Spoon River Anthology* and Sinclair Lewis's *Main Street*. But it lives as Anderson's vision — midway through the second decade of the twentieth century, midway through the First World War — of what was happening to the promise of American life. "These studies," he wrote in November 1916, "will suggest the real environment out of which present-day American youth is coming." It had come out of towns like Clyde and emerged, in the present, in cities like Chicago, "a city of the dead," as he described it the same month to a friend, a city given over to the pursuit of money and status. "In the office dead voices discuss dead ideas," he said, as if he were trying to sound like William Blake in London. "I go into the street and long rows of dead faces march past." It was also a city, a culture, trying to drum up enthusiasm for the Allied cause in the Great War — which, after his brief experience of war, made the prospect of the future all the more disheartening for Anderson. While other famous writers-to-be rushed to the Italian front or signed up to drive ambulances, Anderson thought that what was required was "a leader now for America who will have the courage to ask the people to pray and be sad."

By November, having written half of the Winesburg tales, Anderson saw that his own salvation lay in the fancies that he could express, in the "thousand beautiful children [yet] unborn." He imagined that his mission was to keep alive what he called "the very blood and spirit of all this aimlessness" in himself and in the kind of people that he wrote about. There was still "vastness of possibility," he concluded. If nowhere else, one could see it in the land, and "if we can love *that* we can love America. There is only vastness of possibility." His subject was the common people of America, his task to give them their voice. "A democratic plea," John Updike has called *Winesburg, Ohio,* "for the failed, the neglected, and the stuck."

There were some in Winesburg who were still alive. There was Doctor Reefy of "Paper Pills," who jotted down thoughts on bits of paper, rolled them up into little balls, and eventually threw them away — "Little pyramids of truth he erected and after erecting knocked them down again that he might have the truths to erect other pyramids." So committed was Anderson himself to this figure of open-mindedness that twelve or thirteen years later, he offered a four-paragraph version of Doctor Reefy as his contribution to *The Bookman's* series on "Statements of Belief: The 'Credos' of America's Leading Authors." There was Roy Pearson of "The Untold Lie," who, when asked by a young co-worker what to do about the girl he had gotten pregnant, thought of how he himself might have gone to sea or worked out West rather than get married. But he says nothing, knowing that whatever he advised would be a lie, knowing better than to impose his imaginings on another. And there is George Willard himself, lending continuity to the whole, as one "grotesque" after another opens up to him, and as he himself develops into manhood, learning what it takes to be a writer and a lover.

As was true of some of the men at Taylor-Critchfield, George aspires to writing *lasting* prose; as was true of Anderson, his ambition distinguishes him in Winesburg. George is not above fatuousness on that score, telling Seth Richmond it was "the easiest of all lives"; nor is he above the kind of behavior Anderson had paraded before Hecht, planning to fall in love with Helen White and then having Seth tell her in order to "see how she takes it." But he comes to appreciate his teacher's resonant advice: "You must not become a mere peddler of words," Kate Swift had said. "The thing to learn is how to know what people are thinking about, not what they say." George is ready to fulfill his mother's dream that he not be "a dull clod, all words and smartness," like his father. At the end of the book, his mother dead, George Willard, age eighteen, boards the train for Chicago. So it had been. Twenty years after Anderson had done the same thing, he dedicated *Winesburg, Ohio* to the memory of his mother. He had done what George Willard had set out to do; he had justified his mother's faith.

Not a novel, not just a collection of stories, *Winesburg, Ohio* is precisely what Anderson called it in a subtitle that many editions omit: "A Group of Tales of Ohio Small Town Life." Though he fell prey to the notion that the final test of literary manhood was the ability to write novels, he was not comfortable in what he said was, by contrast to the tale, "the more compact novel form." "A man keeps thinking of his own life," he said. "But life itself is a loose, flowing thing. There are no plot stories in life." Those who wrapped it up in novels or "short stories" betrayed life. Those, like Dell, who later insisted that a story be "sharply definite," that it must have "a beginning and an end," could not appreciate his effort "to develop,

Emma Smith Anderson

Irwin McLain Anderson

The Anderson children, c. 1886.
Standing: Stella and Karl.
Seated: Sherwood, Ray, Earl, and Irwin Jr.

"Jobby"

Bicycle factory, Clyde.
Anderson is fourth from the left.

The Anderson children, c. 1896.
From left: Karl, Ray, Sherwood, Stella, Irwin Jr., and Earl.

Members of Company I.
Anderson is in front, second from the right.

Business Types

SHERWOOD ANDERSON

The Undeveloped Man.

THE advertising man sat upon his upturned grip at a railroad junction. It was midnight, a drizzle of rain was in the air and close about him lay the unbroken blackness of a cloudy night.

Down the tracks in the railroad yards a freight engine was making up a train. The banging of the cars, the rumbling of the wheels, the swinging lanterns and the voices of the trainmen lent interest to a long, dull wait. Suddenly up the track there came a rippling string of oaths, and for the next ten minutes the air was filled with them. In the words of Mark Twain, there was "swearing in that railroad yard, swearing that just laid over any swearing ever heard before."

The engineer swore and he wasn't half bad; the conductor deftly caught up the refrain and embellished it, and then from far down in the yards the voice of a brakeman cut into the game.

It was all about a box car and a coupling pin that wouldn't catch, and it was nothing less than genius the way that brakeman handled his subject. He swore scientifically. He worked over the ground already covered by the engineer and conductor and from it harvested another crop, and then he caught his breath, waved his lantern and started into the dense forest of untried oaths. The best part of it all was the way he clung to that box car, he went far enough afield for words but when he used them they were pat, they were all descriptive of the car and its peculiar and general uselessness.

"He is a sort of genius in his way, ain't he?" said a weak, piping little voice at the advertising man's elbow.

SHERWOOD ANDERSON

"The Undeveloped Man," 1904

Cornelia Platt Lane

The Andersons with Robert and John, and Cornelia's father, 1909

HOME OF ROOF-FIX
(CURE FOR ROOF TROUBLES)

Just a Word in Your Ear

JUST SUPPOSE you were going to buy a new roof this year. You would expect to pay anywhere from $2.00 to $4.00 per hundred square feet, wouldn't you? Now, the interest on $3.00 at six per cent is 18 cents per year. So the cost of the new roof would be 18 cents per square per year, not counting repairs, cost of putting on, or anything.

Well, we have proven to thousands of cases that with ROOF-FIX you can keep the old roof in perfect condition at five cents per square per year. Think it over. It's a dollar and cents matter. Buy ROOF-FIX and keep the price of the new roof in your pocket. Catalog free. Write for it.

THE ANDERSON MFG. CO., Elyria, Ohio

The Anderson Manufacturing Company, as pictured in his catalogue to the top of my bent, my own capacity to feel, see, taste, smell, hear." He wanted, he said, "to be a free man, proud of my own manhood, always more and more aware of earth, people, streets, houses, towns, cities. I wanted to take all into myself, digest what I could."

The sentiments were part Conrad ("My task," he had written in the preface to *The Nigger of the Narcissus,* "is to make you hear, to make you feel — it is, before all, to make you *see!*"), part Whitman ("All this I swallow, it tastes good," he said at the end of one of the longest of his famous catalogues. "I like it well, it becomes mine"). But the idea of collecting the tales and organizing them around a central figure was Anderson's. It was the right form for him, and it was *his* form, his invention, he liked to claim. Though he later read Joyce, he never bothered to compare his own form with the organization of Joyce's *Dubliners,* nor need he have, for the epiphanic moments in Joyce's text do not, and were never intended to, bring a collective people to life. If Anderson knew of what is a closer parallel, Sarah Orne Jewett's *Country of the Pointed Firs,* he never said so. The one precedent he did acknowledge and turn to again and again for encouragement in later years was Ivan Turgenev's *Sportsman's Sketches,* a book of twenty-five pieces that quietly honors rather than makes stories out of the lives of common people. But the sportsman's life does not evolve and so give shape to his sketches. Pressed, Anderson would insist on the uniqueness of his own accomplishment — justifiably. "I can accept no standard I have ever seen as to form," he wrote in 1921; and then in 1938, thinking back on *Winesburg, Ohio* in an effort to regain his writing stride, he added, "It is a form in which I feel at ease. I invented it. It was mine."

Collecting the tales the way he did, he maintained contact with an all but vanished form of social life. It was his way, Antaeus-like, of re-establishing his base, regaining his strength, after too many years of trying to be a financial and social success. Anderson was not writing short stories, "nice little packages, wrapped and labeled in the O. Henry manner," he later said, not writing about or for "the rich and well to do." He was staying "at home, among my own people, people in my own street." He was speaking as one of them, implicitly encouraging them to share one another's lives. After "Tales of Ohio Small Town Life" came other subtitles: "Tales, Long and Short, from American Life" (*Horses and Men*), "A Book of Impressions from American Life in Tales and Poems" (*The Triumph of the Egg*), and

"The Tale of an American Writer's Journey" (*A Story Teller's Story*). These were often about life in the Midwest and usually did not succeed as well as *Winesburg, Ohio,* but each one was an attempt to hear and render the voices of "common" people, people who were not usually welcomed into the community of literary figures, people who often had no community themselves.

Winesburg, Ohio, then, is the book in which Anderson came into his own as a writer, the book in which he found his subject and his style, the one inextricably bound up with the other, and it is about that achievement. It is about what he found it took to be a writer. It is the book in which Anderson begins to come to terms with his protean character as a man. What's more, from 1915 on, after "Hands," he considered himself a man insofar as he was satisfied with himself as a writer. More or less explicitly, he had been writing *about* himself from the start, ever since his first contributions to *Agricultural Advertising.* Now his very style would be the measure of himself as a man.

More crudely, "the theme of the book," as he later put it, "the thing that really makes it a book — curiously holding together from story to story as it does," is: "the making of a man out of the actual stuff of life." While planning to convert *Winesburg, Ohio* into a play, he described Seth Richmond as a young man who wanted to make money, "be a big man," and George Willard as a dreamer, wanting to become a writer "because almost everything in his own life goes wrong and he has a vague feeling that in some novel or story he may be able to build up an ordered fine life." It was to be George's life from then on, sometimes a life of which he would be ashamed, the dreamer, Anderson said, being capable of more brutality than the likes of plodding Seth, but a life, on balance, "of decent manhood."

Insofar as the women of Winesburg tend to be sexual dynamos or predators, the men imagine that in order to be men they must subdue and conquer them. Thus, in "Nobody Knows" George convinces himself that he is "wholly male, bold and aggressive," in order to cope with Louise Trunnion; in "An Awakening," he sets out after Belle Carpenter, "half drunk with the sense of masculine power." Anderson never wholly freed himself from the idea that women possessed power over life and death, that they were mysterious, natural forces to be subdued. Nor was he ever fully sure that he was man enough to do it. But at the same time, he was clear about the limits of such thinking. In "Nobody Knows" George wins only a pathetic victory; in "An Awakening" he is summarily defeated, thrust aside by the man Belle really loves. And by the end of the book, George ceases to think like a stereotypical male.

With his mother's death, George "crosses the line into manhood." For the first time, in "Sophistication," he takes "the backward view of life," and he wants to share his understanding with Helen White. For her part, tired of a world "full of meaningless people saying words" (her college instructor is visiting the Whites), she rushes out into the night to meet George. The setting of their meeting — the fairground the night after the annual fair, the fall night cooler and longer, the town almost all closed up for the evening — is frozen in relief:

> In Winesburg the crowded day had run itself out into the long night of the late fall. Farm horses jogged away along lonely country roads pulling their portion of weary people. Clerks began to bring samples of goods in off the sidewalks and lock the doors of stores. In the Opera House a crowd had gathered to see a show and further down Main Street the fiddlers, their instruments tuned, sweated and worked to keep the feet of youth flying over a dance floor.

Together, they do not profess their love, nor is George put to any test: "He wanted to love and be loved by her, but he did not want at the moment to be confused by her womanhood." They kiss — "but that impulse did not last." When they draw apart, it is as if after another kind of conception: "Mutual respect grew big in them." Finally, from such maturity, *in* such maturity, they descend into youth:

> It was so they went down the hill. In the darkness they played like two splendid young things in a young world. Once, running swiftly forward, Helen tripped George and he fell. He squirmed and shouted. Shaking with laughter he rolled down the hill. Helen ran after him.

"For some reason they could not have explained," Anderson says, "they had both got from their silent evening together the thing needed." Maintaining his ability to dream, but no longer brutish, retrieving the innocence of his youth, George enters manhood, ready to go on and become a writer. Appropriately, one of the last strains one hears in the voice of the writer who imagined the making of such a man is that of "Jack and Jill."

Winesburg, Ohio would not appear as a book until 1919, but Anderson began to publish individual tales (along with "Sister," "The Story Writers," and "The Novelist") in the winter of 1915–16. He and Dell were no longer close personally, but Dell was happy to accept "The Book of the Grotesque" and "Hands" for publication in the February and March issues of the *Masses*. In August, he printed one more: "The Strength of God," concerning the temptations of the Reverend Hartman. The next month Anderson would be forty, rather old for a writer who was just beginning to be published — and whose first novel was *still* not out. He had gotten off to a very late start. But, understandably, he was beginning to swell with pride over what he had accomplished.

It was not acceptance by the *Masses,* though, that filled him with the most confidence. "My crowd," Dell wrote in 1942, "were too rough as playmates for Sherwood." To put it without swagger, their interests were more specifically political, less literary, than Anderson's. What he took as final proof that he had arrived as a writer was the attention paid him by the editors of another periodical — the *Seven Arts.*

Seven Arts began publication in the fall of 1916 in New York under the editorship of James Oppenheim, a poet and writer of sentimental and muckraking fiction. Waldo Frank was associate editor, Paul Rosenfeld the music editor. Among those who sat on its advisory board were Van Wyck Brooks (soon to become an editor too), Kahlil Gibran, Edna Kenton, and Robert Frost. Its prolegomenon, as Frank put it, was *America's Coming of Age,* Brooks's dismissal of the "vaporous idealism and self-interested practicality" of American life and literature, in the name of what he called, rather vaguely, a release of "those personal instincts that have been the essence of art, religion, literature — the essence of personality itself — since the beginning of things."

The one exception Brooks could point to was Walt Whitman. Unlike his British counterpart, William Morris, Whitman had not inspired America with a concrete, social ideal, but he was significant nevertheless. He was the first to give America a sense of something organic in its life. (*Seven Arts* was less hesitant: "The Spirit of Walt Whitman Stands Behind the Seven Arts," their ad ran; he is "your Homer," Romain Rolland wrote in the first issue.) Developing his criticism of American culture in the pages of *Seven Arts,* Brooks said that the American mind had no barriers to throw up against the forces of materialism. The acquisitive life had lost its sanction; it was no longer even adventuresome. Americans were left numb in spirit, without any sense of communal purpose. But the younger generation was beginning to demand more, to demand, in the first place, a literature that was aware of the country's plight and was able to address it. It was beginning to sense the presence, once again, of "some prodigious organism that lies undelivered in the midst of our society, an immense brotherhood of talents and capacities coming to a single birth." In order for that "organism" to come into being, America needed — and *Seven Arts* was prepared to welcome — "a wiser head and a riper heart than we have yet seen."

The stage was set for Anderson. Edna Kenton was the first to hear of him. She had gone out to Chicago the year before in an attempt to interest writers in the new venture. Though in 1915 Anderson was not well enough known to be invited to the meeting she called, she heard about this "bright Chicago advertising man" who wrote stories, and when she returned to New York, she told Frank about him. He pursued the lead and soon received a draft of "The Untold Lie," and then "Mother" and "Loneliness," all on cheap paper, in "long gangling script," Frank recalled, "each word of which looked like a lean hound in full chase across the page." When he read "The Untold Lie," he was ecstatic; it was, he said years later, "one of the great stories of the world." He sent it back, though, pointing out that there was only one small problem: before he bought it, he wanted to see some punctuation. But that was easily solved. Anderson returned it with commas placed after every six or seven words and a note saying that if that wouldn't do, Frank should suit himself.

In the flyer that the editors of the *Seven Arts* sent out, announcing their intentions, they spoke of "a renascent period" in American life. They said they sensed "the coming of that national self-consciousness which is the beginning of greatness," and they cited the arts as evidence. The *Seven Arts* would be a channel, a way for the arts to express the new promise of America. "In short," they concluded, "the *Seven Arts* is not a magazine for artists, but an expression of artists for the community." Whether the Winesburg tales helped inspire the editors to such claims or whether the tales appeared on Frank's desk as their fulfillment, there they were, reporting that life in the service of Mammon was soul destroying, that Americans were lost without spiritual inspiration and communal purpose, proving that there *were* writers out there who had vision. *Seven Arts* would publish four of the tales and a piece titled "From Chicago" in ten months, and it would have published more had the periodical's backer not withdrawn her support after the issue of October 1917. Sherwood Anderson's writings were verification of Brooks's social criticism, and justification for *Seven Arts*'s existence. What was even more exciting, truly extraordinary, was that the man who wrote them lived them, and in writing them showed that America could restore itself.

"His famous flight," as Brooks would later say, "when he 'walked out' of his office" in Elyria, was to become "the symbol of an epoch." When he published his version of *America's Coming of Age, Our America* in 1919, Frank said that "what happened to Sherwood Anderson and turned him from the traveled American part of making-money is of a vast significance: not as regards the life of Anderson alone, but in the life of the United States." Along with Dreiser and a man named Booth, Anderson represented "the one thing needed, the one thing missed: inherent life." When Frank looked back on his days at *Seven Arts,* he said Anderson personified "the fecund sap of what he loved to call Mid-America." And more: "To me, the young New Yorker who knew his Europe well and had scarce seen his own land beyond the Eastern seaboard, Sherwood Anderson was America."

By the fall of 1916, Anderson's prospects as a writer had risen to heights that could hardly have been headier. And by then he thought he was ready to make a new start in his relations with women as well. Ever since his separation from Cornelia he had been opening himself up to the possibilities of new love, preparing himself for another marriage, a different kind of marriage.

He was assisted in his efforts by a woman named Marietta Finley — Bab, as he always called her — a woman who was unlike Winesburg's Helen White in that she was ardent in her devotion to Anderson, but was like Helen in providing constant and enabling friendship. She was a woman who wanted to marry Anderson, a woman, though, to whom Anderson came the closer because he would not do so.

Anderson met Bab in the fall of 1914, after a play put on by Maurice Browne's Little Theatre group in the Fine Arts Building. She was with a friend from Indianapolis, where she lived; he was with some of the "little children" from nearby Cass Street. She was dark-eyed, almost petite, lively — not a beautiful woman, but obviously and immediately attractive. Since she was a reader for the Bobbs-Merrill Company (and an astute one, as her reports on *Mary Cochran* and *Talbot Whittingham* demonstrate), she and Anderson had much in common, but what actually happened that night, or in the months or years that followed, we do not know. One might well assume that they became lovers, but the life we *know* they shared concentrates elsewhere — on Anderson himself, on Anderson as he offered himself to her in his letters. Over three hundred of them survive, the first written in September 1916, two weeks after Anderson's fortieth birthday.

For two years they had been corresponding, for two years they had apparently been exploring their feelings for one another, but in November 1916 Anderson wanted no more of that. "I have an idea," he began, and he went on:

> Suppose instead of just writing you letters which may concern themselves with personal things, a cold in the head etc., I write you instead my observations on life and manners as they present themselves to me here and now. By this plan I may write you at times daily, at times only once a week.
>
> When these things come to hand type them, putting on date and making a carbon copy. At the end of six months, or a year we will see if we haven't material for a book that would be of interest to others.

Whatever had gone before was over, whatever he had put in writing, Bab was to destroy — and she did. There was "but one way by which you can get value out of your friendship with me," he went on coldly. "If the things I write extend or enlarge your own horizon they will be of value to you. You will have to be the judge of that."

She was to be not so much his muse as his sounding board. He was writing in his pride in himself, and he assumed that she would share in it. She would watch and read as he set down the meaning he was discovering in his life. There were times when he could not write, he said, but there were other times when "the whole world is of a sudden alive with meaning. Every gesture, every word of the people carries significance." Anderson would put those moments down for her. Those were the times, he went on, when "the terrible feeling of the utter meaninglessness of life passes. I am carried along through hours and days as by a great wind. I am happy."

That was the way the tales of *Winesburg, Ohio* came, and he would send them all along to her too. There were occasions at the office when, in meeting with men about advertising hose supporters, say, he would want to take out a revolver and begin shooting, but there were other times when he would go happily, because these men's words seemed "just a part of the inexhaustible drollery of life," and he wanted to get them down on paper as well. Bab could write him whatever she wanted, but to him the value of their correspondence was that it allowed him to record his observations about the life around him. "To express these things in even a fragmentary way gives me satisfaction," he said. Assuming she wanted to proceed, then, she could "begin by copying this note."

What Anderson established with Bab Finley was a relatively unattractive version of the situation he had imagined for the writer in "The Novelist," which he published that same year in the *Little Review,* or for George Willard, a situation in which the writer and the lover were one, in which writing was sufficient lovemaking, the pen enough. "I am trying with all my might to be and remain a lover," he wrote Bab in December of 1916. "All this writing is addressed to my beloved." "She" was made up of all the women in the world. In turn, like all the women he had known, in fact and fiction, his mother, Trillena White, Elizabeth Willard, Kate Swift, Janet Eberley, Bab had something of that force, that quality of Woman, in her. In 1926 he imagined her taking the place of his sister Stella, who had died of complications during surgery eight years before, or even that of his sister Fern, who had died in infancy. "Perhaps no woman wants such a position with a man," he admitted, but her "wanting it or not seem[ed] to have little to do with it." Just so long as Bab remained his ideal Woman and did not confuse him with her sexuality or her human frailty, he could respect her. Just so long as she did not "clutch" at him, did not indulge in self-pity, they could be friends. "The light touch is the thing," he said. When she told him she was sick, he replied: "When you are well and strong I will come some day to see you. I will never come to see a sick person." Those standards met, he often stopped by to visit her on his way to or from seeing a client, and they would meet, in New York, or New Orleans, or Chicago. What was most important (to him, at least) was that he would provide her with a running commentary on his life.

In 1914, when Anderson met Bab, he had ostensibly broken with his unclean past, with the business world, with the hypocrisies of his marriage, but in fact he was still working for Taylor-Critchfield, was still an advertising man, and he was still dependent on women for companionship. His need to make money and his need to make amends to his mother — the two inextricably bound since his earliest days — would not be easily satisfied. So dramatic a gesture as his Elyrian flight would not be enough.

But in Bab's presence, so long as that presence was distant, he could begin to break free. He could write not for her but *to* her. In doing so he was selfish, egotistical, even cruel, but he acknowledged the fact many times. And as he pointed out, he had been kind in one respect. "O my dear friend," he wrote in 1927, "when I think back upon it sometimes I think to you at least I have been in part fair. I have at least never married you, have I. I mean only that I am thinking now how horrible it is to be married to such a one."

Anderson kept two of her letters. There was no need for more. The first, written in 1924, told of "a certain litheness of spirit" she felt as she recalled the little boy in him and of her refusal to accept the confessions of selfishness and cruelty that showed up from time to time in his letters. It also harked back to her devotion, her desire for him, but assured him that it was under control. Her physical need, she said, was "disciplined a great, great deal." She spoke of a fund that she had set up that would produce a hundred dollars a month for the support of his children, a fund that she maintained until the Depression made it impossible. In her letter, as if to create a kind of marriage in spite of him, she said that she would continue to send money for the children "for as long as we both shall live." "You see quite frankly," she said, "you and your children are the reality and the meaning of my life."

Four years later, in 1928, Bab married an Indianapolis doctor named E. Vernon Hahn, and then, in 1933, having heard that Anderson had remarried, she wrote Anderson the last letter that passed between them. Picking up on Anderson's suggestion of almost twenty years before, she said that she and her husband were thinking of publishing Anderson's letters to her, and she wanted his permission. As for marriage, she wished him "a good adjustment." That was what marriage was, she realized, "not a goal but an adjustment both pleasant and otherwise." "But worth the effort nevertheless," she added.

In 1962, her thoughts still harked back to 1916, to when she had had to destroy the "personal things" and when the correspondence that Anderson thought might be presentable began. She had agreed to meet with the man who eventually did edit Anderson's letters to her. When he came, she ushered him into her one-room apartment and greeted him with a question. She still wondered what it would have taken to get Anderson to marry her. "Why did Sherwood Anderson marry Tennessee Mitchell?" she asked.

Though Bab may not have wanted to hear it at the time, Anderson had already given the answer in his second surviving letter to her. In this letter he looks back at the evening he and Cornelia had spent with Marian at Rosalie Court many years before, the time when Cornelia thought he wanted her to die. Babs was like Cornelia, he had told her in his letter, "one on whom the door is shut." He himself was the kind of person who did the shutting and was therefore likely to hurt anyone who cared for him, anyone, that is, except those who were delighted when people left — "except the born adventurers like Marian and T."

"T" — or Tennessee Mitchell — had almost literally been *born* an adventurer. She had been named after one of the famous, notorious Claflin sisters, who advocated women's suffrage, free love, birth control, and vegetarianism in the pages of their *Woodhull and Claflin's Weekly,* and she grew up in a nonconformist household (in Jackson, Michigan). She had become accustomed to the presence of freethinkers and spiritualists in her home (she could remember falling asleep on the lap of "the great agnostic," Robert Ingersoll), and was taught to be undistracted in her pursuit of the good life. "Right and wrong were not terms used in our household," she said. Sex was an issue only of "manners." What she objected to when one boy tried to "pet" her, for example, was his choice of venue: a cemetery bench. Becoming a "new woman" was not easy, though. Once when she was driving with her father, the horse had bolted and she had panicked. Instinctively, she had grabbed her father's hand. He brought the horse under control, drove to a fence, and tied it up, silent all the while; and then he took Tennessee down from her seat and spanked her, saying that what she had done was "one of the reasons men distrusted and despised women." Whether she liked it or not, independent she would be.

When her mother died and her father remarried, she went to Chicago, age seventeen, taking her twelve-year-old sister with her. She played the violin and the piano, but having been told she had perfect pitch, she decided she would start out making her living in the music world as a piano tuner. It was, she said, "the next best thing to spirituality."

She arrived in Chicago in the early 1890s, and while Anderson was trying to make money by working at odd jobs in Clyde, she made her way into wider and more various circles. She found a man who would teach her how to tune, and, beginning with pianos in a warehouse, she was before long tuning all over the city, now spending a month at a convent instructing the nuns in music education, now giving lessons on the pianos of the rich. She was, if not convention- ally beautiful, a magnetic presence, willowy, with reddish brown hair, and strong and delicate features. She admired Isadora Duncan, wore big hats, long, heavy earrings, and the requisite floating scarves, and she moved like a dancer. She was witty, she could be sharp, she often resented her pupils, "their automobiles, nurses, gov- ernesses and the surfeits and advantages of which they had little or no appreciation," but as even Bab Finley said, she "had a graciousness in dealing with others," she had "great charm." Her poise made one of her friends think of "an Indian princess." In the eyes of another, she had that "fatal undertow power" that their crowd called, "for lack of a more accurate diagnosis . . . 'a way with men.'"

What appealed to *her* especially were men who lived somewhere between the wealthy and the actors and dancers and musicians she knew, "the great number who have little interest or aptitude for busi- ness," she later called them, and "a yearning for the arts, and lack either a decided talent for or the courage to pursue them." The de- scription fits Anderson, whom she met, along with Cornelia, at Mar- gery Currey's in 1914, and it fits Edgar Lee Masters, with whom she had a tumultuous and painful affair for about a year and a half be- tween 1909 and 1911.

Tennessee met Masters when he paid a visit to the divorced heiress with whom she shared a North Side apartment. He had been pub- lishing syrupy lyrics under the name of Webster Ford at his own expense, and though she did not like them, she liked the intellectual companionship and was flattered when he turned to her for inspira- tion. He was in a marriage that everyone understood to be a formal- ity, and for her part, "I was deriving no benefits from conventions . . . I was alone and had no responsibility except to myself. I felt confident to handle that, his situation was his own affair." In his *Spoon River Anthology* he has "Tennessee Claflin Shope" say:

> *I asserted the sovereignty of my soul.*
> *Before Mary Baker G. Eddy ever got started*
> *With what she called science*
> *I had mastered the "Bhagavad Gita,"*
> *And cured my soul, before Mary*
> *Began to cure bodies with souls.*

And so she did, and in reaction, everything else Masters wrote about her is self-serving, tending toward vicious.

In her version of the story, Masters urged her to escape to Europe with him, but knowing there was no "entireness" in his love and arguing that earning a living was her first priority, she refused. In his, it was she who insisted. The refrain of his "Ballade of Ultimate Shame," published in his *Songs and Sonnets* of 1912 (with "T.M., August 20th, 1909 — May 23, 1911" below the title) is "I loved a Magdalene to my lasting shame!" She is Calypso to his Ulysses in 1921 ("She loved me, wonderful Calypso. / But what is love? It is only love."), and Dierdre in *Across Spoon River,* his autobiography. There, by 1936, she has become as "subtle and designing beyond any woman that I had ever known," "a cold, uncanny, farsighted mind, with a sort of congenital nymphomania." Thanks to this "severe schooling in what was practically erotomania," he had become a better reader of Shakespeare and had written poems he could never have written otherwise, but she was a demon, an enchantress who had "mastered" him until he resolved to "master" himself.

When Anderson met Tennessee there on Fifty-seventh Street after the long nightmare in the Ozarks, she must have seemed everything his wife was not — colorful, bright, irreverent, self-sufficient, and, above all, unencumbering. Whether he had completed the manuscript of *Mary Cochran* before he met Tennessee, or whether she modeled for that independent working woman, she fulfilled all the terms Anderson had laid down. She was a woman who did not seem to need to love and be loved. She could go on unfazed if he shut the door. She could accept that behind it he was absorbed in his own thoughts and dreams — writing. In the months that followed, as stories and tales emerged that proved he was a writer, and as these began to appear in print, into her independent and artistic life he must have had no trouble reading unqualified support for his own.

Tennessee was Woman while seemingly not too much of a female presence — or so Anderson convinced himself. But in fact she defined his newfound freedom every bit as carefully as Cornelia had tried to define his respectability. She even costumed and choreographed it. Going along with his inclination to add dashing touches to his dress, Tennessee decked him out. "There is a blessed flavor about understanding people," he reported to a friend in 1917, and Tennessee was one of them: "She has bought me a little feather to wear in my hat. She has bought me a golden yellow scarf. Tomorrow she will buy me socks all splashed with purple and yellow crystals." Drawing out and then drawing on his desire to break forth in song and dance, she introduced him to the opera (and for such occasions tried to convince him to wear full dress). When she started giving classes in modern dance, Anderson came, wrapped himself in a sheet, and went through motions that he was willing to imagine might express his inner being.

In June of 1916, having written many of the Winesburg tales and with the publication of a portion of them assured, he followed Tennessee to Lake Chateaugay in upstate New York, thirty miles north of Lakes Placid and Saranac, just below the Canadian border. There, beside the lake, a woman named Alys Bentley ran a camp, Camp Owlyout, that consisted of a large rustic building with a screened-in porch, a boathouse, and several cabins and cabinlike tents, pitched on platforms. Like others of its kind that were in vogue both in America and abroad, it pointed the way to healthier eating and freer expression. Those who came (mostly women, women of all ages) came to learn Delcroze eurhythmics, or what Miss Bentley called "motor-mental rhythms," and to improve their diets, with proteins one day, for example, carbohydrates another, and — always — with enormous salads. As many as fifty campers might be present at one time. Arrangements and classes were purposely fluid. The campers' "studio" was a clearing in the woods, surrounded by silver birches; their attire was skimpy, sometimes nothing at all. There they would dance or improvise while Miss Bentley, winding away and shouting encouragement, played Beethoven and Brahms on the victrola. "Let go! Let go!" she would cry, as her pupils moved and assumed poses that they thought expressed the rhythms of their feelings. Or there, for hours, they would just bathe in the sun.

In this new setting, Anderson felt right at home. "This lovely camp of the nymphs out in the open," one of them called Camp Owlyout, "girls dressed in lovely flowing Greek draperies, dancing in the grass with their feet twinkling in the sun." And among them, as free as any other spirit, was Anderson, "the only faun in the camp." He tried to dance with the nymphs, but he had more success gathering them around him, telling them his tales, and questioning them endlessly about their lives, about what it was to be a Woman, possibly a "new woman."

He followed Tennessee first to Lake Chateaugay, and then into marriage. Over the years, Anderson gave several explanations for his decision. He said that he married Tennessee to protect her from a scandal involving Masters, who was under attack by the Hearst papers as Clarence Darrow's law partner. He said that he agreed to marry her when she came to him in tears, saying Masters wouldn't. Reducing the courtship to stereotype, he said that he and Masters were both competing for the same woman and that he won out. Though too much time had elapsed for there to have been intense rivalry or chivalrous gestures, Anderson might well have been moved by jealousy over what he knew of Tennessee's affair. But it was she, in fact, who pressed for marriage. Still, Tennessee had the makings of a perfect wife, he thought, because as he said a few years later, she could be counted on not "to become the wife," and he willingly obliged.

Having been informed of her husband's intentions, Cornelia had filed for divorce in the spring of 1916. She stated that her husband's salary was fifty dollars a week and that his support of his family had been intermittent at best, but she asked for nothing. As for her response to Tennessee, Cornelia later told her daughter that her father always married first-class women. On July 27, 1916, the divorce came through.

Four days later, Tennessee and Sherwood, along with Alys Bentley and at least one attendant camper, climbed into a carriage and were driven the several miles to the village of Chateaugay; and there, in a little ravine, under an apple tree, they were married by a justice of the peace. Tennessee wore a short smock dress, her hair was in one long braid, her feet were bare. Though she was forty-two, she gave her age as thirty-seven. Anderson was two months shy of forty. After the ceremony, the justice said that he hoped he had done a good job, he was assured he had, and the wedding party returned to camp. Since June, Anderson had been staying in a tent, retreating to a cabin or to the big house to write when it got cold. Before the wedding he had fixed it up as best he could in order that his bride might have a "home," and there, in the sylvan paradise of Camp Owlyout, the Andersons lived out the summer.

By 1916, artists had begun to gather around Lake Chateaugay. Alys Bentley's boathouse served as a gallery for their work. The one person Anderson came to know at all well, though, was Trigant Burrow, a Freudian analyst and member of the staff of the Johns Hopkins University Medical School, who was building a cottage across the lake. He would call it Lifwynn — "joy of life." Sometimes Burrow and his wife took the two-mile trip across to have their midday meal at Camp Owlyout; often the newlyweds went to the Burrows' for a "Southern style" breakfast of sausages and waffles. And the two men talked.

In his way, too, Burrow imagined that humankind could live in harmony. His theory was that we had known such harmony before we learned to differentiate between ourselves and our mothers, in a unifying, "preconscious" love that was lost, terribly lost, as the Great War was proving, but that we could rediscover through analysis. To Burrow, our problems were not individual but social; collectively we were an organism that had fallen ill. When Freud asked, "Does Burrow think he is going to cure the world?" Burrow's answer was, "I most certainly do." Early bacteriologists did not take the position that only the families of Pasteur and Koch were to be immunized; and, he argued, "there is no disease more communicable than nervous disorders." Over the years, his patients began to take cottages on the lake and came by special launch to their sessions, and then, when Burrow's belief in the need to cure *social* neuroses led him to question his own authority, he turned Lifwynn into a camp. He added a tennis court, a croquet ground, a softball field, and as the occasion arose, while at play, or preparing a meal, or stacking wood, the group analyzed itself, not for therapeutic but for investigative purposes. In 1921, Burrow pointed out to Anderson that what he was working toward in his novel *Marching Men* was exactly what he had in mind when he spoke of "Our Common Consciousness," and he tried to convince Anderson that they were both just media for the expression of higher truths. For his part, in the euphoric summer of 1916, Anderson was willing to recognize in Burrow a kindred spirit.

But after that summer on Lake Chateaugay, it was the burden of Alys Bentley's cry "Let go! Let go!" that he wanted everyone to hear. The following January, when Bab wrote, still smarting from her hurt, and asked him whether he had ever really known what it was like to give something up, he turned the accusation back on her. It was she, he said, who couldn't give things up, she who couldn't "let go." She let things be taken from her, she was a prisoner of her needs. His advice was: "Cry back to the Bentley physical attitude. 'Let go.'" That, he told her, was what he had come to realize should be the burden of his own song: "Sometime I shall become a God, a new John the Baptist crying in the wilderness and the burden of my cry shall be, 'Let go. For God's sake, let go!'" And then he said that he had read her letter over and that that cry still rang in his head: "'Let go. Let go.'"

It was easy enough to say that to Bab. Rather than marry her, Anderson had cast her in the roles of confidante and literary executor. A new kind of correspondence was under way, and already she had proved invaluable as recipient of his writings: when a fire in his tent at Camp Owlyout destroyed drafts of some of the Winesburg tales, her carbon copies saved the day. It was not so easy to apply his advice to the woman he had married, or what was the real problem, to himself. He had begun to "let go" in writing, to let out exhilarating thoughts about men's better selves, but writing was one thing, his relations with women another. He and Tennessee planned to take modern (that is, separate) residential measures to guarantee them freedom in their marriage, but he still was not sure that as a husband he could "let go."

Arriving back in Chicago (after a short visit with Cornelia and his children on the way), Anderson retained his room on Cass Street, and Tennessee rented an apartment on West Division Street, a few blocks away. It was what Floyd Dell and Margery Currey had done, it was the thing to do, but it was also indicative of just how fearful Anderson was that if he got too close to a woman, something might be taken from him, or that he would simply lose that woman's affection.

After six months of marriage, he wrote Bab that every time he went into Tennessee's house he went "timidly, questioning." He wondered how he would be received. If he felt the slightest hint of her not wanting him he was sure he'd run. Two weeks later, he told Bab it was good to be back in town with Tennessee after a depressing business trip, but that again, he was scared. Tennessee meant so much to him: "I do not dare approach too close to her, make her too close a part of my life because I do not want to take into her life my greyness but to be where she is means everything."

Though he did not make the connection (and though others have made it not to Anderson but to his brother Earl), Anderson was like Enoch Robinson in the *Winesburg, Ohio* tale "Loneliness," frightened by the woman who was seemingly "too big for the room" in which they sat, terrified lest she submerge him in her understanding of him. "I live away from this woman I have married," Anderson said. "I go often to walk alone, to be alone. This also is misunderstood. Rumors run about. The woman is condemned because of the loneliness of my life. She is made to seem hard, cruel and indifferent when she is only big." In fact, he said, like other women, she would satisfy his every want, but he simply could not take it. No more happy in marriage than he had been the first time, though it was she who was condemned, it was he who "shut the door" and fled.

But this time he could distance himself from his uneasiness, this time he had another life that he could lead without feeling guilty. He could walk away from so difficult a situation and he could go on to end so troubled a letter on a jaunty note because *Windy McPherson's Son* had been published in October.

He was learning "to know and not yet to be destroyed," as he put it ambiguously and ominously ("not yet," where he must have meant "yet not"). It was all right. He could seem not to care: he would go and take a walk. In spite of his reservations about the novel form, he could not help thinking that he had passed the big test. "The short story is a solo by the second cornet. The novel is a piece by the full orchestra," he declared that same month. What's more, his novel had gotten good reviews in the right places. His closing words to Bab were: "The Nation for Jan 11 had a wonderful review of my book. There was also one by Hackett in this week's New Republic."

The *Atheneum* found the novel repellent and William Lyon Phelps of Yale University said it lacked artistry, but they were welcome foils. Writing in the *Chicago Daily News,* Anderson said that the novel did not meet even his standards — it was not crude enough, it was not "loose and disorderly enough to reflect the modern American life" — but where it mattered, he was praised. The *Nation* had said that *Windy McPherson's Son* introduced "a new writer of originality and power," and Francis Hackett had said that it had "a freshness that belongs to the springtime of creation." In the *Masses,* Floyd Dell recalled the excitement he felt reading the manuscript three years before, and went on to invoke the Russians, "Turgeniev and Tolstoy, Dostoevsky and Chekov, Artzibashev and Gorky," in an attempt to define Anderson's "spirit." Sounding for a moment like his counterparts at *Seven Arts,* he said that the novel was "all through, an asking of the question American literature has hardly as yet begun to ask: 'What for?'" In his five pages Waldo Frank also spoke of a resemblance to Dostoevsky (calling the novel "a temperamental, not a literary thing"), and then went on to compare Anderson favorably to Dreiser and to Twain. Anderson's was what he called "Emerging Greatness." The fact that it was just emerging, that Anderson was middle-aged, was not surprising given America's cultural condition: "For it has far to come," Frank said. "The European is born on a plateau. America is still at sea-level. The blundering, blustering native was thirty-seven before he became Walt Whitman."

The novel went into a second printing, and Anderson was on his way to becoming another "representative man," the twentieth century's "poet," a symbol of hope to those who thought that America had yet to grow up artistically. "I greet you at the beginning of a great career," Emerson had written Whitman upon receiving a copy of Whitman's *Leaves of Grass*. Many people were preparing Anderson for a similar future, none more enthusiastically than Frank, and Anderson was eager to embrace it.

In January, Frank sent Anderson *The Unwelcome Man,* his own unabashedly Freudian novel about a young man's failure to mature, just published after having been rejected fourteen times. The two men had not yet met, but in Frank's novel Anderson recognized a fellow idealist. He compared Frank to his old friend John Emerson, the former Clifton Paden. They were alike in their intensity, he said, but whereas Emerson had been caught in life's "meshes," "become rich . . . become sordid, cynical," the arts had saved Frank. He had remained alive; Anderson could tell from his book that Frank was willing to open up his mind and soul to everyone, but still: "There was something reeking and vulgar about life you haven't got at." "Why?" he asked rhetorically, and went on in his version of lines from Whitman's "Song of Myself": "Have you been in rooms too much? Have you been doing too much thinking?" The answer was the one he had heard Alys Bentley give at Camp Owlyout: "Oh, so often I want to shake you. To cry, 'Let go, let go.' . . . I like you and what you have done. I just want you to 'let go' more." It was vague advice, he knew, but he would go into more detail shortly. He was coming to New York. Finally, the two of them were going to meet.

In February 1917, Anderson combined a business trip with a visit to the *Seven Arts* office at 132 Madison Avenue, and there, for the first time, he met those who must have seemed to him America's most authoritative men of letters. There was Waldo Frank, age twenty-seven, Phi Beta Kappa from Yale, well traveled, the author of a novel that was not great, but also of a book on *The Spirit of Modern French Letters* that the Yale University Press would have published had he let them. There was Van Wyck Brooks, just a few years older, Phi Beta Kappa from Harvard, also well traveled, and already the author of *The Wine of the Puritans* and *America's Coming of Age*. They were there to welcome the belated arrival of "Genius in America."

What they wanted, or at least what they expected, by the account of the editor, James Oppenheim, was a man who had just stepped out of the pages of *Winesburg, Ohio,* "a shy sort of fellow, a little mussed, slipping against the wall so as not to occupy too much space." But Anderson was more complicated than that. He was a man who had sympathized with the forgotten men and women of America, had appreciated his subjects' worth, but he was also a man who had come to appreciate the worth of his own writing. Though the editors may not have wanted to remember, Anderson was still an advertising man. What they saw before them was "an up-an-coming ad man with a stiff collar," Oppenheim went on, and with "a bit of the super-salesman air" about him. What he had come to sell was himself: one of the purposes of his visit, he said with a laugh, was to argue for more money for his tales.

It was as likely a way as any for him to present himself. He had been an adman off and on for sixteen years, but obviously he preferred the role that they had prepared him for. (It didn't finally matter that he received all of eighty-five dollars for his contributions to their periodical.) It was the role he felt best in, as he told Bab. Though his lack of education and training would have kept him silent, he wrote her before his trip, "perhaps given to scribbling in secret" in France or Russia, here in America he had allowed himself to speak. He had done so because he realized that in doing so he would be speaking *for* America. His wasted years, his struggles — even his ignorance — these were all typically American. The men at the *Seven Arts* had shown him that. Looking back beyond the reviews that had just come out, back to the nights in Elyria when he had escaped to his room to write, he said that this thought had come to him: "'I am an intensification of the spirit of my times.'"

When the editors of *Seven Arts* greeted him as if he were that spirit, Anderson was almost overwhelmed. They had liked him, they had listened to him, listened to his "provincial, middle western point of view with interest." It had been exciting to meet with the approval of Dell's friends in Chicago when he was just getting started, but this was New York and these young men were from Yale and Harvard, they had traveled abroad, they knew the world's literature, they knew what America needed — and what they needed turned out to be the writing he was doing. Having met these men, he felt he had worked his way out past the breakers "into the open sea," he said. "I loved it all, and I felt people loving me."

He knew there was another way to look at his eastern pilgrimage. He knew he had rushed around a lot in New York, that behind his "smiling front" there was "an intense eagerness." He was not so confident as to believe these men implicitly, and after two weeks he was simply confused. What he had experienced was, for the time being, "beyond expression," he told Bab. "Everyone, everything — the things people think and hope of me. It is all beyond expression now."

But for the time being, he would do anything, anything to justify the faith of these men. He would believe he was the man they said he was. He would write. That went without saying. But in his writing he would go on and express the self they said he was. Not only would he "let go"; he would hand himself over. "I want to open my veins, to bleed, to know, to understand," he said. "I dream of that. I come home dreaming of that. I will not be outdone. For the love that has been given me I will give and give." Often, thereafter, in his writing, he would do just that: he would give until he had nothing left except his willingness to give.

SIX

Unrest

1917-1919

BY 1917, Sherwood Anderson had transformed his life. Though he was still an advertising man, his personal life had changed radically since the days of his first marriage. Most important, he had explored and expressed — had re-created — his life in fictions, and he had been recognized and praised for his achievement. He had found himself in writing.

But Anderson was never a man to be sure of himself. He could hold the pose of the confident adman for just so long. He was, after all, his father's son. Figuratively speaking, this was true of him too: if he met a man from Ireland, suddenly *he* was born in Ireland; in the presence of a man from Scotland, a burr would come into his speech. In the next few years Anderson was in constant danger of losing sight of his subject — the man he had been, the men and women he had known — in constant danger of becoming others' simplified versions of himself, their subject, subject to them. It happened most clearly upon his return from New York in late February 1917.

In his elation over his reception among the editors of the *Seven Arts,* Anderson began to write a series of poems — or "chants," as he called them. In them he celebrated America's rural past, confronted the Industrial Age head-on, and pressed forward into the vaguely but undeniably promising future. He was Cedric in one chant, "son of Irwin and Emma . . . here in America, come into a kingship." Otherwise he was a disembodied voice, just "I," "at the beginning of my life," "pregnant with song," "out of the West — out of the land," going "from the place of the cornfields . . . into the new places," "the beginning of things and the end of things." He had no subject, really. He was just being the spirit of the Midwest, or America, the way they had wanted him to be.

He wrote forty-nine poems in all. In almost half of them he returned to corn as a symbol of order and potential. The symbol had always been handy ever since one of his earliest contributions to *Agricultural Advertising,* when he used it to offset the devious ways of the city, and it had figured in the notes he kept during his flight from Elyria, but now he worked it to death: "My head arises above the cornfields," "The corn in its struggle whispers and sways," "I am of the deep fields where the corn grows," "Fields marked for corn to stand in long straight aisles," "The cornfields shall be the mothers of men," "Promise of corn / Promise of corn."

They were poems from "mid-America" and some were about Chicago, but Anderson discouraged any comparisons with Carl Sandburg, whose *Chicago Poems* had come out the year before. *Any* comparison to Sandburg made Anderson nervous. Sandburg was a contemporary, another man from Chicago, a rival, not so good a writer but an equally famous one. He was a notable personage; Anderson wanted not only to best him but also to win his approval. He was not so interesting a man, yet he brought out Anderson's worst fears about himself. Sandburg is "submerged in adolescence," he told Van Wyck Brooks in 1919. "I am in it and of it, but I look out. Give Sandburg a mind, and you perhaps destroy him. I don't know whether this would be true of me or not."

Still confessing to being adolescent, mindless, to being still "the undeveloped man," he held on to the hope that *he,* at least, had some perspective on his own being, that *he* did not have simply an adolescent's view of the world. Anderson knew there was more to Sandburg than his popular image — more than a "He man, an eater of raw meat, a hairy one" — and in later years he tried to do that man justice, but when Anderson was in danger of losing his hold on himself, Sandburg reminded him that he himself was less than the man he wanted to be.

During a spring evening that they spent together in 1917, Sandburg had read some of the chants and said he liked them; Anderson was pleased, but he was also quick to point out that he felt "a suggestion of closed-in icy places" in Sandburg, and that Sandburg's own verses did not "sing." By contrast, he meant his own to soar. In his desire to open up completely, to give all, it was certainly not Sandburg, it was Whitman (Whitman and the King James Version of the Bible) that Anderson had in mind. Publishing his attempts to reach those sublime heights was his way of proving he was willing to bleed. "I would publish the verse for one reason if for no other," he wrote Frank in September. "It will give a rare opportunity to those who desire to flay me."

The handful of reviews that greeted the poems when they were collected as *Mid-American Chants* the next year were kinder than that. They only pointed out that the poems were the material of poetry, not poetry. Citing a version of one of these poems that he had seen in *Poetry,* which began "See the corn. How it aches," a reporter called Anderson "the chiropodist poet." Anderson pointed that out to Frank too. It was as if somewhere he knew that what he was doing was not right, as if he were taking delight not only in trying to fulfill others' hopes but in watching his own being dashed.

In May 1917 Waldo Frank printed "From Chicago," a prose piece that announced Anderson's rebirth in slightly soberer terms. In eight sections, the second of which was "The Novelist," which had appeared in the *Smart Set* the year before, Anderson presented as many versions of himself: "still young and pregnant," trying "to extend the province of his life through his work," or "revealing himself to us . . . shamelessly and boldly." In contrast to the artist who gives us "an almost overwhelming sense of proficiency in his craft," he said he was revising a book (*Marching Men*) that was "partly good, partly bad," in which he himself was the "fine figure" of a labor leader. At the end, he was singing, in the voice of a raftsman in the Ozarks, of a country girl who had been ruined by the city, himself, too, the man who had seduced her. Accepting the title of American Writer, he was confidently making his accession to it the subject of his writing. With a verve, he was playing what he called in the piece "the endless game of reconstructing [his] own life, jerking it out of the shell that dies, striving to breathe into it beauty and meaning." He was many beings but held together by no one of them.

For about six months before even meeting Frank, Anderson had been swept along by Frank's enthusiasm. Now Anderson wanted him to visit on Lake Chateaugay, where he and Tennessee were going to spend another summer. This time they were going to pitch their tent on the other side of the lake, away from Camp Owlyout. "There will be woods and a lake but no people, except when we want to cross the lake to them," he told Frank in the spring. "I've got in some way a big swinging notion to get to you," he went on, his mind overflowing with the language he was working in. "It isn't mine. It belongs to waving cornfields and the marching impulses of men that go on, have to go on, in spite of these things that seem to cloud the world." On a more practical level, he insisted that Frank come in June. That would give them time to think and talk at their ease. After that "a Johns Hopkins man" would be "on the same side of the lake."

They had their week, without their wives as it turned out, but it proved disappointing. During it, Anderson saw a side of Frank that correspondence and sporadic visits to 132 Madison Avenue had not revealed. Frank wasn't so different from John Emerson after all. Along with his energy, along with what seemed his enthusiastic support, Anderson detected "a streak of barely perceptible vulgarity." Frank seemed to have such grandiose notions about himself. He seemed to commandeer. There was such a "quickness and sharpness in getting hold of people and things" about the man. Frank had in fact acted accordingly — he had "run away with one of the girls here" — but that was not so much offensive as worrisome, of a piece with his tendency to ride "life with whip, boot and spur instead of letting life flow into [him]." Anderson was confused, even afraid for Frank.

But there was nothing he could do for him, and the best thing he could do for himself was escape Frank's influence and flee into the woods, where he could could continue to work on his own liberation. "I stretched myself out on the grass and sobbed like a woman to the glory and the quiet of this place," he told Bab. "Deep in the ground my roots and my Gods lie. They are whispering to me."

Anderson was not as surprised when Trigant Burrow proved less than an ideal companion. He had spent time with the man the summer before. It was, in Burrow's case, that he was too much the analyst and was too trusting of his own authority. But now, in his way too, he seemed to want "to come close and close," to take over Anderson's very thoughts. Everyone seemed to distort Anderson's own sense of himself. Juggling his relationships, he wrote Frank in August that Burrow reminded him of Floyd Dell, whom he now considered just a man who wanted to reform him, to remake him. Accepting others' and his own account of himself, Anderson was happy to be all potential, the American man in the making, but even as he slipped into roles others created for him, he wondered: why was it that men constantly got the impression that he was someone "to be molded"?

But, he went on to Frank, "one rather hectic talk on the matter" served to distance Burrow. He could now see that it all had "an amusing and pathetic side," and he promised — "some day" — to tell Frank the story of his "several long talks with Dr. Burrow." Anderson was not one to wait long to cast his experience into words, and that day came soon. In July of the next year, "Seeds" appeared in the *Little Review,* beginning with a sentence that Anderson later cut when he included the story in *The Triumph of the Egg* in 1921: "There was a Doctor from Johns Hopkins talked to me one day last summer concerning universal life and its universal insanity."

"Seeds" is a complicated and revealing piece, more of a theme and variation than a tale this time, that shows Anderson confused but, in the writing, clear about his confusion. Its theme is that nobody's visions can be realized. Nothing flowers the way we want it to.

Anderson dispenses with Burrow early on, sets him up as a nervous little man, exhausted by his efforts to "cure people of illness by the method of psychoanalysis," yet at the same time aggravatingly shrill in his insistence on understanding people, on entering into their lives, on loving them. "I have to try to love. You see how it is? It is the only way," he says. "Love must be the beginning of things with me. There is understanding in that." As he presses on, the narrator turns on him and grows shrill himself: there is only so much you can know about other people, you can't love them by understanding them, he says. But Burrow insists: people's lives are like young growths; they are choked with vines, "old thoughts and beliefs planted by dead men"; we must free ourselves. As for himself, he concludes: "I want to be a leaf blown by the wind over the hills. . . . I am weary and want to be made clean. I am covered by creeping, crawling things." That is what Anderson wanted to tell Frank about Burrow: he was insufferably close.

But the fiction goes on to turn on a version of Anderson himself, the Anderson, specifically, who might have thought he had found the truth of marital love in his second marriage. Most of "Seeds" is about a painter and would-be writer in Chicago named LeRoy (the king, supposedly come to power), who by another lake (Lake Michigan) tells the narrator about his relations with a woman in the boarding-house where he lived. She was a woman who had come to the city "to study advanced methods for teaching music." Burrow was "grotesque" in his faith in the truth of psychoanalysis, this woman in her obsession with sex: "Sex spread itself out over her body. It permeated the very fibre of her being. At last she was sex personified, sex become condensed and impersonal." She would have nothing to do with the men of the house, but, leaving the bathroom door ajar, throwing herself down on the living room couch and lying there "with lips drawn slightly apart," neither would she leave them alone. When the landlady threatens to evict her, she bursts in on LeRoy, her eyes burning, her breath coming in little gasps, and asks him to "take" her: "'Take me,' she said, dropping her face down upon his knees and trembling violently. 'Take me quick. There must be a beginning of things. I can't stand the waiting. You must take me at once.'" The woman was "a little lame" and walked with a limp, and so recalls the woman Anderson met in Jackson Park the night he could not enter Margery Currey's studio; but the strongest impression she leaves is of the Tennessee that Anderson came to believe threw herself upon his mercy after her affair with Edgar Lee Masters. The composite, in his imagination, is overbearing, overwhelming Woman.

To LeRoy she is a woman who, like all of us, needed to be loved: "'What would cure her would cure the rest of us also. The disease she had is, you see, universal,'" he says to the narrator. He had once thought he might have been the one to love her, but like Burrow he had failed — "'I have seen under the shell of life and I am afraid,'" he says — and he ends, the story ends, with the same cries that Burrow had uttered: "Old thoughts and beliefs — seeds planted by dead men — spring up in my soul and choke me. . . . I would like to be a dead dry thing. . . . I would like to be a leaf blown by the wind." Neither analysts nor lovers have a cure. There are seeds, but they produce only choking growths. Right to the end, there are Shelleyan cries to the fructifying winds, but not a breeze stirs.

The narrator is too smart to think otherwise, but then again, the narrator is too smart for his own good, as both the Doctor and LeRoy let him know (in the same words) when he tries to chasten them: "How smart we are! How aptly we put things!" Burrow's optimism was embarrassingly close to Anderson's own; so too is LeRoy's faith in love. Both sentiments prove unwarranted, but so too does the narrator's confidence that they are unwarranted. The last truth the story questions is the narrator's. The lives of the "grotesques" in *Winesburg, Ohio* were stunted. There always seemed to be more to them, waiting expression. In "Seeds," there seems to be little or nothing left of its three figures once their truths are denied. All that remains is the writing, in control as it levels each man in his turn, but leaving nothing after it has done its work.

It was inconclusive. As Anderson was in the habit of saying at the time, good writing had to be. Defending what he was producing, Anderson did not refer readers back to his own state of mind; rather he spoke confidently — or with bravado — of the social implications of inconclusive writing. In fact, not only was it inconclusive, it was unruly — "crude," he called it. Nothing in American life was settled. How could a prose that was truly American settle anything? If it was to be true to the way most men and women lived, how could it be refined?

The year before, Anderson had worried that *Windy McPherson's Son* was not "loose and disorderly enough to reflect the modern American life"; in November, he contributed "An Apology for Crudity" to the *Dial,* recently moved from Chicago to New York (and from literary right to literary left), in which he explained why American literature *had* to be crude in order to be American. "How, indeed, is one to escape the obvious fact that there is as yet no native subtlety of thought or living among us?" he asked at the outset. "And if we are a crude and childlike people how can our literature hope to escape the influence of that fact? Why, indeed, should we want it to escape?" America had given itself over to industrialism. The dominant note, "the note of health," in American life was once that of "the noisy, swaggering raftsman and the hairy-breasted woodsman"; now it was the factory hand's, not the out-of-the-way figures Anderson had created in *Winesburg, Ohio,* but the men who were driving America forward — not Wing Biddlebaum's, for example, but the factory's hands.

Accordingly, in Anderson's view, American writers had to realize that the spirit of Twain and Whitman had passed; they had to forgo the way of "such masters of prose as James and Howells," and of course they had to avoid "neat slick writing." Their chance for a new start lay in immersing themselves in the lives of their fellow men, writing "out of the people and not for the people," sharing with them "the crude expression of their lives." Anderson said he knew that there was "something approaching insanity in the very idea of sinking yourself too deeply into modern industrial life," but he was not one to do things by halves. "There is no other road," he said. He was ready to abandon his careful exploration of what he knew and to set about recording American life wherever he encountered it.

On and off that year he worked on *Immaturity,* a novel about Winesburg after the coming of the factories. By December the book had "gone insane." Caricaturing himself, he wrote Frank: "A really delicious, garrulous, heavy, lame fellow with shaggy eyebrows is writing." "If he is successful, as I pray the Chicago smoke gods he will be, the whole world will be puzzled to know what he is talking about." *Immaturity* never appeared, but finally that same year *Marching Men* did, and the response he predicted for *Immaturity* greeted it. Frank wrote saying that the merit of the novel was "poetic rather than that of objective realism" and that on the whole it was "extremely significant, because it [was] extremely 'expressive.'" Reviewers agreed with Frank's description but did not conclude with his generous verdict, nor did readers generally. Given *Windy McPherson's Son*'s poor sales abroad, John Lane put out no English edition; only about a thousand copies sold in the United States. "It don't matter," Anderson wrote Frank. "I know what I tried to do. In any event, if the thing I wanted is at all there, it will take time to grow and mature in the minds of others."

He ignored his own doubts about the novel's worth. The merely "expressive" had begun to suffice. He had begun to replace his writing. *He* was the work of art; he was not the creative but the created being. People came to see him and to hear him read. When Jacques Copeau, the director of the Vieux Colombier Théâtre, came to the United States, at Frank's suggestion he made a special trip to Chicago to meet this man who represented what was new in American life. For his part, Anderson put in appearances at the Round Table at Schlogl's restaurant and at the Dill Pickle Club, places where writers of the later Chicago renaissance gathered. The former was dominated by reviewers and editors of the *Daily News*, Harry Blackman Sell, Harry Hansen, Ben Hecht, and others, carrying on where Floyd Dell and the "Friday Literary Review" had left off; the latter was part theater, part meeting place, set up in Tooker Alley, near where Anderson lived, by a man named Jack Jones. Anderson would sit back in his chair and watch the proceedings, like some latter-day Whitman in Pfaff's beer cellar in lower Manhattan, or he would enhance his reputation as a consummate storyteller. He had won his way to a similar position four years before on the South Side, on Fifty-seventh Street; there was something farcical about it all this second time around.

Being in the company of ordinary Chicago newspapermen gave Anderson a sense that he was in touch with the actuality and the raciness of men's lives, and they might represent a kind of intellectuality, a kind of peripheral status with which Anderson could sympathize, but they did nothing for his prose. Nor did George Ade or Finley Peter Dunne or Ring Lardner, the stylists (past and present) among them. Fortunately he did not imagine their narrators were "the people" nor try to incorporate their expressions into his own. He had come upon his "colloquial style" independently. It was — and it remained — his and his alone.

Jack Jones spoke with appropriate contempt for what he called "the bourjoices," wore his hair long, and let it be known that he once cracked safes for a living, but he was only what the young bohemian poet, Emanuel Carnevali, called "the emperor of the intellectual flops." If that. At the Dill Pickle Club one might hear Maxwell Bodenheim read his poetry or witness a performance of a play by Ben Hecht, but one might also find a forty-year-old stenographer up on stage, talking about "Men Who Have Made Love to Me." "'I give them the high brow stuff until the crowd begins to grow thin,'" Jones once told Anderson, "and then I turn on the sex.'" He hadn't even had to pay the stenographer for her performance.

No work of lasting importance was being done. Almost everyone had gone East. Nothing, nobody could deflect him from his attempt to render America as he saw it. Anderson was never really confident, never really sure that the praise he got was genuine, but he had little cause to believe or doubt what others said about his work. He could believe both the best and the worst that he thought about himself. There was no one to help him focus on himself. No one else now seemed formidable to him.

Hecht would always reserve a place for Anderson in his affection, and Anderson would always wish the best for Hecht. He was as close to Hecht as he was to anyone at the time, but their relationship was tenuous, insubstantial. Anderson was almost twenty years older, mellower, gentler; Hecht was all dazzling surface. They met, they shared good times, they parted. They were never really close enough to have significant differences.

Hecht placed the Anderson that he knew around 1917 in a novel he published four years later titled *Erik Dorn*. In it, Anderson is Warren Lockwood, a fellow writer for a liberal journal called *The New Opinion*, "a man," Hecht says, whereas the others are only "a group of schoolboys reducing life to lessons." He has "found himself and is trying to shape secrets into words," his "virile gentleness" soothes the book's young hero, but finally he is seen as just too contentedly set in his own unsophisticated ways. Dorn cannot understand Lockwood's taste in art, and Lockwood's response to Dorn's immersion in a steamy nightlife scene is one big yawn.

In his autobiography, *A Child of the Century*, Ben Hecht told of trying to write a play with Anderson but giving up as he watched Anderson stretch the first act on past a hundred pages without a sign of stopping. All Anderson wanted to do, Hecht concluded, was walk up and down his Cass Street room reciting their lines, pretending to be their play's hero, Benvenuto Cellini. That might be yet another fiction, but undeniably Hecht's tolerance level declined.

Anderson's writings *had* offered America a new sense of itself, but Anderson himself was a different kind of man, and there was no one in Chicago to play the devil's advocate — or at least no one he would allow to take that part. He was alone in his pride, alone with feelings that he elevated into a principled avoidance of literary gatherings. "To draw ourselves apart," he had written in his "Apology for Crudity,"

> to live in little groups and console ourselves with the thought that we are achieving intellectuality is to get nowhere. By such a road we can hope only to go on producing a literature that has nothing to do with life as it is lived in these United States.

He did not even want to be associated with a group or a movement that opposed groups or movements. Though he was as responsible as anyone else for it, in the *News*, in February of the next year, he warned against talk about "mid-America" as distinct from any other part of the country, warned that the culture of Chicago was in danger of becoming a culture in only the precious sense of the word. "If we are not careful," he said, "we shall sink into the vulgarity of taking ourselves as seriously as Germany or Washington Square in New York." He had it worked out (and others had tried to work it out for him) so that he and he alone was in touch with "life as it is lived," and so that he could best represent it and present it in his writings, on his own, even without, it sometimes seemed, a readership.

But obviously he wanted to be appreciated. On a more personal level, he wanted friendship, he wanted camaraderie. In fact, there was nothing Anderson wanted more, and he was *most* alone because he had yet to find it. In the late fall he began a letter to his brother Karl by tossing off the bad reception of *Marching Men* again ("As you must know, it is very amusing to me to see our American intellectuals taking me so seriously"), and bracing himself for the reception of *Mid-American Chants* ("It will probably make me the most abused man in the country"), which would be out the next year. He then went on to express his disappointment at finding that the writers he had come upon were, after all, no more supportive, no larger, than business- or advertising men:

> I dare say your experience has been like my own. I came among artists hoping to find brotherhood there, but there isn't much of it. As it is in painting, so it is among writers. Fundamentally most of our American writing men are graceful and facile fanners and whores altogether. If one did not laugh at them, he would go mad.

Though the early days around Fifty-seventh Street had been exciting, he had never found brotherhood in Chicago, nor had he found it in New York.

Waldo Frank was an enthusiast, and for a time he swept Anderson off his feet. He insisted to Anderson that theirs was not an attraction of opposites. "I should be deeply disturbed if you came to prize in me the element which is unlike you," he told him, but that did not stop Anderson from being awed by Frank's Yale education, his knowledge of foreign languages and lands, any more than it stopped Frank from turning Anderson into "inherent life." Frank was in love not so much with the man himself as with the idea of him. (Or perhaps he was in love with Anderson's wife. In one letter he actually mapped out a switch of partners, pairing up the couples, then connecting his wife up with Anderson, Tennessee with himself, and writing the word love where the lines crossed.) "Just like brothers," he wrote. "Do you hear? For, it is ever so much clearer to me, that we are brothers — mystically brothers — brothers out of the infinite."

Though at first he shared Frank's enthusiasms, and responded to his claims of affection in kind, Anderson did not really like Frank's novels, first *The Unwelcome Man* and then another called *Dark Mother,* and after the summer meeting at Lake Chateaugay, he tried to put Frank himself at a distance from which he could keep Frank's talk of "greatness" in perspective. He knew the dangers such talk presented. It encouraged him to make too much of himself. It was hard work trying to be an honest writer, hard enough keeping himself out from between himself and his work, he often said. It was especially hard when all he heard was praise — "The struggle is hard enough without you and your goddam 'greatness,'" he finally told Frank. That kind of talk distracted him; he also feared it would be followed by its opposite.

He was distressed at how people could praise him so when his first novel was published and then turn on him later. "People I had long known and who had looked upon me with indifferent tolerance or even friendliness praised me openly, but in secret did things to hurt me," he said. Perhaps he was thinking of Floyd Dell, whose editorial board at the *Masses* had turned down some of the Winesburg tales, or of Mencken, who, he thought, saved his praise for the tales until praise was common. But without specifying what "it" was, he told Frank that "it has made me a little draw back into my shell. It has opened up to me the fact that men in the arts can be very small and petty." He would try not to think of them and advised Frank to do the same. "What matter Kenton, Fiske, Jones etc.?" he asked. "When you think of them, be Rabelaisian. Fart at the moon."

Anderson had no difficulty keeping Van Wyck Brooks's judgments in perspective. In the first place, they were themselves so judicious. "His is to me the most sustained and thoughtful mind concerned with American criticism," he told Bab in September 1918; in the same month, in a review of Brooks's *Letters and Leadership,* he pointed out that Brooks was "the scholar with the fine spirit, who looks hopefully about him," but "refuses to be sentimentally optimistic about our failures." Also, he knew that Brooks always kept *him* in perspective. He too had his grand ideas about Anderson, but they were relatively harmless for the simple (and to Anderson sad) reason that Brooks could not like him very much. "As for Brooks," he told Frank, "I say frankly I love the man and am not afraid of his judgment of me and my work. He will perhaps be more fair than yourself in not having in him any warmth of affection for me."

And so he was, calling *Winesburg, Ohio* "the most beautiful prose fiction of our time," taking issue with "An Apology for Crudity," regretting the novels and the poetry. But toward Anderson personally, he was only kindly. He accepted Anderson's criticism of his book on Twain (too much the "just judge" in this case, "rather than the sympathetic friend or lover," Anderson had said), and after Anderson died, he recalled how struck he had been by Anderson's "fresh healthy mind and his true Whitmanian feeling for comradeship, his beautiful humility, his lovely generosity and the 'proud conscious innocence' of his nature," but still, he kept the man at a distance. The innocence was, he thought, that of an "animal or flowering tree"; he was unnerved by the sexual implications of Anderson's stories and defended himself by explaining to Anderson that he, Anderson, was "a new kind of animal in literature"; he saw how lonely and needy Anderson was, and balked.

For his part, Anderson had only so much confidence in his own right to be appreciated. When Anderson suspected that Brooks disapproved of the sex in his tales, he started to protest, but faltered:

> I wish you could know how much I have loved, do love, your mind. I've frankly banked on it more than the mind of any other American. Am I right in my secret belief that you, down at bottom, believe me, in my reactions to life — well, not nice?

When Brooks said Anderson did not take "letters" seriously enough, Anderson was quick to agree. Brooks was right, he admitted to Frank; in fact, he went on, "both you and Brooks are more civilized than myself."

In 1923, in a sadder and a mellower mood, Anderson wrote about his trips to New York and what he called the "great vogue for understanding America and Americans." "All the smart keen men were talking and writing articles and books on the subject," and he was taking them all seriously. Now he could see that these men were in too much of a hurry, that the art of a country could move only as fast as the country itself, that too much was being asked; more specifically, he now realized that the burden that had been assigned to him "lay a little heavy." Sounding himself like Nick Carraway, having had enough of Eastern ways, he withdrew into the ranks of his fellow midwesterners — Dreiser, Sandburg, Masters, Darrow, Fitzgerald — all differences forgotten. He had not quite belonged, he realized. He was being used. He was not being accepted as the man he was but was being transformed into the American spirit. On the other hand, who was he, really? What kind of a man? He had to admit he enjoyed the praise. Again, he has us think of his father. Had someone offered him "a drum major's uniform to wear on Fifth Avenue," he would have worn it gladly: "I had enough of my father in me that I would have accepted that with joy, too."

As he looked back, the man who impressed him most among the *Seven Arts* group was Randolph Bourne. Bourne was the most radical among them; it was his pacifist views of the war that led Mrs. Annette Rankin, the angel of the *Seven Arts,* to withdraw her financial support. To Anderson, he was "the most vivid figure," the only man whose political talk interested him. Reading Bourne's essays on youth, on friendship, on feminism, one can imagine that Bourne would have come to know more than the messianic artist and the malleable man in Anderson, but his death in 1918 at the age of thirty-two made that impossible. The only real friend Anderson made in New York was Paul Rosenfeld, the *Seven Arts*'s music critic, but he met him only briefly at Frank's during that visit to New York in February. Anderson would have gravitated toward the more prominent of the *Seven Arts* editors, and Rosenfeld was never one to thrust himself upon anyone's attention. The next year, Rosenfeld left the scene to serve in the Army. Anderson came to know him later, and only gradually, as the excitement Frank generated died down and as Brooks and Anderson settled into what can only loosely be called their friendship

Anderson cut himself off more and more from his associates at Taylor-Critchfield too. By 1918 he had arranged it so that though he still shared fees and cleared his accounts with them, he had his own office and his own schedule. It was an arrangement that would allow him to hold on a few more years until he was confident that he could support himself by his writing alone. In June he thought of resigning altogether and handed Bayard Barton a letter which began thus:

> Dear Barton:
>   You have a man in your employ that I have thought for a long time should be fired. I refer to Sherwood Anderson. He is a fellow of a good deal of ability but for a long time I have been convinced that his heart is not in his work.

"There is no question but this man Anderson has in some way been an ornament to our organization," he went on. "He is a nice fellow," he concluded, but "let's can him." It was an amusing gesture; at the same time, it was typical of the man who, when he stepped back to assess himself, was as likely to want to undercut as to support his own efforts. It might also have been a roundabout plea for more indulgence.

Business associates and friends receded from his life. He valued what he called Bab's "comradeship," but she was a fool, he wrote her, to be kind to him. For Christmas, 1917, she sent him a cigarette box. He too had intended to honor the season, to write letters and buy gifts, but this Christmas was worse than usual, and he didn't do a thing. Christmas morning he retired to his room, lit a candle, and decked himself out in regal colors, like a king — or so he described himself in a note he then wrote Bab. Whether or not he had had too much to drink, afterward he went to sleep for fifteen hours and wrote her again the twenty-sixth, thanking her for the gift that she had sent him. It looked like a coffin, he said.

Nor did Anderson approach his wife. However much they saw of each other and others, they maintained their separateness. During this period, a friend observed how Tennessee's trenchant sense of humor saw her through. Anderson, the friend said, was always "blackly dour." Aimless and frustrated in Chicago, in the spring he weighed the possibility of taking Tennessee with him and moving down to Owensboro, Kentucky, home of his best client. What he did instead was take another leave and go on his own to New York.

A year and a half before, in his excitement over meeting the editors of the *Seven Arts,* he had thought he would probably live in New York one day, "at the edge of the busy intellectual life that goes on there," he told Bab, but upon his return, in the summer of 1918, he just found what he called "a hole" and buried himself in work. He found a room in Chelsea, on West Twenty-second street, near the offices of the *New Republic,* to be sure, but Anderson might just as well have been on Cass Street, so successfully did he lose himself in his work. He had another sparsely furnished room, at the back of a house that was presided over by an elderly Irish woman. She brought coffee, toast, and fruit up to his room in the morning; and there he stayed, still in his dressing gown, unshaven, and wrote each day until noon.

This visit, the man he was most eager to contact was his old friend Clifton Paden (now John Emerson), because he knew Emerson was only too happy to give him a token job in John Emerson–Anita Loos Productions, the movie company that he and his wife had set up. When Emerson asked Anderson what he liked to do, Anderson said, "Take long walks," so Emerson gave him the title of "location finder" and sent him on his way at fifty dollars a week. He also had Anderson write occasional publicity releases ("the provocative trash required by newspaper columns," Anita Loos called it), none of which ever found their way into print. Anderson showed up occasionally at the studio across the river in Fort Lee, New Jersey, and felt some of the excitement of people in the new industry, but having done a chore or two, he would go back to his room to write, or perhaps take the bus up to Central Park where he might also write or just sit for hours.

Soon he made his peace with New York, through his friendship with Anita Loos even more than through his friendship with her husband. "Nita," he once said, "I'm not going to let New York get me down. When I walk along the streets, I brace myself to look everyone right in the eye!" To his longer-term confidante and support, Bab

Finley, he wrote in August, "There is a certain definite sharpness and shallowness about the people here that I like. . . . I love them perhaps most because they are so little a part of myself." He had asked Brooks to help him find a room when he arrived, and he must at least have seen him. He re-established contact with Karl, who had earned something of a reputation, primarily as a portrait painter, won several prizes, and now lived in relative prosperity in Westport, Connecticut, near the Brookses. Tennessee came on for a few weeks, but essentially Anderson was alone.

However much he doubted the integrity of the man and his business, Anderson was not about to refuse John Emerson's patronage. He needed the money, he needed the time. He believed there was truth in his and others' claim that he represented the spirit of his country, but at the same time, for all his ability to lose himself in the adulation of others, he was finally sane and shrewd enough to know that he had yet to make good on that claim. Word of mouth was not enough, not others', certainly not his own. He was tired of talk. Nor could the words he had so far published fully justify his reputation. *Windy McPherson's Son* was derivative, *Marching Men* unsuccessful, his "chants" nothing he could seriously defend. There were his tales, known and admired but as yet uncollected in one book. He had more he had to say, and he needed to say it in a novel. And so, in a matter of months, he wrote a draft of *Poor White,* the best of the seven novels he was to write.

Anderson rediscovered and expanded his subject in *Poor White.* The novel is about what happened to Bidwell, Ohio, with the coming of industry, what happened to Winesburg, what happened to Clyde. Anderson had known it all firsthand. He had celebrated America's "progress" as an advertising man and had tried to contribute to it as a businessman. He knew, again at firsthand, what had happened to men and women in the process. He saw how their relations were transformed by their attempts to modernize and mechanize the world. He knew from his own experience how a man could lose his ability and will to function in a society that rewarded only crude material and sexual power.

Anderson had tried to tell the story several times before: in embryonic verse form in *Mid-American Chants*; in "Godliness," the four-part section of *Winesburg, Ohio* that he wrote the summer before up at Lake Chateaugay; and in the appropriately titled *Immaturity.* In *Poor White,* he finally told it, told it as it had happened to average American men and women he had known. It was once again *his* story, but in the telling of it he was now — after two troubled years — convincingly representative.

He took his central figure from Twain: Hugh McVey, "born in a little hole of a town stuck on a mud bank on the western shore of the Mississippi River in the State of Missouri," son of a widowed drunkard with whom he lives in a shack by the river, later nurtured by an enterprising woman from New England who plays the role of Aunt Polly. There is something in him of the Abraham Lincoln whom Anderson had begun to worship — he is tall, gaunt, roughhewn. A dreamer, feeling "himself a part of something significant and terrible that was happening to the earth and to the peoples of the earth," he is also George Willard now turning his imagination to the task of freeing men and women from the drudgeries of work. He is a good American boy, trying to make a man of himself, as he tells his foster mother, doing so, eventually, by inventing first a plant-setting machine, then a corn-cutter, a coal-car dumper, and other such machinery. Hugh's is not a dream of "acquired wealth." Arriving in Bidwell in 1889, at the moment when "mankind seemed about to take time to try to understand itself," Hugh seems to offer its inhabitants the chance to deepen their sense both of individual idiosyncrasy and of communal strength. Thanks to him, men could smoke and talk while their machine cut corn and bound the shocks. They had time to think, to appreciate "the wonder and mystery of the wide open places." Thanks to him, "a new kind of poetry" could be heard "in railroad yards and along rivers at the back of cities where ships are loaded."

But in the process, Hugh destroys what in "Godliness" Anderson had called an "old brutal ignorance that had in it also a kind of beautiful childlike innocence." Spiritual belief dies, families split, the youngsters become slick. Something approaching class warfare begins, not a war like the Civil War but "a war between individuals to see to what class a man must belong; then it is going to be a long, silent war between classes, between those who have and those who can't get." Anderson knew it all: the industrial heroes and heads of promotion companies, parodies of Lincoln and of Grant, manipulating papers and numbers so as to come out ahead even as the investing troops go down in defeat; those investors down on their knees asking God to protect the inventor on whose machines they bet their savings; the up-and-coming venture capitalist and the town's leading landowner courting each other on a moonlit buggy ride; above all, the hacks who "used their minds and their talents as writers in the making of puffs and the creating of myths concerning the men by whom they were employed."

Confident of what he knew about recent American history and of what he felt about it, Anderson wrote sentences that were both sweeping and cutting:

> And all over the country, in the towns, the farm houses, and the growing cities of the new country, people stirred and awakened. Thought and poetry died or passed as a heritage to feeble fawning men who also became servants of the new order. Serious young men in Bidwell and in other American towns, whose fathers had walked together on moonlight nights along Turner's Pike to talk of God, went away to technical schools.

In one of his boldest strokes, he took the romantic idea that men had become the slaves of their machines one step further: Hugh becomes the ghost of one himself. Trying to gauge how a cabbage-planter might function, he goes out one evening and enacts its possible motions in a field, ignoring the family that was hard at just such work. Seeing "the great length of his figure and his arms . . . accentuated by the wavering uncertain light," his arms going stiffly up and down, the French family crouches, then flees in terror, later declaring that "a ghost had come into the cabbage fields and had threatened them with death if they did not go away and quit working at night." In another, a harness-maker, literally mad over the loss of his trade and of his savings, lunges at Hugh and digs his fingers and teeth into his neck.

"Learn your trade. Don't listen to talk," the harness-maker had said before the coming of the factories. "The man who knows his trade is a man. He can tell every one to go to hell." This did not prove true for either this harness-maker or the one who was Anderson's father, but it had for the son. In "The New Note" that he had hit for the *Little Review,* Anderson had tried to inspire men to "craft love." He had heeded his own call, and he had survived. In much of *Poor White* he explored what happened to men when machines and figures and talk took over. He did so by focusing on Hugh's attempts to redirect his country's progress and on the figure of Clara Butterworth, the leading landowner's daughter and later wife to Hugh, on what she endures because of men who had no trade, because of what they had come to think was required of a man instead.

Clara goes off to Ohio State University, suffers the advances of young men intent upon "making it" as future financiers or, by way of compensation, as uncontrolled libidos, and finds companionship with another woman, Kate Chancellor. Clara feels older and wiser than all the men she meets. By Anderson's scathing analysis, they are of two kinds: "those who are kindly, gentle, well-intentioned children, and those who, while they remain children, are obsessed with stupid, male vanity and imagine themselves to be masters of life." Clara has to contend with her father's need for mastery as well. But though Anderson portrays the androgynous Kate in entirely sympathetic terms, and though he does insist that Clara's life is impoverished for lack of the company of women and has her "caress the memory of her one woman friend" at her wedding feast, he has to have her married. For Clara is Woman. "There was a creative impulse in her," Anderson writes, "that could not function until she had been made love to by a man." And thus Clara is also Mother, mother, climactically, to a son, and mother, finally, to Hugh. She is the "Other," a nurturing and awesome presence, created out of Anderson's sense of the failings of men in the machine age.

"One should be able," Clara thinks, "to find somewhere a man who respects himself and his own desires but can understand also the desires and fears of a woman." But she finds only Hugh, Bidwell's, the era's, substitute for a hero; and their marriage is a sorry one. They are propelled into it because less than a week after their first meeting, Hugh hears three workmen chortling over stories of the trouble Clara had been in with men and is so incensed that he strikes out at them (never having hit a man before); he then rushes off to Clara, well-intentioned child that he is, imagining he can rescue her. When he proposes, she knows that although she does not love him, she will do no better, so she leads him to the barn, hitches up a horse, and drives them to the county seat. On the way back, Hugh sits silent, afraid because he is only a "poor white," resentful at being led, unnerved by the lust he feels. Trying to speak, his mouth opening and closing with no sound other than the smacking of his lips, to Clara he looks "animal-like and ugly." By Anderson's lights, he is modern man, in modern marriage. But it isn't his fault, Clara reflects, she shouldn't have rushed him. And thus: "With bowed heads they rode, each trying to find courage to face the possibilities of the night." Anderson depicts their relation with broad strokes — the way Thomas Hart Benton might have done it for a post office mural — bringing out the individual feelings that prevail and, at the same time, seeming to generalize from them.

On their first night, Hugh finds no courage. To him, sex corrupts;

he "won't let her do it," and the first night he literally flees out the window. For days thereafter, he tries to avoid what he imagines to be his duty to assault Clara's "whiteness and purity," until finally, one night, his foot on the bottom step, she calls to him and breaks the spell:

> "Come here, Hugh," Clara said softly and firmly, and like a boy caught doing a forbidden act he went toward her. "We have been very silly, Hugh," he heard her voice saying softly.

And he ascends to one kind of manhood.

But though she has been in a man's arms, three years later Clara still feels she has never had a lover. There has to be more to men than that. It is then that Hugh is attacked by the harness-maker and then, in saving him, that she realizes that she is "the mother" — "fierce, indomitable" — and that he, "forever after," is "no hero, remaking the world, but a perplexed boy hurt by life."

Anderson was not alone in decrying men's impotence in the age of the machine. Fifteen years or so earlier, Henry Adams had been in the habit of enlivening Washington dinner parties with his attacks on the American male. "The American man is a failure! You are all failures!" he would say. "The typical American man had his hand on a lever and his eye on a curve in his road; his living depended on keeping up an average speed of forty miles an hour, tending always to become sixty, eighty, or a hundred," he asserted in his *Education,* and "he caught the trick," as he put it, "of affirming that the woman was the superior." It was more an obsession than a "trick" of Anderson's. His men are always frightened boys, afraid not only of women but of what they think is the defiling power of their sexuality. But in *Poor White* Anderson was, like Adams, only guardedly autobiographical. In this text, Anderson's social vision is so strong that we do not automatically register signs of his failures to live up to his expectations of himself as a man — until the end.

Four more years pass, and Hugh is on his way to Pittsburgh to see about casting a new part for a hay-loader. He is under considerable pressure because a man from Iowa had already been granted a patent on a similar machine. But in the Pittsburgh station, and then again as he rides past Youngstown, Akron, Canton, Massillon, on his way back to Bidwell, he takes out some brightly colored stones that he had picked up on the shores of Lake Erie while he was waiting for another train on another trip; he watches how the light plays over them and undergoes a conversion:

The same light that had played over the stones in his hand began to play over his mind, and for a moment he became not an inventor but a poet. The revolution within had really begun. A new declaration of independence wrote itself within him.

Sensing, somehow sharing "his troubled state," Clara has been waiting up for Hugh. "Her mother spirit was aroused. He was unfilled by the life he led. She understood that. It was so with her." But in her case, the lack of fulfillment is in the past tense, because she is pregnant with their second child and she has felt what she is sure is *him* move. When Hugh arrives she welcomes him, and together they walk out to the fence to gaze across the open fields; there she tells her news. On the way back, they hear the snoring of an old farmhand, a figure from a better past named Jim Priest; the factories begin to whistle and scream, signaling a shift in crews; and with a more sprightly step than Windy McPherson's son's, Hugh ascends the steps of his house with his wife.

We have been present at the announcement of the birth of two sons. Choirs of factories seem to welcome their poet; the attendant priest is there at least in spirit. Clara is fulfilled, and Hugh will be in the only way a man can be — not as a simple sexual male, not as a master of machines, not by being rich, but by being creative, in thought and with words. In committing himself to that definition of manhood, he had twice declared: "The gods have thrown the towns like stones over the flat country, but the stones have no color. They do not burn and change in the light." That changing remains for him to do. His business is to illuminate the town. And so he would; having written *Poor White,* so Anderson had. Anderson's endings are almost always assertions of beginnings, more or less contrived or strained indications of his own determination to keep on writing. They almost always betray the relatively personal nature of his art. But *Poor White* is, as he said, essentially about Bidwell. It is finally a rendering not so much of Anderson but of what he and others thought he represented — the transformation of American life in the twentieth century.

By December he was back in Chicago, and happily so, as he made clear to Brooks in several ways. He told Brooks that he had been reading *The Education of Henry Adams,* and that for all his admiration he had to say people lived and died "rather better in the Middle West": "Nothing about us is as yet so completely and racially tired." He told him about his falling-out with Waldo Frank (and added that he found Frank's new book, *The Art of the Vieux Colombier,* "very badly overwritten"); he told him too that his dependence on the movie industry had become impossible. He was home, where he belonged: "Back here I almost feel able to say that I don't care if I never travel again. The place between mountain and mountain I call Mid-America is my land. Good or bad, it's all I'll ever have," he said staunchly.

In fact Anderson was about to begin years of essentially nomadic life, but in spirit he was defending himself against Brooks, against his reserve. He was implicitly rejecting social life like Westport's, a life that he thought was secondhand, "too far away from life," a life that he had come to think was corrupting his brother Karl. He was weaning himself from the East.

It was time they came to him. He was thinking of starting a magazine "here in the heart of America," he informed Brooks, and he wanted "you fellows from coast to coast to come here. We have always been going to you. I want it changed if possible." Finally, and most importantly, he was thinking about his own writing, about what he had accomplished in recent months. He had regained confidence in himself. He had finished a draft of *Poor White,* "about laid by . . . in shocks and stood up in the field," he said. "The husking" would have to wait, though, while he corrected proofs of the book that was to win him his fame.

Anderson had collected all the Winesburg tales under the title *The Book of the Grotesque,* and Francis Hackett, whom Anderson had known in both Chicago and New York, had shown the results to Ben Huebsch, a genial and cultivated publisher, famous for his commitment to good books. Huebsch had published Hackett himself, and Oppenheim and Brooks. He was known best for introducing James Joyce and D. H. Lawrence to American readers. After *Mid-American Chants,* John Lane was ready to give up on Anderson. When Lane found the Winesburg tales "too gloomy," Huebsch had no trouble gaining Anderson's release. Changing the title to *Winesburg, Ohio,* he published the book in May of 1919 (reprinting it again in December and then twice in 1921). Though sales were relatively modest — about 1,700 copies in the first six months and just over 3,000 in the first two years — the reviews were good, and Anderson was pleased.

A few reviewers objected to what they considered its unseemly materials. Several years later, feeling unappreciated, Anderson would refer back to them or to a New England library he had heard of that had actually burned the book, but at the time he dismissed the comments of his detractors. The anonymous one who wrote "A Gutter Would Be Spoon River" for the *New York Sun* had to be a woman, he told the literary editor of the *Chicago Tribune,* Burton Rascoe, and added, "I wrote Ben Huebsch to look her up and please find someone to gratify her choked-up desires." He was full of himself, for praise had come from all quarters — even from the *Boston Transcript,* even from William Lyon Phelps. The reviewers who mattered had found Masters and Anderson incomparable. Some thought that there was no use comparing them; as Rascoe had put it: "Into the soul of Mr. Masters the iron has sunk; he is bitter, reproachful, and removed. In Mr. Anderson there is a fraternal pity and a homely tender feeling of participation in human destiny." Others thought that Anderson was so much better, as Mencken had maintained: "Here is the goal that *The Spoon River Anthology* aimed at, and missed by half a mile." In comparisons to Chekhov and Dostoevsky and Tolstoy, Anderson fared very well. The young Hart Crane was so inspired he said he found "the entire paraphernalia of criticism . . . insignificant, erected against the walls of such a living monument as this book," and that "America should read this book on her knees. It constitutes an important chapter in the Bible of her consciousness."

Anderson forged ahead. What was easily the best novel he had yet written was almost finished. All *Poor White* needed was "two or three weeks' steady writing . . . and then a week or two for cutting to shape," he thought. He wrote some of what he wanted to be "a new book of tales," published one tale, "I Want to Know Why," in the *Smart Set,* and had another, "The Triumph of the Egg" (later called simply "The Egg"), accepted by the *Little Review*; he later withdrew it because the magazine had become "too dreadfully inartistic and bad" and published it the next year in the *Dial*. These stories are among his most famous and his best, the former so successful in creating the tortured voice of a young boy exposed to the vulgarity of assertive masculinity that some would think that the author had no other voice.

For "The Triumph of the Egg" Anderson returned to Bidwell, Ohio, to small-town folk trying to make their fortune, and to memories of his father. His tone was now ironic, dry, amused; it was material over which he had full control. The story is about small-town people possessed by "the American spirit for getting up in the world," in this case trying to do so with chickens.

"One unversed in such matters can have no notion of the many and tragic things that can happen to a chicken," the narrator explains. All his family has to show for ten years of raising chickens is "little monstrous things," chickens with four legs or two heads or two pairs of wings, chickens gone "quickly back to the hand of their maker that has for a moment trembled" and now preserved in alcohol in bottles. Trying to make their fortune owning a restaurant, the father insists on keeping the bottles on a shelf. When he fails, he decides the trouble is that he has not been cheerful or entertaining enough, so he tries tricks, making an egg stand up on end, for example, and tries for "something of the jolly inn-keeper's effect." At the story's end, the problem of the egg remains — it will not stand on end, it breaks — as does the fact of something more mysterious and elusive than success.

Anderson himself was not content to repeat what were proving to be successful moves. "I want constantly to push out into experimental fields. 'What can be done in prose that has not been done?' I keep asking myself," he wrote Brooks in March of 1919. His answer was "a purely insane, experimental thing I call *A New Testament*," an attempt, as he put it, to express "the purely fanciful side of a man's life, the odds and ends of thought, the little pockets of thoughts and emotions that are so seldom touched." They were to be like the *Chants* only "infinitely more difficult"; and though they would not come out in book form for almost a decade, examples began to appear (in the *Little Review*, ironically) in October. Anderson thought of combining such "things" with the material of *Poor White* in a book he would call *Industrial Vistas,* an analysis of America, no less, "achieved by the autobiography of the fanciful life of an individual." He even asked Huebsch what he thought of the idea of children's books.

He seemed to be bursting with creative energy; at the same time he was searching frantically for a way out of the life he was leading in Chicago. In the summer, a botanist at the Field Museum lent Anderson his spacious log cabin near Ephraim, Wisconsin, way up on Green Bay, for a few weeks, and Anderson thought he had found his escape. It was Lake Chateaugay all over again. A surge of good writing behind him, he laid claim to being in touch with nature's creative power. "These days out of doors, walking much alone, under trees and swimming in the sea renew me," he reported to Bab. "Deep within me I am at peace. O that I could stay here alone for months."

And he tried to come up with a way. He thought of buying land nearby and starting a summer camp, not just for children but for adults as well. They could all help with the clearing and building, he thought, or do some farming. "Tennessee has genius with children and I could handle the grown-ups," he told Frank. He looked to John Emerson as a possible backer; that failing, he turned to Trigant Burrow and then went on to ask whether Burrow knew of anyone who would give him what he really wanted: outright support. He had proved himself as a writer, as one of America's most prominent and promising, in fact. He was right when he said, "I know of no other man in the country who has got such recognition as has come to me." He figured he needed about twenty-five hundred or three thousand dollars a year to live on. Wasn't there someone who would back him to that extent so he could try to do his work?

On the one hand, Anderson knew he was a famous American writer and thought he deserved support. On the other, he was a man who was forever insecure, most likely to doubt himself just when he had become most excited about his writing. "To tell you the truth," he ended his letter to Burrow, "I know of no reason why anyone should do this." He couldn't see any reason from such a person's point of view anyway. Perhaps he was, after all, "but a man grasping at straws."

In August, he had "gulped the mess again" and accepted the need to continue on as an advertising man; he was even "quite cheerful" about his new arrangement with Taylor-Critchfield. But in December, returning to both of them for encouragement and (the word he used) "love," Anderson complained to Brooks and Frank, telling the one that the advertising business was growing "constantly more like eating my own vomit," and the other that he could not go on, that he had to get out.

All the while, his frustration took its physical toll. At first, as he well knew, it was "an odd kind of psychic illness," brought on by his return to Chicago after his stay at Ephraim and then aggravated by his sense of its "unrest." He sensed the "dull dreary hatred in men's hearts." The war had brought it out — the United States had been drawn in — and that summer of 1919 it was manifesting itself in the worst race rioting in Chicago's history. In one encounter on a Lake Michigan beach, fifteen whites and twenty-three blacks were killed. The whole world seemed sick. "I have a notion the whole world is somewhat ill," he told Bab. "The reports I get from men who have recently been in England and France is that there is a hopeless illness of spirit there."

In a series of letters to her, Anderson ran through all his options (the camp, writing, "being a wandering peddler, a man who lives in a tiny frame house at the edge of a small town") and traced the fluctuations of his feelings. He had tried everything but to no avail; he had hoped someone would come along and rescue him; in his passivity, he was wasting away. Business was "like a prison"; he sprang up and "beat against the bars" and then fell back exhausted and ill. He used the metaphor enough to suggest a real state of mind, one something like that which he had experienced seven years before in Elyria. Using it again, in September Anderson told Huebsch that Chicago was "a madhouse." By the end of the year, he was indeed at wits' end: "I know nothing of how it can be done. I only know it must be done. If it cannot be done, I shall get out anyway and suffer what loss of friendship and what ugly hatred is necessary." And however psychosomatic his malady was at times, there were limits to his physical resiliency. As his forty-third winter set in, he fell just plain ill with influenza.

"It is a tired time filled with tired people," he wrote Bab. "Everyone has a son, a mother, a brother, a wife, someone dragging him back and back. Human relationships in such a time become instinctively clutching." In a word, his wife was "clutching," and he found it intolerable. Their marriage had never been a conventionally happy one, but they had planned it that way and had lived with — or found a way around — strain. Now Tennessee was receding into a depression of her own. She was "breaking under the hard work she does every year," Anderson told Frank. But it was not just the work and not "a temporary thing." Anderson saw that she was unhappy with her life. Though he did not put it in so many words, he knew she wanted more from him. But although he could open up to his confidante, confronted with an ailing wife he shut down.

Writing *Poor White* the year before, Anderson had been a judicious critic of his culture. Now he felt like its victim. He was a prisoner to his job. He wasn't free to write. The very weather oppressed him. Though he did not lose himself so completely as he had seven years before, as 1919 drew to a close, he found he could not stand up under the mounting pressures. Typically, he held out the hope that women were superior to the culture, that he could flee to them, but finding that not to be the case (thinking of Tennessee, for one), he was left only with the idea of fleeing. "I turn to women because men are too concerned with making money and overfeeding their lusts," he said. "I am stupid. I forget that women are as much involved in the tangle as men. So much of the time I do not want hands on me but want to run clean and alone." He reverted to his image of himself as essentially "a clean boy running over the hills," went all the way back to his fictional Camden, it seemed, and determined to make his image his reality. He had beat temporary retreats to Lake Chateaugay, to Ephraim, to New York. In such a mood he had run out on his family and his business seven years before. Now he was preparing for another flight.

This time he had another text, another fictive life, to go by — not Hamlet's but Gauguin's. When Somerset Maugham's *Moon and Sixpence* came out that year, Anderson told Bab that it was "a striking story" that would help her understand him. It was based on Paul Gauguin's life; at the same time, Anderson said, it was a story he thought of writing. In his mind's eye, he saw "the figure of a man walking on the streets of a town on a Summer Sunday evening," and he was "about to run away to create the story of what happened to the man."

In the act of writing, he said, "all staleness in life floats away." That had been true for years. Now he felt that letting anything — or anybody — interfere with him and his writing was cowardly. He had to go.

SEVEN

Alabama and Paris

1920-1921

THIS TIME Anderson went south, south to Alabama. He just put his finger on a map, ran it straight down, and went to where it hit the Gulf of Mexico — not to New Orleans, not to Saint Petersburg, but directly south, to Mobile Bay. All that mattered was that it would be warm, and he would be alone. A new year, a new decade. He wanted to begin all over again, and almost immediately what he called "a new door of the house of the spirit" began to open.

In Mobile, he took a room in an old house where dockworkers boarded. His accommodations were comfortable, he had his own fireplace, and the house itself was surrounded by a brick wall. The first night it was raining slightly, but he walked out anyway, to absorb his new freedom and his isolation. He walked down to the docks, and from a cargo of bananas that was being unloaded helped himself to two or three. He cut back through a little park and enjoyed the smell of flowers in the wet night air. It was about the last thing one could do on a January night in Chicago. Happily losing his sense of time and place, he walked on past midnight, and past where the pavement stopped, until he came to the "negro section" of the city. It was late, but he still heard voices, soft voices, and laughter. Already he felt soothed by the rhythms of this "sleepy old place," Mobile, especially by those who maintained their own rhythms while the city slept. He knew it was absurd, but as he walked back to his room he stopped, held a clenched fist in the air to symbolize what he had been experiencing up north, and then, to mark a new beginning, slowly brought it down and opened it.

He had one errand he had to run: Jack Jones of the Dill Pickle Club had asked him to pay a visit to a woman, a painter named Ann Mitchell, who was staying across the bay in Fairhope, Alabama, weighing Jones's proposal of marriage. Jones now had it in mind to transform his Pickle Club into a real theater; Ann was a painter, doubtful that she could be the kind of help he'd need. Anderson had still graver doubts about Jones and his grand schemes but kept them to himself: she was so evidently in love. Nor, at first, did he think much of Fairhope.

The town had been settled in the 1890s by a small group from Des Moines, Iowa, who had read Henry George's *Progress and Poverty* and had come to Alabama to realize his ideals about equitable taxation of the land. Thirty years later, these "Single Taxers" seemed to Anderson to be only "middle class eccentrics," working for mild reforms while the Western world was torn by war and revolution; or worse, they seemed to be just wealthy and tired old men and women who had come down from Ohio and Illinois and Wisconsin to wait out the winter on the verandahs of smug little houses with names like "The Dovecote," "Westwood," "Idlehours," and "Moss Manor." But what with Ann there, and another artist named Wharton Eshrick and his wife, and another woman who could type for him, Anderson decided that Fairhope would lift his spirits even more than Mobile, and soon he crossed the bay to stay.

He found a little house just outside of town, backed by pine woods and only yards from the water at high tide. It already had a stove and some dishes, a table, a few chairs, and an iron cot. With Ann's help he found bedding. He could easily do his own housework and cook for himself. Fish and clams and crabs were right outside his door. So too — everywhere, it seemed — were brilliant colors. The beaches of the Gulf were milk-white, the land behind him red clay, lemon yellow and blue too, but mostly red. At sunset, after a rain, the clay came down the rivers that fed the bay and turned its waters "warm blood red." Anderson thought he'd found "a golden land," a paradise, in which he said he could live "as the gods live." Or very close to the way they lived. He estimated he had to spend only about five or six dollars a week.

As the days warmed, he walked for hours along the beaches that stretched for miles on either side. On one occasion, he slept out all night and then was laid up a few days by a combination of sand flea bites and some variety of poison ivy or oak. On another, he stayed the night with "a tall gaunt woman" whom he came upon as he was walking up a little cove. She reminded him of his mother. She had three wild sons; her husband was off catching snapper. And he fanned out into the surrounding area, first driving around the town in a little horse and wagon, then going up and down the Tombigbee River on a riverboat, and up and down the Alabama River to Selma and back. Once he went as far as New Orleans. Always he was alone, always trying to appreciate and emulate the slow and quiet pace of life around him.

Nothing impressed him more than the life of blacks. He watched them as he drove through town, he watched them as they docked the riverboats, he watched them unloading cargo ships, he went inland and watched them load lumber onto rafts and harvest sap for turpentine. He marveled at how different they were when they were alone among themselves, and so he made himself inconspicuous, or actually hid himself behind the trees. It seemed to him that all their white foremen did was swear, and that in their presence the black men became self-conscious, imitated their foremen's ways and called each other "nigger"; alone, they had their own language, especially their song. So far as he knew, they were "the sweetest souled people in America," and no one realized it. He hoped no one would ruin it all by writing a book about them.

In the four and a half months he spent on Mobile Bay, Anderson acted out his own improved version of *The Moon and Sixpence*. He was that man he had envisioned back in Chicago, idly walking the streets of town on warm Sunday evenings. He was also Hugh McVey, dazzled by the way light played on some brightly colored stones, and he was furthering his own revolution, revolving and becoming "a poet" once again.

At the same time, the circle taking one more turn, he set himself the task of expressing what it was he was doing. The most obvious way of doing that was to write, and he easily accomplished what he had not been able to do during the past year: he finished revising *Poor White*. So happy was he with his situation and his work in Fairhope that he tried to go beyond words in order to express himself. He went "color mad."

It didn't all start with his reading about Gauguin. In conceiving of himself as an artist, Anderson had never thought exclusively of words. His father's kind of painting did not lift his sights, but his brother's did. Back in 1895, when he enlisted in the Ohio National Guard, Anderson had put down "painter" as his occupation. In Chicago, he had learned something about the Cubists and the post-Impressionists from Karl, more immediately from the Armory Show that Karl had helped to mount. Now, "letting go" again, he did so in painting — and with all the clay around him, in sculpting too. He never did so without being able to laugh at himself, but at the same time, he remained absolutely committed to what he was doing. Before he was through, he was grinding clay in an old coffee grinder in order to be able to have some to work with back in Chicago; and, not surprisingly, he was playing with a fantasy of teaching others how to sculpt and paint and feel what he had felt.

As for himself, he went to one painting class in Fairhope, left before it was over, and never went again. He tried "things," objects he would stare at and try to paint, but that was constraining too. So he looked out his window or just at the rectangular white expanse and the colors there before him and tried to express himself the way he imagined blacks were expressing themselves when they sang. All he wanted was lines and space and then colors to "lay into them." He thought it was to his advantage that he couldn't draw. Though brandishing his brush Anderson might have whispered Gauguin or Expressionism to himself, what emerged were relatively awkward, realistic renderings of a tree trunk or a black man's head, or landscapes that one might conceivably label Fauvist were the colors (ironically) not so tepid. The way their subjects sometimes fill out their compositions, and the quality of an occasional patch of color may make one think of Georgia O'Keeffe, who reportedly liked his work. But he was not trying to paint or be like others.

That fall he had a one-man show at the Walden Book Store in Chicago and the following year, thanks to Paul Rosenfeld of the *Seven Arts,* another at The Sunwise Turn, a bookshop in the Yale Club building in New York. When a woman left a check for seven hundred dollars for two of his canvases, saying they had made her feel the way she wanted to feel, Anderson was pleased that someone had shared his moments of liberation and was of course pleased by the temporary liberation the check allowed, but all that really mattered was the act of expression itself. He wanted to press out, press away. In a flyer he wrote for his shows he said, "There are certain images that haunt the human mind. They cannot be expressed in words except through the poet who occasionally raises the power of words beyond the real possibility of words." It was a gesture toward, an advertisement for, a self that was somewhere out there just past consciousness.

But he was more than half aware that he would not succeed in color: it was simply not his medium. Words were. In words he had moved past words before. In words he had created a better life for himself, a cleaner life, a truer life. And in words he continued to press on. He was writing what he called his "own kind of poetry," a poetry of "mystic, vague impulses" that went along all too well with his painting. The previous fall he had started to publish sections of what he titled "A New Testament" in the *Little Review*; he published ten there by the time he left Alabama in the spring and two more shortly after that; and then he wrote over fifty more that, with a few of the original twelve, were published in 1927. They were not prose, not poems, not prose poems, and not even chants this time, just utterances. In them he tried to get at what "the Hebrew poets" had done in parts of the Old Testament, but this was *his* bible. In it he was trying to arrive at his "own inner sense of what is beautiful in the arrangement of words and ideas." That Whitman inspired him went without saying. But reading his "testaments," one thinks only of the Anderson who allowed himself to play the bard when he was most content.

"If I could be brave enough," one went (in its entirety),

> and live long enough I could crawl inside the life of every man, woman and child in America. After I had gone within them I could be born out of them. I could become something the like of which has never been seen before. We would then see what America was like.

In it he is "A Poet." In others he is God, or Christ, loving his way into others' lives. Or God visits him where he lies on the sand, turns him over and kisses him, or he is on about his father's business, serving female words that have found no lovers, replacing castrated male words — "my book a hospital for crippled words." He is Jeremiah, weeping in the night, the trumpeter calling men to build temples to themselves, the discoverer of a language that will bring down walls. (At his most embarrassing, he is also a man whose very thought might "make Illinois pregnant," or one who declares: "I shall run through life like a little lost dog" and "put my cold nose against the bodies of people.") In "The Red-Throated Black," in "Singing Swamp Negro," in "Negro on the Docks of Mobile, Alabama," blacks are portrayed as "the sweet inner meaning of song," as the song itself, succeeding where the poet fails.

Obviously Anderson does. He has no subject, not blacks (or anything they were singing about), not the cultural situation he had explored in *Poor White,* not that most ready subject, himself. Lover of words that he claimed to be, he did not even have his eye on them. He was just going on about a better language than anyone knew, and about how it would bring people out of themselves and into each others' lives were it to exist. His "testaments" were, if nothing else, he said, "experiments in rhythm," successful because they served to give "a sweeter roll to the old boat" he called his prose. He kept making them with some regularity for at least the next few years. By his reckoning, they were helping him learn some unknown language.

One could say that the terrible "testaments," the painting, and Anderson's being in Alabama in the first place all constituted just another effort on his part to shed the traces of the past, of city life, of financial responsibility, of insistent women. It is as if he were back on Lake Chateaugay, and before that at Union Pier, reaching for ecstasy. But he was not being merely self-indulgent. All the while he was hard at work. He finished his revisions of *Poor White,* he went back to *Mary Cochran* and salvaged two stories from it before dropping it for good, he started to work on tales that he would collect with them (and with "I Want to Know Why," "Seeds," and the retitled "The Egg") as *The Triumph of the Egg* the next year, and he began the novel that would most clearly reflect his experiments, "something looser, more real, more true," as he described it, "a rollicking, Rabelaisian book called *Many Marriages.*"

That spring, Anderson was in what he considered paradise. In that golden land, he had almost no expenses, but more importantly, he was working well. He was in *two* paradises, because he was also alone, but midway through his stay he had to give up one: Tennessee wanted to join him. That she was tired, unhappy with her life, Anderson knew, and he knew too that she had written Frank to ask about analysts in the East "for a Chicago friend of hers"; but he did not inquire as to what was really wrong, or how much he had contributed to her malaise by running off. When she appeared in the spring, he was annoyed.

In late May, as they prepared to leave Fairhope, Anderson could present a decent front. It was he who had persuaded her to come down South, he said, to "be utterly reckless, chuck her job and income"; and she was much improved, "almost well," declaring that he had given her "the golden days of her life these last two months," he reported to Frank. For the time being, he had converted her. He had sat her down in front of some clay, told her to clear her mind, to think not of being a sculptor but of there being a figure there, and that in time, when her fingers began to want to clear away the excess clay, like Michelangelo about to release his *Slaves,* she might begin. Meanwhile he wrote and read to her what he had written. When the stories were collected the next year, photographs of seven "Impressions in Clay by Tennessee Mitchell" preceded them, several being figures of her husband's characters. "O, for a world of people not tired," he wrote Brooks. "What things would come out of them."

That spring, while Tennessee rested and waited and worked on figures from his tales, and in the following months they spent up North, Anderson tried to come to terms not with her, but with the frustration and the misery men felt and caused in marriage. It was not in New York, not in the first draft of *Poor White,* but on board a boat in the Gulf of Mexico that "there came that moment when Hugh McVey crept out of his wife's bedroom." Coming off his "experiments," in "The Man in the Brown Coat," Anderson wrote: "Why, in all our life together, have I never been able to break through the wall to my wife? Already I have written three hundred, four hundred thousand words. Are there no words that lead into life? Some day I shall speak to myself. Some day I shall make a testament unto myself." He still could not say what held him back, but in story after story he tried to say what it felt like to be failing there on the other side of the wall.

Through the stories that he wrote (and that were later collected in *The Triumph of the Egg*) runs his sense that marriage deadens men's and women's spirits, that men and women wanted not to love but to possess, that they were afraid. Through them too runs his understanding of men's sometimes petty, sometimes harmless, sometimes deadly compensations. In one story, "The Door of the Trap," taken from *Mary Cochran,* he told of a college professor's struggles with his desire to use a student as a way out of his diminished, married life. In "The Other Woman," he was more explicit: "she" had come to him the night before his marriage; her faith in her own desires and her courage were forever after an inspiration to him; she remained in his fantasies, a contrast to his wife, who slept in the room next door. In "Out of Nowhere into Nothing," not her father, not her boss, who loves her from behind the bars of his marriage, but an old man from her hometown appreciates the heroine's spirit — which is, as the title implies, small comfort. In "Brothers," the narrator tells of a crazed old man, and then of another man, a stolid, sullen soul who is infatuated with a girl who works in the bicycle factory where he is foreman, and who one night murders his wife. The old man reads about it in the paper and claims he is the foreman's brother — as in his loneliness, in his effort "to reach out to unattainable beauty," he is, and as in his plaintive tone the narrator is too.

In all of the three or four hundred thousand words that he had written, Anderson may not have broken through to an understanding of his wife, or wives, but from the first, beginning with *Windy McPherson's Son,* he displayed his intimate knowledge of lovers and husbands; he also showed he knew that along with their charm went a power to hurt, and that along with their "vague, mystical impulses" went destructive ones. These men were the people he knew best, the figures he set in motion to see how he would act. They are among his most successful creations and are at the same time indicative of his limitation as a writer.

His men are capable of villainy — they could kill — but they are always men we understand, and therefore men we do not finally think of as villains. There is no one in Anderson's writings we can hate. His most compelling characters are the products of his candor, his desire to confess — and we forgive. In a few years, after Van Wyck Brooks had begun his work on Henry James, Anderson started reading "The Master" and didn't like him. James seemed to him a man who did not dare to love, whose characters were unlovable. Anderson had "a fancy" that he ventured: "Can it be true that he is the novelist of the haters?" Anderson was deeply satisfied with the tales he wrote in 1920, and with reason. "Honest to God tales," he called them, "best I've ever done." But hatred would have helped make them even better. Anderson's generosity is one of the most attractive things about him, his ability to survive his own and others' doubts and criticisms one of the most impressive, but he might have gotten past the wall — seen more about himself and others — if he could have paid more respect to the feeling that some people might finally be unlovable, some actions unforgivable.

He had written up his situation with Tennessee, or with women generally, written it up, as he would have put it, "cleanly," but this was not to say that either it or he had changed. In May, Tennessee went back to Chicago and then north to Ephraim again, with a woman whose husband had just died, while Anderson went on to New Orleans, to New York, to Kentucky, primarily "to mend the broken strings of [his] economic life." He had had no steady income for months, and one did not live on six dollars a week in Chicago. In July he joined Tennessee in Ephraim. While he was there, he put *Many Marriages* aside and went to work on a novel that he never published called *Ohio Pagans*. Again the writing went well, again it brought him, as he said at the time, to "the realization of life in myself." When he flagged, he found relief in climbing the hills in back of their house, picking raspberries, or just sitting where he could look out over the waters of Lake Michigan.

But one incident cut right across his hopes that he could repeat the previous summer. Among the people who came up to visit were Ann Mitchell and Jack Jones, who were married now. They motored the many miles up Lake Michigan from Chicago in a small boat that Jones had made — "with my own hands," he boasted — arriving just ahead of a storm. Pure luck, the local fishermen said, and everyone tried to prevent their going back the same way, but Jones insisted. They tried to stop Ann, at least, and failed again. Another storm hit when they were about two-thirds of the way home, just as they passed Racine. Jones managed to lash them to their upturned boat, but by the time they were discovered thirty-six hours later, Ann had drowned, going to her death, Anderson always thought, to save her husband's pride. It turned out later that she had been awarded a prize by the Chicago Art Institute, but the prize was for a living artist, so her achievement went unpublicized and the prize went to someone else. A macabre tale, the moral of which was, as Anderson put it: "The artist in her had surrendered to the egotism of the male." If Anderson applied this moral to himself at all, it would not have been because of his attitude to Tennessee. He would have vowed never to let that kind of brutishness destroy the artist in him. Whether or not he thought of parallels at all, he never saw Jones again.

Having fled Chicago at the beginning of the year, Anderson could not bear to face the city from yet another apartment when he returned in the fall, so he went out past its limits to find a place to live. He went to the southwest to a town called Palos Park. A few trains a day connected it to the city, but it was too far out to be a suburb. Rolling hills and fields lay all around. Just to the west was the Palos Hills Forest Preserve. The house he found was "only a box," but then again, it cost him only $12.50 a month, and its one stove looked as if it would be enough help to enable him to withstand the approaching winter.

Tennessee came out two or three days a week — still unsettled, and unsettling. In November Anderson wrote Jerome and Lucille

Blum, artist friends whom they had known together in Chicago, who had themselves just escaped to Tahiti for a year, saying that Tennessee had really taken to sculpting and now wanted "to sit under a fig tree by a green sea and have beautiful blacks bring her clay to be modeled." (It would be like a woman, he added, to want black male slaves.) Well, she knew the modern terms on which they had married and knew that he was an artist. "The poor woman went and married me and is stuck to make her own living," he said, "and it's hell."

As for himself, he had work to do. He wrote, he continued to dabble in paint. Occasionally he took the twenty-five-mile ride into the city, for he still had to put in appearances at Taylor-Critchfield. He had just learned that Edward J. O'Brien was going to dedicate his *Best Short Stories of 1920* to him. "The Door of the Trap," "I Want to Know Why," "The Other Woman," and "The Egg" seemed to O'Brien to be "among the finest imaginative contributions to the short story made by an American artist during the past year." It was one more reason for Anderson to hope that the day might be approaching when the income from his writing would be commensurate with his rising reputation, when he could pass the agency by, but in fact that day receded before him.

When *Poor White* came out in October, it was greeted by mixed reviews. Mencken praised him in an article that Anderson said was "well thought out, dignified." When Francis Hackett complained about his lack of form, about the abruptness of the ending, for example, Anderson asked himself how he could maintain that "large, loose sense of life" that Hackett also praised him for, and then concluded that Hackett was just "spiritually tired." But Anderson could now see his name grouped with those of the rising authors of the day, such as Sinclair Lewis, whose *Main Street* appeared in 1920, and F. Scott Fitzgerald, whose *This Side of Paradise* was published the same year. Anderson and Lewis exchanged congratulatory letters; although he hesitated about *Poor White,* Fitzgerald would soon pay his respects to Anderson. On the other hand, the sales of Anderson's novel were disappointing. Fitzgerald's novel sold 40,000 copies and earned him six thousand dollars that year. *Main Street* sold 180,000 copies in six months. Anderson was right in assuming that it probably sold more copies in a week than his book did in a year. At the end of November he wrote Huebsch to say that he hoped *Poor White* would not go out of print before Christmas, as *Winesburg, Ohio* had done the year before.

Anderson would have to go on being the extraordinary man who both worked for an advertising agency and wrote highly respected fiction. There was even an exhibition of his art in town that fall. Although he was not yet financially free, he was famous, certainly the most notable writer in Chicago.

In early January 1921, an associate at Taylor-Critchfield named Y. K. (Kenley) Smith invited Anderson to visit the big house where he lived with six or seven young men and women. It was on Division Street, near Tennessee's apartment. They called their place "The Domicile." Smith had visited Anderson at Palos Park. He knew everyone at The Domicile would be honored if Anderson would stop around. They were all trying to earn their living in advertising or journalism or business, and they were all eager to meet this man who had risen from such beginnings to such heights.

It was an attractive group: there was Smith and another advertising man named Don Wright, and Smith's wife Doodles (who, it turned out, was having an affair with Wright), and his younger brother, Bill; there was also Smith's sister Katy, and Edith Foley, who collaborated on articles for magazines like the *Woman's Home Companion*; and Bill Horne, who had been an ambulance driver during the war and would one day become a leading Chicago advertising man.

To Anderson, none was more attractive than a twenty-one-year-old man named Ernest Hemingway. He had written some advertising copy for Firestone tires; he was still sending articles to the *Toronto Star,* where he had worked the year before, but he was drawing regular pay as assistant editor of a magazine put out by a shady organization called the Co-Operative Society of America. At The Domicile, no one worked harder than he did, no one even played as hard as he did. He tried every kind of writing, he did everything he could to get published. Although his ads were mostly burlesques, one for bottled blood from the stockyards, for example, that he called "Bull Gore, for Bigger Babies," his friends said he would have made a great adman. He made a stab at writing a comedy with an old high school classmate. He did satirical rewrites of the news, which *Vanity Fair* rejected. The next year a periodical in New Orleans called the *Double Dealer* would print a prose fragment and a quatrain of his. Anderson knew right away. Saying goodbye to his hosts the first night, he thanked them for introducing him to Hemingway and said, "I think he's going to go some place."

From Hemingway's perspective, Anderson was a man who could help him get there. Anderson did not help him much with his writ-

ing. In a few years Anderson would tell his other great protégé —
William Faulkner — that he would gladly help him find a publisher
for his first book as long as he didn't have to read it. Though he read
more of what Hemingway wrote, Anderson helped him, as he would
help Faulkner, mostly by his example. He represented professional
success, he could say how you achieved it, he could say what you did
to maintain it. He talked on about writers and artists he knew, about
periodicals, about publishers, about fees and reviews. Up until that
time, Hemingway's reading had been mostly in nineteenth-century
British writers. Anderson told him about the people who had inspired him, about Turgenev and Borrow, Frank and Brooks, about
the modern movement in both art and writing. He took him out to
Palos Park to show him how essential it was to have a place apart in
which to work.

Hemingway had probably read some of Anderson's stories in Toronto. He soon read *Winesburg, Ohio*. Again, if only by his example,
Anderson encouraged Hemingway to write about the things he knew,
in his case about a young man's responses to the war and to sexual
awakening. But Anderson had almost no influence on the Hemingway style itself. Having started to imitate Ring Lardner back in high
school, Hemingway was well on his way to finding his own narrative
voice; as a journalist he was already learning to pare down his sentences. If anything, Anderson's manner soon offended him. His
friends could sit and listen to Anderson for hours. They enjoyed his
flamboyance, the way he told his stories, the way he dressed, and
they kidded him. But Hemingway sat on the edge of the circle and
watched, watched, Kenley Smith said, the way a boxer watches,
waiting for his opponent to overextend himself. Wrapped in his own
sense of himself as the center of attention, Anderson could not have
known how he affected Hemingway. Once, just after Anderson had
left, Hemingway muttered that it wasn't right to "let a sentence go"
the way Anderson did. The man's openness had offended him, had
in some way threatened him. He saw a man who was capable of just
running on, letting his sentences say how he felt, a man who left
himself open. Already, in this famous man who was more than twice
his age, Hemingway saw a man with whom he could compete. Many
years later, reflecting back on Anderson's manner, Hemingway said:
"Sherwood was like a jolly but tortured bowl of puss turning into a
woman in front of your eyes." Turning into a woman — it was the
worst thing Hemingway could imagine a man doing.

Anderson and Hemingway saw each other about once a week over a period of only four or five months. In January, out of the blue, Anderson had received a fitting invitation. He had risen to prominence on the American scene. Now Paul Rosenfeld, who had watched the process from the wings of the *Seven Arts,* wanted Anderson to go to Europe with him. It seemed like a reward and a preparation for greater things to come. Chicago had less and less to offer him. He had never been abroad; he could meet some of his famous contemporaries, he could stand before masterpieces.

On a more prosaic level, the invitation was a godsend. The winter took much more of a toll on Anderson than had the one before. Once again it seemed that not just Tennessee but everyone wanted him to lift them up; every time he went into town he felt "sucked dry." It became harder and harder for him to work. It was, he said, "a rotten winter." This time, though, the trouble was mostly somatic. In March he learned that his sinuses had been infected for months, and so he began treatment — three long visits to his doctor each week — and soon improved. Before he left for Europe, he had his tonsils taken out. He had thought seriously of moving back to Alabama, with or without Tennessee, and maybe with their friends the Blums, but Rosenfeld's wire offered an incalculably preferable solution.

Though they had met on only a few occasions, Rosenfeld had liked Anderson from the start. In him he saw a more human, a more likable version of the man his fellow editors had made so much of. He once took Anderson to the Yale Club for lunch and would ever after remember how Anderson made him appreciate people from other, less cultivated walks of life. They were talking about the New York police, when Anderson leaned back in his chair, laughed, and said that for his part, all he could think of was their coming home at the end of the day, taking off their boots, and nursing their feet. Rosenfeld said he felt "an amazing force in the peasant-like and highly civilized being over the table." Finally, both the man and his work convinced him that "a beautiful, extraordinarily humanizing force was active in American life."

He responded to Anderson the way his fellow *Seven Arts* editors did — for them Anderson represented the potential, the vitality of American life — but he imagined Anderson's art performing a different function and imagined himself encouraging it in a different way. Rosenfeld had come by his high hopes for America through music and through painting. (*His* contributions to the first issue of *Seven Arts* were "The American Composer" and, on Alfred Stieglitz's studio, "291.") He did not envision the transformation of American culture in historical or social terms; he did not want anyone even to think of art in those terms. Like Brooks and Frank, he wanted America to aspire to more than material satisfaction, but his touchstones were Stravinsky and Schönberg, the Scriabin concert he had heard in London in 1914, and the one he heard a year later in New York, given by a nineteen-year-old in a black velvet jacket and slippers named Leo Ornstein. Not surprisingly, his prose was ornate, rhapsodic.

But as everyone knew, Rosenfeld was an affectionate and generous man, tireless in his encouragement of others' talents. What Rosenfeld heard in Anderson was a lovely voice and a lovely sensibility, and he wanted to help cultivate it. He saw himself as present at, assisting at, America's birth, never as exemplifying it.

And finally, though Rosenfeld was fourteen years younger than Anderson, the two men were very much alike. Rosenfeld was not egomaniacal, like Frank, nor, like Brooks, aloof. When Anderson lost confidence in himself, he might lump them all together, seeing himself as "stupid," "slow," "a schemer, a chronic liar," and imagine Rosenfeld to be like "them," brought up "in a different atmosphere," having had "the privilege of being serious" (and indeed he had been a year behind Frank at Yale, and like Frank and Brooks, had traveled abroad before). In the thirties, they would differ profoundly over the relevance of politics to art. But for as long as Anderson lived, Rosenfeld would be his friend.

Traveling with him was a pleasure. At first it seemed a bit like "walking a tightrope." Rosenfeld proved a little *too* sensitive: he seemed to react so strongly to others' moods, he could be hurt so easily. Anderson's explanation was that Rosenfeld had never worked, he had "no give and take with people." Others might come right out and say it — the proletarian writer Edward Dahlberg, for example, who said Rosenfeld was "flighty, feminine" — but the two travelers had a talk and soon all was well. Anderson thought there must be "old scars" there that he had overlooked. When he went on to say "there is something of the woman in P.," it was not to criticize.

At first it wasn't at all clear that Tennessee was to come along. There were limits to what Rosenfeld could afford. But then the Andersons found money for Tennessee's expenses, and Anderson wrote

Rosenfeld, assuring him that his wife would make "a great companion." Usually there was nothing that could recommend a woman more than the fact she was a woman, but that did not seem to be what Rosenfeld wanted. What Anderson said on Tennessee's behalf, then, was that there was "a certain thing about her that made her often too decent to be a woman at all."

Rosenfeld tried, but inveterate bachelor and New Yorker that he was, he could not make her feel at home. Edmund Wilson came upon the three of them together in a Paris restaurant, and overheard their conversation. His impression was that Tennessee was a "raw-boned prairie woman," and that Rosenfeld was having a very hard time trying to come up with "a modestly folksy manner" for her benefit. (Rosenfeld would be more at ease with Anderson's third wife. She was "frankly an old-fashioned woman, which every woman really is," he observed. "The greatest of all frauds was the free woman.") Fortunately, on the trip over the trio ran into the Andersons' old friend from the early days on Fifty-seventh Street, Ernestine Evans, and during the Andersons' stay in France, she and Tennessee often went their way while Anderson and Rosenfeld went theirs.

They sailed on May 14, 1921, on the French liner the *Rochambeau*. Arriving in Paris, they stayed at the Hotel Jacob et Angleterre on the Left Bank, just a short walk from the Louvre. While he was there, Anderson did some writing. Like the old man in "The Book of the Grotesque," he found a "little bare raised place" in the Tuileries gardens, rented a chair, and wrote on the low wall in front of him — "an ideal desk." But much of his time was spent just observing, sometimes with Rosenfeld, but more often alone. Almost every day, he said, he would put a few francs in his pocket and "plunge into the city" to see what he could find. What he came up with and recorded in his notebook was an ideal France, a preindustrial France, peopled, as America had never been, with unnamed, consummate artists. Postwar France was uninspiring. Rodin's work seemed too literary, too intellectual. Lesser artists seemed to huddle in groups, trying to find strength in numbers. Jacques Copeau, who had come to see him in Chicago, was now a terrible disappointment, his theater having become a kind of "upper middle class chapel" in which he played the part of a "nonconformist preacher of the new art." But there was the land itself and the people who lived by it, and then there was the incredible art.

When Anderson later went on to London he was disappointed: one expected to come upon a field in one's travels, but "no such luck"; London never stopped. But in Paris one was constantly restored by signs of nature's abiding presence. There was a special "pearly clearness about French skies"; there were freshly cut flowers everywhere; in the small hours of one night he heard a nightingale and then the sound of shutters opening as others seemed, like him, to be carried out of themselves by its song. Though Anderson was no reader of romantic poetry, the cityscape he observes seems obviously secondhand. He seems to come right out of the pastoral age that he so fondly recalled in the pages of his own *Poor White*: he imagines himself a teamster, driving one of those carts he saw, with wheels as tall as cathedral doors, piled high with hogsheads of wine and sacks of grain, drawn by as many as ten stallions. And the stallions! They showed how devoted the French were to the soil. They were not, as they would be in America, castrated. Beside them walked their drivers, cracking their whips. "These are my people," Anderson wrote in his notebook. "These men love the great breasted stallions as do I. They are not afraid. They do not castrate. Here is life more noble than anything machinery has yet achieved."

The art carried him even further back in time and filled him with more wonder. He saw a Picasso exhibition and appreciated Picasso's central position in "the revolutionist movement," but it was not the "new" that impressed Anderson most. When he and Rosenfeld went for their first walk across the Seine and entered the gardens and the parks fronting the Louvre, Anderson stopped, leaned against the pedestal of a statue, and started to rub his eyes. Rosenfeld thought he had a cinder in his eye. But he was weeping. The way it was all laid out, the Louvre, all the tradition it represented; it was more beautiful, Anderson said haltingly, than anything he had ever imagined.

Going on to discover works of the Middle Ages, "the delicate and massive beauty" of Notre-Dame, the "purer" Gothic of Sainte-Chapelle, he was more moved still. He was angry with Mark Twain for having pandered to his American readers' narrow-mindedness with his version of these monuments in *Innocents Abroad*.

The day he and Rosenfeld visited Chartres was among the happiest of his life. Much of their time was spent outside the cathedral, with Anderson quietly observing, and Rosenfeld beside him on a bench, reading in Huysmans's *La Cathédrale*. From that vantage point, and with Rosenfeld's prodding, Anderson reaffirmed his dedication to Art. Hugh McVey was converted by the way light played off a few stones picked up by the railroad track. Now Anderson was seeing the same phenomenon infinitely magnified. Chartres was "almost all poetry in stone," "the last word in beauty." It symbolized the worshiping men could do as they worked with their hands; it was work for no earthly gain; if even signed, it was signed where only God could see.

Two years later, when he used the occasion to climax his *Story Teller's Story*, Anderson joined those craftsmen's company as a writer of tales. As he recalled it, watching people move in and out of the cathedral, the tourists intent upon imprinting Chartres on their memories, the old Frenchwomen, adjusting their shawls about their heads as they went in to worship, he focused on two women and a man, the latter flirting with the one who was clearly not his wife. A little drama began to take shape. The wife, or sweetheart, pretended not to notice what was going on, but after the three went in she emerged alone and stepped aside to cry unnoticed (she thought) before the other two caught up with her. Anderson imagined there was a story there that one day he might tell. The men who had carved those portals and he who would tell the story of the woman who had just emerged through those portals — their aims were the same. Chartres, he said, made one "more aware," as he was at the time. That was his calling too: to make people aware of the stories of others' lives. Finally, to confirm him in his resolve, *there,* seated beside him, was his friend Rosenfeld. "It was one of the best moments of my own life," he wrote. "I felt free and glad. Did the friend who was with me love me? It was sure I loved him. How good his silent presence."

Though Anderson had been reviewed only a few times, news of his achievements and promise as a writer had preceded him to Europe. In a few years, American writers traveling abroad would cause no stir, but while Anderson was in Paris, many came to pay him their respects. Lewis Galantiere, whom Anderson had first met through Floyd Dell and Margery Currey and who was now attached to the International Chamber of Commerce in Paris, found the Andersons and Rosenfeld their accommodations and served as their occasional guide. Leon Bazalgette, the editor of the review *Europe* and a translator of Whitman, came to their hotel. So too did James Joyce. Bazalgette complimented Anderson on giving him the feel of America, on not writing like a European. Joyce was more of a figure, a handsome man, with the most beautiful hands Anderson had ever seen, whose wit and smile, he said in his notes, would light up his otherwise "gloomy" face "like a light brought suddenly into a dark room." Joyce's lot, he went on, was perhaps the hardest of the modern writers, but he was clear about the importance of the man's work (as he had been clear, from the start, about Hemingway's): he said that *Ulysses* might well be "the most important book that will be published in this generation." He saw Joyce several times. One encounter was enough for Anderson and Ezra Pound, however. After it, Anderson wrote Pound off as "an empty man without fire."

The women who met Anderson were charmed. When Galantiere took him to visit Marguerite Gay, who was doing a translation of *Winesburg, Ohio,* she took Galantiere aside and whispered to him that often, while she was at work on the book, she had seen Anderson in her mind's eye — just as he now appeared. Sylvia Beach first saw him pausing on the doorstep of her famous bookstore, Shakespeare and Company, looking in her window at what was the first copy of his book that he had seen in Paris. Having talked to him a while, she saw that he was part boy, part famous writer, part "poet and evangelist (without the preaching), with perhaps a touch of the actor," and she listened in suspense as he gave her a simplified version of how he had freed himself from the bondage of respectability and security, and run off to be a writer. According to her, though her friend Adrienne Monnier had to converse with him in pidgin French and pidgin American, she understood him even better. Monnier cooked her favorite chicken meal for him. In his company she imagined another twist of his kaleidoscopic character: she thought he resembled "an old woman, an Indian squaw, smoking her pipe at the fireside." Old woman? Squaw? The description is not far from one we have of Mme Monnier herself — "stoutish," straight hair brushed back, and dressed in a long skirt and tight waistcoat. It as if Anderson were like his father, this time taking on not only the manner but also the appearance of the next person he met.

In the course of his conversation with Sylvia Beach he told her how much Gertrude Stein's writing had meant to him; and although he needed no introduction, it was she who took him along to 27, rue de Fleurus, in the middle of June to meet Stein. They got along famously. Tennessee went once and tried harder than most wives to join in the conversation, but like all of them ended up talking with Stein's companion, Alice B. Toklas. Rosenfeld does not seem to have gone at all.

There, in that domesticated palace of art, surrounded by the modernists' canvases and drawings on the walls and by *objets* from all ages on the tables and on the mantlepiece, Anderson told Stein how he had discovered her writings back in 1914. He told her how she helped him find his tools, helped him believe in himself as a writer, and she was pleased. Rendering his visit the next year for the *New Republic,* he compared her to the women on whose porches he would stand on Saturday mornings in Clyde, waiting to collect for the newspapers he had delivered the week before. Hers was a "great kitchen of words"; her materials, her "handmade goodies," were like their pots and pans, and their jars of fruits, jellies, and preserves. And like those women he remembered from his youth, she was something of a work of art herself: "If her smile has in it something of the mystery, to the male at least, of the Mona Lisa," he wrote, "I remember that the women in the kitchens on the wintry mornings wore often that same smile."

In the fall, Stein asked him to write a preface for a collection of her writings that she was having published in Boston under the title *Geography and Plays.* When she told him he was "really the only person who really knows what it is all about," she was not just flattering him. The few pages that he would write titled "The Work of Gertrude Stein" are as good a place as any from which to enter the world she makes in words. When she wrote the following January, "I have never had more genuine emotion than when you came and understood me," she was expressing her delight at the prospect of reaching a wider American audience after years of relative obscurity and downright ridicule, but she was also expressing what would be an abiding affection for the man.

They were a good couple. To her, as to many people, there was something boyish (or even girlish) about him. "Yes, undoubtedly, Sherwood Anderson had a sweetness, and sweetness is rare," she would write after his death. To him she was another mother figure, but one who did not distract him with her sexuality. Faulkner would later say that she was one of the few people Anderson could trust. He believed her when she said he was good; he knew she would never do anything to hurt him. In more social terms, though for entirely different reasons, they were both outsiders and, at the same time, explicitly and emphatically, Americans. Anderson particularly liked the way Stein told stories "with an American shrewdness in getting the tang and the kick into the telling." And they were older. Younger men and women were coming over who would be successful writers almost from the start, many of them, moreover, as "expatriate" writers. There were Eliot and Pound, Dos Passos and Hemingway and Fitzgerald, Kaye Boyle and Malcolm Cowley and Alfred Kreymborg. All of them, Stein said, were twenty-six: "It became the period of being twenty-six. During the next two or three years all the young men were twenty-six years old. It was the right age apparently for that time and place." The two of them were in their midforties and never, as Stein wrote Anderson, "never . . . off Americans."

Stein had Hemingway in mind as she described those fortunate young men. When Anderson went back to Chicago he convinced Hemingway that he had to go to Paris to develop as a writer, not to Italy, as he had planned, and Anderson provided him with glowing letters of introduction to many of the people he had met — to Galantiere, to Joyce, to Stein. And from Stein we know that Hemingway learned a lot. When he first met her in March of 1921, much to his dismay, though, all she wanted to talk about was Anderson the man, about "his great, beautiful, warm, Italian eyes" and "his kindness and his charm," which were of no concern to Hemingway at all. He wanted to talk about the stories, about writing. He looked at her, Stein recalled, with "passionately interested rather than interesting eyes." He was interested in his work and its future. "There is the career," she remembers his muttering, "the career."

Personalities were at issue, as were sexual jealousies and preferences. If nothing else, "Hands" had shown Anderson to be sympathetic to those who lived unconventionally; and he himself exuded tolerance as well. In his later years, Hemingway made it very clear that he could not abide what was going on at 27, rue de Fleurus. From the start, Toklas resented his presence in their apartment. But she found Anderson "very handsome and incredibly charming." He had an "all-inclusive heart," she said.

More obviously, reputations were at stake. Professional jealousies were awakened, but literary history was working itself out in impersonal ways as well. Those whom Werner Berthoff labels the "Americans," those writers (of whom Anderson was the most prominent) who believed America was a special place, its uniqueness discoverable in "some morally purer and technically simpler way," were yielding to what he calls the "new men of letters," to those writers who lived and wrote in the world at large. The "Americans" had done their work, they had cleared the way for writers of the next generation, some of whose voices (Hemingway's, anyway) prevail to this day, and as those younger writers took over, they would not be known for their respect for their elders.

Anderson had described the process as far back as 1916, in a short piece on Dreiser in the *Little Review*. Soon, he had predicted, writers would have a sense of humor, grace, "lightness of touch," qualities one was not likely to find in his great contemporary. Having it, like little children, they would run through the streets, shouting: "Look at me. See what I and my fellows of the new day have done." What they would have forgotten, or would perhaps never have known, was Dreiser, the man whose "heavy feet" had cleared a path for them in the first place. "Their road is long," he said, "but, because of him, those who follow will never have to face the road through the wilderness of Puritan denial." Dreiser they might ignore. Anderson himself they would pummel mercilessly.

But in the early 1920s, if you had told Anderson that his day would soon be over, that he had done most of the writing on which his reputation would rest, you might have tapped his worst fears, but you could not have convinced him. If you had announced Anderson's demise to the general reader, you would have had an even harder time. Anderson would in fact become more and more popular, even as his reputation among writers declined. His writings would always be accessible, his faith in common people inspiring. In the spring of 1921, he could worship at the shrines of Art, could meet others there and be seen as one of its leading devotees. Whatever any other writers might be doing to overtake him or to brush him aside, he could walk through the streets of Paris with total confidence.

But after a little less than three months abroad, Anderson had to get back, back to America. "When he grew to be a man Tar saw Europe and liked it," Anderson wrote of himself a few years later, "but all the time he was there he had an American hunger and it wasn't a Star Spangled Banner hunger either." By the middle of July he was ready to say that one of the main things he had learned from his trip was how much of an American he was and how much he wanted for America. Just as a generation of young writers was gathering in Europe to say not only that America had come of age but that, like the West, it was beginning to die, Anderson and Rosenfeld were agreeing that though neither of them was young in years, they were both "young enough." They were young, he said in *A Story Teller's Tale,* "with that America of which we both at that moment felt ourselves very much a part."

In late July they crossed over to England, and there Anderson felt even more appreciated, ironically more, perhaps, than in the United States, he wrote his brother and Bab Finley. He met Arnold Bennett and Ford Madox Ford and John Masefield. From Oxford he wrote that he was about to play golf with "the director of the Moscow Art Theater, a hindu Prince and an Englishman." He actually spent time with Edward J. O'Brien and with the novelist John Cournos, both of whom had already paid their respects in print, the one in his short story anthologies, the other in a highly favorable review of *Poor White*. But in the only thing he himself published during the summer, a piece called "Hello Yank," which appeared in the English Tory weekly *Saturday Review* on August 6, he stressed the fact that he was an American, a typical American, and went on to say that what he disliked, what all Americans disliked, was being patronized. True, Americans might be childlike and "dreadfully unsure" of themselves, but only a small portion of them were sons of England; true, they spoke the same language (or didn't, many Englishmen would say), but just possibly they were "making a new language," a language enriched by their own special experience. Four days later, on August 10, 1921, he boarded the ship that would take him back to resume the task of finding that language.

EIGHT

Another Flight

1921-1922

BOTH IN THE UNITED STATES and abroad, Anderson's fame increased. When his collection of stories — *The Triumph of the Egg* — came out in the fall of 1921, it met with the highest praise Anderson had as yet received. As he said, the reviewers greeted it "with fire and feeling." There was talk of "unbelievable and glamorous beauty," of "strange beauty and unmistakable power" from H. L. Mencken and John Peale Bishop. Others used superlatives to sum up Anderson himself. Mary Colum (an Irish critic who was not given to saying kind things about America or American writers) said Anderson was now the country's "most significant writer of imaginative prose." In England, Rebecca West wrote that he was "one of the most interesting personalities writing in English today." "Of all the younger American writers," she went on, he was "the one we have most reason to envy."

"Younger American writers" — it was a category that Anderson was forced into in the most significant gesture of all: in October, he learned that he was to receive the first *Dial* award for service rendered to letters by "a young American writer." The prize was two thousand dollars, which was to Anderson an enormous sum of money. In its turn, the *Dial* received unqualified praise for establishing the award and for its choice of the winner. "If the *Dial*'s award each year finds an artist so promising," the *Nation* said, "and helps assure him a period of leisure for further work it can become a priceless element in American literary life." It was a very high honor. After Anderson, the award went to T. S. Eliot, to William Carlos Williams, to Ezra Pound.

It was also a very heavy burden. Anderson began to feel as if his life were being taken away from him, used by others, and returned in forms he could not live with. In December, when he went to hear Francis Hackett give a talk, he was appalled when someone interrupted in a loud voice to announce Anderson's presence in the audience. A few nights before, he had gone to meet with a group of supposedly "revolutionary painters." When he saw that they had invited a photographer and a newspaper reporter in hopes of getting publicity through his presence among them, he swore and left. Francis Hackett literally illustrated what was happening. He sent Anderson a drawing of him fleeing from a mob of fat and well-dressed men. He called it "Celebrity — or the Price of Fame."

Anderson was hardly one to avoid attention. He asked for it. He seemed to thrive on it. He was delighted to imagine that intelligent people were beginning to appreciate him. But this was too much. For all his showiness, he was not a public man. There was "a distinct flavor of vulgarity" in all this "coming out into the open," he wrote his publisher. On the most practical level, it distracted him from his work. He had to begin each day, he said, "by shoveling mud out of the temple." But more seriously, he thought that if he were to accept the idea of achievement, he would be accepting old age and death. It was what he was doing and could do that mattered, not what he had done. What cut most deeply of all was that the forms of life he *had* to live with, had to enter into or else lose all respect for himself, began to avoid him. There were times when he felt he couldn't do what he was meant to do. There were times when he simply couldn't write. "The figures of the fancy slip away," he wrote in November, "the thing within myself that so often makes any and all life possible, doesn't happen." Ostensibly he was a "young" writer with all the time and money in the world to create, a man who could go off and demonstrate how deserving he was of such special treatment. In fact he was a forty-five-year-old man who could not get any writing done.

He need not have seen what that might portend for the future. The immediate contrast was dispiriting enough. At the end of the year, he went east with Tennessee for the holidays to New York, where they stayed with their friends the Blums, and to Westport, where they saw Paul Rosenfeld and Van Wyck Brooks and spent Christmas with Anderson's brother Karl and his family. In January he went back to New York to accept the *Dial* award. At the ceremony, he spoke haltingly about how hard it was for artists to survive in America, and about how he had managed to do it. One friend said he sounded like a Civil War veteran.

Dispirited, he then went through almost exactly the same moves he had gone through the year before, just a little more elaborately now, this time in New Orleans, and this time entirely without Tennessee. By mid-January he had a room on the third floor of an old house on the corner of Royal and Saint Peter streets, in the heart of the French Quarter. He had a table big enough for his books and his writing materials. He had a fireplace. Over its mantle was a picture of the Virgin, beside it two glass candlesticks with crucified Christs on them that would figure prominently in the rush of writing that would come in the two or three months that he stayed. There was a long French window, and a wide gallery where he could pace.

In no time he had established his old routine: in the morning the landlady brought him coffee, he worked until noon, and then he sauntered out, to talk with people or just observe. On a late January day that he described in a letter to Karl, he saw the world's oyster-opening championship settled after lunch, walked on the wharves among "singing Negro laborers" in the afternoon, and watched a prizefight in an outdoor arena at night. He had some money now, not just prize money. His books were finally selling well. After having had a good start, the sales of *Winesburg, Ohio* had fallen off. In the two years since its publication in 1919, it had sold only a little over 3,000 copies, but when it came out in a Modern Library edition in 1922, it sold as much in a month as it had in all of the first year. *The Triumph of the Egg* was going into its third printing; by the end of April, 4,500 copies would be sold.

He felt strong, or at least he did not tire easily. And he was alone the way he liked to be alone: no wives, no lovers, just a waitress he walked with in the afternoons while she was off duty. He wrote Bab Finley about her. She was one of the most beautiful women he had ever known, he said. "She gives me more richly than any one I've known, a sense of a life I'd almost forgotten." He was also saying that though he was alone, and though he knew Bab would gladly join him, *their* relationship was unchanged. "Well," he added, "she has something to teach every other woman I've ever known."

Fairhope had no more than a few artists, but New Orleans, or, more specifically, the hundred or so blocks known as "Le Vieux Carré," had begun to draw a large colony just before Anderson arrived. As New Orleans was becoming the nation's second busiest seaport, the Vieux Carré was becoming the Greenwich Village of the South, rich in history and in its extraordinary mixture of people. Because philanthropists and artists were only just beginning to discover it, it was still affordable.

And New Orleans had its own periodical, started the year before, called the *Double Dealer*. It was to be a "double dealer" (they took the name from the title of a William Congreve play) because it was going to fool both the South and the nation by giving them something other than the "treacly sentimentalities" that usually passed for Southern literature. Like two of the few existing magazines of which the *Double Dealer* editors approved, the *Dial* and the *Little Review*, they published experimental work, in 1922 the first works of Hemingway and Faulkner, works by Hart Crane, Jean Toomer, John Crowe Ransom, Allen Tate, and, most prominently, Sherwood Anderson. Six months before he arrived, they had published an intelligent appreciation of him by Crane. Three years later, they printed an article entitled "Sherwood Anderson and Our Anthropological Age," which claimed that with him "our literature has definitely turned its vision inward." While he was in New Orleans, they published the first of several of his "New Testaments" and an essay entitled "New Orleans, the Double Dealer and the Modern Movement," in which Anderson mentioned the periodical but mostly celebrated New Orleans as the most cultured city in America, *culture* meaning "first of all the enjoyment of life, leisure and a sense of leisure."

The magazine was edited by Julius Friend; its offices were in a loft in a business district on the edge of the Quarter, loaned to them by Friend's uncle. It was the gathering place for writers and artists, "itinerant literary men, restless painters, and all manner of odd fish," James Feibleman, a young poet among them, later said. When Anderson walked in they all stood up, and not surprisingly, he found them delightful, but two weeks later they seemed just overprivileged boys who spent their evenings with society women. Never having encountered "that crew" before, he was curious. He went out with them a few times and found that a few times was enough.

Besides, he had gone off to be alone, which is to say, though he might find a muse, someone to play the role of Woman, he had gone off to be with the best version of himself that he could discover — in writing. This time it was *Many Marriages*.

He tried to go on with *Ohio Pagans* but flagged. It was a version of Clyde, of "Bidwell" life, long stretches of which ended up in his next collection of tales. As the title suggests, it was that life transformed by Anderson's experiences in the South, but given his mood the subject was still too constraining. It was like *Poor White,* it had social implications, but Anderson was ready to move out beyond. Who knew to what, but that was the point. He just had to express himself. His goal was to give "the whole expression of [his] own impulse toward life." He was prepared go on for three or four or five volumes, following wherever that impulse led.

He wrote "like a man gone mad," right from the moment he had gotten off the train in January, he told Gertrude Stein. A month later he informed Ben Huebsch that he had written fifty thousand words. He was entering a new phase, writing a new kind of prose. He had it all mapped out. First there had been those imitative "realistic" novels; then, thanks in part to the *Mid-American Chants,* the period of *Winesburg, Ohio, Poor White,* and *The Triumph of the Egg.* Now, having written most of *A New Testament,* he was launched into another "mood in writing," a mood represented by *Many Marriages.* In it, he was struggling "to get a quick nervous rush to the thing, something intensely suggestive of modern life." He was after "big game," he said. Some days he had to force himself to leave his writing table; some days, after a morning's work, he found he could hardly walk.

But in trying to construct a "self" that would express something so vast and vague as "modern life" Anderson only limited himself. The self he came up with was really quite familiar. One could remember hearing about it in his previous (and superior, more textured) work. It was the self that had grown up in relative poverty, had a strong mother and a weak father, tried one way or another to make it in America, and ended up aspiring to create a better life for itself than the dominant culture offered. Now he focused primarily on one stage along the way, on how that self had become entrapped in a bad marriage and how it would escape. For all the copies it would sell, critics and readers would recognize that self and begin to turn away from Anderson, not allowing for the possibility, the fact, that he was more resourceful — a better man — than that. There would be another mood, another phase. But it was true for now. Though Anderson would become more and more visible and his life no less various than before, the quality of his writing fell off. And he knew it better than anyone.

The previous December he had published a story in *Broom* about marriage that he called "The Contract." The man in it is an attractive visiting speaker at a discussion group, the Thursday Club, that reminds one of the Round Table Club that he and Cornelia had joined in Elyria. The woman is the local Eve — she understands "the depth of his stupidity." He is no match for her. When they are seen together on an outing, she fears scandal, feels beaten for a moment, but then becomes quite sure of herself. "The whole fact of organized life stood back of her trembling figure," Anderson writes. So she secures a "contract" — he says he'll marry her. Anderson described the aftermath in stark, grim terms. When he looks at her, he feels "like one condemned to beat with bare hands against a cold stone wall. The wall was as hard as adamant, but was surfaced with some warm soft growth." Having proposed, "he felt like a beast who in playing about at night in a forest has suddenly put his foot into a trap."

It is a tight story, the frustration and rage nicely understated, but Anderson wasn't satisfied. In January he told Crane he agreed with him: no, it didn't seem to "come off." Whether he believed that or whether he was just being gracious, he was soon happily absorbed in writing 260 pages about breaking such a contract.

Here is what Anderson means by "many marriages," in what is the new manner — both looser than the prose of the second phase and, at the same time it seems, one long, pained gasp:

> One might think of people constantly passing in and out of each other. In all the world there would be no more secrecy. Something like a great wind would sweep through the world.
> "A people drunk with life. A people drunk and joyous with life."

Or:

> If one kept the lid off the well of thinking within oneself, let the well empty itself, let the mind consciously think any thoughts that came to it, accepted all thinking, all imaginings, as one accepted the flesh of people, animals, birds, trees, plants, one might live a hundred or a thousand lives in one life. To be sure it was absurd to go stretching things too much, but one could at least play with the notion that one could become something more than just one individual man and woman living one narrow circumscribed life. One could tear down all walls and fences and walk in and out of many people, become many many people. One might in oneself become a whole town full of people, a city, a nation.

The man possessed by this vision is John Webster, a washing-machine manufacturer, breaking out of his marriage and about to run off with his stenographer.

He begins by coming home from work one day, taking off all his clothes, and pacing up and down in front of the mirror, admiring himself. When his wife and daughter come in, he tells his daughter how his marriage has declined ever since he first came upon his wife, lying naked at a friend's house, and agreed to marry her to save her from her shame. His daughter sits on his bed in her nightgown, and as he tells his tale, he strokes her leg, squirms on his belly, kisses her feet. Horrified by what seems like a violation of her consciousness, the psychological equivalent of the consummation of her marriage, his wife sinks down "like some great animal on all fours" and then retreats into the bathroom where she poisons herself. (Small wonder that the painter Balthus admired Anderson above all American writers and considered *Many Marriages* the best of all his books.)

At one point in the middle of the novel, Webster has an image of himself standing in front of a picture of the Virgin, with two candlesticks with their crucified Christs on either side, opening up a box, taking out a silver crown, putting it on his head, and declaring: "I crown myself a man." He deserves it, the text suggests, because he has been so open, because he has the courage to leave. In the foreword Anderson asks his reader to reflect with him on those seemingly trivial moments that become suddenly gigantic undertakings in altered circumstances, entering a room, for example, when you want to say to the woman seated there: "It is not my intention to continue living in this house." "Why has it become so difficult for you to take the three steps towards the door?" he asks. "Why do your hands tremble like the hands of an old man?" At the very end he has the same image of himself, standing before his mantle, placing the silver crown on his head. As Webster and the stenographer were on their way to catch the 4:00 A.M. train to Chicago, he worried that she would wake people up with the sound of her heels on the sidewalk; at first he didn't have the courage to tell her. But he musters it, he tells her to walk on the grass, and that makes him worthy of his crown, it makes him a man. The man who can dissolve a bad marriage and go on to tell his stenographer to walk on the grass is a man who can take all nations into himself. In Webster's mind, and in the mind of the man who made him, they amount to the same thing.

"After it is all over with some woman, what does he do?" Anderson asked of a writer ten years later, in his second-to-last novel. "He makes literary material of it" is his answer. "He fools no one. Every one knows." Nor was anyone fooled by *Many Marriages*. Because it was so clearly Anderson, Stein did not like it as a novel, but liking the man so much, she registered her disapproval gingerly: "You do a little tend to find yourself a little more interesting than your hero and you tend to put yourself in his place." When he reviewed it for the *New York Herald,* F. Scott Fitzgerald said that it was "the full-blown flower of Anderson's personality," but *he* liked it. Rather than regret the absence of any social context, he marveled that the narrative existed in what was almost "an absolute vacuum." A month later he wrote Anderson, saying the book had stayed with him, he liked it even more than he had said in his review, it was "a haunting book."

Judgment seems beside the point. *Many Marriages* is a bad novel, but who else could write a novel so bad in just the way *Many Marriages* is bad? It is one volume (as it turned out), devoted to a transition in one man's life, and on and on it goes. As Stein put it, "There should be a beginning a middle and an ending, and you have a tendency to make it a beginning an ending an ending and an ending." One might criticize the lack of impersonality, or of form; one might criticize the lack of novelistic detail; on the other hand, one might well be mesmerized. As for Anderson, he had something he had to tell himself: he had to get out of marriage, he had to end, and end, and end.

Certainly "The Contract" and, all told, *Many Marriages* seem to emanate from Anderson's feelings about his first marriage, but his feelings about marriage in general had come to be so strong he did not need to specify. When he went back to Chicago in March of 1922, he entered what he called "a god-forsaken time." It was as if there were nothing there, no friends, nothing in his marriage. Tennessee's building on Division Street was being renovated, so she came out to Palos Park to stay. It was clearly something he didn't want. He had "invited her," he told Lewis Galantiere, and then, as if to comment on his lack of feeling, asked sourly: "Am I not a generous cuss?" Her presence in his little "box" in the middle of nowhere soon proved more than he could stand, so in June he moved into an apartment on the South Side, and she went back up north to Ephraim. Then in early July he fled the area altogether, in a secondhand Ford. Ben Huebsch said he could use his apartment on Saint Luke's Place in New York. After that, he didn't know. Perhaps he would go to Europe for a year or two. In August he put the matter squarely to Stein: "Have run away from all my friends, including friend wife."

With *Many Marriages* Anderson did start something new. For six or seven years he continued to try to express his "own impulse toward life." He did it in prose, in what would turn out to be his most immediately popular novels, in several more strictly autobiographical volumes. He did it too in his movements from place to place all over America. Nineteen twenty-two was the beginning of what Brooks called "his roaming years." And in 1922, ten years after his flight from his office in Elyria, he resigned from Taylor-Critchfield. Without any fanfare, that year he finally cut all his ties with the advertising and the business world.

Before leaving Chicago, Anderson reminded Bab Finley that he had "a half diseased desire" to make himself appear heroic in such circumstances, but this time he wasn't going to give in to it. He wasn't even going to take her up on her invitation to stop by and see her in Indianapolis. He was under no illusions about what he had done, and he didn't want to cause any more pain. He didn't even want to be known: the recognition he had achieved for himself seemed a mockery. "I have thought the remedy to be a long period of being unknown," he wrote Rosenfeld on his way east, "even if necessary losing my name."

On the trip, he had a taste of anonymity, and he enjoyed it. A group of friends and acquaintances from Clyde had organized a celebration for him on the shore of Sandusky Bay, a big cookout, "with wine and song." One of them told him that they were proud of him; they were not sure why, they didn't know what he had gone on to do in the world, but they were proud of him anyway. The residents of Clyde were in fact very slow to honor him. When he left town as a young man, he faded from their memory. Just before he died, he was still wondering whether the library had or even wanted copies of his books. But on this occasion, he was happy not to be reminded that he had made a name for himself as a writer.

A week later he looked up Hart Crane in Cleveland and had further cause to regret being a famous man of letters. He came to dinner, and by the end of the evening their friendship was over. He had enjoyed the young man's praise and had reciprocated with intelligent criticism of Crane's verse. His feelings were more than usually paternal, given Crane's desire to abandon the family candy business. The evening began well, with Crane now, finally, able to express his long-standing admiration for Anderson to his face, but after dinner Anderson got into an argument with Gorham Munson, who at twenty-six, had just founded *Secession,* a little magazine that welcomed younger, more experimental writers than Anderson. Munson did not share Crane's enthusiasm for this honored (and, as far as he was concerned, pretentious) guest. He cared even less for Anderson's friend Paul Rosenfeld. Munson was writing a book on Waldo Frank, Rosenfeld had panned Frank's *Dark Mother,* Munson attacked Rosenfeld, Anderson defended him and called Munson "a colossal egotist." They almost came to blows. Anderson should have known better. It was the sort of thing he liked least in the world, he wrote Crane the day before he left town. What he regretted most was his own "stupidity in being drawn into a literary argument." He was sorry he hadn't made any effort to see Crane before he left, but in his mood it was best for him "to hunt solitude."

He found it in Ben Huebsch's apartment and set to work — again — "like a crazy man." Trying satire, he wrote a piece on the industrialization of his native state ("Ohio: I'll Say We've Done Well") that appeared in the *Nation* in August, and another on modernist movements in the arts ("The Triumph of a Modern") that he would include in *Horses and Men,* his next volume. The secret of the genre, he told his brother, lay in writing delicately, sympathetically: "Any sign of patronage would ruin it." But right then, he had no sympathy, least of all for himself. His tone was cutting, wry:

> I once had a perfectly good little factory over in Ohio, and there was a nice ash-heap in a vacant lot beside it, and it was on a nice stream, and I dumped stuff out of the factory and killed fish in it and spoiled it just splendid for a while.

Nor did he imagine anyone could do anything about the ruination of the environment and the degradation of men's lives. There were a few green spots left here and there throughout Ohio, he said. In Cleveland, you could get a glimpse of the lake. But a little more effort and there would be nothing but houses "blacked up with soot" and factories in which men drilled holes in pieces of iron all day — 23 million in a lifetime, by his estimate. His faith in politics was at its lowest ebb, just where it had been the spring before, when he had thought for a moment of the efforts of a "Big Bill" Haywood or a Eugene Debs, men trying to make life "easily wonderful," and written: "As the flapper on the streets says, 'where do they get that stuff?'"

At the end of August, he told Karl that as well as the satires he had written "five short stories and a long poem." They were about what interested him most: himself, what kind of a man he was, what kind of a man it was who would leave Tennessee.

The most startling result he titled simply "A Man's Story." It was about stepping all over a woman. He had introduced the idea many years before, in writing *Talbot Whittingham,* just before separating from Cornelia, but the form for it was not right. Now he had it — "a longish short story" — and, fueled with the urge to explain (and with whiskey), he filled it out. Like "Hands," it came in a rush, twelve or fifteen thousand words, all one night and into the next afternoon. Like "Hands," it was always a favorite.

It is not Poe, certainly not Chekhov, but Anderson *in extremis.* It is about a man, a poet, who in passing through Kansas City meets a druggist's wife, who in turn is so attracted to him that she leaves with him for Chicago. There she devotes herself to him completely, earning their living as a wardrobe woman in a theater by day, and at night sitting in silence, "like a boat in which he had floated on the sea," while he writes. "Your mind should have been a boat in which we could lie together, sleeping and resting," he said in what is presumably the long testament he wrote that fall, "but I am afraid that I should have become truly insane and run away in the night." It is the intimacy, the devotion, that a man cannot stand. In "A Man's Story," he does not flee. Instead, as he is walking along with her one day, a crazed admirer from the theater shoots her. He hardly notices. When they go back to their grimy quarters, she builds a fire and finally collapses at his feet, having been alive in dying as he had been dead to the world. And then there arises Anderson's problem: how is a man to get out with a dead woman (or a woman whom he considers dead weight) blocking his way to the door? He nudges her with his foot, and when that doesn't work he does what he had done before: he steps on and over her, and departs.

But then there are further questions: What are we to think of such a man? What is he to think of himself? Or, as he poses it at the outset of the story:

> "Can a man be wholly casual and brutal, in every outward way, at a moment when the nearest and dearest to him is dying, and at the same time, and with quite another part of himself, be altogether tender and sensitive?"

The answer would seem to be yes, yes he can. He had concluded so before: along with his boyish sensitivity and desire to create, there was cruelty; along with his desire for "many marriages," there was his beastly sexuality. "One was a male and at the proper time went toward the female and took her," he had John Webster explain to his daughter. "There was a kind of cruelty in nature and at the proper time that cruelty became a part of one's manhood."

In a long section of another story, "Broken" ("A Chicago Hamlet," when it was collected in *Horses and Men*), Anderson has an adman tell of an adventure with the wife of an Ohio farmer for whom he once worked. She is another "other woman," a version of Gretchen, the housekeeper, in his very first story, of the baby sitter, of the tobacconist's wife, and he, he is a man who has retained an "almost holy modesty" that prevented his achieving "the kind of outstanding and assertive manhood we Americans seem to think we value so highly." But he is also a brute. One night the farmer's wife, a German woman, comes out to the barn where he sleeps. Not a word is exchanged, just one embrace, one kiss. He feels no desire, in fact he is rather contemptuous of women. Just one kiss, and ever after this Hamlet has an image in his mind of a woman, of Woman, walking away from him, "her body a broken thing" — "fairly rushing along, and yet, you see, she was all broken to pieces."

Ultimately Anderson was exploring the question of manhood; ultimately he was asking what it took for a man to grow up (at whatever age). He asked that question specifically in a tale that drew on his memories of growing up in an all but fatherless family, a tale he called "The Sad Horn Blowers." "One stood face to face with manhood now," he wrote:

> One stood alone. If only one could get one's feet down upon something, could get over this feeling of falling through space, through a vast emptiness.
> "Manhood" — the word had a queer sound in the head. What did it mean?

For the time being, he settled the issue most successfully in the best of the stories he wrote in the fall, "The Man Who Became a Woman." Men's efforts in "The Sad Horn Blowers" are, as the title suggests, quite puny. In other stories they are bewildering, at best. Perhaps a man could happily be a man if he could be a woman first.

Like Anderson, the central figure, Herman Dudley, left home at nineteen. (Unlike Anderson — or anyone else in Anderson's writings — he is, as he tells his story, happily married.) Like Anderson (once a "chambermaid in a livery stable"), he spent time in a kind of latency period among the types that frequent country racetracks, in the soothing company of horses, a symbolic gelding in particular. He was happiest with his friend Tom Means, something a man grown up in a homophobic culture has to admit to cautiously:

> To tell the truth I suppose I got to love Tom Means, who was five years older than me, although I wouldn't have dared say so, then. Americans are shy and timid about saying things like that and a man here don't dare own up he loves another man, I've found out, and they are afraid to admit such feelings to themselves even. I guess they're afraid it may be taken to mean something it don't need to at all.

Anderson had tried to combat those fears before, most famously in "Hands." Now he would defend a different kind of man, not just the grotesque Wing, encouraging boys to dream, but the likes of those boys themselves, being (in their friendship), dreaming of, and becoming something more than what the culture says is manly. In Herman's case, the something more is woman — thus his name: Her/man.

Tom is Herman's idol. Tom wants to be a writer, to write a book about the great racing driver Pop Geers, "to show that there was at least one American who never went nutty about owning a big factory or being any other kind of a hell of a fellow." Herman is that writer, the narrator, telling his story, telling it in a tentative, gentle voice — tending to his knitting, as he says — that verifies his extraordinary claim.

The effects of that other kind of manhood are all around, on the infernal landscape, like the one Anderson wrote about in his satirical essay on Ohio, all lit up by coke ovens; but most immediately and terrifyingly, the effect can be seen in the figure Herman meets in a bar where he goes one night, to live it up, perhaps to find a whore, and be like other men. When that figure, a ghostly redhead, beats up a man who taunts him, and, once the man is down, crushes his shoulder with his boot, Herman's response is . . . to become a woman. He looks in the mirror behind the bar and sees the face of a woman. He knows what it must be like to face the brutality of a man. That is what it is like, again, when, actually mistaken for a woman, he is attacked by two black swipes as he is about to fall asleep in the hayloft. He escapes, flees into the dark night, and stumbles through a horse's skeleton; he is born again, "all that silly nonsense about being a girl" burned out of him.

But he has *known* what it is like to be a woman. To him, women can no longer be whores, the means to specious manhood, nor can they be the opposite, the other specious means: virgins, made for him, "by God, perhaps," "shy and afraid" of everyone else but him. In the confusion of his adolescence, Herman dreams of both but comes to feel how women really feel.

It is not that Anderson opted for sensitivity in the course of writing these tales that fall, or that his brutishness fell away. He always encouraged sympathy and understanding; but he was no clearer about what to do with the fact that men were sexual beings. Nor did he ever free himself from gender stereotypes. For all his sympathy, women remained "women." A man might become a woman and gain by it. He was not likely to be drawn by a woman who had become a man. But in "The Man Who Became a Woman" Anderson imagined as much about a man as he ever had, or did. No "grotesque," no simple "hell of a fellow," Herman *is* more of a man for having had a woman in him and for sharing that with us.

Many of the tales concerned men and manhood, and so it was appropriate that when he collected them the next year in *Horses and Men,* he dedicated the volume to Theodore Dreiser, a man whom he had always admired. He prefaced the volume with the short tribute to Dreiser that he had published in the *Little Review* in 1916; the dedication took this unusual form:

> *To Theodore Dreiser*
> *In whose presence I have sometimes had*
> *the same refreshed feeling as when in*
> *the presence of a thoroughbred horse.*

That fall Anderson saw something of his idol for the first time, if only by virtue of living nearby: Dreiser was staying three doors down on Saint Luke's Place. Anderson soon learned that Dreiser was indeed that man whom he had heard about, and had described in his earlier tribute, as so sensitive that when he once paid a visit to an orphan asylum he was reduced to tears watching the little children file past him. (He also learned that Dreiser had taken no offense at the dedication, as he had feared he would.) Now Anderson was so in awe of his neighbor that he could barely bring himself to knock. When he did, Dreiser came to the door, and Anderson announced himself — and Dreiser shut the door in his face. Anderson was furious, but later in the day he received a note assuring him that Dreiser was indeed the man he thought he knew and loved. Dreiser explained that when he saw Anderson at the door he was embarrassed too; he was very sorry, and would Anderson come to a party, a bachelor party, he was giving.

There is some question as to whether Anderson in fact attended the party or whether he just repeated the story of what went on as he heard it from a critic of the day named Ernest Boyd. The guest list was impressive anyway: besides Boyd, H. L. Mencken, the critic Carl Van Vechten, the writer Llewellyn Powys, and Burton Rascoe, then a reviewer for the *New York Tribune,* were there. It was potentially a lively group, but they all sat around the walls of a rugless room, waiting for Dreiser to offer them drinks, and in the meantime making increasingly futile stabs at conversation. Relief seemed to come in the form of F. Scott Fitzgerald, bearing a bottle of champagne with which he hoped to honor his host, but Dreiser promptly took it to his icebox, and the dashing young author was reduced to joining the others along the wall and to reaching into his overcoat to draw on his own private stock. To Anderson, it was all fine, proof of Dreiser's greatness, of a piece with his sitting there, folding and refolding his handkerchief at the orphan asylum, with his inability to confront Anderson at the door. Perhaps Dreiser was the most important writer living, Anderson wrote his son a few years later, and not just because of his writing. In fact his prose could be crude, as everybody said. He was great because he had in him "the most male tenderness." "Manliness — maleness really — implies tenderness," Anderson said.

In 1922, the country began seven years of economic prosperity and high living. The government spent $10 million a year trying to circumvent rumrunners, but Prohibition brought with it a world of speakeasies and nightclubs and, by 1926, $3.5 billion of illegal trade. In New York too, Stein might have said, everyone was twenty-six. Anderson was forty-six, a famous writer, but too old to make the requisite trips up to Harlem — or out to Long Island.

After time abroad and in Saint Paul, Minnesota, the Fitzgeralds returned to New York that fall to satisfy the city's expectations of what "the Jazz Age" was like, and in late September or early October, they invited Anderson and John Dos Passos up to the Plaza to have lunch. Nothing as flashy as diving in a fountain, but still, a gathering of stars. Both Anderson and Fitzgerald had praised Dos Passos's *Three Soldiers.* Dos Passos had told Anderson: "There's nobody in the country such a note means so much from as from you." Fitzgerald admired

Anderson. It started as an elaborate affair, with champagne and lobster croquettes. During lunch Dos Passos took refuge in talk with Anderson about writing as Scott and Zelda tried to embarrass him with probing questions about sex. And then, as if it were a preview of a scene from *The Great Gatsby,* the Fitzgeralds said they wanted to go out to Great Neck, Long Island, to check on a house that they had rented, and said they wanted to see Ring Lardner, who lived there. Dos Passos regretted the part he was made to play. He went, and was embarrassed by Fitzgerald's mockery of the real estate agent's pitch, then depressed to find a Lardner too drunk to talk, and finally fed up when a ferris wheel ride they took on the way home to salvage the excursion turned sour. If for no other reason than that he was too old for it, this was not Anderson's kind of show. He had gone back down to Saint Luke's Place after lunch.

Anderson was drawn into the circle of artists (among them Marcel Duchamp and Carl Van Vechten and the dancer Adolph Bolm) that constituted the salon of the Stettheimer sisters on West Fifty-eighth Street, and again, though he may initially have been pleased to join in, he ultimately realized that he did not belong. This time the gatherings were just too precious. Sister Florine was a painter, and her studio was draped in cellophane curtains of the sort she would use for the Gertrude Stein–Virgil Thompson opera *Four Saints in Three Acts.* Sister Ettie aspired to be a writer. Anderson did strike up a correspondence with her, and in a passage of the *Notebook* that he published in 1926, he recalled that the two had felt something for each other when they met. She seemed like "some warm exotic plant," and it may have been that she sensed the earthiness in him. But then he dismissed her, as he had been tempted to dismiss Rosenfeld, as being out of touch, as being "born rich." And as for her books, the people in them had no roots, and the elegant houses in which they lived, he implied, were uglier than anything he had seen among the poor. "Wriggling" in response, she wrote Anderson that she was "quite normal," that she could sew and scrub and cook as well as any working woman. As for what she found attractive about him:

> I did not feel you particularly as "of the soil"; I felt in your presence a sense of life such as one feels when holding a bird in the palm of one's hand in the quiver of its beating heart.

But after number fifteen of the "Notes Out of a Man's Life," their relations were few and formal.

In the fall of 1922, Sherwood Anderson was as respected as any writer in America. Each of his last three books had been more warmly received than the one before. Most of *Many Marriages* was being published serially in the *Dial,* and in the three months following its publication in book form the following February it would sell more than nine thousand copies. There were parties in his honor, and there were honors, like the *Bookman's* placing him on its "Committee of Contemporary American Fiction," along with Willa Cather, William Allen White, and others. But one never feels that Anderson fit in. The great were too great, the young moved too fast, the rich were too fine.

But he did find another friend in Alfred Stieglitz. Stieglitz was another great man, but this time one who was twelve years older and a master at encouraging younger artists. Ushered there by Rosenfeld, Anderson had been in Alfred Stieglitz's presence before. He had seen the Georgia O'Keeffe show at Stieglitz's famous gallery, "291," in 1917 when he came east and met the editors of the *Seven Arts.* The work that Stieglitz showed and produced, and the integrity of the man in doing so, had already driven home to Anderson "the old lesson," as he put it, "that one cannot muddy oneself and be clean." But he did not get to know Stieglitz until 1922. When he did, he could face him as well as look up to him.

He saw Stieglitz as "Poet" (the title of the "testament" he dedicated to him), "Poet" incarnate, hurling himself against the iron gates of life, "joy and love and faith" shining in his eyes; and Stieglitz saw Anderson in the same lofty, potentially embarrassing terms, and he told him so. The year after they met, Stieglitz wrote Anderson that he would never forget what Anderson made him feel when he walked into Stieglitz's apartment on Sixty-fifth Street, where he and O'Keeffe (though not yet married) were staying: "Strength and Beauty. Or should I say simply Great Beauty for Beauty is always strong." They had not seen each other often, he went on, but every time they did he noticed changes in Anderson, his face undergoing a change — "ever beauty but coupled with a haunted moment" — and as a result he came to like Anderson more and more.

However much their personalities differed, the two were equally idealistic, idealistic about the possibility of catching the truths of their feelings in their art, and idealistic about America. (One cannot help thinking that Stieglitz's famous photograph of a gelding, for example, with its ironic title, "Spiritual America," was inspired by Anderson's interest in the symbolic possibilities of horses.) They were equally convinced that Woman was closer to nature than men, that she felt and perceived the world differently. As Stieglitz put it, she "receives the *World* through her Womb. Mind comes second." (For him, O'Keeffe's greatness lay in her having fearlessly expressed that supposed truth.) And at the time, the two were striving equally hard to transcend themselves, or move past their respective realisms, Anderson in his testaments, Stieglitz in his cloud series. Only their media differed, as Stieglitz pointed out. "That's all we are here for — to aid each other in realizing Self," he wrote, "as beings with potentials far beyond all skies and stars":

> There is a reality — so subtle that it becomes more than reality. That's what I'm trying to get down in photography. — That's not juggling with words. — I feel you are after a similar thing and are working at it in *your* way as I work it out in *my* way.

But at more than midlife, both men had reason to seem "haunted," for both were working against the sense that they had done their best work. Finally, in their personal lives, both men were trying to extricate themselves from marriage and to begin anew.

No evidence of Stieglitz's sympathy and respect for Anderson is more compelling than the photographs he took of him that winter. No evidence of what strength lay behind Anderson's gentleness is more moving. William Faulkner said that Anderson trusted only Stein, but he must have meant among writers. In Stieglitz's presence Anderson inspired a different image, still a tender one, but this time not a quivering but a rooted one. It is as if Stieglitz knew that like himself, Anderson could always renew himself. The photographic images show Anderson open, sensuous, inviting, but not appealing. In several of them, behind Anderson there is something like a tree. "You seemed to stand there in my forest like some wonderful tree that had no name," Stieglitz wrote him, "a large simple tree — with some branches and tender leaves." The most famous of them, slightly blurred, Anderson later called "the turgid head of Anderson."

What Anderson saw in Stieglitz he celebrated in a short article that he published, along with his "Impressions" of Stein and Rosenfeld, Lardner and Sinclair Lewis, in the *New Republic* in October 1922. Lardner and Lewis appear as undeveloped men, Lardner like the shy boys who used to hang around the "town toughs" in Clyde, ashamed to admit they hungered after beauty; Lewis, unable to admit to a love of life, and so delighting in imagining that other men are dead. Stein and Rosenfeld, of course, Anderson said, knew no such fears. Two weeks later, Anderson unveiled the figure of his new friend: "As for myself," he said, "I have quite definitely come to the conclusion that there is in the world a thing one thinks of as maleness that is represented by such men as Alfred Stieglitz." In Anderson's mind, Stieglitz represented maleness because he remained a crafts-man, in love with his tools and his materials, in a mechanical age. He represented it simply because he did not need to question it. "True maleness does not boast of its maleness," Anderson wrote.

> Only truly strong men can be gentle tender patient and kindly; and sentimental male strutting is perhaps always but an outpour-ing of poison from the bodies of impotent men.

With and about Stieglitz, he was sure of what it was to be an American man, as clear as he had ever been about the shortcomings of what others thought, confident about the kind of man he was himself.

But though Anderson valued friendship more and more, for him it would never be enough. That fall he also fell in love. It was far harder for him to avoid doing that than to stay clear of a literary argument, especially now that he was once again radically cut off from any kind of family or home. Without love he was lost. He had to have it — such was the pattern — in order to be able to be alone and to work.

NINE

Tutoring Faulkner and Hemingway
1922-1926

ELIZABETH PRALL SEEMED PERFECT, Cornelia and Tennessee in one. Physically, she was like neither of them. She was smaller, more delicate, less of a presence. But like them both she was from the Midwest, and like the one she was very proper, like the other, able to move with confidence through bohemia. She had gone to the University of Michigan and had come to New York to go to library school. By the time Anderson met her in the fall of 1922, she was running the Doubleday bookstore in what had been the carriage driveway of Lord and Taylor's on Fifth Avenue, and she was living on the top floor of a brownstone she owned in the Village, on Charlton Street.

Margaret Lane, Cornelia's sister, shared her quarters with her. Edna St. Vincent Millay lived nearby, as did Max Eastman, editor first of the *Masses* and then of the *Liberator,* and his sister Crystal. Elizabeth had not known them at the time, but some of her tenants had known Anderson ten years ago during the renaissance days in Chicago: Susan Glaspell occupied one floor; in the basement apartment, Floyd Dell lived with a woman who Elizabeth said was "clearly not his wife." It was there that Dell was handed a subpoena to appear in court for having defended conscientious objectors in the pages of the *Masses.* After Dell left, Stark Young moved in. He was a friend and former teaching colleague of Elizabeth's brother; at the time, he was a critic for the *New Republic.* (On Young's recommendation, Elizabeth hired William Faulkner as a salesman in her bookstore. "Very elegant and distinguished," she said. "He fitted perfectly into the genteel atmosphere" of her store.) There were other literary personages in the neighborhood, Maxwell Bodenheim, for example, whom she called "one of the filthiest poets around, physically and poetically," but she managed to keep her distance. "We had a clique of our own," she said, "that had nothing to do with the more garish and more outlandish personalities of the village."

Dell told her about the early days in Chicago, Margaret Lane about her former brother-in-law and his "determinedly 'emancipated'" wife, Tennessee Mitchell. Before she even met him, Elizabeth had an impression of "this great free spirit of the mid-West" that she ought to get to know. When they met, he gave an irresistible performance: his striking costume, the shock of what was now gray hair that complemented it, the extravagant stories, the way he told them, playing all the roles himself! She thought he was courting Margaret and went about her business — which undoubtedly made her all the more attractive — but soon he was taking her to places he had discovered on his walks, sitting her down in little bistros and talking endlessly about himself. She sat and listened, as intent upon his dark eyes as on anything he was saying, and he was inspired by her attention. "I ran into the road, plunged into the road," he wrote in a "testament" he titled simply "An Emotion: to E.P.":

> My torn feet were touched by the golden dust of the road. My fingers tore at the gold and silver gown that wrapped her about. With a little whispering laugh she passed into me. I was drawn into her and was healed.
> The little bells were calling, calling.
> She came with me in at the door of my house. My house stands at the edge of the road, at the edge of the forest. The little tinkling bells sound in the rooms of my house.
> The little bells are calling, calling.

Elizabeth was almost forty. Anderson was forty-seven. He was a man wearied from traveling, recalling places where he had stopped, recalling Clyde and Palos Park, and he was an adolescent, hanging on to the skirts of his virgin queen. Other men might pause a while, but he was one to think of marriage right away.

By the end of the year, Elizabeth had thrown up her job and gone to California to be with relatives, in part because Tennessee had spread the word that Elizabeth was breaking up her marriage, in part to prepare herself for the new life that Anderson had described to her.

"Like a teenager," she said in retrospect, "I was running away from my home in New York to find adventure." Thinking he had finally found a woman whom he could happily take into his home, Anderson prepared to go to Reno, Nevada, to obtain a divorce from Tennessee.

The train ride west in February was long and boring, but also welcome. He had had too much, Anderson said, of "New York and the neurotics" and too much of his own prominence. Nineteen twenty-two had been a year of "devastating intensity of feeling." His nerves were shattered. Going out West would do him good. He was going, he thought, to get a quick divorce. There in Reno what he called in March "a sort of process of internal adjustment," "a kind of inner distillation," could begin. As it turned out, the proceedings dragged on for more than a year, but that gave him plenty of time to confirm himself as his newfound man in the most explicitly auto- biographical writing he had done so far.

In 1923 Reno was a quiet, friendly, unusually tolerant small town, even as it was well on its way to becoming "the biggest little city in the world." A famous divorce involving a steel magnate and a showgirl and a wife who had come there to make her case had put Reno on the map in 1906. By 1910, the town was turning out 300 divorces a year (by 1931, over 4,700). The residence requirement was six months and a professed intention to make Nevada home, one that reformers fought but that was reaffirmed by an initiative measure the year before Anderson arrived. Soon the residence requirement would be reduced to three months and then, what with competition from other states and the fact of a profitable business during the Depres- sion, to six weeks. A solid middle-class town, it had its share of churches and fraternal organizations, and it had a small state univer- sity. It had more than its share of law offices and beauty parlors, and legal gambling and prostitution. "We have six laws," the saying went, "four of them are unconstitutional."

On the streets, along with Reno's middle-class citizenry, one could see cowboys, Indians wrapped in gaudy blankets, flappers walking dogs, or other future divorcées in jodhpurs. One found the prostitutes on the outskirts of town in what was called the "bull-pen," a ring of little one-room cottages, fronted by a boardwalk and surrounded by a high board fence. Through town ran the Truckee River; out beyond, stretching back east, were sagebrush deserts, and to the west, the snowy peaks of the Sierra Nevada. At an earlier time and in another mood, Anderson might have sought refuge among such characters, but this time he followed the river and the roads out of town.

For all his attacks on men and their machines, their cars especially, Anderson loved to drive more than anyone. He bought an old Dodge roadster and spent countless afternoons driving out into the hills. There was more expanse than he had ever seen, one rise receding before him as he drove, which, when reached, was succeeded by more desert flatlands and more rises. Once into the hills, he walked for hours in the upland valleys and fished. Sometimes he went with a young man he thought was "rather a gentleman," some sort of relative of the Gould family, who liked to "tramp," but mostly he went alone. He took up his painting once again and, admiring craftwork as he did, rented a sewing machine and tried to make a few colorful shirts for himself. He declined an invitation from Mabel Dodge Luhan to visit her in Taos but did accept one to speak at the university. In talking with his hosts he found that they had never heard of the *Seven Arts*. They had "faintly" heard of Carl Sandburg, because of "his *Shows*." "It was a little like talking to the people of Mars," he told Paul Rosenfeld.

The one man whose company Anderson enjoyed was Judge George Bartlett, the man who would eventually grant him his divorce. (Clarence Darrow was Anderson's lawyer back in Chicago.) Bartlett was a crusty soul, whose experiences in Reno led him to write a book called *Men, Women, and Conflict,* later retitled simply *Is Marriage Necessary?* It was an issue Anderson enjoyed debating. (He also cuffed the judge's pants on his sewing machine.) Otherwise, the men Anderson saw only made him depressed about American manhood and about America in general. Infants, he called them. The natives, the cowboys, the gamblers seemed like "noisy brutal children." The only men he could stand were the Basque sheepherders, "silent sheep men," whom he came upon on his walks.

One day Anderson drove out into the country with four men who wanted to see about buying a gold mine. They wanted him along, he suspected, on the off chance that, being a writer, he might publicize their venture. It turned out to be just like a business trip to Cleveland in the old days. Out came the whiskey and the cigars, and the talk of gold soon degenerated into crude, clichéd talk of woman. When he got back, in a letter to Stieglitz and O'Keeffe he registered his shock at coming upon "the immaturity, the badboyishness of men" after trying so hard to imagine "the tender realities" in people. Why couldn't they see the beauty around them? Or "in one's own work sometimes, too," he asked. As it was, "each is afraid of his neighbor, outdoes him in vulgarity to seem manly."

Meanwhile, Elizabeth had received enough entreaties from Anderson to prompt her — much against her family's wishes — to come to Reno. Whether it was lawyers' advice or a matter of propriety, they certainly couldn't stay together. When Elizabeth's brother David came to visit from Berkeley, where he was now teaching philosophy, he warned them against being seen even kissing. But Elizabeth rented a cottage, and there Anderson could come from the little house that he had rented on East Liberty Street, and work, and take his meals.

By mid-June, Anderson's self-distillation process was well under way. He wrote Rosenfeld, telling him that as he must know, he, Anderson, was subject to fits of depression, which seemed at times to approach insanity, and that his only escapes were work or "a few people in whom I feel the power to love" — or, we might say, people who would love him enough to allow him to escape into his work. Elizabeth had proved to be one of those people. She was "a steady sanity" on which he could lean, "a power to love and give real companionship day after day with no mean inferiority in her nature." What she determined to do was avoid the mistake that Cornelia and Tennessee had made: she would not try to change this man, she would just try to adapt herself to his ways.

Each morning Anderson started by writing letters. He would joke that he did it "partly as a substitute for drink," but it was in fact his way of approaching the fictional world, the recreated world, in which he sought to know himself. It was also his way of tightening and securing the network of his friends. In several letters he sifted through his list. In the spring, he named Stein, Dreiser, Rosenfeld, Brooks, Stieglitz. He included nobody from the literary crowd in Chicago (except Ben Hecht "when he isn't being a smarty"), or in New York. They were only "book-made men." In the fall he added Jean Toomer and an admiring English professor from Pittsburgh named Roger Sergel, with whom he had started a correspondence, and Brooks began to fade in his esteem.

In an attack on him in the September issue of the *Dial,* Alyse Gregory had quoted Brooks as saying that Anderson was "bogged and mired in adolescence." Anderson had few illusions about Brooks's view of him, but the news came as a shock, as did the fact that it came in the quarterly that had honored him so highly just the year

before. Brooks explained that he had meant the remark to apply to
D. H. Lawrence and said that Gregory shouldn't have used a remark
dropped in conversation, but Anderson replied that he didn't think
that he *or* Lawrence should be called immature. In fact, wasn't it
Brooks's emotional skittishness that deserved the name? "My dear
Brooks," he wrote, "isn't there at least a chance that the fear of emotional response to life may be a sign of immaturity as anything else?
It does seem so to me." By contrast, Rosenfeld was openly supportive, and Stieglitz had become the source of Anderson's most gratify-
ing reflections of himself.

In May, Stieglitz sent some of the pictures he had taken of Anderson a few months before in New York. In two of them Anderson saw
himself "disintegrated, gone to pieces, fallen down before the ugliness in himself and others." In the "turgid head," he saw the man
who had truly accomplished something. "In that one thing you make
me respect myself," he wrote back. "It is surely a great piece of
work." In the months that followed, he tried to reproduce that second
man in a story of his life, a story he ended up dedicating to Stieglitz
himself. Stranded in Reno, he produced a work that asserts that in
the very act of writing he was a man who could serve as a model for
American men everywhere.

After playing with other titles, like *Immaturity* (which he'd used
for a work he would never finish) and *Straws* (which sounded much
too negative), Anderson called it *A Story Teller's Story*. The repetition
was appropriate: it was the story of the emergence and development
of the equivocal and problematic state of being that was his as a
writer. It was akin to the work he once projected as "the autobiography of the fanciful life of an individual." It was the story of how
he came to have faith in his ability to tell stories, it was his defense
of himself as a creator. At the same time, it was his defense of himself
as "the American Man." The one was the product of the other: the
man coming into being because he was creative, the man being a
man because he had the courage to be a writer, because as a writer
he could expand himself beyond others' confining definitions of
manhood.

In May he wrote Stein, telling her that what he was writing would
cure him of his tendency to be so interested in "the self," that he
would "unload it, — as it were," and she thought so highly of the
result that reviewing it, she put his name on a short list of those
American writers (the others being James Fenimore Cooper, William

Dean Howells, and Mark Twain) who she thought had "essential intelligence." Anderson also thought well of what he did. To him it
was a "gorgeous book," a book every young writer ought to read, a
book that never got the attention it deserved. He asked his son John
to read it as his father's attempt to prove that "the artist man" was
"the most masculine and manly of all men." Though few have shared
Stein's and Anderson's high estimation of the book, it does do that.

It was, by another of his definitions, the story of a man's "adventures with men," a story that began with his realization that there
were no leaders in his life, no men he could respect. Anderson himself
looked for his ideal in Abraham Lincoln. He read everything he could
find on him that summer and wrote about seventy pages on him that
he titled "Father Abraham." He felt that he had grown up with Lincoln (as against that Sunday school teacher, Robert E. Lee), out of
the same soil. When Waldo Frank sent him a biography of Lincoln
in 1918, he wrote back saying that with "no presumptuousness" the
book might have been a study of himself. Now he got more specific:
there was a sensual side to Lincoln that the man was afraid of, he had
an embarrassing visionary for a father, he knew how to step outside
himself, he was a great storyteller. But finally Anderson couldn't
make Lincoln fit his mold. Though he was "a man's man," Lincoln
could not find inner satisfaction in the world at large. He was not,
after all, a writer.

Among the stories that Anderson told for the first time in *A Story
Teller's Story* was a long one about a woman named Nora, who lived
in the house where Anderson had stayed when he first went to Chicago. It was new, but in that it was about male posturing before
women and about their using women when their manhood failed it
was quite familiar. The other "adventures" focused entirely on men,
more specifically, on their impotence as revealed in their stories.
There were those he had heard in the Chicago warehouse and, before
that, in the bicycle factory in Clyde, those he had heard on his trip
to New York to meet the editors of the *Seven Arts* (in pages he tact-
fully cut from the galleys), and those he had watched moviemen
churn out when he went back the next year. He devoted pages con-
trasting an embittered judge, a homosexual, who cynically advised
him to take the material age for what it was worth, with a man who
was literally crippled, but who was strong in his emphatic sense of
other men. In an epilogue, he told of a writer of poison-plotted foot-
ball stories who did not have the courage to grow up and follow the

dictates of his fancy. In each case, he detected self-delusion or dirtiness or fudging — all signs of impotence.

The book being a fanciful rendering of his evolution as a writer, Anderson began with his father and included more sympathetic reflections on him than he ever had before. Irwin appears as the disappointment that he was, but also as a man of unrealized potential. He was a bad actor, he hedged with words, but now Anderson sees him as having lived at the wrong time, a time when the only way a man could dream was through building railroads and factories or drilling gas wells. He had been robbed of his inheritance. The next generation was more tolerant; so the son had been able to develop the father's power with words. In keeping with this reading, Anderson refined the years surrounding his flight from Elyria down to such an extent that the pages in question could be titled simply "When I Left Business for Literature" and published separately. For the climax he used the story of his day at Chartres with Rosenfeld, the day, he now said, when he accepted himself as a storyteller, "come that far on the road toward manhood."

In an essay on "American Fiction" that she wrote in 1925, Virginia Woolf singled out *A Story Teller's Story* as enabling her to understand "the nature of American writers' problems before we see them tussled with or solved." She noted that Anderson kept repeating, "I am the American man," repeating it over and over again "like a patient hypnotising himself." And that was his problem. That was the trouble with American writers: they kept on worrying about the fact that they were American. Woolf acknowledged that in his fiction Anderson had achieved what, after all, very few writers had achieved — he had made "a world of his own" — and her defense of his "softness" could effectively mute the criticism of many of his detractors. He was not a typical American male; as a writer he was no model of impersonality. But he had dared to question the value of the heroic westerner; he had tried to bare his soul. "The softness, the shell-lessness of Mr. Anderson are inevitable," she said, "since he has scooped out from the heart of America which has never been confined to a shell before." But she wished that he would recognize the solution to his "problem": Yes, he was an American. There was nothing he could do about it. He would be much better off if he would just forget the fact and write.

In a few years Anderson would recognize what Woolf was talking about. He would feel that with *A Story Teller's Story* he had begun a period of self-exposure, and he would again "want clothes." But that spring and summer and fall in Nevada he wrote with a "gaiety" he would not experience again in writing for another ten years. By October he had written four hundred and fifty typescript pages. He was delighted. He thought he had solved his "problem" by the very fact that he had isolated and named it.

That of his divorce would not be solved for many months. It was he who had come to Reno and filed for a divorce — on the grounds of desertion. It was a charge Tennessee had little trouble denying, and she did so at first because she did not want the marriage to end. She raised questions about payment for the illustrations of *The Triumph of the Egg,* which Anderson interpreted simply as her unwillingness to let go. Finally Tennessee asked that they delay long enough for her to get a teaching job she wanted, that she be allowed to secure it before there was any adverse publicity. That put him at "the mercy of her whim," he said. "Naturally I am going right ahead." Tennessee's response was that he was like Hemingway: though professedly a realist, he was one of "those great romanticists" who "jump reality without regard for those they jump on." The divorce did not come through until April 1924.

After the divorce, Tennessee developed her skills as a sculptor and continued to teach music and dance. And like Cornelia, she looked back on her marriage a bit cynically — but also with something like nostalgia. In fact, the two of them looked back together. "The most amusing thing," she reported to a friend:

> I hear that S feels that having lived with an artist and then being deserted has made me a sculptor. I told Mrs. A. No. 1 whose reply was — He made me a school teacher and you a sculptor. What a pity it is he doesn't work faster so he can do more for women.

And then Tennessee added, "It's foolish of us to be down on him. He's as he is, a very charming person — maybe it's too much to expect more."

As soon as the divorce was final, Anderson and Elizabeth Prall crossed the border into California to get married. They were met by Elizabeth's mother and brother, her sister Dorothea, Dorothea's husband, Max Radin, and their daughter Rhea, and they all piled into the Pralls' new robin's-egg blue touring car, and, eluding reporters, went in search of a minister who would perform the marriage ceremony. After being turned down by one who would not marry a man who had been divorced, they found a more obliging one on the outskirts of Martinez, California.

After a wedding lunch back in Berkeley, Elizabeth and Sherwood managed to avoid reporters once again and went to San Francisco, where Anderson resorted to the old trick of registering in a hotel under an assumed name for the new purpose of spending time alone with his wife. When they returned to the Pralls' home in the Berkeley hills, however, Anderson invited reporters in and gave them not only the stories they were looking for but also drinks.

For a few weeks, he "had a violent case" on all the Pralls, and there was talk of the Andersons' building there in the neighborhood that consisted of Elizabeth's brother David, their mother, their sister, a violinist who taught at Mills College, and the Radins. With the possible exception of Elizabeth's mother, who was a little overwhelmed by Anderson, they all liked him, but they were, as Rhea Radin put it, "shockingly intellectual" (none more so than her father, who was a biblical and classical scholar as well as Boalt Professor of Law at the University of California), and it soon became apparent that there was no way Anderson would fit in. First there was a dinner at the Radins' that erupted when a couple of local artists attacked "the moderns," among them Stieglitz. Anderson could see that the men were threatened, just taking refuge in the old line that something was being put over on the public, and he could see that there was trouble ahead when one of the artists' wives took his side. As had been the case at Hart Crane's, Anderson should have known better, but some of these artists under discussion were his friends, one in particular, and in such circumstances, he said, "I spit out." It was "a peculiarly emotional evening," after which Elizabeth went upstairs and cried over the fact that people could hurt each other in the name of beauty as well as ugliness. On another occasion, Radin made the mistake of voicing his reservations about *Horses and Men*.

David Prall liked him, but found he had to shout to be heard; and in turn, Anderson thought David was only a "little philosopher . . . from a land far away" who did not expect much from life. If he thought the atmosphere was rarefied in Westport, in Berkeley he must have thought he was in a vacuum. Elizabeth summed up the problem more graciously: Anderson "had very little formal education," she said, "and it contrasted sharply with the bookishness of my family." Elizabeth and Sherwood stayed in Berkeley for a few months, during which time it became obvious that they would be better off in some other part of the country.

While he was there, Anderson gave a lecture at the university entitled "The Modern Writer." Before so many people that he had to
give the lecture twice in one afternoon, he presented himself as the
enemy of shoddy, slick storytelling and of the culture that rewarded
such corruption, and the defender of the "modern movement," which
he defined as workmen's attempts to regain control over the tools and
materials of their crafts. He made the transition and switched roles
by telling his audience that he was from Chicago and quoting an old
Chicago motto: "Put away your hammer and get out your horn."
Chicago was where he was from, but contemplating his next move,
he doubted whether he would ever move *to* Chicago again. He
thought of Mobile, Alabama, but he decided on the most recent place
where he had been at home. For the next two years he would blow
his horn in New Orleans.

Arriving in July 1924, Anderson and Elizabeth rented a stately,
high-ceilinged apartment on the second floor of the Lower Pontalba
Building. From its wrought-iron balcony they could look out over
the city and down on what was once the Place d'Armes. With its
equestrian statue of the city's savior as its focal point, it had been
Jackson Square since 1856. To the left was the Cathedral of Saint
Louis. In September they moved to a house on Saint Peter Street,
nearby but closer to the wharves, where Anderson loved to stroll. By
then, he was one of the main attractions of Le Vieux Carré. Wherever
he went, he was a spectacle. He walked with a blackthorn stick and
with something of a swagger now that he had put on weight. He
wore brown suits that wouldn't show the dust of the racetracks where
he often spent his afternoons, fancy corduroy shirts, kerchief and finger ring, woolen socks spilling out over his shoes. All New Orleans
knew Anderson — "strangers would know that he was something
special as he strolled down Bourbon Street," James Feibleman later
wrote — and as Elizabeth said with some pride, they knew all of
New Orleans.

Anderson was more comfortable with small groups of men who
liked to hear him talk. He re-established contact with the *Double
Dealer* crowd. Feibleman, Julius Friend, the future Louisiana novelist
Hamilton Basso, others from the *Double Dealer,* the *Times-Picayune,*
and Tulane University would meet at one of the less expensive restaurants, such as Gallatoire's, or at a newspaper hangout called Max
in the Alley, or at the Absinthe House, a famous speakeasy, and
always Anderson would be the center of attention. He drank hardly
at all. Elizabeth said she saw him drunk only once in all the years

she knew him. It was his own high spirits that carried him and his listeners along. He was the one among them who had risen to the top; more important, he was the one who had the best stories to tell, and he told them marvelously. His timing was perfect by then, as were the modulations of his deep and ringing voice.

He was what Basso called "our Royal Personage" — theirs in the French Quarter and also, increasingly, in the eyes of those outside. His readership increased with everything he wrote. Abroad, he was published not only in England and France, but in the Soviet Union, Germany, and Sweden. But in one respect he was an obvious commoner: he needed money. It had been good for the soul for him to rid himself of his advertising accounts, but he soon learned that he could not depend on a steady income using the right kind of words. It was extraordinary. When he had come down to New Orleans two years before, he had the *Dial* prize money in hand and the sales of his books were rising, but the $2,000 was long gone, and sales had fallen off. Nor could he depend on what he might make from what he was currently producing. He had sold "A Man's Story" for $750, more than he had made on all his other stories up to that time; then a magazine called *Phantasmus* promised him $3,000 for printing two excerpts from the childhood section of *A Story Teller's Story*. But *Horses and Men* (which contained "A Man's Story") didn't sell well, and after printing excerpts in May and June of 1924, *Phantasmus* simply folded and paid him nothing. The sales of *Many Marriages* declined when the Boston Booksellers' Committee spread the word that the book might be in violation of an obscenity law. Anderson was not exaggerating wildly when he said just before coming to New Orleans a second time, "I was rich and suddenly I am poor."

Once there, he had to consider expenses that hadn't seemed to exist as he was coming into his own as a writer, expenses a family man might face. He had kept in touch with his children through the years. When he lived in Chicago he often went out with Tennessee and his friend George Daugherty to visit his children in Michigan City, Indiana. Tennessee had taken a particular liking to Mimi and tried to make her entrance into her teens a bit more exciting than it would otherwise have been in Michigan City. She gave Mimi hand-me-downs from her wealthy students; she even brought her into town so that she might attend the Francis Parker School for a term. But Anderson had not spent much time with his children since he left Elyria in 1912.

Now his older son, Bob, was eighteen, a high school graduate, and he was determined to be with his father. He followed him to California, hitchhiking much of the way, and then went with him and Elizabeth to New Orleans. He wanted to be a writer, he said. What Anderson could see was that he was "starved for affection." He was confused, and in his confusion, he drank more than he could hold. As for being a writer, Bob seemed to Anderson to be all assurance without anything to back it up, and Anderson felt responsible and tried, he said, "to make him see himself." Since the father and the son were very much alike and were never comfortable with each other, that proved difficult, but Anderson spent time with Bob and tried to launch him on a career. He thought college might help, perhaps Tulane, and then he got him a job on the *Times-Picayune*, but that didn't last. His son John would prove easier to love and would soon show evidence of an artistic talent — as a painter — that was truly promising, and that Anderson happily encouraged. Now that the children were growing up, he wanted to be more of a father to them.

One solution seemed to be a house. Anderson had a memory of the rooms in which he had lived that was like "a desert trail," he had written in *A Story Teller's Story*. "In a sense they haunt my whole life." He set about looking for a house to buy in New Orleans. He wanted his own roof over his head for the first time in his life. He wanted a place where his children could come and be with him. In March of 1925 he wrote Stein, saying he would do anything to get a house — "lecture, spit over the top of boxcars, do anything to get it but make love to ladies I do not fancy."

In January of that year, Bab Finley had set up her fund for the children. His old friend John Emerson lent him money. Elizabeth tried to help by opening a decorator's shop in New Orleans with a friend. He himself had already gone forth to lecture.

He had signed up with the Leigh Lecture Bureau in New York, and that first fall and winter of 1924–25, and again the next fall and winter, armed with three lectures ("The Modern Writer," "Mid-American Writing," and "America: A Storehouse of Vitality"), he virtually toured the country, lecturing in (at least) Boston, New York, Philadelphia, Cleveland, Pittsburgh, Indianapolis, Urbana, Chicago, Nashville, Birmingham, Topeka, Fort Worth, San Diego, and Seattle.

After his first tour, he told what it was like in "When the Writer

Talks" in the pages of the *New York Evening Post Literary Review*. It was exciting, he said, it awakened the actor in him, but then there were those questions afterwards, questions about what it took to be a writer, questions he had spent books, his writing life, it seemed, trying to answer. He would grow impatient, and just as he was about to come up with some "smart impertinent" answer or fling his watch at someone, he would be rescued by his host. Others' reports are less dramatic. People turned out in great numbers and heard "sound and honest doctrine" (as Donald Davidson described his talk at the Centennial Club in Nashville). If they expected to hear something shocking from the author of *Many Marriages,* they were disappointed, but on the whole, they were appreciative.

One who was not was the young William Saroyan, who, when he heard Anderson on the West Coast, thought his idol looked "soft," and that he was "squawking," or nagging, he said, as if American life's not being what it should be were the result of some deliberate plot to embarrass him. "I saw him fat when I was lean and hungry," he wrote. "I felt ashamed for him, because I couldn't understand what he was doing in front of a room full of middle-aged clubwomen, talking." His response was relatively kindly, but he could also sound like another of the younger generation, waiting his turn: "'I'll never get fat,' I thought. 'I'll never do that. Stand there like a blithering idiot.'"

Anderson could make as much as five hundred dollars a lecture, but he was still scared about money matters. He thought he could help himself by changing publishers. During the fall of 1924, Horace Liveright had come to New Orleans, looking to expand his already impressive list of writers. He was a colorful and persuasive man. Handsome, dark-eyed, and pale-skinned (he was once described as looking like "a referee at a snake race"), he was a gambler and a play-producer, as well as a publisher. His offices were as likely to be filled with actresses and showgirls as writers. Elizabeth didn't like him. He seemed the kind of man who would take your hand under the dinner table. And Anderson himself described him as "an eager rather corrupt (I'm afraid) child," but it was Anderson who first broached the possibility of abandoning Ben Huebsch, the man who had published *Winesburg, Ohio,* and thus introduced him to the world. "[I] felt like a dog," Anderson confessed, "wanted to do it and at the same time didn't want to." But eventually he did.

In contrast to Liveright, Anderson thought Huebsch was an "honest, fussy old maid." Honest, and intelligent. Huebsch had taken a chance on Anderson when it wasn't an obvious thing to do. He was inefficient, but to the man whose reputation involved scorn for slick business practices that seemed almost a virtue. On the other hand, *A Story Teller's Story* had come out in October; the year was almost over, and Anderson had yet to find a copy of it in a New Orleans bookstore, he told Liveright.

In April 1925 Anderson signed an agreement with Liveright whereby he would receive a hundred dollars a week as a kind of advance. He would receive 15 percent of sales, and 10 percent from Modern Library reprints (which meant *Poor White* as well as *Winesburg, Ohio* by then). For his part, Anderson agreed to produce some sort of volume once a year. The agreement was for five years. This arrangement promised to relieve Anderson of worries about money once again, leaving him free to write. In June, Anderson learned that his announcement of the switch hadn't reached Huebsch before he heard it secondhand and that Huebsch was mad. Salesmen were going around saying Huebsch was comparing Anderson to Judas. That he couldn't believe; it didn't sound like Huebsch, and besides, he was sure any soreness would wear off. "A man can't stay sore about such a matter," he said.

Liveright came to New Orleans on business. Others came just to visit Anderson or to pay homage. John Dos Passos had chosen New Orleans in retreat from New York, perhaps specifically because Anderson was there. Anita Loos did too and there, at the Saint Charles Hotel, wrote *Gentlemen Prefer Blondes*. Down for Mardi Gras, Ring Lardner called up Anderson, and Anderson took him out to dinner. Edmund Wilson stopped in and appeared "likable" to Anderson but "very much the intellectual." He seemed to see everything through books, Anderson wrote Bab: "Nothing comes to him direct." On a tour that Anderson gave him, they saw "the negro stevedore, the night watchman on the docks, the pilot on the river boat, the street car conductor — All these smile and nod at me," he reported. "They feel something of themselves in me. I feel something of my self in them." The itinerary, of course, was Whitman's.

With hindsight we know that the most interesting person to come to the city was William Faulkner. He came first in November 1924. He was twenty-seven. He had read some Anderson and liked it, *Horses and Men* especially. Later he went so far as to say that one work in it, "I'm a Fool," was "the best short story in America." His friend Phil Stone encouraged him to go over to New Orleans to meet this famous writer. He was hesitant, but having worked for Elizabeth in

New York two years before and knowing she admired him, he went to Saint Peter Street, and the Andersons welcomed him with an exceptionally high-spirited dinner party. After Faulkner left New Orleans, in December, his book of poems, *The Marble Faun,* was published, and shortly after that, he returned to the city with Stone. This time he went in search of a job on a ship bound for Europe but also to go on with his conversation with Anderson. The *Times-Picayune* ran a picture of him under the heading "Southern Poet in Orleans" and described him in the caption as "visiting Sherwood Anderson here."

By the time Faulkner and Stone arrived, Anderson had gone off lecturing, and for what she said was "an uproarious week" Elizabeth went sightseeing with the two young men by day and then off to Bourbon or to Rampart Street at night. Soon they began taking their meals with her, and then when Stone had to go back to Oxford, Mississippi, Faulkner moved into the Andersons' spare room.

When Anderson returned in March, he really didn't want the young man living there, but the Andersons knew that Bill Spratling, a young architect from Tulane who lived around back of the cathedral in "Pirate's Alley," had an extra room. Leaving some of his belongings with the Andersons (mostly half-gallon jars of corn liquor, Anderson later said), Faulkner made the move, and then Anderson began to enjoy his companionship.

After his usual morning's work, Anderson might emerge to find Faulkner waiting for him in Jackson Square. Faulkner proved to be not only a good listener, but a man who could match Anderson telling tales. The best one spilled over into letters they exchanged. It was about a descendent of Stonewall Jackson who raised sheep in the swamps, about the transformation of those sheep into aquatic beasts, about one of them in particular who had some Jackson blood in him and went along the shore annoying the girls who were swimming. They talked of printing up their results, but only Faulkner did. He included some of his contribution to the Jackson tall tale in his second novel, *Mosquitoes.* Their conversation would continue as they walked down to the water, Anderson pointing out the sights, Faulkner walking beside him with a slight limp, the result, he said, of a war wound, and looking up to him not only as an authority but because Faulkner was three or four inches shorter. Often they would meet again in the evening, and drink, and talk on into the night.

One occasion Anderson wrote up as "A Meeting South" and published it in the *Dial* in April 1925. It was about the time Anderson took Faulkner to see a former madam named Aunt Rose, one of the most colorful mother figures Anderson had ever found. Towering over six feet tall, red-haired, she had survived the closing down of the Storyville district and now lived on Chartres Street. In the story, Anderson makes nothing of the name here on this side of the Atlantic, in the City of Man, but much of young "David," who on their visit talks about his daddy's dying plantation and his war wound, about how much he likes Shelley, and about how he has to drink to get himself to sleep. The piece ends just that way, with "a small huddled figure of a man" lying asleep on the bricks of "Aunt Sally's" patio in the shadows of a banana plant, and with Anderson overjoyed that he has brought these two people together. It has something to do with their being kind of aristocratic, he muses to himself as he walks away, and something to do with his pride in the fact that he, an outsider, can understand and appreciate them.

Typically, Anderson was not altogether sure of his own position. For several months, Anderson took Faulkner under his wing, but in no time he realized that Faulkner would not stay there long. He told Faulkner to move on to prose, and he told him he had to have a place from which to start, and that that place was what he was, "what he was born." Not that Faulkner necessarily understood (though understanding might come in the writing). What was important was that he remember where he came from and not be ashamed. In his own case it had been "Winesburg" and the Midwest; in Faulkner's case, it was "that little patch up there in Mississippi."

That spring Faulkner published sketches in the *Times-Picayune* and the *Double Dealer* that are obvious responses to Anderson's recommendation. "Cheest," for example, as the tone of the voice in the title alone suggests, is Faulkner's homage to "I'm a Fool," *his* attempt to register how young boys talk at the track. Little pieces like "Jealousy," "The Liar," or "The Cobbler" are, in theory, like Anderson's portraits of the "grotesque." But they did not finally sound like Anderson. They were just proof that Faulkner could easily absorb an influence on his way to forging his own style. If anything, this young man had too much talent, and Anderson warned him: "You can do it too easy, in too many different ways. If you're not careful, you'll never write anything." Perhaps there was an edge to what he said, perhaps the slightest hope that he could slow Faulkner down, but all that Faulkner chose to remember was a man who insisted on the highest standards.

What he said in the appreciation that he wrote in the *Atlantic* in 1953 was that Anderson was

> warm, generous, merry and fond of laughing, without pettiness and jealous only of the integrity which he believed to be absolutely necessary in anyone who approached his craft; he was ready to be generous to anyone, once he was convinced that that one approached his craft with his own humility and respect for it.

He liked this man who was more than twenty years his senior. He said that Anderson was the one man he knew whom he "could have shared a desert island with." He was also grateful. Late that spring in New Orleans, he gave Elizabeth the completed manuscript of a novel in hopes that Anderson could be persuaded to read it. She came back with word that Anderson would recommend it to his publisher provided he didn't have to look at it. In June, Anderson recommended Faulkner to his new publisher as "the one writer of promise" he had met in New Orleans, and the next year, 1926, Liveright published what became *Soldier's Pay*. Three years later, Faulkner dedicated *Sartoris* (the first of the Yoknapatawpha novels) to Anderson, with an inscription that began: "through whose kindness I was first published."

Faulkner knew that it was sometimes hard for the man before him (the man this time in the "bright blue racetrack shirt and vermillion-mottled Bohemian Windsor tie") to believe in *himself* as a writer. With more confidence than usual, Anderson had recently declared himself a writer and a man in *A Story Teller's Story*, but Faulkner sensed how easily that confidence could be shaken. In Faulkner's eyes it had nothing to do with money or with family troubles. It was entirely a question of his style — "Just style," he said in his "Appreciation," "an end instead of a means." If Anderson could maintain *it*, then everything else would follow: "What the style contained would have to be first rate: it couldn't help but be first rate, and therefore himself too." Faulkner knew how much Anderson hated "glibness." But he also saw how much Anderson feared that he himself was glib. He knew how hard Anderson worked for "purity," how he was always "fumbling for exactitude." But Faulkner knew too, as he put it, that there were times when Anderson stood "a little bigger, a little taller than it was," times when the style failed and what remained was only Anderson — trying, in both senses of the word.

Hearing him going on a bit too long, sensing his vulnerability, some would not be able to resist being cruel. Faulkner always could. But still, within a year, their relationship was essentially over. Anderson would continue to take an interest in Faulkner's career, and he still had advice for him, but someone else would have to pass it on. He no longer liked "the man personally very much," Anderson told Liveright in April 1926. Faulkner had done something "so nasty" to him.

What it was, no one knew for sure, not even Faulkner. All he knew was that while he was away, Anderson had "taken umbrage" at him, and when he saw him again the next year in New Orleans, Anderson wouldn't speak to him. Was it that he found out that Faulkner had lied to him about being wounded in the war and therefore made him look silly in a story he himself had written? Did Faulkner insult an old friend of Anderson's, a University of Chicago historian named Ferdinand Schevill, who was visiting the Andersons in New Orleans? Was it that they argued over race relations? (This is a much-favored explanation, and one that Anderson offered in a piece he wrote in 1930 about young writers, called "They Come Bearing Gifts.")

Perhaps it was that Faulkner had called Anderson's writing into question, that he had publicly surveyed Anderson's writing and found some of it wanting. A review of Anderson's work that Faulkner had written for the *Dallas Morning News* in April 1925 could have been it — assuming Anderson did not see it until months later. Faulkner's praise for *Winesburg, Ohio* and *Horses and Men* would have gone right by him. What would have stuck were his statements about *Many Marriages* ("Here, I think, is a bad ear"; "humor is completely lacking"), his (seemingly innocent) comparison of Anderson's Ohio manner to Warren Harding's, and, above all, his criticism of *A Story Teller's Story*. The first half of the book was excellent, he said, especially Anderson's portrayal of his father, but the second half displayed "an elephantine kind of humor about himself"; it showed that Anderson did not have "enough active ego to write successfully of himself," that he was not yet mature. The verdict would have been hard enough for any man to take as he began to look ahead to his fiftieth birthday, but if Faulkner was right, if this man had come to depend so much on his style, then to say he wasn't in it, or was not there yet, was to say he did not exist as a writer.

After publishing his review, Faulkner took two more playful swipes at Anderson. In December 1926, he focused on Anderson exclusively in a little book called *Sherwood Anderson and Other Creoles.*

He had him appear in what he called Anderson's "primer style," as the supposed author of a five-hundred-page introduction to a series of drawings that Spratling had done of the habitués of Le Vieux Carré. "First, let me tell you something about our Quarter, the Vieux Carre. Do you know our quarter, with its narrow streets, its old wrought-iron balconies and its Southern European background?" it began. The first drawing was of a pudgy, slightly seraphic Anderson, all dolled up, filling up an upholstered chair, his hands cupped around his knees, his cane and his latest publication at his feet. After thirty-seven mild caricatures came Spratling and Faulkner at the drawing board, behind them an air rifle and a sampler saying "Viva Art," and at Faulkner's feet three jugs. In the foreward, "W.F." speaks of the richness, the good fellowship, and the "soft laughter" all around, and in little plodding steps ends with an appeal to Americans' "one priceless trait," their sense of humor. "One trouble with us American artists is that we take our art and ourselves too seriously," he says. As the *Times-Picayune* put it in its review, *Sherwood Anderson and Other Creoles* did not contain a malicious line. The local audience that bought up the first printing of four hundred copies in a week could not have thought there was. Though he was hurt, neither, really, could Anderson. The serious damage had probably been done in April of the year before.

Another swipe was the result of an outing Anderson organized. Buoyed up by Liveright's support, in July 1925 Anderson hired a yacht and invited about a dozen people for a day's sailing across Lake Pontchartrain. Besides Faulkner, Lillian Marcus, the *Double Dealer*'s angel was aboard. So too were Spratling, and the Antonys, who owned the building where Faulkner and Spratling stayed, and several people from Tulane, including Basso, then still a student at Tulane. He literally, others metaphorically, sat at the feet of the honored hosts, the Andersons. All of them appeared in Faulkner's *Mosquitoes,* which he finished in September of the next year.

The day itself was a disastrous one. It stormed, the engine stalled. Wherever the excursioners took refuge, in the cabin or on the shore nearby, there were mosquitoes. Faulkner's friends buzzed on like characters (as he acknowledged) in Aldous Huxley's *Point Counter Point.* Prominent among them is Dawson Fairchild, talking at length about the demasculinzation of men, about writing ultimately to please women, about how words seem now to fail him. Faulkner was hardly flattering "Fairchild" when he said he looked more than ever like a walrus, "a deceptively sedate walrus of middle age suddenly evincing a streak of demoniac puerility," and had him crudely flirting with the ladies; but satirizing Anderson's talk, he is, like Hecht in his portrayal of Anderson as Warren Lockwood in his novel, *Erik Dorn,* relatively gentle. "That first infatuation," he has him say, for example, "that sheer infatuation with marveling over the beauty and power of words. That has gone out of me. Used up, I guess. So I can't write poetry anymore. It takes me too long to say things, now." It is something that Anderson might have said to Faulkner as they walked along, without appearing ludicrous. After the way Faulkner had already characterized Anderson in his review, his presentation of him here was not likely to offend.

If Anderson had seen Faulkner's review in the *Dallas Morning News,* there would have been anger when he said to his wife: "I'll do anything for him so long as I don't have to read his damned manuscript." If he had not seen it, with an air of casualness and at the same time with a sense of urgency, he was saying he had to get on with his own work. Specifically, he was in a hurry to get *his* latest novel off to Liveright.

It was *Dark Laughter,* at once an astonishingly bad book and by far his most popular. He had written a draft of it in the fall of 1924 with more than his usual speed, "the whole thing in about two months." Having signed with Liveright, he was now working all day every day on it and wishing he had the strength to carry on into the night. It was even more intense, he said, than *Many Marriages,* "even broader and has a greater swing to it." And like so much that he had written before, it was going to be "by far the best novel I have written."

Into it went not just the familiar story of his broken marriages and of his youth and early manhood, but also his thinking about war and about manliness, and about the differing ways men and women were creative. Into it too went his memories of Chicago, the advertising and newspaper businesses, and Fifty-seventh Street, and of Paris, especially of what was only a "sex orgy" in a small entry in his notebook then, the Quatre Arts Ball. It was "a fantasy," he told Rosenfeld. In it he wanted "the War, new sex-consciousness, niggers — a slow, fantastic dance of sounds and thought." In the foreground he imagined "neuroticism, the hurry and self-consciousness of modern life"; in the back, "the easy, strange laughter of the blacks."

For a plot he took another Dudley (this time surnamed Bruce) out of a first marriage, out of the newspaper business and a bicycle factory, and put him to work in the garden of the town's leading industrialist, and then whisked Dudley and the industrialist's wife off to the approving — the "dark" — laughter of the Negro servants. "In the road before the house one of the negro women now laughed" is the way the novel ends:

> There was a shuffling sound. The older negro woman tried to quiet the younger, blacker woman, but she kept laughing the high shrill laughter of the negress. "I knowed it, I knowed it, all the time I knowed it," she cried, and the high shrill laughter ran through the garden and into the room where Fred [the abandoned husband] sat upright and rigid in bed.

But one does not so much follow a plot as marvel at the convergence of what seems to be everything that was on Anderson's mind — and converging not to the rhythms of a dance, but cacophonously. When it was finished, he wrote Stieglitz that he had tried to give "the sense of a dancing, shifting world of facts, moods, thoughts, impulses," but this time added what one senses most: an almost manic Anderson. "That's me, anyway," he said. "I'm not very stable."

New Orleans came out like this:

> Niggers on the docks, niggers in the city streets, niggers laughing. A slow dance always going on. German sea-captains, French, American, Swedish, Japanese, English, Scotch. The Germans now sailing under other flags than their own. The Scotch sailing under the English flag. Clean ships, dirty tramp ships, half-naked niggers — a shadow-dance.

This leads to:

> How much does it cost to be a good man, an earnest man? If we can't produce good earnest men, how are we ever going to make any progress? You can't ever get anywhere if you aren't conscious — in earnest.

And Woman, on the other hand:

> The woman. Mystery. Love of women. Scorn of women. What are they like? Are they like trees? How much can woman thrust into the mystery of life, think, feel? Love men. Take women. Drift with the drifting of days. That life goes on does not concern you. It concerns women.

The sentences chop on. The questions pop up. (Anderson must have set some kind of record for the number of questions in a single novel.)

The narrative jerks back and forth, the switches signaled by such chapter openings as "Heat!" or "Other strange memories for Bruce, walking with Sponge," or "Marriage!" or "First one thing and then another."

The summer before, Anderson had said that Joyce's *Ulysses* had been his "starting place for the prose rhythm of the book." His more general claim to be in league with D. H. Lawrence is much easier to accept. Though he was critical of the fictions after *Sons and Lovers* and of what he thought were Lawrence's neurotic dreams of being "the great, dark animal," as evidenced by his *Studies in Classic American Literature,* Anderson was forever loyal to him. He would write glowingly of Lawrence when he died, of his being another "man's man," of his representing "Kingship," no less. In the middle of writing *Dark Laughter,* he declared: "That Lawrence. He is in the modern England what I am in the modern America. That I know."

The most obvious thing that Anderson was trying to do in *Dark Laughter* was discover himself through the "niggers." When he first discovered "them" in Alabama in 1920, relatively few "fools" (as he called them) had preceded him. Shortly thereafter, Hart Crane wrote in the *Double Dealer* that he hoped Anderson would try to "handle the Negro in fiction." He thought Anderson could do it without "sentimentality or cruelty." *Dark Laughter* proved him wrong.

After his first trip south, Anderson made more and more of the men he watched work and heard sing, or rather projected more and more onto them. All the clichés emerged: they experienced life differently, they were somehow more "real," more in touch, more beautiful. Writing Jean Toomer in December 1922 he said he didn't want to write *about* the Negro. He knew he wasn't one of them, so he couldn't portray them with any authority. But still, he wanted to write the way the Negro *was,* the way he responded. He didn't want to write "of the Negro," he said, "but out of him." When he despaired of doing that, he tried painting: "There was less mind, more feeling." Then he wondered if it could be done at all. That is where Toomer came in: he was one of the moderns, one of "us," the "nervous distraught ones," but he was one of "them" too. It was wonderful, Anderson said after reading *Cane,* "to think you belong also to the men I saw working on the docks, the black men." Toomer proved that a man could be a modern writer and still tap whatever source it was from which those body movements and those sounds on the wharves emerged. In *Dark Laughter* Anderson tried to prove that he too could be that kind of man.

As he told Toomer, he wanted whatever this was that came "out of the Negro" to appear in works of art in its purest form. He didn't want it to be just "Negro art," he wanted it to make for art, he wanted it to be available to *him*. Ultimately, he wanted it for himself. He had met a woman in London who was "a bit too Negro," he said. She thought too highly of the work of blacks, because it was done by blacks. Toomer's idea of starting a magazine, a possible way, he hoped, of "giving the Negro to himself," was a bad one. "The important thing is that there be artists," Anderson said. Though skeptical at first, in writing *Dark Laughter* he was confident that it danced the way Toomer's writing danced and that he himself was inward with the ways of blacks.

And he was encouraged to think that he could succeed. In the first place, the times were encouraging him. He did not have to go up to Harlem himself to know that blacks and their music were fashionable. In 1925, when *Dark Laughter* appeared, Anderson was far from alone in thinking he had written something literally "jazzy," or something significant about blacks. There had been Waldo Frank's *Holiday* (1923), Eugene O'Neill's *All God's Chillun Got Wings* (1924), DuBose Heyward's *Porgy* (1925). Carl Van Vechten's *Nigger Heaven* would be out the next year. Nor had he proceeded without specific encouragement — from Crane, and from Toomer himself. Toomer told him that he himself could not have matured as an artist without having read *Winesburg, Ohio* and *The Triumph of the Egg*. He said that Anderson had "evoked an emotion, a sense of beauty that is easily more Negro than almost anything" he had seen, and he inscribed these words in the copy of *Cane* he sent Anderson when it came out in 1923: "To Sherwood Anderson whose rich glow and beauty opened those emotions which in this book are most pure."

And the book-buying public led Anderson to believe that he had succeeded. They had learned to expect authenticity from Anderson. Ever since 1917, when he walked into the office of the *Seven Arts,* he had been groomed to be vibrant America, and he had run willingly and well. He was said to have given America back to itself more creatively than had ordinary self-made men, and he had. Now that he was giving life to them in this suddenly popular form, they responded enthusiastically. If in this latest effort he was less restrained, less intellectual, if he was more primitive, more shocking, even if he was vulgar and degrading, the more interesting he seemed. He was called all these things. But he was still what *Vanity Fair* called

"America's Most Distinctive Novelist." In December the magazine printed a full-page picture of him by Edward Steichen, underneath which they quoted H. L. Mencken as saying that *Dark Laughter* was "one of the most profound novels of our time." But even if you did not agree with that particular judgment, you had to read the novel because it was by Sherwood Anderson. Also, there was the simple fact that it was well distributed and well advertised, now that Anderson had gone over to Liveright.

Dark Laughter was Anderson's one best seller. It came out in September of 1925 and sold more than twenty-one thousand copies in the first three and a half months, and went through eight printings in the first nine. At the same time, with the book's publication, Anderson was more exposed, more vulnerable, than he had ever been. Having always sought to be honest and open, and, at least since the writing of *Many Marriages,* to express himself without worrying about literary or social form, he was now out there, it seemed, with more material than he had ever tried to get into one book and, what mattered most, out there in prose that he thought captured the rhythms of both modern and some more basic form of life.

But he had come to a dead end. As he would soon discover, he had written himself out. Indefatigable changeling that he was, he would find another route, a whole new way to write, but after *Dark Laughter* he lost first the respect of the writers who would succeed him, and then the respect of readers, and he would never fully recover either.

Fitzgerald, who had written his editor, Max Perkins, in June of 1925 that Anderson was *"one of the very best and finest writers in the English language today,"* wrote him in October that *Dark Laughter* was just *"lousy."* Two months later he wrote scornfully of the press's response to it. It wasn't those who waited for the "Winesburg" stories as they were published one by one in the *Little Review* who praised it, he said, only "the other boys who find a new genius once a week and at all costs follow the fashions." When Faulkner looked back and said that with *Dark Laughter* Anderson should have stopped writing, he can't have meant that Anderson had done the best that he could do. What Faulkner and Fitzgerald thought Anderson never knew, but Hemingway's response he could not ignore. It was a direct and public shot — a little book called *Torrents of Spring.*

Inspired and advised by Anderson in Chicago in August 1921, Hemingway and his new wife, Hadley, had gone to Paris in the fall. Before he had sailed, Hemingway had come to Anderson with what food he had left, an occasion Anderson remembered affectionately in "They Come Bearing Gifts." Anderson knew the man was going to go places, and now he was off, "coming up the stairs, a magnificent broad-shouldered figure of a man, shouting as he came." From Paris, Hemingway was again all excitement and gratitude — "lots of things happen here. Gertrude Stein and me are just like brothers. . . . Joyce has a most god-damn wonderful book. . . . I've been teaching Pound to box wit [*sic*] little success" — and in the months that followed, he went to school with Stein.

One or two of the stories that he wrote look back to Anderson. "Up in Michigan" is about sexual initiation. But it was apprentice work; Stein thought it was cluttered, and Hemingway dropped it after its first publication in *Three Stories and Ten Poems* in 1923. "My Old Man" is told from a young boy's point of view, and as if to underscore both the connection and the younger man's succession, Edward O'Brien published it in *The Best Stories of 1923* and, on the basis of it, dedicated the volume to him. If anyone was tempted to imagine later traces, in "The Battler," say, or "The Undefeated," Hemingway did everything he could to erase them. When Edmund Wilson said he heard echoes in "My Old Man," Hemingway said no, though he knew Anderson "pretty well" and was "very fond" of him, he hadn't seen him in several years, and he certainly wasn't inspired by him. The man had written some good stories, but all that too was in the past: "His work seems to have gone to hell, perhaps from people in New York telling him too much how good he was." Meanwhile, Anderson went right on admiring Hemingway, both the writer and the man. The blurb he wrote for the American edition of *In Our Time,* published in 1925 by Liveright, began: "Mr. Hemingway is young, strong, full of laughter, and he can write." He had no idea *how* full.

When *Dark Laughter* came out, Anderson had Liveright send copies to several of his friends in Paris, to Stein, to his French translator, Madame Gay, to Hemingway. In the same season, Hemingway picked up some of the Turgenev that Anderson had recommended, and also Donald Ogden Stewart's *A Parody Outline of History,* with chapters on "Cristofer Colombo," "The Spirit of '75," "How Love Came to General Grant," and the like, done "in the manner of" James Branch Cabell, Lardner, and others. From the former he took his title, from the latter his idea, and in ten days (according to the text), seven, or six (according to letters in which he tried to make lighter and lighter of what he did), he had written *Torrents of Spring,* his parody of *Dark Laughter.* And then he ran around Paris and made himself hoarse reading it to friends.

Nobody ever said it was a nice thing to do. Hearing him, Bernadine Szold, a friend of Tennessee Mitchell's, was appalled at what seemed to be Hemingway's gloating over the damage he hoped to inflict. Tennessee's response was more complicated: "I always knew him for a cruel beast," she said, "but I didn't know how clever." Fitzgerald's friend Gerald Murphy was dubious when he heard it (his wife Sara fell asleep), Dos Passos tried to discourage him from publishing it, Stein, of course, was "very angry." Pauline Pfeiffer, Hemingway's wife-to-be, was almost alone in finding it hilarious. Hadley, his wife, "thought the whole idea detestable."

As to *why* he did it, his looking up at Anderson's picture on Sylvia Beach's wall and vowing to be there too one day suggests the obvious explanation. More immediately, he wanted to move over from Liveright to Scribner's, and he figured that Liveright would loosen his hold if he offended Liveright's most prized author — and he was right. In this he was encouraged by Fitzgerald, who recommended the book to Liveright, saying on the one hand that it was "about the best comic book ever written by an American," but on the other, confessing that he hoped to see all those writers of his generation that he admired "rounded up in the same coop" with him at Scribner's.

But whatever were Hemingway's intentions, the fact is, *Torrents of Spring* succeeds as parody, and it succeeds in parodying not just *Dark Laughter,* but other of Anderson's books as well (*Marching Men* and *Many Marriages* especially), and not just Anderson, but Stein and Mencken and any other literary figure (or organ) that came into his mind's eye in those few days. In his zest, he did not spare even himself.

Frequently explaining to the reader where he was, and how he got there, and where (with luck) he might expect to be a few pages later, Hemingway satirized Anderson's seeming inability to plot. In meandering himself, he hit on many of Anderson's favorite topics. There were those men who worked with their hands. "Why shouldn't a man work with his hands?" he asked. "Rodin had done it. Cezanne had been a butcher. Renoir a carpenter. Picasso had worked in a cigarette factory in his boyhood." There were all those wives. Scripps O'Neill had two: "As he looked out of the window, standing tall and lean and resilient with his own tenuous hardness, he thought of both of them. One lived in Maneslona and the other lived in Petosky." There were the "natives." Mostly they were Indians (and here Hemingway recalls his own renderings of them), but now and then one hears chuckles from behind the bar or from the kitchen. It is a Negro — or "perhaps the chap was only sooty from the stove." From Paris there are memories of the Beaux Arts Ball, and naturally no geldings, for "all horses were stallions."

But above and over all, there was Anderson's "affectation" of the simple, the innocent, the naive. It was that, as the epigraph from Henry Fielding has it, that was to Hemingway "the only source of the true Ridiculous." He caught the choppy rhythms ("Night in Petosky. Long past midnight. Inside the beanery a light burning."), especially as they carried along those disconcerting questions of Anderson ("Well reader," he says in the "Author's Final Note to the Reader," "how did you like it? It took me ten days to write it. Has it been worth it? There is one place I would like to clear up. You remember back in the story where the elderly waitress, Diana . . ."). Put in these terms, the idea of the American man as a gentle man came out absurd:

> A man was inside the station, tapping something back of a wicketed window. He looked at Scripps. Could he be a telegrapher? Something told Scripps that he was.
>
> He stepped out of the snow-drift and approached the window. Behind the window the man worked busily away at his telegrapher's key.
>
> "Are you a telegrapher?" asked Scripps.
>
> "Yes, sir," said the man. "I'm a telegrapher."
>
> "How wonderful!"
>
> The telegrapher eyed him suspiciously.

The idea that he is a representative American man was that much more absurd:

> Tears came into Scripps's eyes. Something stirred inside him again. He reached forward to take the elderly waitress's hand, and with quiet dignity she laid it within his own. "You are my woman," he said. Tears came into her eyes, too.
>
> "You are my man," she said.
>
> "Once again I say: you are my woman." Scripps pronounced the words solemnly. Something had broken inside him again. He felt he could not keep from crying.
>
> "Let this be our wedding ceremony," the elderly waitress said.

Scripps pressed her hand. "You are my woman," he said simply.

"You are my man and more than my man." She looked into his eyes. "You are all America to me."

By the end, there was little left of Anderson, but one need not think only of him and his failings, or of the insensitive, hardly "magnificent" Hemingway, clamoring up the literary ladder. One may think too of Hemingway the writer, intent upon perfecting his own style, full of energy, and funny, if only in the way a sophomore can be funny.

That is why he had done it, he wrote Anderson. He had had fun. Moreover, he had made five hundred dollars doing it. Also, he said in another letter, writers shouldn't have to pull their punches. If they did, when "somebody starts to slop they just go on slopping." He had trouble saying it, trouble trying to explain how he was separating his affection for the man from his impatience with his writing, and Anderson called Hemingway on what he thought was his patronizing tone. "You always do speak to me like a master to a pupil. It must be Paris — the literary life," he said. "You didn't seem like that when I knew you." But the facts remained: Anderson had slipped and Hemingway was disappointed. Speaking more frankly to Perkins than he had to Liveright, Fitzgerald wrote him that *Torrents of Spring* was "almost a vicious parody," but he went on to say that he agreed with Hemingway: Anderson had let everybody down who believed in him.

It could happen to anyone, as Anderson well knew. Any writer could fail at any time. His style could fail him, and he would have to pay. Ten years after *Torrents of Spring* was published, Anderson invited Dreiser to survey the literary landscape with him. "Today, for example, Hemingway is the new man," he wrote him. "What praise lavished on him. Look out, Hemmy, they'll be trying to kill you off tomorrow. Or is it Bill Faulkner, or Thomas Wolfe."

With Faulkner there was a reconciliation of sorts. In 1937 they were at a party together in New York. Anderson tried to avoid a meeting, but Faulkner persevered, pulling Anderson aside, saying, "Sherwood, what the hell is the matter with you? Do you think that I am also a Hemmy?" A month later, Anderson went to see him at the Algonquin. Faulkner had passed out and, coming to, had asked for him. As Faulkner said on several occasions, Anderson was the literary father of his generation, and he wanted that known. He had no intention of killing him.

At that time, to Anderson the difference between his two protégés seemed that stark. In Faulkner (or Wolfe) you feel "an inner sympathy with the fact of life itself," he said. But not in Hemingway. In him there was "the desire always to kill." There was a need to go for people out of a fear that they were going to attack him first. Anderson even imagined Hemingway being his own worst enemy, doing himself in, as it were. He told Ben Hecht there was no need to hit back. "Ernest is such a shut-in, fathead sort of writer that he's going to end up burlesquing himself," he said, not without some enjoyment of the prospect. "And," he added, "he'll do it a lot better than I could." In future years, whenever he heard of Hemingway's "glums," he found it ironic that what he liked to call "the hard-boiled guys" were no more impervious to depression than anyone else. There seemed no limit to Hemingway's success, but Anderson knew that any success was temporary. Hemingway's lean, tough style seemed to have won a culture over, but Anderson knew that it might not be much more enduring than his own.

But in their correspondence right after *Torrents of Spring* was published, Anderson was anything but combative. He slipped into Hemingway's terms: "Come out of it, man. I pack a little wallop myself," he said. "I've been middleweight champion. You seem to forget that." In doing so, however, he sounded plaintive. He sounded like a man who was about to retire from competition. In those same terms he pointed out to Bab Finley that he'd had his "fill of hitting" long ago.

Far from trying to retaliate, he continued to admire from the sidelines. It was as if he didn't mind being bested by this man. In July he wrote Hemingway that there was something impressive about his getting five hundred dollars (in contrast to the three hundred dollars he'd gotten for *Winesburg, Ohio*), that there was his "vitality — the ability to take it," his ability to get through his early years as a writer. Most "so-called artists" didn't have it, he said. In October 1926, in his last letter to Hemingway, he expressed his disappointment at hearing from Hemingway that he had been "this side of bughouse" with insomnia for months. He was "shocked." "Aren't there any real huskies in the world?" he asked.

TEN

Withdrawal

1926-1929

ANDERSON FULFILLED HIS OBLIGATION to Liveright with
not one but two volumes in 1926, neither of which was
"husky" in the least. One was *Sherwood Anderson's Notebook*, a compi-
lation of previously printed pieces, interspersed with rambling reflective passages on men and women and the modern world under the
heading "Notes Out of a Man's Life." Among the pieces were "From
Chicago" and "An Apology for Crudity," only nine years old but
seemingly from the very distant past.

The other was *Tar: A Midwest Childhood*, mostly tales of his youth,
or what he called "his childhood dramatized and lived in the person
of Tar Moorehead." He began writing it in the first person but
switched to the third, thereby coming closer to the truth of his experience, as had been the case many times before, by indirection.
One tale was a version of "Death in the Woods." Others, with titles
like "A Small Boy Looks at His World" and "Tar's Wonderful Sunday," appeared in the *Woman's Home Companion*. The book's manner
was, as he said, "gentle and whimsical" but with enough "dramatic
force" to carry the reader along. Here, for example, is Tar at the time
of his sister's birth:

> Tar lay, listening intensely. He was like a young quail crouched
> under leaves when a dog is ranging a field. Not a muscle of his
> body moved. In a household like the Mooreheads' a child does not
> run instinctively to the mother. Love, warmth, the natural expres-
> sion of tenderness, all such impulses are buried away. Tar had to
> live his own life, lie quiet and wait. Most Middle-Western families
> of the old days were like that.

It was no attempt to register the pulses of "modern life," nothing like *Dark Laughter*. Not many reviewers and readers even noticed *Tar*. But it is all the more attractive for calling so little attention to itself. It changed at least one man's life. In 1927, when James T. Farrell read it in a filling station at Thirty-fifth Street and Morgan Avenue in Chicago, his drab surroundings, the ugly factory walls and the noisy street corner, seemed to vanish, and it seemed to him he was living in the countryside with Tar. *Tar* gave him "a means of re-affirmation of self," he said. It strengthened his ambition to write, to write about his own boyhood. "Here was one of the seeds that led to *Studs Lonigan*."

But with *Tar*, Anderson was running out of things to write about. He seemed retiring as a writer, and there seemed little reason why he and Elizabeth should not retire from New Orleans as well. Early in the summer of 1925 he asked several friends if they knew of some out-of-the-way place where they could go, some place where they could live economically and he could fish. He asked Julia and Julian Harris (the son of Joel Chandler Harris, creator of the "Uncle Remus" stories), whom he had met while lecturing at the University of Georgia, if they knew of any place in the mountains of Tennessee or Georgia, or maybe Virginia, and they did. They knew a family named Greear who had a farm in a little town of two or three dozen people in the southwestern corner of Virginia, in the foot-hills of the Blue Ridge Mountains. They had lost a lot of money recently when the furniture factory they partly owned went out of business and their bank stock fell, and they were hoping to make a new start by taking boarders in.

In July 1925, the Andersons went by train to Marion, Virginia, and from there took an old lumber railroad twenty miles or so back into the hills to a town with the alluring name of Troutdale. There the Greears welcomed them, and some of their boys (they had five, and one daughter) prepared a place where Anderson could work. They swept (or shoveled) the dust out of a little cabin on the property, built him a rude table, and brought a chair out from the farmhouse. The Greears thought twelve dollars a month for both of them (laun-dry and meals included) would be fair, but Anderson insisted on two dollars a day for the two of them.

It was a paradise very different from the one he had conjured up in Alabama. He developed a healthy dislike for chickens. They ran in and out of the farmhouse, their droppings were everywhere, but otherwise he was ideally situated. The farm sat on top of Locust Ridge, looking out into North Carolina to the south, to mountains all around. In front, a meadow sloped down to a creek and railroad tracks a mile away, beyond which lay the town. Anderson loved his cabin even more. He had a view of Pine Mountain. All manner of bugs and birds flew in and out of his open door. He could hear cowbells, and the wind's whisperings in the cornfields, and the sound of the springs that trickled out of the surrounding hills. There he finished *Tar,* and there he began quite consciously to contemplate his own decline.

It is hard to think of a time when Anderson was more at home. He still stood out. He arrived in a white linen suit, bright blue shirt, and a cardinal-red tie, wearing a Panama hat, but to the Greears he was not so much a "personage" as a benign presence. He had "the gentlest, kindest, most musical voice I thought I had ever heard," Caroline Greear said. "His eyes were very black, soft, but penetrating." At one point when her husband was away trying to mend their fortunes, she wrote to him about Anderson, saying, "He's like no one we ever knew, you can tell him anything and he understands what you are trying to say before you can find the words." The family marveled at how much mail he got, but nobody knew who he was until a girl came running to the house one day with an old copy of the *Literary Digest* that said he was one of "greatest writers in America." Having finally found anonymity, he wasn't pleased to lose it, but the Greears protected him, telling the president of a nearby college that he had gone away, for example, when in fact he was quietly working in his cabin.

In New Orleans, Elizabeth's social life had been quite her own. Here she had hardly any life at all. She tried her best, but she seemed much harder to get to know than her husband. In the evening she would retire while he sat up late and talked. In the morning he would come down early and sit in the kitchen while coffee was being made. When it was ready he would take Elizabeth's breakfast up to her in their room, and then come down again and drink his coffee while he looked out at the valley from the porch. After a morning's work he was likely to walk out on the hills, or to tour the countryside in a buggy that the Greears had found for him to rent. That summer, Elizabeth went back to New Orleans before he did in order to tend her decorator's shop.

When Anderson returned to New Orleans himself, he determined that what he wanted was not a house in the city but "a little house by a brook on a side road, the smell of grass, all the things that nature means." They were the things that appealed "to those who are no longer young." "Soon," he said, "I shall begin to grow old." And as a result of his wanderings around Troutdale, he found that idyllic spot.

The area was lovely. It was also very poor. The best of the lumber was gone. The attempt to bring in a furniture factory had failed and had impoverished the hopeful townsfolk even more. There was something appealing about that. Anderson was relieved to find people who did not read and were not falsely educated. "It does so beat talking to pretentious half-artists," he wrote Stieglitz in August. And they were so friendly, inviting him in for moonshine and, if he wanted, for the night. But Anderson knew well enough that his was a version of pastoral, that he was part of the new world, coming into the hills along with the paved road and gas stations, and making himself feel at home by converting these "natives" into happy, virtuous souls.

If he forgot, he was reminded. Having heard that he was a writer, one woman confronted him with the simple fact that no one around could afford a book and that besides, most of them could not read or write. He later wrote about another who was young, unwed, pregnant, and seemingly helpless, to whom he offered twenty dollars — and who reponded by telling him "to put it somewhere, I won't say where." He met another by Ripshin Creek (so named because of what happened to your shins when you tried to cross it). She owned a farm, and, across the creek, a cabin where she lived. She said she wanted to move to West Virginia, and Anderson agreed to buy her out, on the spot, without a word to Elizabeth. He gave her a downpayment of $50. The farm cost $1,450.

Anderson had a cabin built for him over the winter while he and Elizabeth were back in New Orleans. It was like the Greears', on a hill across the creek from the farm, this time amidst dogwood and flowering ivy and mountain laurel, and looking out over hills whose lines, Anderson was fond of saying, were so sensual that a puritan would probably want them clothed. In March, he and Elizabeth had their New Orleans friend Bill Spratling draw up some plans for a house. When they returned in May, as construction on it started, they moved into the garage, which they had had renovated.

Their neighbors seemed to come out of the late Middle Ages,

"mostly English stock — much of it uncrossed." John Greear had recommended as foreman of the crew that went to work on the house a man named Marion Ball, who reminded Anderson of one of the gravediggers in *Hamlet*. After years of constructing sawmills, "old man Ball" couldn't make much sense of Spratling's drawings. And besides, he had his own way of doing things. On occasion he would hire a man to drive him around the hills while he drank moonshine in the back and bragged about building "that millionaire down there the finest house was ever built in this country." Three or four days later he would return, feeling rested, he would tell Anderson.

The result was impressive, imposing: four bedrooms, three baths, kitchen, large dining and living rooms, numerous fireplaces, all in stone, the lumber seasoned oak. Ball said he would build a house that would stand until Gabriel blew his horn. The walls were eighteen inches thick. The house had two wings made out of logs; in back there was a screened-in porch, in front, a terrace and eventually a lawn, walled in by an elegantly curved stone wall, where Anderson and his visitors played croquet. He paid Ball about sixty cents an hour, his crew anywhere from fifteen to twenty.

He called his house "Ripshin," after the creek that ran through the property. In time Anderson hung a large painting that Karl had done of him. It showed him glancing out at the viewer. Behind him was Ripshin, rising out of the valley, its scaffolding still on, like some Gothic structure he was building to save his soul. As for his earthly goods, the house used up almost all of them. He had earned eight thousand dollars from *Dark Laughter* in the first year. Ripshin cost him ten.

By the fall of 1926, though Ripshin was not completely finished, the Andersons were country gentry. Anderson bought a setter — "got me a dog," he said in localese — then another, so he had Rip and Shin. In the next two or three years, in addition to furnishing the house, Elizabeth tried to raise turkeys and geese. They gardened successfully, but left farming to a hired hand. They had two horses and got in trouble when one of them roamed to neighbors' haystacks for its meals. There was talk of raising sheep ("being shepherds," Anderson wrote Elizabeth's friend Stark Young), but fortunately only talk. In 1927, Elizabeth bought twenty-five or thirty acres of the lovely, rolling orchard and farming land around them, thereby doubling their holdings.

They had visitors and, suddenly, more family than Anderson ever imagined when he first considered owning his own home. In July of 1926, Paul Rosenfeld came for the first of many visits. Charles Connick, an artist in stained glass, came down from Boston with his wife. An editor from Liveright came to talk about *A New Testament,* the collection of "testaments" that Anderson began writing in 1919, which would be coming out the next year. One after another, Elizabeth's siblings came. In the summer of 1927 Lucille Swan (now the former Lucille Blum) took up residence in a nearby house to paint.

Anderson started to draw his children closer to him. With the help of Herbert Croly, the editor of the *New Republic,* he tried to get them college scholarships. Especially Bob, he thought, needed to be with people his own age. He was not successful, with regard to the scholarships, but Bob would start at the University of Virginia in the fall of 1927, and John at the University of Wisconsin the following year.

Anderson tried to reconstitute the family he grew up with as well. His attempt was inspired by the news, arriving by telegram on February 17, 1926, that his brother Earl had been picked up on a New York street, having suffered a near-fatal stroke. During the many years since Anderson had last seen his brother, in Elyria, Earl had been a sailor, an unsuccessful commercial artist, and, for the last four or five years, a baker's assistant. And always, in his own mind, unwanted. In the room Earl rented, Karl found some drawings, copies of his famous brother's books, and sixty-five dollars, all the money he had. Among his effects at the hospital where he was taken was the unsent letter to Sherwood that told how he felt everyone in the family had turned their backs on him. Earl was "a small silent fellow," Anderson had written in *A Story Teller's Story.* "If I was silent," Earl's letter said, "it was because I was afraid to court hostility."

Feeling guilty, or perhaps feeling his brother's sense of unworthiness as his own, Anderson lunged at him. He wanted Earl to come stay with him in Virginia. That being impossible, he went to see him at Karl's, in Westport, Connecticut, where he was recuperating. He saw him only a half a day, but in that time, he told Bab Finley, he thought he loved more than he had ever loved. He found Earl "the most beautiful man I ever saw . . . the truest finest poet I have ever seen." Upon his return, in the back of a book he wrote words to Earl he probably never sent, telling him he was the brother to whom he most clung, that he needed his love as he needed nothing else in the world. In a letter he did send, he generalized from his feelings: "Men think they seek passion in women. They seek a deep passion, the passion of life itself. No man can live alone. It may be a man can live in another man. I think so."

In March Sherwood's brother Irve came down to New Orleans from Baltimore, where he worked as a factory superintendent for the American Can Company. Though he had had little or no contact with him since Clyde, Anderson had always thought of Irve as the one among his brothers who could stand up to anything, but here he was, his nerves quite "gone back on him," in need of help. "First Earl and now Irve," he wrote Bab, and there seemed very little he could do to help, but he brought Irve on with him to Ripshin in the spring.

During the summer Karl came down and tried in his way to bring the brothers together — in a work of art — but he succeeded only in accentuating their differences. He painted Sherwood and Irve, and when he went back north, he painted in Earl, who had by then been moved to the Marine Hospital in Newport, Rhode Island. The result has Sherwood seated front and center on a sofa, looking hale, and in his light suit, relatively large. His arm is thrown around the sofa, around the space to his left, from which a bespectacled Irve stares out, and in back on his right is Earl, slumped over, clearly beaten. Four years later, Anderson would read a message in his brother's portrayal of him. He knew he had been "arrogant and terrible" at times, he told Karl: he "felt the reproach . . . and it was earned."

It was Earl who mattered most. What was beautiful in Irve was covered up, Sherwood told him. As for Karl, he was, "in a strange way a shadow." Soon after Karl left, as if to make amends for his unspoken feelings Sherwood wrote him to say he'd often been unfair to him, that watching him painting he had been ashamed. If only he could make Karl feel how intensely he admired him, that would be some consolation. But he didn't, really. The next year Karl had a crisis of confidence himself, and Sherwood wished he could help but he was doubtful. In 1929 he told his son John that though Karl had money and social status, he never discovered any truth as a painter. In fact he suspected Karl hated it. "I don't believe it would be possible for him to love either a woman or a landscape," he said. In turn, and around 1929, Karl expressed his own reservations again, in another portrait (this time in a long, unpublished novel) of a writer, nicknamed "Swat," who was a womanizer and a defiler of his mother's memory.

His siblings' troubles would have loomed less large had he been writing well, but after finishing *Tar,* Anderson could find less and less reason to be proud of his own work. Though he wrote a lot, he completed relatively little. "I'll Build My House," "Another Man's House," and "Other Men's Houses" are among the titles of his attempts, but this time reality won out: he was in fact spending much of his time watching Ball's crew work on Ripshin. He contracted to write twelve articles for *Vanity Fair* at three hundred dollars apiece, and in the next few years he wrote at least that many, but what is most apparent about them is their thinness. Some are about places where he had lived (Chicago, New Orleans, the Far West), several are about aspects of where he was living (a mountain dance, county jails, country "squires," or justices of the peace), others are about "the lives of the inconsequential," "small town notes." At times there is a poignancy about them. Always there are short, declarative, or fragmented sentences, questions thrown out not for answers but to suggest childlike wonder or bewilderment, and interruptions and digressions that make for embarrassment, not suspense. It was as if, having written about so many of his subjects so many times before, he was saying: Here, you do it.

As the construction of Ripshin dragged on, Anderson began to sink into depression. In late August he wrote his friend Roger Sergel, telling him how he had gone "creeping to Elizabeth, tears in my eyes," despairing of ever writing anything "decent" ever again and questioning the worth of everything he had ever written. In September, he wrote Karl, telling him that "Another Man's House" wouldn't take shape and that the day before his nerves had gone "rather to pieces."

Nineteen twenty-six had been a difficult, an almost overwhelming year. Earl had appeared and, Anderson must have known, would soon disappear. His feelings for his brothers, or for Elizabeth, were none too sound. His sense of his children's futures was far from clear. In December he published a story in *Scribner's* titled "Another Wife." Its hero was forty-seven but to himself still childlike, the words with which he enters his new marriage surely a reflection of Anderson's spirit this third time around:

"O Lord. I've got me a wife, another wife, a new one," he said to himself as he went along the road in the darkness. How glad and foolish and frightened he still felt! Would he get over it after a time?

He seemed thrown back to childhood as a writer too. Hemingway's and others' criticisms had at least registered on him, but what was worst of all, this time he could not write away to prove them wrong.

On the one hand, there was Ripshin, solid symbol of his success and security; on the other, "Another Man's House," failing to materialize on the page, proof that he was worthless after all. "This year, I undertook too much," he had said to Sergel, "a house and a novel too." At the end of the year he and Elizabeth went to Europe for what was, at best, a diversion.

In late November 1926, he stopped in Newport, feeling "very humble and useless," and saw Earl for the last time. (Earl died just a day before the Andersons returned in March.) In early December Anderson's son John and his daughter Mimi, the one almost eighteen, the other fifteen, showed up in New York, Mimi having been pulled out of class by her mother only the day before and told she was going to Europe. Elizabeth managed to buy her a few dresses before they all sailed on the SS *Roosevelt*; and on board she started to get acquainted with them and to like them both (she soon found that she liked John much more than Robert), while Anderson got to know the crew and the workings of the ship.

Anderson was sick with the flu by the time he arrived in London, and he went on to spend his first ten days in Paris in his room. Almost nothing recalled his glorious days abroad six years before — except by contrast. After meeting with Arnold Bennett and Frank Swinnerton in London, he was displeased by what he thought of (in Bennett's case, at least) as writers selling out to "cheap romancing." In Paris he tried to set up his old routine of writing in the morning, but nothing came. The one person who might have lifted his spirits in Paris didn't. In a few notes he kept about his trip he said that he expected Gertrude Stein, at least, to be the same, and indeed she was, but though they had some conversation, most notably (and futilely) about the possibility of collaborating on a biography of Gen. Ulysses S. Grant, nothing could bring back the excitement of their first meetings six years before. They joined together on social occasions, but Anderson avoided the most important one: a party she gave in his honor. He had Elizabeth go with his excuse about his flu, while he nursed his depression with whiskey.

He had Elizabeth meet with James Joyce alone too, at a meal that was over in record time, Joyce ordering only milk. She had not read *Ulysses,* and before she went out she announced she had no intention of doing so. She was not prepared, she said, to learn a special language, to which Anderson replied, "If you don't understand it, don't read it." But when Anderson joined Elizabeth and Joyce on a subsequent occasion, it went no better. This time Joyce ordered oysters all around, and Anderson, not liking them but not having the courage to make his distaste known, sat in awkward silence.

The day before he left, Hemingway came to his hotel and invited him out for a beer. Hemingway later told Maxwell Perkins that they had had a fine time together, that Anderson was pleased to have received $750 from *Scribner's* for "Another Wife," and that he "was not at all sore" about *Torrents of Spring.* Anderson later wrote that all Hemingway had done was lift his glass, say "Here's how," turn, and walk away. But whoever was or was not cordial to him, however much attention he got, Anderson was too wretched to respond. Shortly after his return, he ran on about his trip like this:

> Sherwood Anderson —
>   A man's name.
>   You hearing it around.
>   Presently a kind of deep sickness. . . .
>   Hemingway made a damn fool by it; Joyce, too. I saw it popping in them both.
>   I am Joyce.
>   I am Hemingway.
>   Christ!

At the same time he wrote to his son John (who had stayed over in Paris to study art) that what he had witnessed was his father at "a dead, blank time." He would remain stalled for much of the following year. "A dumb summer after a dumb winter," he wrote Stein in the fall.

All the while, Elizabeth acted on her belief that the only way to make marriage work with this man was to adapt to him. But she was wrong and increasingly unhappy. In Paris, she got so tired of fronting for her husband or just tagging along that when the inevitable question as to what *she* did came up, she took to answering, "I raise pigs." The one bit of relief came in the person of a former student of her brother's named Ralph Church, who came over to see the Andersons from Oxford; it was relief, really, for them both. With him she could snicker at a poetry reading at Natalie Barney's "Académie des Femmes," while Anderson was trapped in the row in front of them with Stein and Alice B. Toklas. But though they all might share light

The Andersons in the Ozarks, 1913–1914

Anderson back at Taylor-Critchfield, 1914

Tennessee Claflin Mitchell

Members of the Fifty-seventh Street colony at Union Pier, 1914.
Anderson is on the left, Tennessee in the dark robe,
and Margery Currey lying in state.

Marietta ("Bab") Finley

Anderson on Lake Chateaugay, 1917

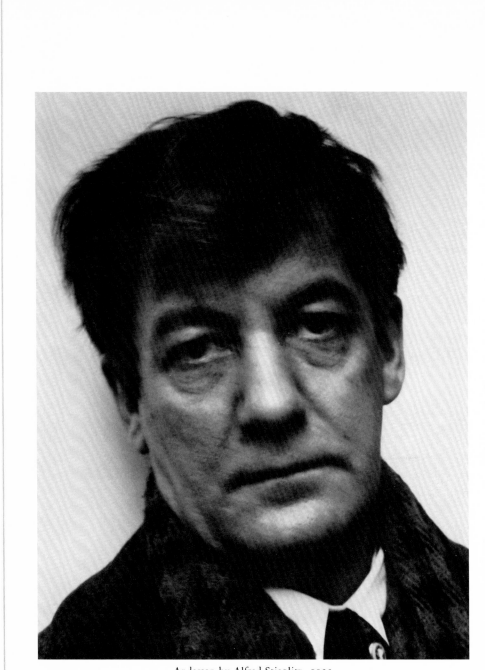

Anderson by Alfred Stieglitz, 1923

Elizabeth Norman Prall and Anderson, by Imogen Cunningham, 1923

Anderson caricatured
by William Spratling
in *Sherwood Anderson and
Other Creoles,* 1926

*He left his factory where he found it—by the side of a stream that
flowed under a bridge in a little Ohio town—at a time in his life
when most men are saving for a soft berth in old age*

"He left his factory where he found it,"
New York *Herald Tribune,* May 16, 1926

Ripshin

Eleanor Copenhaver

Eleanor and Sherwood, Boulder, Colorado, 1937

Anderson and Thornton Wilder aboard the *Santa Lucia*, February 28, 1941

moments on occasion, what Church saw clearly and reported back to his former teacher was that the Pralls had been right about the folly of Elizabeth's marrying Anderson.

After their return to Virginia, she was inclined to agree with them. She later recalled one incident in particular. The two of them were out driving through the countryside as they often did, this time going so far as to cross the North Carolina border. They were shrouded in silence, when suddenly Anderson said in what Elizabeth remembered as "a strange blank voice," "I wish it were all over," and he turned the wheel sharply. The car went off the road but did not flip. When it came to a halt in a field, the two of them sat in silence, and then, after a time, Anderson set about the task of getting the car back on the road, while Elizabeth watched. That accomplished, they drove home to Ripshin in more silence. What filled his were thoughts not only of divorce but of death. Looking back on the year from another gloomy Christmas, he wrote Bab, "Lots of times I said to myself — why don't I die."

If in her pain her vision was sometimes blurred, Elizabeth's understanding of her husband's problem was precise: "He simply could not write and it destroyed his peace of mind." He knew it, and it became more and more evident to others. In August, a review of *A New Testament* in the *New Republic* said what he was feeling. "Sherwood Anderson: Sick of Words" was its title; "The author of 'Winesburg, Ohio,' is dying before our eyes" was its conclusion. When he read it, he said, it made him sick to his soul, and he spent a few days trying to deny what it said, but then he straightened up and asserted that it was the kind of criticism the country needed. He was not a man to dwell on defeat. He was what Virginia Woolf called "shellless," soft, but he was not self-pitying. "We are all too damn tender" — and besides, he said, the man was right. "Let us admit the Sherwood Anderson of *Winesburg* not only dying but quite dead," he told a friend. "Well, let him die. The question that interests me is as to whether there is another Sherwood Anderson coming slowly to life."

"I want a new youth deep down in me," he wrote Bab. And one could hear it coming into being. Other attacks would soon follow, one, by Cleveland Chase the same year, assuming the proportions of a small book. But though he was hurt, his response was fatigue at all the attention and, above all, determination to see if there was yet another Sherwood Anderson.

By the end of September 1927, he had "come to a resolution." He set it down in many letters, this being the version he sent to the Pralls' friend Ralph Church:

> I have decided that for my soul's good, I have got to give up the notion of living by writing. This idea that one must produce constantly, or starve, is terribly detrimental to any sort of freedom of approach.

He had decided to give up making his living by writing and just go out and make his living. The hundred dollars a week that Liveright had been sending him had become a terrible burden, constant reproof for his failure to produce. As soon as he could find another way to make money he would refuse the money.

He was, as he had written Rosenfeld, "too old a bird" for anything to be final for him. He had "waded through other long swamps" before. If he couldn't fly he would slog. He was nothing if not resourceful and, in his way, courageous. As Faulkner said in a very different context, "It takes an awful lot of character to quit anything when you're losing." In fact Anderson would make his living by writing once again, but he would no longer try to live by his writing. He would no longer try to lose himself in his writing. Rather, writing, he would get out and live among others. He had decided to buy — and edit — not one but two newspapers and the printing business that went with them. He thought the ones he had in mind were bringing in about six thousand dollars a year. With great relief, he told Liveright to stop sending money.

Entering the newspaper business wasn't anything he had planned to do. In fact, though he had enjoyed the company of many newspapermen in his day, he had prided himself on writing more durable prose. But the last two or three years, he would soon claim, had been the most miserable he had ever spent, and he was ready to try anything. Sitting in the grandstand at the Smyth County Fair in Marion, Virginia, sometime between August 30 and September 3, watching the trotters and talking to the man next to him, Anderson learned that the two weekly papers in town were up for sale. One was the Republican *Smyth County News,* which had been coming out in an eight-page edition, the other was the *Marion Democrat,* which came out in four. Acting on the information, Anderson launched himself into a new career, started at an earlier stage, even, than George Willard, who, already a reporter, had left the fairgrounds in "Sophistication" to enter into manhood — or he came full circle, having been what George set out to become.

All he needed, he soon found out, was money — $2,500 for each paper — and he knew where he could get it. For a year and a half he had been corresponding with Burton Emmett, another advertising man who had turned to books, but in his case, as a bibliophile. Emmett was highly successful in his business, cofounder of one of New York's largest advertising agencies, and he collected books and manuscripts, American first editions in particular. Even before they met, Anderson opened up to him about his financial and less tangible worries. He wrote Emmett from his Paris room to ask whether he knew of anyone who might be able to "insure" him for "say $2000 or $2500 a year" and thereby enable him to experiment and, perhaps, write well once again. After Anderson began to sell him manuscripts and it looked as if a meeting was about to take place, he admitted that a man who had written so much ought to be more confident of himself but confessed that he was worried: "Suppose you do not like me — at close range."

But now Anderson was if not totally confident, enthusiastic and persuasive. He came away from his first meeting with Emmett, in New York in October, with two notes worth $2,500 apiece, payable in four and five years (though, as both might have foreseen, never to be collected), in return for which Anderson agreed to turn over what manuscripts he could find or produce and for whatever help he could give Emmett persuading other writers to deal with him as well.

Preparing to take over the papers, Anderson came in to Marion from Ripshin more and more that month. On Tuesday, November 1, he owned both of them. The one came out that day, and he was immediately under pressure to get the other one out by Thursday. In less than two months on the job it seemed to him "the most fun of anything I have ever done in my life." For the last two or three years, as he looked back on them, nothing had interested him. He had been spending all too much time with one Sherwood Anderson, and he had never grown so tired of a man in his life, he said. "He crowded himself in between me and everything, the fathead," he wrote Stieglitz and O'Keeffe. Now, thank God, he was too busy to think about him. He was in business now, he was even in advertising once again, with no time for anguish.

He kept his papers' affiliations the way they were, which is to say he retained the postmaster and the local sheriff in their positions as spokespeople for their parties, and made for clearer parity by increasing the length of the *Marion Democrat* to eight pages. He attended to the least details. He might help a man with a handbill announcing

245 · Sherwood Anderson

the sale of steers, or spend an hour arguing with a farmer who wanted twenty-five cents taken off his subscription price. But he was thinking big as well. Within a few weeks he was telling Emmett that when the papers went to the post office there were crowds waiting for it. Subscriptions were coming in from all over the United States. He was thinking about syndicating a personal column he was writing, about putting ads for his papers in the *New Republic* and the book section of the *New York Times*. Also, local advertising was showing results, so he didn't think the men in Emmett's agency need have any hesitation about recommending the papers to their clients.

As he also implied to Emmett, his "having something definitely ahead to do" made his life with Elizabeth much more tranquil. They had had a long talk in which she had accused him of being greedy, of wanting everyone to love him, and he had admitted that she was right. And she had agreed to "break in at the paper" with him. He was not paying her the highest of compliments when he said that he was making her his "Morals Editor," but on the whole he seemed appreciative that she was able to "hold yours truly down." Soon she was working at his side, paying bills, handling subscriptions, ordering type, and happily watching him absorbed in work. By the middle of November, the Andersons had moved into a hotel in town, going out to Ripshin on weekends. In the winter they would just stay in town. In December Anderson wrote Church assuring him that things had changed. They were both leading happier, saner lives — "being very busy."

All through the year, he wrote away. He had a personal column he called "What Say," he wrote editorials, he invented a character named Buck Fever (suggesting a young hunter's nervousness), and wrote enough columns and snippets under his name to fill a volume. When there wasn't enough material, or because the spirit moved him, he printed any and everything, from a poem by Maxwell Bodenheim, to one of his own stories, to any essay by Max Radin on "Crime and the Public," to a letter Emmett sent him from Java, to the Book of Ruth.

He wrote about the seasons and the time of day; he said what he thought about work or "group feeling" or the encroachments of city life; he told about a trip to New York and another to Washington, D.C., where he interviewed then Secretary of Commerce Herbert Hoover, and about the various cats that lived or died around his Marion Publishing Company. He lobbied for the construction of a school for blacks and for the cleanup of a lot across from his office (he called it H. L. Mencken Park, and in appreciation of his efforts the citizenry renamed it Sherwood Forest); he reported on boxing bouts and baseball games, on Kiwanis and Odd Fellow and Rotary and Town Council meetings; he covered court cases involving theft, vandalism, domestic disputes, and the production and consumption of alcohol.

Reading "Buck Fever" we are reminded of previous newspaper creations by Ben Franklin, James Russell Lowell, or Finley Peter Dunne; but Anderson had his own views about country journalism, about its power to strengthen a community's sense of itself and to protect its inhabitants against the leveling influences of other media, coming from other sources, and he wrote and lectured on them frequently.

He managed to keep on writing about the things that were dearest to him, about a slightly Southerly version of mid-American life, about a way of living that was not yet wholly mechanized, about the possible existence of a community. He had done so without having himself intervened, without, it almost seemed, thinking about writing. He was doing so much writing he didn't see it as writing *himself* into existence, but once again that is what it was. After being so exposed for so long, however, he had begun to find some proper clothing. He was surrounding himself with the people who he always claimed were his own, but with whom he had yet to feel at home, with whom he had not even lived since leaving Clyde thirty years before. In the past he had expressed himself, told of his own evolution, or of his liberation, or did so by defending the worth of the overlooked, but now he was being brought out as Communal Man, a man who for the first time might belong.

He had taken up residence in Marion, a town of about four thousand, tucked in among the lovely rounded mountains that edged the Blue Ridge. The very landscape felt old, settled. Anderson's explanation was that it had come "up out of the sea earlier than most places in America." It had had time "to soften its outlines." There was a factory, another furniture factory, but most of its inhabitants lived by operating small businesses that served the farmers of the area. The land around was as yet unspoiled by the industrial giant Anderson had railed against so often — but in his current mood he was not likely to rail about anything. For example, he owned the papers a year before Buck Fever would have to comment on the installation of street lights on what he called the "Rialto," and when he did, he said the huge concrete posts were "darned good looking."

He was at the center of things. Not only was he the town's newspaper editor, but he made the office of his publishing company a kind of library and art gallery, bringing in more than a thousand volumes for people to borrow, and lining its walls with reproductions of works by Renoir, Gauguin, Van Gogh (more and more, his favorite), and originals by Charles Connick and Wharton Eshrick and Stieglitz. He was Marion's celebrity, but he was also one of the men who traded stories on the courthouse steps or in what was called the "Senate Chambers" at the back of Doc Thompson's drugstore. Among the friends he made, his best was a lawyer, Charles ("Andy") Funk, whose sense of humor and way with a tale inspired Anderson as he turned out his Buck Fever entries. He and Elizabeth came to know one of Marion's prominent families, the Copenhavers — Mr. Bascom E. Copenhaver, a lawyer and chairman of the school board, his wife Laura, a lively and intelligent women with whom Anderson argued about the Civil War, and their children, among whom the most adventuresome was Eleanor, who was in her early thirties and working in New York for the YWCA. "It is education — here in Marion," Anderson wrote in his papers after almost two years. "Here I am closer to life than I have ever been. The court, the field, the country road, the farmhouse, the street. It is a school when you have a definite place in it."

But there was always another side to Anderson, always, one might almost say, an opposing side to Anderson. In Marion, even as he claimed to fit in, he feared that as a newcomer he did not, or worse, that he was destined to be an outsider forever. He expressed his fears near the beginning of *Hello Towns!*, a collection of his newspaper writings from his first year. He did so in something like his old staccato style, only now it was tempered, now it convinced:

> An editor's thoughts — not published. Terror. These people. Suppose they find me out.
> Can I do this thing? What do I know of all these lives?
> I have been out of a small town too long. How close it is here. I cannot breathe.
> These people have known each other always. They must know everything about each other. I could not bear to have everything known about me.
> I do not want to be intimate with people.

In his columns he never stepped outside the social structure of the town, but he expressed sympathy for those who had, worrying about conditions in the local jail, for example, or empathizing with the

boys who got drunk and made a row on Saturday night, or with those
who were caught robbing houses. He went further and said that when
he walked into the jail he couldn't see the difference between the
people in there and those outside, that he couldn't see the difference
between them and himself, anyway.

There was the outsider. Less dramatically, there was the man who
simply could not stay put, the man for whom a possibly comfortable
and secure position was "too close." And that meant, of course, that
not only the town and the job but also his marriage would inevitably
begin to feel like a prison.

It had felt that way at least since Paris, certainly since that terrifying ride into North Carolina. Elizabeth had tried, but she had never
liked Virginia half so much as her husband. As for the newspapers,
she knew they had saved him, but not her, and finally not them. As
for friends, she really didn't have any. Even the Copenhavers were her
husband's. She had many in New Orleans, in Paris she could make
do with Alice B. Toklas while her husband talked to Stein or she
could share a sacrilegious moment with her brother's student, but
though "nice enough," the women of Marion were essentially church-
goers, "very uninteresting and highly opinionated." She had gone
along with Ripshin but as if with a vengeance. She had furnished it
in the grand manner, and that began to annoy Anderson. It accentuated his worries about money, it seemed to defeat the purpose of
their venture. It was "wild purchasing . . . purchasing of baubles,"
Anderson said, but even as he said it, he knew that it was also her
solace, a way "to compensate perhaps for love [he] could not give."

In December 1928, just before the Christmas holidays, Anderson
encouraged Elizabeth to go out to Berkeley to visit her family while
he went to Chicago to lecture. He thought they could afford it, and
she ought to go where it was warm and see her family, none of whom
she had seen in a long time. Once there she received what she thought
would be one of those long letters of his, those gleanings of his latest
reflections. It was a note instead. It simply stated that he wished she
would not come back.

She can't have been surprised. Their separation was abrupt, hurt-
ful, inexcusable from her point of view, but there was little more to
say. Her belongings were shipped west. Though the divorce was not
final until 1932, the proceedings were smooth, the settlement was
just. "The Princess," as Anderson had started calling her, made a
minimum of fuss.

For a few years Elizabeth ran the Stanford University bookstore in

Palo Alto, California, and then, having gone to Taxco, Mexico, to visit an old friend from New Orleans and finding Bill Spratling had moved there too, she stayed until she died in 1976. "I really loved Sherwood," she told a young scholar in 1947, "but he got tired of me, and there was nothing more to do about it. It was as simple as that."

From his point of view, there was only slightly more to say. He saw the pattern clearly. "Poor E. is very very nice," he wrote friends, "much nicer than I will ever be — and I do not want her anymore. C. and T. were nice too. Why should I not face myself a wanderer." A wanderer and, he still hoped, an artist. That was the last self, the one he ultimately depended on, the one that could find material in the worst of his failures and the depths of his loneliness. *He* may not have been dependable, but that in itself was potentially lasting: he walked all night, Anderson said, thinking, "This sheer loneliness I feel is a part of my materials too. It is like paint. I shall brush it into a canvas tomorrow."

That January he said the same thing to Bab Finley, after seeing her in Indianapolis on his way to lecture in Chicago. When they met in his hotel room, he was again like Winesburg's Enoch Robinson, terrified lest a woman steal his being. She still wanted him, he felt, but he knew he had to be alone. She offered her continuing support, but, as he wrote her when he was back in Marion, he would no longer accept help from anyone, "least of all from any woman." "You have, my dear, as much right to all you feel, as woman, as I have to what I feel as artist and man," he said. "But now I am separated from that. I have fought to get here in this room alone."

He meant his metaphors. He was living in an apartment above his office, and he had everything he needed, primarily a small kitchen table, three feet by two, and a kitchen chair. He was "at the end of *things*," he was going to sell Ripshin. He wanted only to work, to write. If Bab wanted to be a friend to the artist in him, well and good, but: "As to me, as a man, it should be forgotten now." And so it was. There were a few more letters, a meeting in the spring of 1932, at which Anderson met her future husband, another in 1938, and her request in 1933 that she and Dr. Hahn might publish his letters, "the impersonal ones" with his "running commentary on life and living."

Women seemed intrusive; so too did the daily routine of running two newspapers — the whole business surrounding the newspapers, in fact. His son Bob helped him avoid the routine. After a year at the University of Virginia and having gained some experience working at the *Philadelphia Bulletin,* he moved in with his father over the printing office and soon began to take over the responsibility of running the Marion Publishing Company. (On January 1, 1932, Anderson turned the company over to him officially, splitting the proceeds between his two other children. In March of the next year, Emmett canceled his debt.) In response to Emmett's dissatisfaction with the paucity of collectable items he was receiving as payment for his loan, all Anderson could say was that he was sorry, he didn't blame Emmett, but what with the breakup of his third marriage and, as he now saw it, his having no time for his "real work," it had been "a bad year." If it was any consolation, owning the papers had "saved [him] from insanity," and as Emmett would see in April, he had dedicated *Hello Towns!* to him and his wife, Mary.

In February 1929, Anderson published a piece in *Outlook* titled "Let's Go Somewhere." It took the form of a letter to Charles Bockler, a young painter tied down to a job in a New York bank, whom he was trying to help. In it, he rambled back through places he had been, Mobile Bay, Louisville, the city of New Orleans, and concluded by saying, "Come on, let's go South." And for a month he did — alone. He also went to Washington, D.C., where he made friends and later corresponded with a German baroness and with a man, Maurice Long, who owned a laundry there. Much of July he spent with Bockler and his wife in a house he enabled them to rent in upper New York State, and in spite of his resolve he became involved with Bockler's sister-in-law, a woman named Mary Greer.

The visit with the Bocklers did not go as planned. Charles was there to paint, he to write. But Bockler's wife turned out to be pregnant, and in his narrowed frame of mind, all Anderson could focus on was the sounds of her misery, and he did so unsympathetically. Six months before, what he had heard was "But you do not love me," he wrote the baroness; now it was Katherine's whining and the sounds of her morning sickness — "echoes of my own married life." He went back to Marion, and he spent most of the fall in Richmond, Virginia; then in December he went to Chicago for two weeks to see his daughter Mimi, who had begun to study at the University of Chicago. By the end of the year he was in Saint Petersburg, Florida, and there he heard much more disturbing echoes: he heard that Tennessee was dead.

In December she had written Bernadine Szold that there was "another ex-wife of Sherwood." A friend had told her that Anderson claimed men wouldn't suffer so were it not for women and that he would never marry again, "but," she said to Bernadine, "that person is subject to change without even short notice." Though she was defensively wry about Anderson to others, she had begun to write him letters from Chicago, where she still lived, after five years of silence. When Anderson was in the city, they talked on the phone several times, and one night Tennessee was to join him and Mimi and his friends the Schevills for dinner. At the last minute someone came to see her and she couldn't, but she was anxious for him to come to her apartment. She displayed "a certain crudeness of approach," Anderson said when he heard the news of her death. Perhaps she had been too bold, but Anderson knew full well that she needed "a little love and comradeship" and that he didn't give it to her. He never saw her. On December 26 she was found dead in her apartment. She had been dead for several days, probably from an overdose of pills.

"Women do get me," he confessed at the time of his divorce from Tennessee, "and then I lose them utterly." He lost them to his work, he said. It was the only place where he could grow. She wasn't to blame. "Perhaps the bare truth," he said, "is that T. was sacrificed to that by some inner voice that said over and over, 'Do it, do it.'" Now, on the Gulf once more, he wrote the Schevills, "I could wreck myself forever on this shore. The whole coast is alive with the jagged rocks of my unkindness." And he told Mimi, Tennessee "had so many fine qualities that it is horrid to think how many times I hurt her." "But," he went on, "if I began thinking of that I would go crazy."

As the year and the decade were about to end, knowing that three marriages had ended too, Anderson stood on the pier for a while, looking out over the waters of the Gulf and down at the rocks along the shore — "the jagged rocks of my unkindness." He knew just how cruel he could be, but however critical he was of himself, Anderson was not one to "wreck" himself forever. So he turned around and retraced his steps back to land.

ELEVEN

The Political Years

1929-1933

THOUGH HIS WRITING had not gone well for years, Anderson had never given up. In 1927 the *New Republic* had said he was dying, and the next year Dwight MacDonald, then managing editor of the *Yale Literary Magazine,* said much the same thing in what Anderson himself called a "funeral oration." Reviews of *Hello Towns!* were numerous but bland, except one, again in the *New Republic,* that began, "Hello, readers of the *New Republic. I* have been reading a book by Sherwood Anderson. He liked to write it more than I enjoyed reading it." But Anderson was not daunted. Typically, he had written MacDonald to say he might well be right, but people had been reporting his death even before *Winesburg, Ohio.* All he could do was try new approaches. If he failed, he had failed before — in fact his artistic failures were the "only decent thing" about him.

That year his failure was a 350-page novel he tried to write in Richmond. He titled it "No Love," or "No God," then "Sacred Service," and then "Beyond Desire." As he had told MacDonald, it seemed always necessary for him "to live first what may possibly later be distilled into what I want and need." The living, he had said, had recently been "very very difficult." "No Love" was about that living, about the contrast between the old ways of women, represented by the hero's wife, who bought too many antiques and whom he would have divorced had she not been killed in a car accident, and the new ways that he learns to accept, the ways of "the young female kid of today" who is sexually liberated. The familiar figure of the artist who marries a woman with money and then runs away from her and their children figures in it, as does a version of Maurice Long. It was never published and, according to a note in Burton Emmett's will, Anderson never wanted it published, if for no other reason, one imagines, than that he knew it was terrible.

Writing to both his son John and Charles Bockler in October, he said he had gone as far as a man could go "on the road of feeling." More specifically, he and his generation had gone "a little nuts" about sex. As he announced to correspondent after correspondent, he was tired of it. "No Love" didn't move, he wrote Liveright, because it was about "middle-class people in love." He was through with them and their problems, through with what he described to Roger Sergel and his wife as "the story of sex, what man does to woman and woman to man, what marriage does, etc." He was out of the stage of his writing that had begun at least as far back as the spring of 1920 in Fairhope, Alabama, when he started *Many Marriages*.

Nor did he want to have anything to do with the life he saw all around him in Saint Petersburg — which was not middle-class people in love, but middle-class people in what they imagined to be financial straits, retirees worrying about how they would be affected by the Depression. The Panic had set in a little over two months before, in late October. Within a few weeks, $30 billion of capital values had been swept away. Having foresworn *things,* having vowed to live on next to nothing, Anderson did not feel involved. More important, he had his own depression to worry about.

Anderson reacted against what he considered the "dreadful kind of slack middleclass oldness" of the residents of Saint Petersburg as if it were contagious. They were not old like Alfred Stieglitz, say, still struggling, still alive. They were just "dreadfully old." All they did was play shuffleboard and talk about money. "By God, man, the people," he sputtered to the Schevills, "they are old, they are diseased, they stumble horribly, they play little games in the park, they are all so rather middle-class." If the Schevills could be there with him, lying in the sun, talking about something other than the stock market and how fast their cars would go, he could imagine staying and resting his nerves. But as it was, he had to get out, had to go back up North.

Though there was much in his personal life that threatened to overwhelm him as the year and the decade came to an end, Anderson was through with himself in only the most positive sense. He had found something new to write about. He had a new subject. "As regards my work," he said to Bab Finley, "I have felt . . . a going back toward my own people, working people." He was going north to get back in touch with *them*. In their midst, he said, his nerves would disappear. He wished he were thirty rather than fifty-three, but as he emerged from the depressing state of Florida, he had plenty of energy to spare.

He had discovered "working people." More specifically, he had discovered the labor movement, not the common men and women whom he had written about in his most famous book, or those whose news he had been publishing for several years, but workers — other "poor whites" — particularly mill workers, whom he had just begun to meet in his wanderings around southwest Virginia and over the border into North Carolina and Tennessee. He imagined he had never been out of touch with these men and women. Remembering how hard she had worked, how she had taken in other people's wash, he wondered if in coming upon them now he wasn't responding to his mother's call. But he had yet to write about them. Now he had a feeling that their story was "the great, big story of America" and he was going to be the one to tell it. He wrote Bab that the reality of labor's life might prove more fantastic than anything he had ever imagined.

He had first heard *this* story from Eleanor Copenhaver one time when she had come back to Marion from New York to visit her parents. In her work in the Industrial Division of the YWCA she had come to know much more about the subject than he did. That was one of the most attractive things about her. She had been interested in the plight of working people, of working women in particular, for years.

Anderson had had his initiation some time in early 1929, when he had gone down through the mountain valleys of eastern Tennessee with her, to Elizabethton, where the workers in two rayon plants there had organized themselves. Perhaps he joked about the name Elizabethton, said something about the "Princess" who was now in California, but for once he did not do most of the talking. Eleanor was there on business. She was going because of her work in the Industrial Division. It was she who had a story to relate, the story, the undeniably true and moving story, of the condition of working women in the mill towns of the South.

When they arrived, Anderson saw what he had written about in

Winesburg, Ohio and *Poor White,* saw the transformation, the degradation, of a town (and by extension, a society) with the coming of industry, and saw what happened to its citizens, especially its women, in the process. There were the mill or factory hands whom he had said in his "Apology for Crudity," way back in 1917, were "the dominant note in American life today," but whose lives he'd only imagined since he left the bicycle factory thirty or forty years before.

Now the very buildings of Elizabethton told a story that he took down. The earlier structures were made of brick and timber, their outlines clean and strong. The ones built within the last five years were mere "box construction . . . cheap buildings with cheap dodads on them." The dirty sinks and the fragments of soap in the washroom were enough to sum up the "new" hotel where they dined. But what impressed him most in Elizabethton were the women — the girls — who worked in the rayon mills. They were shockingly young, twelve or thirteen years old at most. What with their developing goiters and thin legs and stooping shoulders, though, their "mill age" was two and three times that.

The girls were woefully underpaid and powerless, but one day — spontaneously — they had led a walkout, and though management had dealt with the workers with brutal casualness and they had returned to work, they had begun to form a union. The A.F. of L. having sent out an organizer, they now had a local of the Textile Workers of America.

The night Anderson and Eleanor were there they attended a meeting. A few hours before, they had seen the mill workers coming out of the factories. At the meeting, the workers seemed wholly different beings. The men seemed more dignified. Excited, the little girls stood up straight and their delicate features shone. Fifty workers joined. There was joy in the room, applause as each new member was sworn in, and there was total dedication. Anyone who couldn't pay his or her dues was spoken for by another. When it was reported that the company would fire anyone who joined, one man spoke up for everyone: "I lived on birdeye beans before there was any rayon plant in these hills and can live on birdeye beans again." Anderson himself had to confess he did not know what would come of all the activity, but he felt that these men and women, and thus "men everywhere who work in fields, in factories and shops," were closer to him than any other men or women would ever be. There was what he called "a kind of religion of brotherhood" that to him, if not to Eleanor, was more important than any wage increase that they might win.

In the light of what was revealed at that meeting, he rewrote his youth, spoke of it in letters as having had him working in factories for years, and he resolved to write his future by it. He knew he was no longer a working-class man but a member of "the artist class." Still, he would share these workers' sense of purpose, accept the men as brothers, the girls as sisters. And in fact he was faithful to his new calling for the rest of his life.

Eleanor had pointed the way. She was a small, quick, energetic woman, eager to confront and bring out the best in the people she met. Anderson described her as "a little dark-eyed, Italian-looking woman," thereby tracing her lively spirit back to what he liked to imagine was the source of his own. She resembled Bab Finley in her appearance, but her sights were set not only on Anderson, but on her own goals, her own work. With Bab and with his wives Anderson turned inward, and when he did he made his own life, his own career, their mutual concern. By the very fact of having another life, Eleanor led him out of his own.

Her education, her experience, everything about her situation set her farther apart from Anderson than any woman he had known intimately before. He was a man with the equivalent of a high school education, a man who had constructed himself out of very raw materials. From Marion, Eleanor had gone to the University of Richmond, and then on to Bryn Mawr, where she earned a certificate in social work in 1920. That same year she began what would be her forty-year career in the YWCA. When Anderson first knew her, she was also working toward the master's degree in political economy that she would receive from Columbia in 1933. She was twenty years his junior, seemingly just the daughter of his friends the Copenhavers, home on vacation from her job in New York. As she herself said, the Copenhaver he seemed most drawn to at first was her mother, who was only eight years older than he. Yet Eleanor's difference made him all the more at ease with her.

How soon they became lovers we do not know, but from what Anderson said, "love" at first was not the point. After three marriages, he had few illusions about his ability to sustain that emotion. In his contribution to a volume called *The New Generation,* which came out in 1930, Anderson said, disarmingly, that he really had nothing much to say. The "young" (who included Eleanor) had new attitudes towards such things as sex and socialism, war and family. life. As for himself, he had found that he only hurt people when he got involved. He had become "a bearer of poison." It was better that he not "try to live too close to a woman" or to his children. Speaking specifically of the men who had been through the war, he said that in their presence he felt more like a child than a father: he was "a man who needs to be taught, not one who feels himself capable of teaching."

In November 1930, in a letter to his brother Karl, Anderson said as much about his relation to Eleanor. In it, he is all passivity, a man directed; she is his teacher, a sterner and more demanding one than he had ever known. He admitted how much he was influenced by women — "They are such an important and necessary part of my life" — and indeed, another woman had come along and "got at" him, he said, but she had done so "in a new way." This time it was not just a love affair, "an amorous matter." Eleanor was "a woman of brains and purpose," and she had work she wanted him to do. She had "got ahold of [him] rather for a purpose of her own." She felt that he was wasting his time, he said. She felt that *all* American writers were wasting their time insofar as they were overlooking the hardest economic facts of contemporary life, and he was persuaded she was right: "No one was going into the factories, seeing the life inside factories, seeing modern machinery at first hand, noting its effect on men etc. and she got me interested."

In *Perhaps Women,* the first book that Anderson wrote about his new brothers and sisters in the working class, before her he is the lowliest of creatures:

> It was a woman who had got me to do it.
> She had come to me, to where I was staying, in a small town.
> I had escaped from the roar of the big industrial cities.
> I was in a quiet place.
> I was like a turtle with his head drawn in, sleeping under a bush.
> The woman had poked me with a stick. She had forced me to crawl out from under my bush.
> I can remember the scorn with which she spoke to me.

She said he was a coward, she said "cowardice was the note in American men now." They were like little children, with their eyes closed, crying. Fixated on sex, the writers among them missed what changes were occurring in the age of the machine ("as though there were no

impregnation other than sex impregnation," she said); the hard-
boiled types, the young engineers, the financiers, accepted everything
("achieving thereby," she went on, "a shallowness almost inconceiv-
able"). "But what am I to do?" Anderson asks. "Go and look," she
replies:

> "Stay looking.
> "Come out of your shell.
> "Go to the factories, it is a new age. The new age is to be worked
> out inside the walls of the factories."

And so he would.

Unlike Elizabeth Prall, Eleanor had no qualms about trying to
influence Anderson. She had a purpose. She made that clear. And she
succeeded where Cornelia and Tennessee did not. She succeeded because she was not so exclusively concerned with him. It was American
society, and Anderson as he and his writings could contribute to the
betterment of American society, that she had in mind. And accordingly, he became less self-absorbed than he had ever been before.
Eventually, in July of 1933, the two would marry. But marrying was
not what they set out to do.

Having come to know Eleanor, Anderson determined to escape not
only the middle-class manners of Saint Petersburg but also his own,
which, he realized, were not all that different. He was divorcing
Elizabeth, but there was still Ripshin, associated in his mind, with
"baubles," with "antique furniture, dresses, fur coats," and, not so
indirectly, with the shoddy writing he had been doing. Thousands of
dollars had gone into the place, and in order to come up with them,
he had rushed into print, skimmed the milk, as he put it, "before
the cream had time to rise." He wanted to be rid of it. Mrs. Copenhaver had set aside a room in Rosemont, their handsome house in
Marion, where he could come and write. When he was not on the
road he would be staying with his son Bob, over the print shop.
When Bob married a teacher at the local college in December
1931, Anderson rented a room from the Sprinkle family, who lived
nearby.

He didn't need Ripshin. But he did need the money. Bab Finley's
fund for the children had long since dried up. He wanted to help
John get a start as a painter. He had taken over the responsibility of
Mimi's education, and he wanted her to stay on at the University
of Chicago. And in general, after his exposure to the mill villagers of
Elizabethton, he felt that he no longer belonged among the landed

gentry: if he belonged anywhere, he said, it was among "the defeated people."

His initial scheme was to turn Ripshin into a club for, say, six members, including himself, the others putting in three thousand dollars apiece, and he sent out word to those who could afford to pay that much (Burton Emmett and Alys Bentley, for example) or knew others who could. It was a wild if not a shady idea, one he might have thought up in Elyria. When nothing came of it, he said he would accept any offer over five thousand dollars. In July of 1932 he made the futile suggestion to the Mountain Mission Associates that they convert it into a health center for their nurses. Finally, what with his marriage in 1933, he reconciled himself to its attractiveness as a country retreat. He withdrew from Marion, its ways having long since seemed dull to him, the point of view of its citizens "a bit too childish," and from his newspapers.

Anderson never was confident in his handling of money. He was never sure he had enough, even while he worked for Taylor-Critchfield. If he had money, he spent it, and spent it generously; when he did not have it, he panicked. If Emmett sent him five hundred dollars he considered himself rich, and then when his balance went down below five hundred dollars he would start to worry. During his recent periods of prosperity, before his conversion to his faith in working people, he had been uncomfortable. He had been concerned that his having Ripshin set him too far apart from his neighbors. The very fact of his having money seemed somehow wrong. There was Dostoevsky, he wrote Emmett in 1927, and then, contemptuously: "Me with my full belly — 5 suits of clothes, a stone house."

He wanted money to write, release from financial worry, but when the money was given to him to *produce* or if it was for work he disapproved of, he could not write. "It is perhaps only when we try to bend the arts to serve our damn middle-class purposes that we become unclean," he wrote on his way north from Saint Petersburg. He was as good as his word, he acted on it. After all, he had had Liveright cut off his allowance. When Eleanor returned to New York in early 1930, she tried to interest the Straights, the "angels" of the *New Republic,* in financing Anderson's efforts to understand the labor movement, but in March he stepped in. There were so many other needs that were more pressing, he said. He would get by. What he published he would publish in magazines that didn't pay very well, or in labor papers, many of which could not pay at all. After a year of trying to fulfill the task that Eleanor had set him, he estimated he had passed up the chance to earn as much as three or four thousand dollars writing "for popular magazines."

He was by no means well-to-do; he made sacrifices, but he respected himself the more for making them. Nineteen thirty, his first year in the field, was a happy, purposeful one. When he left Saint Petersburg, he knew where he was headed and what he was looking for. For the better part of three months he drove through Georgia and South Carolina, and then, after resting in New Orleans, he made his way back to southwest Virginia. From there he took trips to other parts of the state and over the line into West Virginia and North Carolina. He stayed in a lumber camp, visited a sugar refinery, planned "to tackle the inside of steel mills." He enlisted Emmett's support in his efforts to persuade cigarette manufacturers to let him tour their plants. Mostly he concentrated on textile mills and the little mill villages, like the one in Elizabethton, that had sprung up in their shadows. He talked to mountaineers and farmers, factory and mill workers, garage attendants, hitchikers, to anyone he could get to sit down with him where he or she worked or in the lobbies and restaurants of the small hotels in which he had stayed. As had been the case in Chicago or New Orleans, in his presence these people, who might well have been suspicious of this colorful stranger who approached them, felt that they could tell him their stories. Willingly they became his "feeders," sources sometimes for tales, but more urgently now, for his report on the condition of factory workers in America. At the end of the year, he was on the one hand chastened, struck by how ineffectual he was in these new writerly circumstances, and on the other he was as excited about his work as he had ever been: "Perhaps I have got, in a queer way, a new sense of God," he wrote Charles Bockler in November. "Well, I do not say 'God'; I say 'The Thing.' I mean a going toward something, find this way and that, as you painters do." He was as excited as he had been fifteen years before when he knew, without a doubt, that he could write, and when in writing he had created — in his imagination, *lived* — a life of which he was not ashamed. The language is the same. Like George Willard, he was approaching "the thing," "the thing that makes the mature life of men and women in the modern world possible." About three times George's age, and for the tenth, or twelfth, or fifteenth time (who could say?), Anderson stood on the threshold of maturity, of manhood.

"The original revolving doorman of literature," Harry Hansen called him after his death, but Anderson might have come back with Gertrude Stein's proposition that there was no such thing as repetition. "We inside us do not change but our emphasis and the moment in which we live changes. That is it is never the same moment it is never the same emphasis at any successive moment of existing," she said. Our responses, our writings can never be the same: "No matter how often what happened had happened any time any one told anything there was no repetition." At least they could never be the same so long as what her mentor William James had called "the Will to Live" was operating.

Certainly it was in Anderson. He was still Sherwood Anderson, genial, cagey, buoyant, sympathetic, trying to understand and write up the lives of the "defeated"; but not to speak of what he had been through personally, this time around, the world, the "environment," was different. This time it was the Southeast. He had left the industrialized Midwest and Northeast behind, he cared not at all about the fluctuations or the steady decline of the stock market, nor even about their effects (not yet, at least), and he never would survey the ravaged, dusty western plains. This time it was agricultural territory, filling up with machines and factories and mill villages, like Clyde or Bidwell, only in a different place, at a different time. His writing about it would be recognizably his, but different.

He would not be working from memory, nor would he concentrate on fictional versions of himself. In Whitmanesque terms, he would sing less of himself, more about the results of his being the man who was there. And he would find the form to match. He would continue to sing, or chant, but as he said to Bockler, he could no longer "concentrate on pure storytelling":

> The artist is, after all, partly a product of his environment. . . .
> He does not escape the general tone and mood of the world in any
> event. It is antagonistic now. We can't escape the fact. We have to
> participate.

The results, the pieces that he wrote on and about his travels, were titled "Factory Town," "Night in a Mill Town," "Machine Song," "Loom Dance," "Cry in the Night," "It's a Woman's Age," titles that suggest how he combined narratives of sorts and elements of the discursive essay with something like his chants and testaments to convey his special sense of labor's movements. In his *Memoirs* he called *Per-*

haps Women, the little volume in which he collected most of them, "the work of a metaphysician." More modestly in the preface he wrote to it in April 1931 he called it "nothing but an impression, a sketch." A few years later he thought it might have the makings of an opera. In the mix, at the very least, one hears how eagerly Anderson wanted to "participate."

Thematically too, *Perhaps Women* presented a new version of Anderson's thinking about men and women in the machine age. In his prefatory words, it expressed his "conviction that modern man is losing his ability to retain his manhood in the face of the modern way of utilizing the machine and that what hope there is for him lies in women." His theory was that men had lost their power to machines, lost touch, their lives become vicarious. They had accepted, as if it were their own, for example, the power to get from one place to another in a car, and the idea of superiority over the next man because of owning a fast car; they had even accepted such power without paying for it, power on the installment plan. Men were "on the road of impotence." But women were not, women were not controlled by their machines, women could outlast them, and so, once again, to women fell the responsibility of patiently waiting for men to come into their manhood.

Though he had forsworn writing about middle-class people in love, and wondered if his generation hadn't emphasized sex too much, he had no reservations about bringing out the sexual implications of his analysis. Men were becoming impotent, he said, because they had indulged themselves so long they could "no longer stand erect." The machines had put them to shame. No wonder the women worked at their machines so lovingly: they would never be touched with the delicacy their machines displayed as they produced cotton balls. "Here is always hardness," he said. "Here is always the thing done, accurately and truly. No blundering here." One hears cries like Anderson's in the work of previous and later American romantics, from Ralph Waldo Emerson to Henry Adams to Amiri Baraka to Norman Mailer. Yet though he too deplored how machines were running or emasculating men, only Anderson could have imagined that the women were erotically drawn to them.

If he had an idol at the time, though, it was not an American, it was D. H. Lawrence. They had never met, but they had commented on each other's work respectfully, and they would forever be compared or lumped together. Now Lawrence had just died in 1930, and

Anderson wrote a review essay for the *New Republic* and another one two years later, claiming Lawrence as his own. Lawrence represented "the whole notion of Kingship in men." Nobody seemed to understand, not John Middleton Murry or Catherine Carswell or Mabel Dodge Luhan. At least nobody put it the way Anderson did: Lawrence represented true maleness; he was too good a man to sneak around, to treat women casually; he had transcended individuality, he was a giver, a teacher, the ideal worker. Anderson ended his second essay with the curious image of blood from a cut on his hand smeared on the paper before him:

> Little red blotches of my blood covering the sheets on which I try to write of D. H. Lawrence, dead.
> Spoiling the sheets.
> Blood spoiling clean white sheets of paper.
> Not quite. Blood is nice on white sheets on which a man speaks, even falteringly, of a man's man like D. H. Lawrence.

At the very least, he imagined Lawrence as his blood brother.

Of course Anderson's were cries one also heard in his previous work (and though not so clearly, they were still susceptible to autobiographical readings), but unlike the romantics and himself, now he was going to show that men could appreciate and stand up to the machine. He began *Perhaps Women* with "Machine Song," a "Song written at Columbus, Georgia, in a moment of ecstasy born of a visit to a cotton mill." "I am sick of my old self that protested against the machine," he wrote. "I am sick of that self in me, that would not live in my own age." And he went on to sing of the glories of a car ride from Chicago to Miami, of "going at forty, at fifty, at sixty miles an hour," not hearing but feeling new music in his nerves:

> *Touch this key — a field.*
> *That key — a sloping field.*
> *A creek covered with ice.*
> *A snow-covered field.*
> *Curves in the road.*

He went on to sing of losing himself "in a hundred thousand men, in a hundred thousand women."

He wrote of a "Loom Dance" in which a "minute-man," no heroic patriot but an efficiency expert, was driven out of a mill for having tried to coordinate weavers' movements to the movements of machines. When he tried to clock a woman's trip to the washroom, her husband and all their fellow workers knocked him down and trampled him, their legs "hard and still like legs of looms," and afterward they all danced and shouted in the yard. In "Cotton Mill" Anderson tried to render the processes of thread making and the thread's transformation into cord and cloth. So many writers had interpreted machines as dehumanizing, alienating, and the like. Anderson himself saw such results in his "minute-man," but he also saw the marvel, the delicacy, the challenge of the workings of machines. Anderson compared them to natural wonders and said the girls were "half in love" with them.

He had had "a change of heart," he wrote the editor of *Household Magazine,* where "Machine Song" first appeared. He used to be "one of the outstanding little protesters against the machine age," but now he was trying "to go to machinery as a man might go to the mountains and to the forests and rivers." He was not going to be awed by the machine like Henry Adams, or like the Eugene O'Neill of the recent *Dynamo,* nor was he simply going to welcome in a technological utopia. He had no admiration for the young technocrats he encountered on his tours; and while all America praised Charles Lindbergh for the individual heroisms of his flight three years before, Anderson saw him as "rather nice" but basically "all machine" — another cog. Anderson was calling for men to be men again, masters of the machines they had — after all — built themselves. He had real craftsmen in mind, craftsmen comparable to, "as important in the life swing of mankind, as the [men] who built the Cathedral of Chartres."

Finally, of course, he was thinking of what he was trying to do as he wrote. In a section of *Perhaps Women* titled "Ghosts," he said that in spite of what others might think, some of his friends, for example, who thought he was physically large, his own image of himself was "often enough" of "a peculiarly small and ineffectual man," and he wondered: maybe that was why he wrote with such bravado, such assurance; maybe he was trying to be, at least in writing, the man he feared he could not be in life. Maybe, "'I am trying,' I tell myself, 'to find in words a boldness not in myself.'"

He was trying to live up to Eleanor's expectations, and eventually he did, but he was not optimistic about most men's ability to be valorous. How many men, for example, could find themselves as craftsmen at the present time? "Perhaps women," perhaps women would save them, perhaps they would oblige. But *Perhaps Women* does not inspire confidence. The women in it loom larger than almost all previous Andersonian teachers, lovers, wives, and mothers.

Now as one piece has it, "'It is a Woman's Age,'" a factual age, "and in a factual age women will always rule." By Anderson's reading, Woman was in control, especially at home, her image well established in comic strips and magazines, "bringing up father," or as the harridan whom pathetic husbands wait on hand and foot, Thurber's woman-as-house, the suburban Venus flytrap, waiting to devour her prey. In the J. J. Lankes woodcut that introduced Anderson's text, she is high in the saddle, leading a slumped and sad-faced man on a donkey out of a factory town. It was an image the more powerful, Anderson thought, because men depended on it for assurance that at least some other poor devil was "getting his."

After he had seen "Woman" in her youth in Elizabethton, driving out of town, he thought the town's citizens should have erected a monument in her honor. Touring, he had seen her at her machine and imagined her untouched, physically tired but alive in spirit because she was for all time, fruition of a profounder sort. She was not just producer, but reproducer: "She remains, she will remain," he said, "a being with a hidden inner life." Men's one hope was that however seductive the machine was, it could never bring children into the world. Women needed men. They would help men check the power of their magnificent machines. Like Hugh McVey in *Poor White,* they would have to make it possible for men to work shorter hours, spend more time outdoors and with each other — in sum, "get men back, so that [women] may continue to be fertilized, to produce men."

That women might not oblige is evident from the final, macabre tale, "The Cry in the Night." In it, Anderson tells of visiting a factory one night when an accident throws it into darkness. The machines roar on. Above the noise, he hears a woman laughing hysterically and shouting, "Kiss me. Kiss me while the lights are out." A man speaks up, wearily, "Who? Me?" and when she says "No, not you," others try: "Me?" "Me?" To all of them she answers, "No, not you. None of you. I want a man," and other women take up the laughter. The tale and the book end with the mill superintendent's explanation that the women often mock the men that way, implicitly with Anderson's fear that women couldn't care less, with the kind of fear, we might say, that comes of paying women such excessive respect.

His imagings of women's power had always elicited his most drastic responses. Socially and politically, his participation was more tentative, more judicious. He was a writer, somewhat removed, imagining how the world might be improved. "The better living is the end," he put it in November 1930, again to Charles Bockler. An artist could participate, he said awkwardly (foreshadowing the difficulty he would have determining just *how* he should participate), "without quite thinking that what might be called propaganda for better living is an end in itself." Socialism was not the goal, "certainly not wholesale Communism" — just "better living is the end." It was what painters aimed at. Bockler would know. There was Van Gogh, for example, whose chair, whose room, whose workman's boots, told of the artist's intense responsiveness to and respect for the humbler things and people of this world, and whose letters (Anderson's favorite text at the time) told of "the need of love as an integral part of work."

Under the pressure of events, everyone seemed to be joining up, taking a stand, but at first Anderson tried to see the merits of every argument. That same November, at a debate between Stringfellow Barr and John Crowe Ransom over "Industrialism vs. Agrarianism," Anderson was literally a moderator. Thirty-five hundred people, including the governor, the mayor, and various college presidents, came to the Richmond City Auditorium and heard Anderson read eight long, typewritten pages by way of an introduction to the evening's proceedings. After some words about the unfulfilled promise of "bigness," he expounded on his ideas about vicarious power, about the differences between the North and the South (and as he had done ten years before in Fairhope, he brought down his clenched fist and gradually opened it, to symbolize the difference), and about his own anomalous position. "If I am in any sense at all a son of Virginia," he said, "I am an illegitimate son." He introduced the speakers, gave them each a hearing, and yet — by his own account, at least — he came close to stealing the show himself.

In his "introduction," he also took time to deplore the fact that Sinclair Lewis had just won the Nobel Prize for literature. It should have gone to Dreiser, he thought. It had been given, instead, "to a hater, not a lover of American life." Four months before, *Scribner's* had given Anderson's "Cotton Mill" pride of place, and introduced it, appropriately, as a "protest against an unbalanced view of industrial life." Originally the piece had been a direct attack on Sinclair Lewis (and titled "Labor and Sinclair Lewis"). He had been "laying for that bird," Anderson told the first editor to whom he sent it, ever since *Main Street*. In fact he had sent on some kind words to Lewis when the book came out in 1920, but two years later, in his "Four Impressions," he did take a swipe, registering his "sense of dreary spiritual death in the man's work"; and on numerous private occasions, before and after, at gatherings, in letters, Anderson let loose with what were for him unusual expressions of jealousy and resentment. It was not just the magnitude of Lewis's success that irritated him, not just that it had so far exceeded that of writers (Dreiser, himself) who had first turned American readers' attention away from English fictions. It was that unlike Hemingway and Faulkner, he came by his success with such safe, such artless writing.

Now, in 1929 and 1930, Lewis was on what Anderson called his "labor lay." He was going to do a job on Anderson's territory. He was visiting textile mills and mines, with an eye to writing a novel about them. Anderson was sure he would "do to the factories what he did to the small towns, the doctors, the preachers, etc." — stereotype them, demean them — and he "wanted to skin him alive." In "Cotton Mill" he does not even mention Lewis. But no one could mistake what he had in mind when he deplored that quality in "a certain very popular novel about an American small town" that "arouses people's contempt," and regretted that in the minds of people all over the world the American small town was a hot and acrid place, filled with "pretentious people, mentally dishonest people."

Lewis had written an account of the famous strike in Gastonia, North Carolina, a little booklet titled *Cheap and Contented Labor,* that Anderson describes as containing "the usual stage figures," members of Kiwanis and the Rotary, reduced to "bullies swaggering through the streets." Then Anderson tells of an experiment he conducted after reading it. In the document there had been a "maiden lady" clipping coupons in some distant city, supposedly issuing orders that made life miserable for "little mill girls" in the South. One Saturday afternoon Anderson had gone to one of the worst of the mill villages, and to the house of such a girl. Walker Evans might have photographed it: "The walls were dirty. There were old newspapers pasted on the walls to keep out the cold." Other girls wandered in and out, and he described the "lady investor" to them, blamed her for their poverty. Their response was to drift off into fantasies about what *they* would do with all that money, and then when he pressed his case, to protest: "'Ah, you let her alone,' they said; 'what does she know about us?'"

Anderson knew that "labor in America, and in particular in the

South, has got a long struggle ahead of it." He knew and was writing on the breakup or demoralization of families, on the process by which owners replaced fathers (the so-called mill-daddies) with children and women, whom they could hire at lower rates. He knew that machines were throwing men and women (and children) out of work altogether. He knew how town and city dwellers looked down on mill villagers (or "lintheads") living in their midst or out beyond the tracks. But all popular writers were doing on the subject, he said, was giving us "new people to hate" (while investing in who knew what stocks and bonds), and he made his liberal plea: "The situation is infinitely complex. . . . Working people are people. . . . The woman investor in a cotton mill is just a woman, caught in the trap as we are all caught."

Taken out of context, or when he himself ignored their political context, his charitable and elevating defenses of the individual could ring hollow, or become music to mill owners' or investors' ears, but Anderson was right about the simple and venomous portraits in *Cheap and Contented Labor,* and as the Depression deepened, he tried to make a more knowledgeable and practical contribution to labor's struggles himself.

In November 1930 he went over to Danville, Virginia, where the workers at the Dan River cotton mills had been out on strike for over a month. The immediate cause was a proposed 10 percent reduction in their wages, but what soon became more important was their right to have their own union rather than be represented by "the worker's congress" set up by H. R. Fitzgerald, the company's president. The following January he went again and on the thirteenth addressed a meeting held in a hall owned by the Ku Klux Klan. A huge cross was propped up in the corner, the light bulbs on it wired to make it "fiery." The hall seated six or seven hundred people, but many more squeezed themselves in and waited two hours for the occasion to begin. Hymns were sung. Accompanying himself on a guitar, a small boy sang "Cotton Mill Colic," its chorus:

> *I'm going to starve*
> *Everybody will*
> *Cause you can't make a living*
> *In a cotton mill.*

When Anderson spoke, he called upon the workers to redress a situation in which they were relatively powerless. He asked them to do what only management could do, asked them to bring to pass what he'd all but assumed men *couldn't* bring to pass: namely, shorter work days with no decrease in pay; "less profit for the few"; and playing, reading, spending more time with the children (in his notes he crossed out the thought that they oughtn't to give up the struggle any more than one ought to give up on a failing marriage). He presented them with his hope for "better living." But in the process, he dignified the idea of being a worker, a worker with one's hands, and he dignified these workers' desire for union by placing it in grand historical perspective. He compared them to the first settlers, dreaming of a classless land, and to those before them, who had forced a king to sign the Magna Charta. Theirs was a fight for humanity, a fight to save civilization. "It is all very simple," he said. Were machines going to enslave men? Or were men going to "use the machine for the benefit of all"?

It wasn't really up to the workers of Danville to decide, but the speech was well received. *The Hosiery Worker* printed brief fragments and described it as "one of the most remarkable statements ever delivered to a group of workers on strike"; the *Trade Union News* printed it in its entirety. But in his account of his visit, published in the *New Republic* on the twenty-first, Anderson was less enthusiastic. It was as if he knew he had tried again to find a boldness that he did not feel.

He was struck once more by the energy and fellow feeling of men and women out on strike. The "marching men" of his early novel had come alive: "These people want only to stand shoulder to shoulder." And he was struck by their decency. "What do they believe?" he asked. "They believe in people," he said, even in Mr. Fitzgerald ("Oh, he's all right. He's a good man," they said), certainly in the famous writer who had come to speak to them. Looking at himself from their perspective, he wrote:

> There they are. They crowd into the little halls. They cheer you when you come in. Faces peer up at you. There is hope, love, expectation in the eyes of the people.

And looking back at them, and at the occasion, what he saw most clearly and sadly was the "futility of what might be called goodness," the futility in all the people he had met, the futility of his speech. He had stirred them up, but to what purpose? He sensed that the strike would soon be over and that Mr. Fitzgerald would concede nothing, and it took about a month to prove him right. After Danville, Anderson took sides.

All his life he had avoided making political commitments. In 1916, impressed by what he thought was the "real knowledge of poverty and real tenderness for the poor" evidenced by *Windy Mc-Pherson's Son,* Upton Sinclair wrote Anderson, trying to convert him to socialism, but Anderson wrote back saying he didn't know who was right, who wrong, that he didn't want writers distancing themselves from their materials as "socialists, or conservatives or whatnot." He wanted them to be "something of a brother to the poor brute who runs the sweatshop as well as to the equally unfortunate brutes who work for him." The following year, hearing young writers in Chicago talk about "the politics of poetry," he wrote them off as "part of the shrillness of the times." "With war and government," he said, "the artist has simply nothing to do." And for years he acted accordingly. When the International Committee for Political Prisoners asked him to write something on Italian dictatorship in 1926, he declined, saying he had "no political turn of mind." The same year, in a *Vanity Fair* article, "A Great Factory," he declared: "Nothing in the world could ever make me a socialist," and while acknowledging that factories had changed the quality of American life, he justifiably struck the pose of one who for twenty years had not had one political thought, "no scheme for changing anything in the social structure."

But the Depression drew him in. "I seem to be getting into current things more and more," he said to Bockler after his first trip to Danville, "but I do not care much," and for a few years that last clause meant only that he no longer had many reservations about getting politically involved.

He went on to side with the Danville strikers, and then later that year, with the miners of Harlan County, Kentucky. In December 1931 he addressed a meeting in New York of the National Committee for the Defense of Political Prisoners on behalf of the efforts of Dreiser and other writers who had gone to Kentucky to investigate the miners' working conditions and to call attention to the terrorizing methods the Coal Operators Association had used to prevent them from organizing. Anderson had not gone himself, but he titled his remarks "I Want to Be Counted."

In them he said he knew from his own experience that labor had been driven into a corner: there were always people who would work for less; the machines at which they worked were out of their control. Rising to eloquence, he gestured toward "this beautiful new majestic thing in the world, the machine, now crushing millions of people under its iron heel, this thing that sprang out of the brain of men, out from under the cunning fingers of men," and went on, unhesitatingly, to attack the technocrats, the "money brains. Soap brains, Wheat brains. Shoe brains. Clothing brains," who reaped the benefits. He also attacked the social organization, the press, the schools, the churches, "pretty much the whole middle and professional classes" that effectively disenfranchised workers. He told of the excitement and the camaraderie that he had discovered during strikes, referring to them (as only Anderson would) as "operatic"; and then he seemed to drift off, or to descend to self-defense, as he paid tribute to Dreiser for having held out against the corrupting influences of money and of promises of social distinction. But what he was doing was supporting the investigators in their effort to do what he thought members of the "the artist class" could do to help: he was applauding their commitment to true storytelling. Dreiser had been accused of criminal syndicalism. If that was what it was, Anderson said, let there be more of it, more hungering after the truth together. The country was too much of a "speak-easy country" as it was.

If "criminal syndicalism" was a fancy way of saying "Communist," Anderson would have none of it. Whether or not Dreiser or Anderson joined the Party, which neither ever did, whether or not they went to the Soviet Union, which Dreiser did and Anderson did not (though he made plans to in 1932), as Anderson knew full well, the Party wasn't terribly interested in the likes of them. The Communist Party was a working-class party, and they were members of "the artist class."

Anderson was sympathetic toward the Party and active rhetorically, but he did not travel very far with it. Even as he became more involved, he knew that he could not lose his sense of "the other thing," his artistic integrity, his delight in the very richness of human experience for its own sake. Even if it did not get expressed, he said at the time, "what is the difference? It is like love. In a way you can keep loving." A year later, when he saw himself actually "becoming more and more a communist," when he said "it must be coming nearer — an inevitable thing," he was not signing up, but welcoming the long-awaited arrival of an age in which people were not so cut off from each other and from "life" by money.

His commitment to that prospect could take odd forms. In the same paragraph in which he spoke of the possibility of becoming a

Communist, he told Charles Bockler he hoped he'd get the mail carrier's job that he'd applied for. It seemed to him "the right thing — taking letters and packages to people." He told his brother Karl that the Depression was good for people, good for "their goddam childish souls." It would show up "big business men and financiers" especially. They were just "another lot of vain children, they with their eternal dabbling in the arts, etc." In the new age, all men's vision would be like the artist's, he thought, and the *true* artist's vision would be common to everyone. Men might come to recognize the beauty of their fellow "grotesques" after all.

There was also a kind of religious appeal for this man who never had a thing to do with organized religion. In his New York speech he said that not being a political economist he couldn't tell the "technical difference" between socialists and Communists, but he felt it nevertheless: "I guess the Communists mean it," he said in his speech in New York. He did too, and for about a year he tried to believe in "it" as well. It was, he told Eleanor's mother, like her Lutheranism, something he chose to believe in, "something to check life by." "I have always wanted, and I'm sure have needed, a religion somewhat more definite than the poet and dreamer's romanticism about the importance of his own life," he told her. Like a twentieth-century version of Matthew Arnold's flimsy God — "something not ourselves that makes for righteousness" — "Communism" was a resource Anderson called on in his final project of escaping the confines of himself.

His version of the party line on socialists was that "when the rub comes, they always cave in. There is too much sweetness in that crowd." He worked on, but never completed, his own *J'Accuse,* "an indictment of all our crowd," he called it, for not providing revolutionary leadership, and in the spring of 1932 he joined John Dos Passos, Waldo Frank, Lewis Mumford, and Edmund Wilson to issue a manifesto that cavalierly called for "a temporary dictatorship of the class-conscious workers." In June he gave his name to the Communist-affiliated Prisoner's Relief Fund (and later withdrew when he found they were sending out documents that he had never seen with his name on them). In the summer, along with more than fifty other artists and writers, he signed another manifesto, drafted by Matthew Josephson and James Rorty, the one an expatriate literary man turned political writer, the other an editor of the *New Masses.* The manifesto declared that "as responsible intellectual workers, we have aligned ourselves with the frankly revolutionary Communist party," and he thereby became a member of the League of Professional Groups for Foster and Ford, the Communist ticket in the presidential election of 1932. The manifesto, expanded into a pamphlet titled *Culture and Crisis,* urged fellow writers, artists, scientists, and teachers — "all honest professional workers" — to "support the communist Party or the political campaign now under way." The league's members almost surely did, but by Rorty's count only four to six were ever actually Party members.

In August, his way probably paid by a wealthy New York woman interested in pacifist causes named Edith Cram, Anderson went to Amsterdam as one of thirty-two American delegates to the World Congress Against Imperialist War. Its organizers did not intend that the congress oppose all wars. Indeed, war was inevitable, they argued, so long as capitalism and imperialism existed. But the spirit in which Anderson participated all along was in keeping with that of the American committee that later formed, the spirit of the World Congress Against War. By Anderson's account, it was "an attempt on the part of intellectuals, to get together with the workers of thirty-five nations for direct action against war and [it] was very exciting."

On the trip over he declined the first-class accommodations that had been arranged for him, went third-class instead, and spent his time, as he had on his last trip abroad six years before, with the workers and students, with "the young dreamers." "There is a gentleness and sweetness in them that is amazing," he wrote the Emmetts from on board the ship, "a kind of inner decency and goodness that is charming." At the conference, he limited himself to a one-minute statement about the writer in America, for it was the workers, not the intellectuals, who seemed to him to speak most movingly, none more so than a young sailor from an Italian warship who spoke out passionately against Mussolini. The image of their marching was more moving still. It was as if Anderson were reading a page out of his second novel. In his mind any differences between Communists and social democrats and trade unionists blurred. What he saw was the streets filled with "marching thousands . . . a mass of workers, from many cities, having sincere feeling for each other."

That was the gist of his report to the readers of the *New Masses,* dated August 28, 1932. When he explained to them "How I Came to Communism" in the September issue, again he showed how little Communism or any party affiliation, how much more "the other thing," finally mattered to him. *Winesburg, Ohio* was as revolutionary as anything he would ever be able to write, he said, in that it introduced readers to common men and women (and workers, he added for the occasion). You will get most out of the likes of us, he said, by leaving us "as free as possible to strike, by our stories out of American life, into the deeper facts." Though he did not say it in so many words, his language did: his real activity was metaphorical. *His* strikes were movements of the pen.

As always, individuals and their stories were what interested him. The only way he could transcend his selfhood was to tell them in his own, distinctly individual way. V. F. Calverton posed several questions for him and other writers that summer in his *Modern Quarterly*: "What should be the relationship between a writer's work and the (radical) political party? Should he strive to conjoin Art and Conscious propaganda?" Anderson answered: "He should perhaps keep clear. . . . He should try to tell the story, [leaving] plenty of room for the critical attitude." With such an attitude, there would be no room for him in any party.

Some stories, no matter how politically correct, he would not tell, Tom Mooney's for example. The famous labor leader, convicted of murder in 1917 (and pardoned twenty years later), was a "cause" incarnate. Sinclair Lewis visited him in San Quentin and promised him his help, but when Anderson visited him, he found him to be only "a bad actor" and preferred the company of two young workers in for life for having killed people while blowing up a newspaper office they thought was unoccupied. Mooney had sauntered into the visitors' area, dressed in white, black tie flowing, and pronounced to Anderson: "You be the American Zola. I'm the American Dreyfus." The two young men, by contrast, wanted to talk about books and the writers he knew. What was also appealing about them, as Anderson looked back on the incident a few years later (writing in his *Memoirs*), was that they didn't ask him "to sign any petitions, write letters to any governors."

Anderson's most publicized activity during this period, the activity that resulted in his most public statement, was a trip he took to Washington, D.C., on the eve of his embarkation for Amsterdam, to register his protest against President Herbert Hoover's treatment of the Bonus Army. The "Army," or "Bonus Expeditionary Force," as it was called, had come that spring from all over the country to ask that the "adjusted compensation certificate" given them as veterans of World War I be redeemed before the promised year 1945. Essentially they were an army of the unemployed, many of them with families, twenty-two hundred or three thousand strong; they occupied half-demolished federal buildings in the city and camped out on the marshy Anacostia Flats four miles outside it. After the congressional bill that would have immediately given them their bonus was defeated in June, most of them stayed on. The next month they turned down the offer of monies intended to enable them to go home. Most of them had no place to go. They *were* home.

The people in the army constituted the kind of a group or gathering that Anderson loved. They were marching men, the ranks of Amsterdam, villagers, swollen to massive proportions, and among them, all geographical and racial and ethnic differences were leveled. They were patriotic too, the Communists having failed utterly to influence them, and peaceful, but there was enough commotion when they were finally evicted from the government's buildings that Hoover felt justified in calling out the troops — "four cavalry troops, four companies of infantry, a mounted machine gun squadron, and six whippet tanks," by one account — under the command of Gen. Douglas MacArthur (with his aide, Maj. Dwight D. Eisenhower, at his side, and George Patton among his officers). They marched through the crowds and on out over the Anacostia Bridge, where they set fire to the veterans' shacks and teargassed them and their families off the land.

Shocked, Anderson agreed to go down with Waldo Frank and three others to confront the man whom he had interviewed four years before, when he was secretary of commerce under President Calvin Coolidge. This time it was Hoover's birthday. The Girl Scouts had sent a bouquet, a delegation from the Chamber of Commerce a cake. Frank insisted that they were important people, but the president would not see them. Instead, a secretary, Theodore Joslin, lectured them on their obligation as writers to "spread the truth" of how the mob, "turning from their own leaders to the leadership of radicals and communists, made an organized attack on the police of the District of Columbia." When he had gone to Hoover's office the first time, Anderson had spent the morning in the Freer Gallery, enjoying the Whistlers and the Chinese art. He especially liked a seventeenth-century painting called "The Waves at Matsushinea," and one of the Chinese Emperor Ming Huang with his concubine, Kuei-fei, and another of an emperor and a sage, meeting on the island in a lake.

He found Hoover to be the Republicans' ideal of a president (there would never be any paintings of *him* walking in a garden while a lovely lady sang, he noted), and he left feeling he had gotten nowhere with the man. So he went over to the Freer for one last look, but when he got there, he found that it had closed. On this, his second visit to Hoover, though the city police reported that the delegation went on to a Communist headquarters, he just went with his fellow petitioners to get a drink.

Anderson did write Hoover a letter, on August 10, saying that what had happened to the Bonus Army seemed to him like "Tsardom" and asking him to tell the electorate what he planned to do "to help all of us" were he to be re-elected. The next day, he wrote a longer, public letter that was printed in the *Nation*. It was more Anderson's style. "Men like me don't want to be radicals," he said. "I am myself, a story-teller. I would like to give all my time and thought and energy to story-telling. I can't." He couldn't because of what he had seen the last few years driving around the country. What he wanted to say to the president was this: he was "too much separated from the actuality of life. Everything has been very highly organized and centralized in America. Perhaps *you* have been organized and centralized out of our common lives." If Hoover had been there, for example, he would have known that the idea of the Communists' having any effect on the veterans was absurd. Anderson's "radical," ironic, but (one imagines, knowing Anderson) not entirely facetious suggestion was that Hoover sneak out of the White House some night and go around with him for a few weeks to see with his own eyes what was happening to millions of Americans. There is no doubt he meant it when he wrote a year later that had Hoover just gone over and talked to the Bonus Army they would willingly have gone home.

The next year, 1933, the trip to Washington was itself just a good story — published in *The New Yorker* — called "Delegation." In it, Anderson is all coyness, feeling "silly," not sure what was going on, not sure what the Communists were up to, not sure he and the men he had come with "represented anything much." ("The Communists," he said, "go in deep for mystery. I am a little uncertain as to whether I ever met a real one.") The high point of it all comes as Anderson and (it seems) Frank, emerging from a speakeasy, share their delight in what they both noticed was Joslin's fear of them. The piece is merely anecdotal, almost cute. It is a measure of how far and how fast Anderson returned from his three-year engagement with the politics of the Left.

During that engagement, he returned to the lecture circuit, adding a talk on women in industry to his repertoire and offering readings from *Perhaps Women*. He attended the Southern Writers Meeting held at the University of Virginia in October of 1931, and the next month, in New York, he took part in a public debate with Bertrand Russell that was sponsored by the Discussion Guild. In it, he defended parenthood against the notion of the family as prison, the irony of which was not lost on his children. And all the while he was at work on a novel, the first he had completed and published since *Dark Laughter* seven years before. It is the final and clearest indication we have of the fact that Anderson's sympathies for the more vulnerable people of America could never be contained or defined by party lines.

Beyond Desire is about Red Oliver, caught between all the worlds Anderson can think of to create: mother–father, black–white, North–South, mill village and town (and women associated with each), party allegiance and individual (the "critical") attitude. It is another variation on Anderson's most constant theme — a young man's emergence into manhood — though this time his hero does not quite reach the steps or the threshold, or board the train.

The novel begins with word of Red's old college friend and of the "modern" relationship that friend has with a politically committed woman that takes them "beyond desire." By contrast, Red's desires are forever being frustrated, most notably at the hands (quite literally) of a restless librarian who pins him on the table where he is reading his Karl Marx. Red tries to eschew romance by working at the mill, by playing on its ball team and not the town's, and by fighting for workers when they strike, but he fits in nowhere. In the writing, the awkwardness of his presence on the team, the panic that overcomes him during the strike, and his anxiety in the presence of tramps because he has seven dollars in his shoe are all deftly rendered by the man who understood his own estrangement from the people with whom he so strongly sympathized.

In the final section of the book ("Beyond Desire" itself), Red tries to live down his previous failures by defying the National Guardsmen at what is Anderson's version of the Gastonia, North Carolina, strike of 1929. "It is time now for men to prove themselves in a new way," he says to himself, his thoughts centered at the time on the farm girl who has taken him for a Communist organizer and has brought him to her barn. He wants to prove himself both ways, but assuming the role of "Red," he is shot in a Hardyesque climax on the orders of the Guard commander, a young college graduate (and ball player too), who for his part is trying to will himself into beliefs about Communists and the threat they pose that are not wholly his. When reviewers accused Anderson of being confused, he had reason to resent their simple identification of him with "the story of a confused civilization" that he was trying to write, but it is not unfair to say that the book reflects Anderson's inability, or refusal, to align himself politically. His speeches and his endorsements notwithstanding, that had been the story of his last few years.

The book also reminds us how few fictions Anderson had completed in recent years and of all the kinds of writing he had tried. One relatively pleasurable way to read *Beyond Desire* is as an Anderson anthology. There is the story of Red Oliver, so rigidly controlled by Anderson as to seem a compendium of thoughts and opinions that Anderson tried out in his letters and essays. Within it there is Red's father's relationship to a black woman that seems lifted right out of *Dark Laughter*. By far the longest section of the book is a realistic narrative of the librarian's efforts to fulfill her desires, many of those efforts spent in a thinly disguised and by now repellent version of the Chicago literary and advertising scenes, all of them topped by her stepmother's efforts to seduce *her*. The shortest, and what has been for many readers the most successful section, "Mill Girls," is about the heroic young figures and the machinery of *Perhaps Women* done up in Steinian prose.

After a meditation on what he takes to be the language of the Communists and its power to create "queer new alignments" and on the discrepancy between the songs the Communists teach the strikers and the strikers' ability to comprehend, Anderson concludes thus: "There is something more than exact meaning in words. Words have a life of their own. They have relations to each other. Words are building stones with which dreams are built." *Beyond Desire* leaves one with the distinct and moving impression of a man still trying to build, or rebuild, with the same old stones.

Even he was not surprised when the book was not well received. His first, defensive explanation was that it was "disturbing," "too close to real life" for his readers, but then he admitted that the "beauty" he had hoped for "seemed so far off." He also knew that in

1932 people were eager for answers, "a definite statement — Communism, Socialism, the finding of God, the finding of one another, something they can take hold of" — and so it was that Reinhold Niebuhr reported that *Beyond Desire* did not go far enough to make it into the Communist canon, the *New Masses* applauded the fact that it went as far as it did, and Granville Hicks said it did not go far enough. But Anderson never satisfied anyone by giving a "definite statement."

By the time the First American Writers' Congress convened at the Mecca Temple in New York in April 1935, the Left had long since given up on Anderson. As Daniel Aaron has said in *Writers on the Left,* no one at the congress "confused political correctness with literary talent," no one wanted propaganda, but Anderson's name came up only as the author of a "so-called communist novel of three years ago, *Beyond Desire,* which sentimentalized and priapified" workers' lives, "made them smell of sex," and as the founder of the "I-Am-Dumb school" of short-story writing. It was Malcolm Cowley who deplored *Beyond Desire,* James T. Farrell who deplored the influence of the Anderson of "I'm a Fool."

The workers in *Beyond Desire* are not that preoccupied with sex, but the novel is. Anderson had by no means gone beyond his concern for men's and women's lives as they played themselves out in sex. If anything, as *Perhaps Women* had made clear, he thought the presence of the machine made that play more central, its outcome more ominous. Nor did he stop dropping hints about his own marital pilgrimage. There are traces of Cornelia and Tennessee in the Chicago section, and at the end of the novel, it is clearly a version of Eleanor who plants the seeds of doubt in the young guardsman's mind. A young woman, "small like her mother," "bright as hell," she is back from Columbia, where she has been doing graduate work in economics, filled with radical ideas about how the machine had made a joke of the American ideal of equal opportunity and about why the middle class was doomed. Hearing her, her father has to admit, "The future, God knows, may after all lie with our women." And less thematically, Anderson has both him and his son agree: "God, but she would make some man a good wife."

Beyond Desire is dedicated to Eleanor, or "Elenore," as Anderson often spelled it, as if somewhere he heard an echo, saw in the unusual spelling a sign of the Elsinore he had been trying to reach twenty years before. As he was the first to acknowledge, she had brought him as far away from the abyss he had wandered into in 1912 as he had ever been. Ever since she had taken him to Elizabethton, she had inspired him to look at his country and his writing with new eyes. She would indeed make a good wife, but as late as 1932, when *Beyond Desire* was published, it still was not certain that she would be Anderson's.

In July of the next year, Anderson wrote a long letter to his old friend Paul Rosenfeld, regretting that they had drawn, it seemed, so far apart. Adhering to his belief in the purity of art, in a *Scribner's* piece two months before, Rosenfeld had objected to writers' slumming in politics, to their having ceased to consider "the use and administration of material possessions in sympathy with 'vision'" and taken up the question of "possessions" itself, of having abandoned their "historic cause" in favor of that of Foster and Ford (or Hoover or Roosevelt or Norman Thomas). And in a letter to Anderson, he had personalized his attack. In response, true to form, Anderson shaped his past so as to enable the two of them to go on being friends.

Four or five years before, he explained, something had gone "very wrong"; he had withdrawn, or had "rather gotten on the other side." Virginia had been proud to have him as a son, he had been invited to the governor's mansion, senators had invited him to their homes. "The trouble with all this," he said, "is that I am not respectable and do not desire to be." And so he had entered "a transition period." In it he had made mistakes, signed manifestoes and declarations that might be "at bottom nonsense," he might even have gotten "reckless," but he was not, he said, "a politically-minded person." The one good thing that had resulted during that period, though — thanks to Eleanor — was that he had returned to his people. Now, once again, he wanted "to participate in life at any cost." As for his relationship to Rosenfeld, he preferred attacks to silence, but he had an objection of his own to register: Rosenfeld (and Brooks) had hurt his feelings by saying nothing about his last book, *Death in the Woods and Other Stories,* particularly about one story, his most recent one. It was they who were lacking in "the real Communistic spirit" by not mentioning it. It was good ("one of the finest I've done," he had written Ferdinand Schevill a few months before, "and I even dare say one of the finest and most significant anyone has ever done"). It alone, he told Rosenfeld, would refute everything he had said about him.

The story was called "Brother Death." And it is an extraordinary tale — intricate and wide ranging, controlled and easeful and moving. It is more fable than tale, something of a new mode for Anderson, though still unquestionably written in art's cause. It is as if he had distilled into it all that his social conscience had told him over the years. (It is also indicative of how much went into it that as late as the preceding January, it existed as a potential novel.)

"Brother Death" is about two brothers, the one eleven, dying of "some kind of heart disease," but alive to all that is going on around him, the other eighteen, already successful as a cattle breeder and a producer of corn, but at the same time experiencing "a kind of death" because he is learning, in his struggles with his father, what it is to take command, to take over possession of the land. The immediate issue is two oaks — like great bonfires, "so nice against the hills," the mother says; shading too much grass, the father maintains. The oaks focus broader issues too: husband against wife, old families against new (the mother's had planted the trees before he bought them out), the father against his oldest son (who sides with the mother), and finally the mother against that son, if only because she is his father's wife. The oaks come down, the son stalks off. When he returns in three or four days, his father says only that the corn cutting has begun: "'It will be yours soon now,' he said. 'You can be boss then.'"

The story begins and ends with descriptions of the younger boy and his sister putting their fingers on the stumps, wondering if they had bled, arguing over whether only men had their arms and legs cut off, in accidents and wars. One thing is certain: among men's deaths, better the dying boy's. He had lived freely, never having had "to make the surrender his brother had made — to be sure of possession, success, his time to command." Had Rosenfeld written "The Authors and Politics" a few months earlier, we would say Anderson had written "Brother Death" to order. Anderson's story was Rosenfeld's kind of criticism, implicitly advocating (in Rosenfeld's words) "things produced out of feeling: things having the quality of life and awakening feeling and bringing men into touch with its divine source and object."

Anderson's book *Death in the Woods and Other Stories* began with the title story, and "Brother Death" was its complement, the collection's climax. Anderson had high hopes for the volume, but the pieces he put in between what are two of his best stories were uneven. He went back eight years to retrieve "A Meeting South" and a story called "The Return," about a man's unsuccessful journey back to his old hometown. He selected several *Vanity Fair* pieces on southwestern Virginia mountain life. He produced lively satiric work on jealous husbands ("There She Is — She Is Taking Her Bath") and Chicago ladies looking for culture in Paris ("That Sophistication"), both proof that he no longer took the problems of such people to heart. Some reviewers thought they were in the presence of the old Anderson and welcomed him back, but the reception was modest, if for no other reason than that the book was released at just about the time Liveright's publishing firm went down along with his investments in the stock market. There was no one to promote it.

Anderson would never need to begin again in his relations with women, but he could never be satisfied that he had settled anything as a writer. In fact, he had many starts to go. Right up to the day he died he would try to realize himself in writing, working over old material in new modes and new media, rejuvenating old forms with new subjects. Social criticism, a relatively political novel, stories in the old and in altered veins, reportage, satires — Anderson had written them all since his departure from Saint Petersburg in January 1930. By the time of his letter to Rosenfeld, one kind of attempt, one phase, seemed to be over. With *Perhaps Women* and *Beyond Desire* behind him, he no longer seemed so interested in conducting political inquiries and writing social criticism. In fact he would return to them, but meanwhile he was eagerly trying yet another genre. In 1933 what he most wanted to do was write a play.

Anderson had thought about writing plays off and on for years. Jacques Copeau had come to him at 735 Cass Street and had not only urged him to dramatize *Winesburg, Ohio,* but had also left him with the fantasy that he might be "the American dramatist" without realizing it. In the years that followed, he made tentative and at the same time eager moves to see if it could be true. In 1920 he accepted the invitation of Rollo Peters, then a prominent figure in the New York theater world, to discuss Peters's attempt to act on Copeau's suggestion. If we can believe Ben Hecht, Anderson derived at least private satisfaction from working on a version of Benvenuto Cellini's life. In 1925 he said he wanted "passionately to write for the stage" and had the surer satisfaction of attending on at least others' success in putting his work on stage. Beginning in February, an adaptation of *The Triumph of the Egg* was performed twenty-two times as the curtain raiser for a revival of Eugene O'Neill's *Different* by the Provincetown Playhouse in New York. Ten years later his moves were more enthusiastic and wilder. "I have a hunch that this playwright thing is really my meat," he wrote Roger Sergel. Perhaps *Dark Laughter* could be made into a play, or more likely, *Poor White*. A few months later he was working with the themes of *Poor White*, "but different — new characters, etc. I call it *They Shall Be Free*," and then, in the next breath, he was going on about how one might stage *Marching Men*. At the time, he was fired up because he had had, finally, one sustained and moderately rewarding experience with the theater. It was, as Copeau had imagined, because of *Winesburg, Ohio*.

In the fall of 1932, in the loaded atmosphere of a party at Horace Liveright's, Anderson had met a young freelance writer and former vaudeville actor who went by the name of Arthur Barton (his real name being Hartmann). The man told Anderson about a drunken actor he knew who would take any occasion he could to read aloud from Anderson's book, and he went on to say he would like to turn it into a play himself. Caught up in the enthusiasm of the moment, Liveright said he would produce it. By the end of November, Barton came up with a synopsis and Anderson set about writing scenes. In the spring, ominously, another play Barton collaborated on was going through its seven performances in New York before closing. It was called *Man Bites Dog* and was "pure horrible," Anderson wrote Laura Copenhaver (Walter Winchell's headline had read "Barton's Dog Won't Bite"), but, he went on, the whole experience had made Barton nicer. He was "really a swell fellow at bottom," and Anderson went ahead and invited him and his family to Ripshin so that they could work more closely together.

The fate of Horace Liveright cast another dark shadow across Anderson's prospects that spring. In May, on a visit to New York, Anderson went to see him in an apartment a friend had let him use. Liveright was still in his pajamas, sitting on a couch. A few hangers-on were there. His firm and his fortune having collapsed, Liveright had just come back from an attempt to find a future in Hollywood. Seeing Anderson and seemingly ashamed of his surroundings, Liveright got up, put his arm around Anderson's shoulder, and ushered him out of the room. He tried to put a good face on things. "Well, what the hell, Sherwood. I've sunk," he said, and then went on to depict the sale of his publishing house as a promising reorganization, and to gloss over his having failed in Hollywood. But neither man was fooled. Soon Anderson would need to find another publisher.

On the same trip, he met with Paul Muni to discuss the possibility of their working together on a film version of "a mining story," but the *Winesburg, Ohio* project was foremost in his mind. He and Eleanor were to have dinner with the Emmetts at their house in Washington Mews, and he planned to approach his benefactor for financial support. The foursome dined, but as they were all leaving the dining room, Emmett stopped him and asked if they could talk a moment. Though not financially like Liveright, Emmett too was failing. He had been suffering from arthritis, but now his pain went deeper: he feared he was losing his will to live. He appealed to Anderson: "Tell me something Sherwood," he said, "that will make life taste a little sweet to me."

There was little he could do at the time, but when he returned to Ripshin, Anderson wrote Emmett a long, empathic letter, encouraging him to call out to people from the "dark valley" he was in, and then in another letter he tried to ask for money. But the second one he couldn't send. Emmett would think that their friendship depended on his ability to provide. That was the trouble with rich people, Anderson told Barton, that was the trouble with money: it confused relations, it threw up walls. He had said in his first letter that he and Emmett would understand each other better if they were "two penniless tramps" with only a loaf of bread between them. As it was, he would do what he could himself. *He* need not fail; it would be better for him and Barton, better for their work, if he were his own "angel."

He tried. He went out and bought two large tents, fourteen feet by sixteen feet, set them in the orchard, had floors and siding put on them, furnished them, and then promised to lend Barton a hundred dollars if he could scrape up what money he needed to make it to Virginia. In June, the Bartons came down, but their visit and the collaboration were a complete disaster. The way Anderson explained it to Barton was that he had no understanding of "the real story of the play." Barton's problem was one that Anderson himself had finally overcome: he continually got in the way, he insisted on placing himself between himself and his writing. Barton was too close to Arthur Barton. Someday, Anderson said, his feelings for the play's characters might be as tender as those he had for himself, but right now, he still had to confront his own intrusive self. From his years of experience, he advised, "If it breaks your neck make him get to the place where his absorption, at least a part of the time, is altogether centered in his materials and, for God's sake, every time you write a smart or a clever line be suspicious of it."

And Anderson had gotten a lot better at making breaks. Early the morning of July 4 he slipped out, but he left a note explaining his reasons for their failure, asking that the Bartons be gone by the time he returned, and detailing how Barton could have his trunks taken to Troutdale, from there to Marion, and then shipped home. As for the loan, the money was in the bank, and Barton could have fifty dollars if he still needed it. In fact Anderson had to go down to Hendersonville, North Carolina, to pick up Eleanor, who was working at a YWCA camp near there. He wasn't due until the fifth, but he just couldn't stand it any longer. He drove sixty miles an hour almost all the way, checked into a hotel, slept all afternoon and night, and in the morning worked happily on his play. From his hotel he wrote Sergel, telling him that he had tried to be nice, had even tried playing croquet, but that finally

> Barton got me — the eternal sadness and lack of courage either to really get into the play, walk out or punch my nose. I hadn't the courage to go through another scene with the man begging off, clinging on, even weeping etc.

So "suddenly [he] decided to boot him out — as gently as [he] could but effectually." It turned out, however, that Barton was not only what Anderson called a "clam" but a shyster as well, having taken out a copyright on the play in his own name while telling Anderson that it was in both their names. The "Barton mess," as he called it, would not be cleared up until years after Anderson's death, but that November, in his final letter to Barton, Anderson said that it was he who had been taken in, been "rather a chump," and that Barton was "not to blame for that."

In late June and early July 1933, Anderson's tolerance level sank unusually low. On July 4, he couldn't get away from Barton fast enough, and for a very good reason: having decided at some point in the spring to get married, he and Eleanor had chosen July 6 as the date.

TWELVE

Finally at Ease

1933-1940

IN 1926, in *Tar,* Anderson had written about his sister
Fern, who had died in infancy but whom he still imagined as about twenty years his junior, and he went on to explain
the advantages of that fancied sibling relationship:

> Older men like the notion of some woman about eighteen with
> the wisdom of forty and the physical beauty and sweetness of girl-
> hood. They like to think of such a one as attached to them with
> iron bonds. It's the way older men are.

Fortunately, he predicted only the age difference right. "Sweetness"
was not among Eleanor Copenhaver's most prominent virtues, nor
did Anderson (now in his midfifties) make the mistake of trying to
bind her to him. If anything, he was bound to her, first to her political and social theories, then to her as an independent being, a woman
who would not "clutch," with whom he could finally grow up. "I am
trying . . . to keep my love for Eleanor a mature love," he wrote her
mother in 1931:

> I am trying not to be just a boy, like Bob, for example, seeking
> just a woman to love because I need love in my life. It's all right
> for Bob to be so because he is a boy in years. I myself have perhaps
> but a few years to be a mature man if I am to be one before I die.
> It is the challenge for me.

He did not try to make *this* woman just a foil, nor could he have
done so had he tried. In January 1933 he told Eleanor's mother he
thought he would be courting her all his life, and that prediction

proved wholly right. Eleanor would be devoted, she would accommodate, but there would always be her life as well. In *Poor White*, Anderson had had Clara Butterworth wish for a man who respects himself, "but can understand also the desires and fears of a woman." Anderson could be such a man with Eleanor.

As he had with Tennessee, Anderson insisted on openness, on men and women "letting go." Laura Copenhaver was wrong in recommending anything less to her daughters. There was, he told her,

> a certain determined thing I've noticed in you — that your daughters shall — in a certain subtle way — keep free from their men — whereas I believe the real freedom comes, not in that way — I mean keeping something back — but rather it comes to men and women — really, I believe, by giving all — absolutely.
>
> I've an idea a certain self-respect comes from that — the best sort.

What mattered was that *he* gave more this time. He did not protect himself by expecting others to "let go" first, "let go" for him, nor did he protect himself, as he had with Bab Finley, by ruling out marriage. As the two of them traveled together, or in the hours they spent up at their favorite spot, the Round Hill Cemetery on the western edge of Marion, looking down into the Holston Valley and out on the higher hills on almost every side, Anderson talked about his life. On New Year's Day, 1932, he began writing a "Letter a Day" to her, telling her everything that was on his mind. Finally, after so many years, he was at home with a woman.

In the beginning, Eleanor's schedule determined where and when they were together. In the spring of 1931, while she was in New York, Anderson holed up in a hotel in Elizabeth, New Jersey. The next year, he scheduled lectures in California to coincide with the governor's conference on employment that she was attending in San Francisco. While she was conducting surveys in Kansas City the following year, he lived at the Hotel Puritan there. Given the clientele, "little ham actors, prize fighters, ball players, whores and auto salesmen," he enjoyed the irony of the name, but he did not mingle, as he might have done at an earlier time. He stayed in his room, stuck to a Spartan diet of grapefruit, figs, and nuts, and wrote, or else he chauffeured Eleanor while she went around interviewing people. A portion of the work he did was for her — compilations of statistics he had gathered (on the city's electrical power, on agricultural output, the number of tractors presently in use), collations of her questionnaire results (on premarital sex, on church attendance), and possibly contributions to speeches she was to give. On Saturday nights he got Eleanor to go to one of the city's two big dance halls with him. Otherwise he considered himself lucky when he had lunch or dinner with her.

Anderson was not wholly sympathetic, however, with what Eleanor was doing. From Kansas City he wrote Laura saying he didn't think the work of organizations like the YWCA addressed the real problems of the Depression. "When a world is cracking up this mending broken chairs for fat women to sit on isn't so hot," was the way he put it. In subsequent years the problem was more obviously that Eleanor was spending so much time serving *others*. "As regards E.," he wrote Roger Sergel in 1935, "do you really think (I'm a pig you know) that she will feel more valuable, filled, giving her mind — and body for that matter — to YWCA or anything of the sort than the help she can give me." A few months later, he reported that Eleanor had "chucked" her job, she would go wherever he wanted to go. They were going to be "citizens of the vast unknown." But only "temporarily," as he well knew. Soon they were back on the road, going to conferences and meetings, to Niagara Falls, Atlantic City, Macon, Atlanta, West Palm Beach, Tampa, or Milford, Iowa. In 1938, Eleanor became head of the National Industrial Division of the YWCA; the demands upon her time increased the more, and Anderson could not keep up with her. He complained. They had kept Ripshin, and he wanted to spend more time there — and not alone. "I should have two wives," he once joked. But he knew that four was enough.

They began as friends, and as love grew, they tried to keep it secret, lest they endanger Eleanor's position with the YWCA. (Anderson's daughter Mimi was often commissioned as a chaperone, but she cannot have been hard to elude.) They talked of marriage, and they talked of having children (which, to their disappointment, never happened). They approached marriage cautiously. As late as February 1933 Anderson freely confessed that they both were "afraid of marriage," afraid it might limit them, afraid of their depending on each other too much; and his record being what it was, Anderson gave her family every chance to object. Laura was all sympathy and support, her husband Bascom, like the fathers-in-law who had known Anderson before, very skeptical. "I am sorry and hurt that the occasion of our marriage should not be a time of joy and gladness," Anderson wrote "Mr. Copenhaver" (as he would often call him). "I wish with all my heart I had found Eleanor earlier. I didn't. I would like to be friends." But for all his ingratiating attempts, "Mr. Copenhaver" never warmed to him. Still, they went ahead with their plans. In June Anderson wrote Mimi, saying he hoped Eleanor would marry him by July 1, 1933. "Poor as I am at marriage, I always need it," he said, "and I do think it is rather courageous and fine of her to tackle it." They married on the sixth in Marion, in the library of Rosemont, the Copenhaver home. Eleanor's parents, and Anderson's son Bob and his wife, were present.

Then Anderson forged ahead on two fronts: he finished his play and saw it through production, and he got involved in politics again. And the two activities were, oddly, mutually supportive.

For *Winesburg, Ohio*, the play, Anderson halved the number of characters (and added a father for Helen White and another friend for George), streamlined the plot to make it more of a battle between George's parents for his soul, and ended with a newly renovated Willard Hotel's going up in symbolic smoke; but the play remained structurally loose, its dialogue undifferentiated, and without something like Anderson's narrative voice, something like that of the stage manager in Thornton Wilder's *Our Town*, for example, providing a compensating sense of a world. The Theatre Guild took an option on it and released it a year later, but in the spring of 1934, through his friend from Fairhope days, Wharton Eshrick, Anderson met his ideal collaborator and producer in the person of one Jasper Deeter, founder and director of the Hedgerow Theatre in the Philadelphia suburb of Rose Valley.

In Deeter's hands, *Winesburg, Ohio* did not do badly. One hundred and sixty-seven people filled the auditorium on opening night, Saturday, June 30, Theodore Dreiser among them. Almost as if for old time's sake, the *Chester Times* thought the play was dominated by "depravity, blasphemy, vulgarity, and banality," and a disgusted few stomped out in the middle of one performance, but the reviews (most of which were local) were appreciative of the company's efforts, and the play remained in its repertoire for three years. But however gratified Anderson may have been by the performance and however inspired by its modest success to think of writing more plays, it was the company itself, the Hedgerow Theatre under Jasper Deeter, that meant most to him.

It was a community more than a company, its history going back to 1923, when Deeter left the Provincetown Playhouse to create his own avant-garde experiment in a century-old stone mill, and in spirit it went back before that to the arts and crafts movement associated with John Ruskin and William Morris. "In his patient, persistent way Jasper Deeter has been able to make his little repertoire theatre Hedgerow a way of living for his people," Anderson wrote.

Most of the company, more than twenty actors and actresses, lived in a big frame house on a hill above the mill, the remainder in a rented house nearby. Behind the house was a barn they used as a workshop and chicken coops converted into tiny quarters for those the houses could not hold. Everyone shared in every task: washing and ironing clothes, selling tickets, shifting scenery, driving the bus to the trolley station to pick up audiences coming out from the Sixty-ninth Street Station in Philadelphia to see their plays. Anderson would either come over from Wharton Eshrick's house in Paoli, ten miles away, or he would stay with the company. He loved it that he might see the woman who played Elizabeth Willard, sitting in the sun in back of the theater, surrounded by twenty-seven pairs of shoes that she was happily polishing, or that he might hear a woman planting cabbages in the garden suddenly cry out to the man working next to her, "It is not true. I have not misled you. I have not deceived you." She was practicing her lines. "Playing is a group matter," Deeter would say in coaching his actors and actresses. Echoing him and evoking his own experience of the group's life off as well as on the stage, in a lecture he gave at Johns Hopkins University, Anderson said that the drama was the most important of all the arts because it was the one in which its practitioners did not have to work alone.

Hedgerow provided Anderson with an image of what he had said was his aim as he prepared to become involved politically in 1930. "The better living is the end," he had told Bockler. He returned to Hedgerow year after year because there he could experience that "living" personally. The players were a family, and he felt a part of it. They also embodied ideals he had implicitly defended all his writing life — communitarian ideals. By the time he married he had backed off from politics again and, as he tried to assure Paul Rosenfeld, begun again to concentrate on his writing for its own sake, and even as he was trying to write plays and get them produced, he kept his country's fate in mind.

More specifically, for about two years, starting in the fall of 1933, while he was strengthening his ties to Deeter's group, Anderson wrote often and enthusiastically in support of the Roosevelt administration's efforts to give Americans the "new deal" FDR had promised Americans in accepting the presidential nomination the summer before. Anderson was no longer actually "participating," but with the otherwise unlikely pair of Jasper Deeter and Franklin Delano Roosevelt as inspiration, he wrote on, bearing his ideal of a democratic community in mind and reporting on where he found it realized.

As always and for the rest of his life, nothing would be more important to Anderson than his friendships and his writing. Rosenfeld need not have worried, but Anderson had become, and to some extent he would remain, "politically-minded." Toward the end of 1933, he found a more congenial politics, and his politics became more acceptable. He no longer put his name to anything except what *he* wrote, but in extensive writing he did not discuss with Rosenfeld, he continued to observe at first hand and to apply his criticism.

What still most mattered to him were individuals, common people; what still most disgusted him was masculine assertiveness and acquisitiveness. What he focused on, though, was not a vision but the constant presence of average American men and women who just wanted to work, especially those who wanted to work (rather than work over) the land. At times he was dismayed by their acceptance of their lot; on the whole, though, he wanted to report that they would endure the hardships of the Depression, become the stronger for it, and that now, more than ever, they were acting *as* a people. At times his reading of the country's future was regressive, a simple version of the pastoral, but in the main, he was right. Grasses would not break through freeways, nor farms take over factory sites again, but neither would there be, as so many were predicting, any other kind of revolution, or "popular" alliance either.

Anderson struck such notes in several of the pieces he wrote between May of 1933 and August of the following year for the *American Spectator,* an offshoot of the *American Mercury,* on whose editorial board he served (or rather to which he lent Dreiser his name as a way of offsetting what Dreiser feared was Broadway's influence on the periodical). He wrote a satirical piece called "The Nationalist" that reminds one of the tall tale about Andrew Jackson's descendants that he had put together with William Faulkner. It was about the archetypal businessman who had cornered the rat market, organized muskrat trappers, and had a mind to shoot the egret (characterized as a foreigner, eating "our" fish) and sell its feathers. In his first contribution he spoke of his travels through the South, the lesson of which, he said, was that given the promise of the land he saw spread out before him there was no need for economic depression. In his second, "Sherwood Anderson to Theodore Dreiser," he reported that he saw no signs of a coming revolution. Quite the contrary: the very word conjured up images of violence, and workers were suspicious; they wanted work, and if they had dreams, they were of becoming capitalists. In a little squib in February's issue, he said he had been watching the unemployed march in a miserable little mining town and had noticed the magazines for sale on a rack near where he stood: *Sweetheart, True Confessions,* even *College Humor.*

He doubted that the *American Spectator* "ever added anything to the cleaning up of the confusion of the American world," but he had high hopes for *Today.* Edited by Raymond Moley, who had been a key adviser to Roosevelt and for a short period of time his assistant secretary of state, the magazine provided a platform from which Anderson urged Americans to believe in themselves and in the leader who had, at last, arrived. In the fall of 1933, Moley wrote Anderson describing *Today* as "an American political weekly, independent of, although sympathetic with the administration," and defining politics in a way he hoped would induce Anderson to contribute. "Politics," he wrote, "has to do with civilization in its collective aspects and nothing that is human is quite unrelated to its problems." It was likely to appeal. What Anderson got to know of the administration itself was totally convincing.

Late that summer, Roosevelt's secretary of commerce, Henry Wallace, had come to Ripshin with his son and a man from his department for what turned out to be just Anderson's kind of visit. "You see this Henry Wallace doesn't strike you as a fighter," he wrote in what was his first piece for Moley. There was still a lot of Iowa, still a lot in him of the man who could have stayed home and edited the family newspaper, *Wallace's Farmer.* There was "no swank," as he titled his article, nothing fancy about the man who walked through the orchard or sat behind the house with him and talked. Anderson saw him again in Washington, in October when Eleanor had to go to an A.F. of L. meeting, and they discussed the possibility of his doing some public relations work. "Some new workers educational scheme wants Eleanor," he wrote her mother. He himself might be "a kind of underground ambassador to the backwoods and to the writers." He was happy with all the administration was doing to bring the country out of the Depression, and he liked all the men he met: "They are trying. There is a really corking spirit. They are not chuckle-headed or high-hat." He didn't want to stay, to tie himself down in Washington, but for almost two years, in more than twenty articles (at $250 apiece, all expenses paid), he happily performed ambassadorial tasks for Moley.

His second article was on Roosevelt himself, a president whom he never met but one he felt he knew, one who had made people feel close to him — simply by talking to them. Roosevelt had made it clear that he had gone through his own hells and emerged still able to laugh. Unlike Hoover, he had broken through the barriers that separated him from "the actualities of life." Thanks to the media, he had come out into the night. He had, in fact, begun his "Fireside Chats" many months before, but Anderson was still encouraging him: if he was lonely, he said, as all men in high positions probably often were, "he would gain something very real by making his talks to the rest of us over the radio a regular part of our lives." What he would gain was what Anderson had always asked of writers, especially himself: sympathy, "man-to-man understanding." Then in article after article, he told of the democratic spirit that was still alive in the land.

In November and December of 1934, he and Eleanor set out in their car to gather material for his articles. Their first stops were in Ohio — in Camden, Caledonia, Clyde, Springfield, Elyria — towns most of which he had not seen since he had left them thirty, or forty, or fifty years before. Then they drove through Indiana, Illinois, Wisconsin, Minnesota, South Dakota, Iowa, and Missouri, and then back to Marion. No longer a flamboyant figure, decked out in loud colors, Anderson now looked like just a country man, far from trim, his hair thinner and more gray than black, his shirt sleeves rolled up. He met people in small towns, in union meetings, in places famous writers and social critics were not likely to frequent. And he listened. The ideal community he had imagined as "Camden" had not come into being. In fact, it might have seemed it never would. But Anderson still heard how strong and decent people were.

In East Saint Louis, for example, "a town in which lives practically no man who owns anything in the town, who owns a store or house to rent, who owns stock in factories or mills," Anderson saw how drifters, wanderers, itinerant workers, "the down-and-outs," had converted an unused government building into a home for themselves, complete with laundry, delousing facilities, bakery, and infirmary. He saw how people could work with each other for a common good. He saw that no revolution was in the offing, that there was no danger of fascism either, no talk of "the state drawn up into the figure of one man."

He saw just individuals, strong individuals like the woman he picked up hitchhiking, who had walked out on her husband when he hadn't the courage to strike, or the electrician not minding panhandling until he could get work because it gave him a new slant on life, or the black miner and preacher, out of work because he had been labeled "a trouble-maker":

"We have been like hogs rooting in the woods for acorns," he said.
"We have had our eyes on the ground but now we are beginning to look up.
"We are going to try to find out where the acorns come from.
"We are beginning to look up.
"If we do not make good some day it is our own fault."

Often they were all but beaten, like the widower who had lost his farm and was planning to move in with his daughter and perhaps plant a garden. Often they were like the black preacher, moving examples of what would later be called "the hidden injuries of class": they blamed themselves.

When he collected over half of his contributions to *Today* as *Puzzled America,* in 1935, Anderson stressed in his introduction that there was "a hunger for belief, a determination to believe" out there, and that it could be found "in one another, in democracy, in the leadership we are likely to get out of democracy." Anderson's last image of the Danville strikers five years before was of a thousand eyes looking up, looking for someone "to come and make what they want understood to their boss, to all bosses." A year later they elected such a man; they had gotten the right kind of leadership. Nor is it too simple to add that what the country seemed eager to accept Anderson himself had always wanted: someone who would realize the potential of American resources without creating divisions among people, some wise man who might wield authority gently.

Roosevelt had talked to the bosses, and having sat in on some early hearings held under the National Recovery Administration, Anderson thought they would cooperate, raising wages and reducing hours, while the government helped regulate prices. It seemed the hopes he raised at Danville might be fulfilled after all. "Of course it is crude and there will be no end of crookedness and objections, etc.," he said, "but I think an entire new principle in American life is being established."

Among the New Deal programs that meant most to Anderson were the Civilian Conservation Corps (CCC) and the Tennessee Valley Authority (TVA), programs that cared for the land. When he first started to work for Moley, he had traveled for two months in the South, accompanied part of the way by Roger Sergel, to assess the results. There too he found new principles at work — government, a farmer told him, but "a different notion from what we have had." Anderson lost no opportunity to say how the ways of the pre-Depression South had failed, mocking those who had taken "their stand," those who had ignored the poorer souls of the "beaten, ignorant, Bible-ridden, white South." He was especially scornful of men and women who considered themselves aristocrats and yet left the land worse off than they had found it, and of what he called "New Tyrants of the Land," the once "poor whites" who bought up land, drove tenants off it, and grew only cotton. And finally, he dismissed that familiar argument of the well-to-do that had it that America was the land of opportunity and that because they had made their way it somehow followed that "there was a good deal of nonsense about all this poverty." "Come on," he wanted to say to them, "let's go look."

He witnessed how successfully the rugged individualism that had so influenced him in Clyde and, later, in the business world had been tempered for the common good. The CCC brought otherwise idle and delinquent city boys out into the country to work ("Tough Babes in the Woods," Anderson called them); foresters came down out of the hills to tutor them in their camps. Evidence of the success of the program was there to see at Hungry Mother Park, just a few miles north of Marion. The TVA harnessed the energy of the Tennessee River to power industries, rejuvenate farms, and light homes throughout the South; after a day's work, engineers went to country schoolhouses to explain erosion so that farmers could save their land. "The depression had given them their chance," Anderson wrote of the foresters, and they said the same of their charges and their land:

> "Hurrah for the Depression," one of them said to me. They are making a new kind of American man out of the city boy in the

woods, and they are planning at least to begin to make a new land with the help of such boys.

It was a liberal paradise, everyone acting freely for the common good of all.

When it came out in 1935, *Puzzled America* was widely noticed. Some reviewers noted with relief that Anderson had discovered no signs of an imminent Communist or fascist takeover. At another extreme, some derided him for ignoring the potential for radical change. Others played on the book's title, saying the problem lay in its author and not in his country, but in a review for the *Chicago Tribune* that was almost exclusively (and tediously) such play, Gertrude Stein drew the proper distinction, saying: "Yes he undoubtedly is America and American and it is puzzled his America but he is not puzzled he America." She then called it "one of the very best things that Sherwood Anderson has done and that means that is one of the best books that an American has done."

He was forever exposing himself, making himself vulnerable. As another socially committed novelist, Josephine Herbst, said, "Of all the writers of his day, he was least ashamed of a loving nature." In the last decade or so of his life, many took aim, in harsh reviews, in parodies. The most resounding blow was an essay by Lionel Trilling, written just after Anderson died. From *en haut* he told of his impression of the man: there was "a certain serious interest [Anderson] would have in the person he was shaking hands with," and "a certain graciousness or gracefulness which seemed to arise from an innocence of heart," but, Trilling went on, having never outgrown his own adolescence, Anderson would have greatest influence on those who read him at an early age. "What exasperates us is his stubborn, satisfied continuance in his earliest attitude," he said; there is in his writings "no social experience."

Windy McPherson's Son, Winesburg, Ohio, Poor White, Beyond Desire. . . . All of them reflect Anderson's "social experience." *Puzzled America* is only the more directly, the more explicitly informed. To be sure, in it one still hears the voice of the youthful enthusiast and notes the folksy mannerisms. Anderson used more than enough "kind ofs"; the reader is still accosted by "You, the reader" and "Let us say," and asked to pause for "But I am trying to tell you this story now" or "What I am trying to say." But he warned at the outset that he had tried but found "the impersonal tone" would not do, given what he called the new "governmental" situation ("governmental," because politicians seemed to him irrelevant to what was happening). Undeterred by Anderson's stylistic lapses, Irving Howe called it "one of the few books that convey a sense of what it meant to live in depression America"; and surveying American novelists of the day in his *Last of the Provincials,* Maxwell Geismar said there was no one "able to reach down into these particular American lives so deftly as Sherwood Anderson, so native himself, and directly after so long a struggle to achieve his nativity."

Anderson had changed publishers late in the summer of 1933. Horace Liveright had indeed gone into bankruptcy in the spring. In August, Maxwell Perkins wrote Anderson with the idea of Scribner's becoming his publisher, and at the thought of the association Anderson's spirits rose. He respected Scribner's, and "instinctively," he said, he liked Perkins. Their relation at its best would be "a kind of intellectual marriage," one in which neither side "should be too positive." Perkins wanted Anderson's first book with him to be "either a novel or a continuous narrative," something like *A Story Teller's Tale,* and inasmuch as Anderson was embarking on just such a project, something that he was calling *I Build My House* (which would eventually become his *Memoirs*), he thought he could easily oblige, but he did not want to be held to that. He had already sent on his new play based on *Winesburg, Ohio* for Perkins's consideration. In September Liveright died. The Andersons were staying at the Emmetts', as they often did while the Emmetts were at their summer residence on the Hudson River, and Anderson attended Liveright's funeral — he was one of the few who did. After it, he had lunch with Perkins.

In 1934, Anderson published a small collection of writings titled *No Swank* with the Centaur Press in Philadelphia, in a limited edition, as befitted it. Besides the title piece, it included tributes to Charles Bockler, Trigant Burrow, Theodore Dreiser, J. J. Lankes, Maurice Long, a defense of Gertrude Stein against B. F. Skinner, and reviews of Margaret Anderson and D. H. Lawrence. It was a gathering of old friends and other sympathetic figures. *Puzzled America* was Anderson's first book with Perkins. The book was hard to classify. It was neither programmatic nor profoundly analytical, its imaginative sympathies and insights ran along no narrative line. Though it raised Anderson's hopes by making $536 in the first six months, ultimately it did not sell well.

The following year he published *Kit Brandon* — his last novel. It

was different from all the others in having a woman for its protagonist, and it was more successful than most for being modeled on a
real person, operating in territory and in a situation that, as a relatively long-time resident of southwestern Virginia, Anderson knew
well. It has more of a life of its own, or rather the life that Anderson
had entered into during the last eight years or so and had often written about. In December, he wrote Dreiser saying that with this novel
he was trying "to get a bit more outside, not quite so much surrender
to pure feeling, more observation — more mind, if I have it," and
while Perkins was reading it the following June, he said that he had
intended to make it "much more objective" than his others. In this,
at least, he succeeded: *Kit Brandon* is hardly *his* story at all.

He had once reported on a "character" similar to Kit for his own
weekly papers, but Mamie Palmer, his subject in 1928, ended up in
the Marion jail with consumption, the occasion for only a few small
articles on jail conditions and the stoic spirit. His model for Kit, one
Willy Carter Sharpe, "the Queen of Rumrunners," came to Anderson's attention when then Treasury Secretary Henry Morgenthau approached him in June of 1935 and asked him to write up the trial of
some rather prominent Virginia bootleggers, among them the grand-
son of Robert E. Lee. (Willy's claims to attention were her womanhood and her diamond-studded teeth.) In response to Morgenthau,
Anderson followed the trial closely, filling up a scrapbook with clippings about it. The immediate result of his investigation was not just
a study in local color, but "City Gangs Enslave Moonshine Mountaineers," an astute analysis of big-business practices, especially the ex-
ploitation of the "little men" who take the risks, which was published
in a magazine called *Liberty* in November.

The material found its way into *Kit Brandon*, but the novel is
mostly hers. Its subtitle might have been "Perhaps Women Like
Kit." But this time Anderson wrote not just about a woman waiting,
like Clara Butterfield of *Poor White*, or the countless women Anderson
saw tending their machines, but about a woman making her own
way in the world. After her flight from her father and her mountain
home, she works in a cotton mill, a shoe factory, and then a five-and-
dime. We hear echoes of the factory section of Lawrence's *Sons and
Lovers*. During the earlier stages of Kit's pilgrimage we think Anderson is updating *Sister Carrie;* at a later one he has Kit take the book
out of the library for instruction. What Anderson tries to gain for
her is what he found momentarily for George Willard and Helen

White: "self-respect." Now it had to be reached in a culture that was explicitly acquisitive and corrupt, in spite of or through machines, and Kit errs where many Andersonian men had erred before. Kit obsesses over cars ("I'd like to get in her and give her the works," she says at one point), marries a man for the one he drives as much as for anything else, and becomes an expert runner for her father-in-law, counted on as one who "puts the stuff through." She dresses for success; she is fearless:

> She was neatly dressed but not flashily dressed, in a well-fitted suit, certainly well-tailored, and there was something quiet and steady in her eyes. "They don't rape my kind. I've got something they won't dare try to touch."

In a word that summed up many of his objections to his masculinized culture, she is "hard-boiled."

Anderson always imagined his women wanting men, and without their lacking total womanhood, or, as his metaphors suggest, possessing too much masculinity; so Kit is not just alone but lonely. She is a female version of Sam McPherson or Hugh McVey, in need of a mate. She is like and likes her boss, but his is "the story of every big industry." He is greedy and therefore weak. Others' impotence is familiar too: rich boys trying to rebel against their heritage, two men physically doomed as well. The man Kit marries never emerges from his father's shadow or from the women's boudoirs that he frequents. The best he can do is gun his father down in cowardly rage (by mistake) in a shoot-out that serves as the book's climax.

But with about ten pages to go, one *man* emerges, Joel Hanaford, a drunk, an outcast, the local judge's son, no model except that he accepts his failures and helps Kit escape. Gassed and wounded in the war, Joel could almost be Anderson's answer to Hemingway's Jake Barnes. One of Kit's aliases is Mrs. Erskine Hemmingway (*sic*), and Anderson throws out an aside about her weak husband's being a likely "big game hunter" ("How much false hair grows on the breasts of some men?" he asks). He has Joel say to Kit: "I'm only half a man and you want a man," but she sees "a kind of bitter resistance to life in him that she liked. He had been defeated but he was mature." More than Brett Ashley saw in Jake, it is enough to send Kit on "a new kind of adventure": "She would get into some sort of work that did not so separate her from others. There might be some one other puzzled and baffled young one with whom she could make a real partnership in living."

In his self-effacing letter to Dreiser, Anderson had said that he knew Dreiser didn't think the novel was his field but that he might "make it yet." To Perkins he said halfheartedly that he thought the book had "a pretty good chance of catching a rather wide public." To no one's surprise, it didn't. But *Kit Brandon* does not deserve neglect. At times it is stirring, more filmic than any other work of Anderson's. Often it is simply informative about a section of the country and a proletarian subject that had been too often glossed over by sentimental romancers like John Fox, Jr. But not many readers were interested in Anderson anymore. The combined sale of the three books that Scribner's published, *Puzzled America, Kit Brandon,* and (in 1937) Anderson's *Plays,* was fewer than 6,500 copies.

The *Plays* was mostly *Winesburg, Ohio* and a long dedicatory essay on Jasper Deeter, but it also included the play version of *Triumph of the Egg,* a one-act play titled "Mother," which had been performed at Johns Hopkins ("a rotten play," Anderson called it in his diary), and another, "They Married Later," which was all that came out of his idea of dramatizing *Poor White.* Whatever the reviews said (and they were not all bad), Anderson knew the truth: he was quoted in a *Washington Daily News* story as saying the book would sell about eighteen copies.

"Sherwood Anderson Says He's Glad Celebrity Days Are Over," the story's headline read. In the terms that most mattered to him, they were indeed — and he was remarkably valiant in coping with the fact. Artists who took responsibility for their art were bound to suffer, he wrote in November 1935, and they had two choices:

> They become silent or resentful . . . this probably from the notion that they and they only have been so hurt . . . or they get what I like to call "inner laughter," and I wonder if that isn't just maturity.

He chose the latter. "He was defeated but he was mature," he had said of Joel Hanaford. That much proved autobiographical about the novel he was writing at the time.

In a more superficial sense, his "celebrity days" continued. He was still in demand. He continued to lecture on numerous college campuses, to city clubs, to various organizations, and he accepted a few positions as "writer-in-residence." But he took on few of these roles wholeheartedly, and his performances were uneven.

In the summer of 1937, after only two days as "Visiting Novelist" at the Writers' Conference in the Rocky Mountains at the University of Colorado in Boulder, he was ready to leave. The idea that "writers may be made in a school" seemed absurd to him, the discussions and workshops he took part in (with John Peale Bishop, John Crowe Ransom, Ford Madox Ford, and others) bored him. He thought the only thing worth noting about his own short-story class was what he said about racehorses. It was evident that he was beginning to tire. "Though only sixty," one participant later wrote, "he looked ten years older." His face seemed puffy, his fingers forever trembled on what had become his paunch. He rambled; people had to lean forward to catch what he said. He was happiest when he was left alone, or when he escaped Boulder and the Chi Omega house where they had put him up to drive out into the mountains or (on his first Sunday there) to Denver to watch the Negro all-stars play in a double-header.

He also went to talk at Antioch College, and at Wells College, where his friend J. J. Lankes was teaching art. When he went in 1939, he didn't prepare and was, by his own admission, "rotten." On the other hand, that year he worked hard on a fine lecture he gave at Princeton called "Man and His Imagination," which he then expanded for inclusion in a volume entitled *The Intent of the Artist*. And he enjoyed three weeks of teaching at Olivet College so much that he returned the next year and even began to wonder if he mightn't be happy associating himself with a college in some way for seven or eight months out of the year.

There were periods of depression, usually during the winter months. To combat them he and Eleanor tried a remedy that he had tried for years: travel to warmer climates. In 1935 and again in 1937 he was in Corpus Christi, Texas, in 1936 in Tucson. In 1938 he went to Mexico, in 1939 to California. The Andersons included New Orleans in several of their tours. Their 1935 visit is notable for Anderson's having squired Gertrude Stein and Alice B. Toklas around town when they stopped there on Stein's famous American tour. It was the last time the two old friends were to see each other. In Mexico Anderson ran into William Spratling in Acapulco and went boating with him one day, but he passed up Spratling's suggestion that he see Elizabeth Prall one more time. "Bill, I simply couldn't face it," he said. "After all, I guess that was one time I behaved really badly."

On several trips the Andersons were accompanied by Mary Emmett, now the widow of Sherwood's long-time benefactor and friend. The three of them traveled in a little white truck that she had purchased for them. Her husband having died in May 1935, Mary wanted to contribute three thousand dollars a year in return for what he called "a feeling of something like a family" with them. Anderson balked at that but continued to accept money and hospitality as he had from her husband, and, as had been the case with her husband, his relations with her were complicated.

After her husband's death, Mary Emmett often came to Ripshin, and the Andersons tried to keep her busy, helping her start a garden, for example, but she grated on Anderson's nerves. "I think she a little worries the plants," he noted in his diary. In the fall of 1936, when Eleanor went to New York on business, Anderson was sick and took the drastic measure of leaving town under false pretenses ("doctor's orders") to escape Mary's natterings. The Andersons usually stayed with her when they went to New York in the fall, but in 1936 there was a flare-up that resulted in the Andersons' moving uptown to the Hotel Royalton. In 1937, finding he could not work at Washington Mews ("Too much ringing of phones," he said, "and besides, Mary is too rich"), Anderson went around the corner and rented a room at the Broadway Central Hotel. There he wrote and delighted in being considered an embodiment of "culture" in the minds of the clerk, the chambermaid, and others who seemed to know his work. But by the time of the trip to Mexico, he could laugh at the trio's situation. She was "our amazing Mary," as he reported to Eleanor's mother, "always with that amazing innocence of hers that makes you forgive everything. Anyway we got her here alive and as chipper as a sparrow. She is rather gorgeous at that."

At least until her promotion to head of the YWCA's Industrial Department in 1938, Eleanor bent her schedule to accommodate her husband's, going where he had speaking or teaching engagements, following him to the Southwest. She often handled his correspondence. His note is unique among the "Notes on Contributors" to the fifth in the *American Caravan* series for being written instead by a spouse. Its tone is high-spirited, affectionate. It ends:

> He is a passionate traveler and only visits his own home at rare intervals and wherever he goes he always wants everyone to go with him. He does seem to enjoy writing and people. He is almost annoyingly healthy.

But it was not just he who enjoyed himself. Traveling suited them both. In February 1936, for example, Anderson wrote his brother Karl from Tucson, saying that they would be there until the middle of March, when they had to go to New Orleans, "where Eleanor has to do some lifting of the proletariat." Anderson had addressed the Friends of American Authors in Chicago, after which they had driven through Missouri, Kansas, Oklahoma, Texas, and New Mexico. "There are such strange towns, strange places," he said. "I really think sometimes I shall travel always. Even the worst of hotel life is so good compared with family life . . . so impersonal, nice, free." There is nothing to suggest Eleanor disagreed.

The remedy he put most faith in, though, was friendship. He had always wanted it, but in the past so many had disappointed him, either because the men had not lived up to his standards, or because they were not as drawn to him as he was to them, or simply because time brought out deep differences. Now he felt he needed it more than ever — that all men needed it. With the opening of the new year, 1936, he wrote Dreiser and explained.

In writing to him, Anderson admitted that he was trying out what he wanted to say to writers and artists all over America. "Now what I have been thinking," he said,

> is that we need here among us some kind of new building up of a relationship between man and man. I feel so strongly on this matter that I am thinking of trying to get my thoughts and those of others who also feel this thing into form. I think even of a general letter or pamphlet that I might call "American Man to American Man."

This "thing" (this time) was a feeling that "we — and by the word 'we' I mean artists, writers, singers, etc." had not supported each other over the years. For one thing, living in so vast a country, without a London or a Paris, "we" were too dispersed. Thus the idea of a newsletter or a pamphlet. But also, in recent years, "we" had been too distracted by politics; and "we" had allowed ourselves to be too exposed to the power and whims of critics, who constantly brought on new talents in their efforts to do away with older ones. What was more important than politics or prominence was "this need of man for man in the imaginative world."

It was Anderson's own problem, to be sure, but it wouldn't be fair, he said, for people to go around saying "Well, well, Sherwood is down." A few years before Anderson wrote Dreiser, both Hart Crane and Vachel Lindsay had committed suicide, and he was still thinking about them, he said, and wondering if such a network might have saved them. He was also thinking about "the bitterness of a Masters" (and in fact he wrote Masters the same day suggesting that he meet with Dreiser and himself and talk). Years later, when the writers of their generation had come to seem to Van Wyck Brooks "as solitary as the rhinoceros roaming the veldt or as lone wolves drifting about a wilderness" (the generations having been collapsed into one with the passage of time), even he spoke with sympathy of Anderson's proposal.

Over the holidays, some of the "grand little theatre kids" from Hedgerow showed up in Marion while on tour to confer with Anderson about the company's future plans. Afterward, he wrote one of the actresses and asked about Jasper Deeter. With all of them around him, did he feel isolated? Or did he when he went to New York? He must have felt abandoned when Eugene O'Neill "had given himself to the N.Y. thing." Anderson said he knew it was impertinent to ask these questions, but he was considering "some sort of communication, constantly kept up between say twelve or fifteen men" and wanted to know if she thought the attempt was worth making.

The previous spring he had visited O'Neill in Sea Island, Georgia, on his way back north from New Orleans and had come away thinking only of O'Neill's loneliness. "He needs his fellow men," he wrote Roger Sergel. "I felt him clinging to me rather pitifully." It did not help, he thought, that O'Neill's new wife seemed "cold, calculating. Certainly . . . not one of the women who make a house warm." Certainly that was one of the issues he wanted to address in promoting his idea of men's friendship, but not just because he was inclined to project his fears onto women. He knew men better than that. As he put it in his letter to Dreiser: "I think it is our loneliness for each other that has made most of us throw too much on woman . . . making women carry more than their load."

"For a long time now I have been trying to get straightened out in my head — perhaps as a theme of a novel — the thing that happens to men," Anderson had written Emmett ten years before. Now, almost sixty, he dwelt not only on the need of artists like himself to band together, but more generally (and with not much more hope of success) on how all men could benefit from friendship. He worried that his idea for combating the loneliness of artists would "only lead to a lot of sentimental gush," or, as Deeter had said, when Anderson went ahead and broached the subject, that he might be flooded with letters from young men and women who wanted "to push themselves forward by crawling into bed with some man, or men, who they think has, as the saying is, arrived." "It's pretty grubby," Anderson told Dreiser. In celebrating men's friendship — not male bonding, not homosexual relations, or patriarchal domination by another name, but friendship — he certainly knew he would run smack up against his homophobic culture. In its terms, in the terms he played with in his great story, he was asking men to become women.

In the fall, he had written Sergel several letters about an idea, not very definite, "an attempt at expression of a need, not just my own," he called it, "for a kind of male, if you will, getting together." He was hesitant, but Sergel was more so, having confessed to writing long letters to men, "as a kind of relief," and then not sending them, and Anderson was trying to coax him out. Did he have "a kind of inferiority bug"? Did he think a man had to be "some big shot or something, to have value — surely a childish enough notion"? "What is really wanted," he said, "is something like tenderness that dares to go on and on." What he did not mean, "as is the case of man with woman," was "the going to the flesh," although he was not so skittish as to deny that friends might be physically attracted to each other or that they might find a woman more beautiful for being loved by a friend. What he wanted to do was block men's retreat to women and to sex.

"We men feel starved," he wrote, his letter turning into something of a tale. "Then the woman appears. How eagerly we go toward her — how hungrily we go toward her — how hungrily," especially we men of words. He was clear about his own excesses. He knew that both as a writer and as a lover he had given in to the temptation to say more than he felt, in the hope that the feelings would then appear — "because expression itself creates feeling." Imagining himself in women's place, he said they knew and they resented it.

The example he gives is of a time when he was out gathering "brick-top mushrooms":

> It was just night, and the little mushrooms here thick in the woods as I presumed they would be — cold and tender, masted from light straw-yellow to deep orange to the edge of red.
> The silence of the wood at that hour — the sky to the west — the low hills — just watching the growth on the ground — a sudden quick recognition of something.

"You want simply, suddenly, a comrade who feels as you do, sees what you see," he told Sergel. "There's woman." But what Anderson suggested in the very act of letter writing was that there was also what Whitman called "male comradeship." "Male comradeship" would prevent a man from using women, would "stand like a wall between man and a tendency to sell himself out and in doing so to sell out others."

It was Anderson at his best, not only conscious of his attempts to fool himself and others, but reimagining men's and women's lives in a way he had not quite done before. His concern for their communal life was as great as ever, but he was not expressing it in visions of solidarity or in cries of ecstasy. He saw his own moves as representative, imagined how women felt, and then presented his modest solution: men could be friends, be open with each other. *Then* they could approach women.

Anderson's last years were the more pacific and his marriage the stronger for his having such friends as Lewis Galantiere, Paul Rosenfeld, Ferdinand Schevill, and Roger Sergel, men who looked up to Anderson and tolerated his excesses. They and others contributed to what was often a steady stream of visitors to Ripshin. In less than three weeks, in the middle of the summer of 1936, for example, the flow in and out consisted of: the Antonys, friends from New Orleans; Paul Rosenfeld; Y. K. Smith and his wife; the Sergels; a couple from Washington; another from Baltimore; Schevill; and, on August 16, four people from Knoxville. Among the many who came out from Marion were Anderson's son Bob and his wife Mary; his best friend in the region, Andy Funk, and his wife; and Eleanor's mother and aunt. His son John stayed at Ripshin for long periods of time. His daughter Mimi had moved with her husband, Russell Spear, to Madison, North Carolina, just over the border, where together they ran a newspaper. Though he had little patience with his grandchildren, Anderson loved it that he could often gather his children around him.

One of those days included swimming and a dinner for twelve at Hungry Mother Park, after which Anderson concluded: "The present way of life is no good — too complicated. It is too hard on E." And he could not work, but still, while in Virginia, he depended on the constant companionship of not only Eleanor, but her mother and, among the men, Andy Funk. With him Anderson ran the danger of being one of the "boys" he had always tried to avoid — "Evening with Funk. We both too masculine," he noted after one visit — but nevertheless, he went into Marion regularly to be with him, to make wine with him in his cellar or croquet pegs on his lathe, to play cards with him, and to talk.

Among the visitors, no one was more important to Anderson than Paul Rosenfeld. In 1935, two years after their exchange over the relations of art and politics, Rosenfeld resumed his visits to Ripshin. They still had their differences, however. After his trip the following year, Anderson wrote Rosenfeld a long letter, saying there had been "so much suggestion of the tower" in many of his friend's remarks when he was there that he seemed to assume the existence of a proletariat, "a sullen and ugly folk," living somewhere beneath them (a proletariat that included a man and woman who worked for the Andersons, moreover). Anderson then went on to defend the humanity of his caretaker and to evoke the memory of his mother, "washing the dirty linen of pretentious middle-class women not fit to tie her shoelaces." He never sent the letter, however. "Too smug," he wrote on it.

Nor was his friend all that precious or finally all that aloof from politics. On one of his last visits to Ripshin, the two went off to the White Top Folk Festival, which had been held in the region since 1931, and Rosenfeld was no more fooled than Anderson. Ostensibly the festival was a celebration of local culture in the lovely hills of southwest Virginia, but in fact the occasion was carefully rigged. Anderson saw through the idea of the "FOLK." "Young men from New York's eastside put on faded overalls, tie red handkerchiefs about their necks and get all the prizes," he observed. In *his* report on the festival, "Folksong and Cultural Politics," Rosenfeld proved to be, if anything, the shrewder political analyst of the two, pointing out how blacks had been systematically excluded by the "sophisticates" who organized it — in order to "'save' the highlanders and their song."

Whatever the disagreements, they diminished, or the two men learned to contain them. Between them they created an example of what back in 1922 Anderson had described to Bab Finley as a presence — "The Third," he called it — that was always there when two people met, a composite of their two beings. In most cases, he said, "The Third" was half-formed, a "grotesque," a body with no arms, or its eyes crooked; but at its most beautiful it settled "the question of loneliness." It appeared at its best with Rosenfeld. The two men remained close until the end. After Anderson died, Rosenfeld gathered together and published a version of Anderson's *Memoirs* in 1942, and then the substantial *Sherwood Anderson Reader* in 1947.

Young writers remained interested in him. Hamilton Basso insisted that Anderson visit him in North Carolina in June 1936. Later that year he met two other Southern writers, James Boyd and Paul Green, and saw them off and on in the years to come. In 1939, the Steinbecks brought him out to their ranch near Los Gatos, California, but Anderson was relatively unmoved. Shortly after his visit he commented to the Galantieres: "It seems I've become a kind of Papa, 'Reading you is what started me writing,' etc. etc., so I sit like a wise owl."

In the one instance when he enthusiastically reached out to a young writer, he failed, as he had failed before with Crane and Hemingway and (to some extent) Faulkner. The only difference was in intensity. In 1935, having read *Of Time and the River,* Anderson wrote Thomas Wolfe a brief note saying that all these years he had been trying to write novels and here was this book that showed him he couldn't. It was "a gorgeous achievement." But then the next year, Anderson heard that Wolfe had proclaimed his virtues before a bedridden James Boyd — "in a voice to be heard all over the hospital" — saying Anderson was "the only man in America who ever taught me anything. Anything I know of writing I have from him." That gave Anderson heart as he tried to finish *Kit Brandon.* They finally met in April 1937 through Perkins, and in the fall of 1937, Wolfe stopped by for a night at Ripshin. Again Anderson was inspired. "The man is a flood, a continent, but he is generous and full of fine feeling," he wrote Perkins afterward. The only problem had been finding a bed long enough for the man. A few weeks later, when Wolfe wrote telling of his worries about getting published, Anderson told him about the troubles he and Dreiser had had and said, "Every man of force and originality has some trouble." His closing words were: "I love your guts, Tom. You are one who is O.K."

But in a few months the friendship was over. In December, at Mary Emmett's, Wolfe took offense at a flip remark of Eleanor's about his possibly being Jewish, and then, a few days later, he stormed over to the table at the Brevoort Hotel where Anderson was having lunch with a woman who was doing an article on him, and began berating him, telling him that he was "woman-ridden" and that he was "done as a writer." Wolfe later apologized and the two men agreed not to let anything come between them, but Anderson was inclined to let that be their last encounter. He had heard enough versions of those charges. Toward Wolfe he was finally understanding, sympathetic. He knew Wolfe was subject to such tirades. "God, the poor man must wear himself out with these outbreaks," he wrote Perkins, and added, "there is something very real and sweet about him under it all."

At this late stage in his life, Anderson belonged with his oldest friends. As for his relationship with Dreiser, theirs was a long story, going back to 1916 when Anderson had asked Dreiser for help in getting *Windy McPherson's Son* published. Through most of it, Anderson had been all but adoring. Dreiser was, Anderson once said, "the most important American writing. More than that — the most important man writing in English." He followed in Dreiser's footsteps even onto political platforms. When Dreiser closely followed in his, publishing a prose poem in 1926 that was clearly lifted from Anderson's *Winesburg, Ohio* tale, "Tandy," Anderson hardly gave it a thought. When the possibility of plagiarism was raised, Anderson said Dreiser was too great to need help from him or from anyone else.

Dreiser, on the other hand, was never ardent in his feelings. In fact, during the brief resurgence of their friendship in 1935–36, as Anderson sounded him out about American Man communicating with American Man, and in other letters pressed him to agree that the sexes were absolutely different or played the Luddite, he grew impatient. "You are a provoking devil, but just for the same reason you are almost impossible to deal with," he said. "I think you go around producing intellectual sweats." But at the same time he never lost sight of Anderson's virtues. Even as he bridled, he told Anderson outright that he had a "kindly and beautiful mind," and looking back over almost thirty years, in his tribute that introduced *Story's* commemorative issue in 1941, Dreiser said that his old friend had always been "a comforting figure" to him — a "wise, kind, affectionate, forgiving" man.

Travel diverted Anderson, his friendships sustained him. When the flow of guests was modest, life at Ripshin was idyllic. In 1938 he set about having at least the images of just those friends he wanted to see. He wrote Brooks, Frank, Rosenfeld, Stein, Mencken, Stieglitz and O'Keeffe, the Emmetts, John Emerson and Anita Loos, Sergel, Schevill, Dreiser, and others, asking them if they would please send him a photograph of themselves. The walls of two rooms at Ripshin were lined with them. There was no great influx of people into the area. The hills around remained untouched. The house was more than comfortable. Anderson had his cabin across the creek where he could retire and write. What competitiveness was in the man found expression in games of croquet. It was the game his father Irwin had gone out to the Faris farm to play in 1872, but he had ended up courting Emma Smith instead. His son played the game with a passion.

But, as had been the case since at least 1915, when he wrote "Hands," Anderson felt that a part of him was missing if he could not write. He tried, or he had considered trying, almost every medium in the thirties. After *Beyond Desire,* he embarked on at least seven novels, or long prose works, only one of which, *Kit Brandon,* was published. He imagined a four-volume work on the relation between the Civil War and the rise of industrialism. He wanted to convert the figures he had invented for his papers, Buck Fever and others, into the material of nationally syndicated newspaper contributions. He imagined having them ingrained into people's consciousness the way comic strip characters were. He thought of working on operas, one based on *Poor White,* another on *Perhaps Women,* still another on the history of the Mississippi River, with Louis Gruenberg, who had turned O'Neill's *Emperor Jones* into an opera. For all his scorn for Hollywood, he met a man from Paramount Studios to discuss filming one of his stories and entered into fairly serious negotiations over making a film version of *Poor White.* He dreamed of making *Kit Brandon* into a movie and asked Laura Copenhaver to keep an eye out for the right woman to play the heroine. Not to leave out radio, he toyed with the idea of reporting imaginary small-town news on a weekly basis, provided "a really decent sort of sponsor could be found."

Writing on, he did so for money and at the same time tried not to forget his vows of purity. Stories and essays appeared in a host of periodicals. Though he would not go so far as to say it was "the turning aside of a great writer, literature robbed, any such nonsense," he knew it was "pretty temporary work." Looking too long at the pile of "*New Republics, Nations, Surveys,* the People's this and that," strewn on their bed one time when he and Eleanor were in New York, he wanted to cry out "the hell with all of it," the hell with these immodest voices so busy defining a better world. He had been rereading Turgenev's *Sportman's Sketches.* It was such "better revolutionary stuff, really."

But when *Story,* or *The Writer,* or the *Canadian Forum,* or the *Saturday Review of Literature* asked him to say what it was like to be a writer, he would oblige with essays on "Why Men Write," "The Story Teller's Job," "Why I Write," or "So You Want to Be a Writer?" He would go over his days in advertising and business, and, what with the benefit of many years separating him from his experience, give an elevating version of how he had outgrown them. He would recall his years of political involvement and now say the writer's business was just to be curious, to tell his story with some grace, if he could, and that that way "the social implications" would come in "almost unconsciously." He told anecdotes about the pettiness of those seeking fame and about the awkwardness of those who hung around the famous. He took these assignments seriously. In the *American Magazine* for October 1939, for example, in a short piece titled "I Lead a Dozen Lives," we can still hear echoes of the voice of the man who had given elementary explanations more than twenty years before in the *Little Review* of why he had turned to writing and how others ought to do it:

> You must begin by a conscious effort to separate yourself more and more from yourself. Use your imagination for that purpose. Try having it lead you into the lives of others.

But he knew that he himself was no longer going to lead with his example.

He had more to say about writing as he succeeded less himself, but he did write several stories at this time that rank among his best, even though he never collected them in any volume. He reworked old materials: he drew on episodes from his advertising days for "His Chest of Drawers"; in "Two Lovers" he went beyond the "Untold Lie" by adding the lovers' — men's — need for each other, in keeping with his beliefs at the time; and as always, he tried portraits of women, a cutting one titled "Nice Girl," about a girl in pursuit of her sister's husband, for example, and "Not Sixteen," a witty lesson in how to keep young men at bay. On a somewhat grander scale is "Daughters," the story of two conspiring sisters and their father, an old logger, who spies on and finally attacks the more seductive one because her ways and her easily managed suitor's ways remind him of when he was a boy, looking longingly and tearfully at the girl from the city who was visiting her grandparents.

In "A Moonlight Walk," published in *Redbook* in 1937, Anderson wrote of a country doctor who told him how he had resisted the temptations of one woman, who would have set him up in practice in the city, and of another, a Polish maid, who seemed to have chosen him for her first lover. The narrator and the doctor are like the "brothers" in the story by that name, the plot has the makings of another "The Other Woman" (both in *The Triumph of the Egg*). But this time, what the two men share is poise, appreciation for the married loves they have, and "something — "

> -shall I call it inner laughter? — or, to speak in the terms of fighters, "They can take it." They have something — it may be knowledge, or better yet, maturity — surely a rare enough quality, that last, that maturity. You get the feeling from all sorts of people.

In all, the prose is more or less chastened (in the case of "A Moonlight Walk," chastened with considerable help from Laura Copenhaver's editing), as if the lives rendered have been lived through before, as if an older man had come through the trials of his youth.

This is true of none more than "The Corn-Planting," a short parable about acceptance. In it, a farmer and a former schoolteacher marry late in life. Their farm and their son are their whole existence. The boy goes to Chicago and makes enough money selling his drawings for advertisements to go out every night and still have enough left over to send home. Every week he writes. And then he is killed in a car accident, and the narrator goes with a friend to break the news. The best he can do is blurt it out, withdraw, and wait. In his conclusion — in his muted, storyteller's tone, in the rhythms of Anderson's sentences — the obvious symbolism of the title is resonant:

> It was an incredible thing. The old man had got a hand corn-planter out of the barn and his wife had got a bag of seed corn, and there, in the moonlight, that night, after they got that news, they were planting corn.
>
> It was a thing to curl your hair — it was so ghostly. They were both in their nightgowns. They would do a row across the field, coming quite close to us as we stood in the shadow of the barn, and then, at the end of each row, they would kneel side by side by the fence and stay silent for a time. The whole thing went on in silence. It was the first time in my life I ever understood something, and I am far from sure now that I can put down what I understood and felt that night — I mean something about the connection between certain people and the earth — a kind of silent cry, down into the earth, of these two old people, putting corn down into the earth. It was as though they were putting death down into the ground that life might grow again — something like that.

By way of summary, the narrator says, "The two old people must have thought of their son Will always in terms of life, never of death." It was to be, in so many words, Anderson's own epitaph.

But in the spring of 1939, he was at work on another book. As he told Roger Sergel: "I'm trying again . . . a man has to begin over and over." And he meant from the start that he was trying, he said, "to think and feel only in a very limited field, the house, the street, the man at the corner drug store." Specifically, he was writing *Home Town,* his last book, a long essay really, with numerous illustrations from the files of the Farm Security Administration.

By 1939, or 1940 when *Home Town* was published, the small town was well on its way to being exclusively a metaphor, sucked up by the media and then broadcast as a tranquilizing notion, an over-the-counter alternative to facing the facts of contemporary life, or the memory of the Depression, or the prospect of entering a war. Although he had been attacked for doing precisely the opposite in his most famous book, with *Home Town* Anderson seemed to be paying homage to the myth.

In preparing the volume, he wrote to Roy Stryker, chief of the Historical Section of the FSA's Division of Information, giving him a long list of "shots" his photographers might want to get, shots of the county courthouse, the justice of the peace, the lawyers, the jail, the bowling alley and skating rink, a birth scene, a strike scene at a factory gate, young men in an old Ford "with sentences scrawled over it," mountain people — what he saw in and around Marion, in other words. But Stryker seems to have ignored Anderson's suggestions. In the book there is no jail, no strike, no birth.

In a draft of his essay, Anderson still tried to look faithfully, including a section on the jails and concluding with one on Saturday night, complete with a drunken father coming home and terrorizing his children, but again the editors had something more soothing in mind. In what remains, Anderson acknowledges the power of the media and the mail-order business, the automobile and the city. He knew, in other words, that the small town's days were numbered, but what prevails over all is a sense of the rhythms of the seasons, of the churches, of school days, town characters, boyhood friendships. It is very seductive. "One of the most perfect pictures of American country life that has ever been made," William Allen White called it in the Book-of-the-Month Club News.

Anderson made the "small town" serve several purposes. He said that it was still the testing ground of democracy, the place where we started, and where we could still prove ourselves as a nation and as individuals. It was also the place, the very image of smallness itself, to which he wanted to return in spirit. On the first page he advised young men with "a burning desire to remake life, the whole social scheme," to stay put. It was a strategy that young idealists might follow, but it was also a safe one for a man his age. His gloss on his advice was:

> In saying that, I had in mind staying closer home [sic] in our thoughts and feelings. The big world outside now is so filled with confusion. It seemed to me that our only hope, in the present muddle, was to try thinking small.

It was a sensible way of dealing with his near (forced) retirement as a writer. "If we could only learn to be very small," he wrote a prolific Wisconsin author, August Derleth, in response to his defense of Anderson against his critics, "walking quietly and not asking much. For example a man like me. I will have no quarrel with what they have done to me."

But the book was also, as he had said to Sergel, a place from which to begin again. One idea he had was for "a high-grade child book." After *Home Town* came out, he wrote Stryker saying that children no longer knew where their food or clothes came from, and that he wanted to write a book "in simple direct prose, and in pictures" about "the drama back of the production of almost everything that makes the child's life comfortable." He thought of those weekly broadcasts from an editor of an imaginary small-town newspaper. He corresponded with Maury Maverick, the mayor of San Antonio, whom he had met on his western swing in 1939 and on whom he wrote an article for the *New Republic,* suggesting that he commission a play about the early days of his city. He ought to get "a good man to do the play," he said, "someone like Paul Green or Sherwood Anderson to write it and train the players." Nothing came of any of these projects. But Anderson had another idea: he wanted to go to South America.

THIRTEEN

Starting Out Again

1941

SHERWOOD ANDERSON was a man who constantly re- newed, remade himself — after every failure, but after every success as well. Having found his own voice writing the *Winesburg, Ohio* tales, he strained it with his *Mid-American Chants,* and then went on to write his best novel, *Poor White.* Having succeeded with that, he insisted on trying something he thought had never been tried before and came up with his "Testaments." All they inaugurated was a relatively barren period, but from it Anderson emerged a newspaper editor and, later, a political journalist.

In his personal life, he was no less determined to better himself. The transformation was not as simple as he often made it out to be, but within a few years he went from being president of a manufacturing concern, through a breakdown and the failure of his business (and his marriage), to being one of America's most important writers. He was disappointed by a few men who he thought were, or who he wanted to be, his friends, and he tried the patience of others. He wanted nothing more than to commit himself to marriage, and he ran away from three of them. But eventually he established a network of friends that was sustaining, and he made what he considered an ideal marriage.

The way he put it in his diary was that he seemed "to be able to be a son of a bitch and pop right out of it as gay as a lark." He could make the transition a bit too easily. But on the other hand, he was forever turning on himself, recognizing how heartless he could be — recognizing, reflecting, writing out the workings of his fears and cruelties as best he could. He tried to hide nothing from himself. If he seemed to forgive himself, to move on too fast, the people he hurt, women especially, were not far behind him. He was a loving man, and there were few who wanted to resist him.

The reach of his sympathies — both as a writer and a man — was limited, but he always wanted to learn more about people and to appreciate their worth. And he wanted others to do the same, not just in the name of human decency, but because that, for him, was what was distinctive about his country. He did not actually express his feelings in political terms until the 1930s, but his defense of the individual was democratic all along. He tried to imagine not only the worth of each person he met, or created; he tried to imagine what more they could be. His greatest concern was that there be more to men than the self-made men, or the warriors, or the "hard-boiled" types that succeeded each other as models for men during his lifetime. He had looked to each for guidance, and he had followed, but then he had seen their limitations, seen them in himself.

Often he said it was industrialization that was at fault. America's most powerful men — even its most famous writers — had made themselves all wrong, he thought. They had steeled themselves, they had not matured, they were less than men. So he looked to other men, to blacks, to men who worked the land, to writers, and he looked to women, hoping to find proof in them that American life was still creative. In his beginnings as a writer, he discovered their presence all around him in the Midwest. After that he set out to find them, first in the South, then in the Southeast. Finally, at the time of his death, he went looking in South America.

In the latter half of 1940, Anderson made plans to go on a kind of good-will tour there. He intended to go through the Panama Canal, then down along the west coast of the continent. His plan was to settle for three or four months in a South American town of about five or ten thousand and get to know the people — "much as I have always tried to do in relation to life in our own North American towns." He thought the common men and women of their respective countries ought to get to know each other.

He gained unofficial support from the U.S. State Department, and then in order to meet his upcoming expenses, he began to negotiate with the *Reader's Digest* about articles he might write for them. He began to correspond with an Argentine writer and a Chilean publisher as well. He wrote about his expectations for the trip and about publishing, but also about the larger question as to how they might create a greater flow of ideas between North and South America. What he and many "ordinary North Americans" feared was "the growth of imperialism," he said. America had become "so powerful, so rich." If any common understanding was to be arrived at, it would have to be through artists' efforts, not politicians', not businessmen's.

While he was in New York, Anderson went down to Bank Street three times a week to take Spanish lessons from a woman named Margarita Madrigal. Dutifully he filled notebooks with vocabulary words and tried to practice a few hours a day with a "Linguaphone." Like a child with a new toy, he wrote Anita Loos, saying, "I put the records on the phonograph so that I may hear the actual spoken language. I think the outfit would be a big help to you."

You have to learn to do everything, even to die, his friend Gertrude Stein once said. He had thought about that often enough to be prepared to do it well. Perhaps he had started ten years before, when he told his future mother-in-law that the time had come to be a mature man before he died. He once said that the trouble with his making statements and what made him "a bum revolutionist" was that he was "not terribly interested in arriving," but emotionally he had. Happily he could begin to die. What that meant he did not know, but one answer might have been the one he gave to Emmett when Emmett asked him for something with which to sweeten his life. We have to "live a little in others" and gradually "get away from self," he had said. "As for the end," he went on,

> I have often thought that when it comes, there will be a kind of real comfort in the fact that self will go then. There is some kind of universal thing we will pass into that will in any event give us escape from this disease of self.
> I believe, Burt, that it is this universal thing, scattered about in many people, a fragment of it here, a fragment there, this thing we call love that we have to keep on trying to tap.

In 1936, he published a defense of euthanasia as part of a discussion occasioned by Charlotte Perkins Gilman's having committed suicide after finding her cancer was incurable. "I have nothing but respect for the woman Charlotte Gilman," he wrote. "My hat off to her. I wish I also could be assured of the same sort of clean departure, of the courage and the sanity of it." ("The little white pill," he wrote Sergel three years later. "The hell is to know when to swallow it.") Ever conscious of the artfulness of his life, he wrote in his *Memoirs* that his life had begun at just the right time, and he hoped that it would end at the right time, "not carry on too far."

By 1940, Anderson was no longer what Eleanor had called "annoyingly healthy." For years he had been plagued with sinus troubles. He smoked, he often took a drug to help him sleep. Though his drinking by no means rivaled that of other famous writers he knew, in his later years, by his own reckoning, he drank too much. He put on weight. Looking back on their outing in Acapulco in 1938, William Spratling remembered him as "seminude and flabby . . . suddenly very vulnerable and almost senile." Resentment over Anderson's treatment of his friend Elizabeth Prall may have informed his description, but undoubtedly Anderson was in decline. Yet he would die no ordinary death.

In mid-October 1940, Eleanor left Ripshin for New York, and Anderson came on two weeks later. She met him at the station, "looking lovely," he wrote in his diary — "very happy to be with her again." And for a time he continued in the highest of spirits.

There was still a place for him in the limelight. Edward Weeks of the *Atlantic* interviewed him on NBC radio. A reporter did so for the *New York Post*. His whereabouts having become known, an electrician from Camden, Ohio, his birthplace, came and "hit him up" for seven dollars. As if to signal how far he had come in his almost sixty-five years, how far his reputation had traveled, a Greek came too, with translations of his poems and stories.

The Andersons always led an active social life when they were in New York. That fall they saw the Schevills, the Galantieres, and Paul Rosenfeld. They went up to Croton-on-Hudson to visit Max Eastman and his wife. Francis Hackett, whom he had not seen in fifteen years, was there with his wife. They dined with Mary Heaton Vorse, who had also written a novel about the strike in Gastonia. They went to parties, one at the Stettenheimers', into whose circle Anderson had been introduced back in 1922. At another Anderson met Somerset Maugham. Anderson also saw his brother Karl and found him dispirited, but spent a pleasant evening swapping tales with him.

The war in Europe threatened to involve the United States, and the thought of its approach weighed heavily on Anderson. "It will be a great sickness on everyone," he wrote. But at home there was hope. On November 5, he and Eleanor joined the crowds at Democratic headquarters and then in Times Square to celebrate President Roosevelt's re-election.

All the while he wrote — or dictated — his *Memoirs,* and much of his activity went into deciding who should publish them. He met with Stanley Young, who had been trying to entice him over to Harcourt, Brace for months. At the Galantieres' he met Max Schuster, who also wanted his *Memoirs,* as did Lippincott. Though they made what Anderson considered "a fine offer," it seemed to him that Scribner's hadn't done enough for him, that Maxwell Perkins was more interested in younger writers than in him. In November he wrote Perkins in terms that followed on those he had used when they had begun negotiations seven years before. Then he had imagined "marriage." Changing publishers was, he now said, "a good deal like getting a divorce." He had gone through "a little kind of private hell," but he was switching over to Harcourt, Brace. He hoped that they would still be friends.

Anderson also met with Carlos Davila and Roberto Rendueles of the Editors' Press Service to discuss publishing possibilities in Chile, and the more immediate possibility of getting a discount on his boat ticket, but then on December 18 came the shocking news that Eleanor's mother had died in her sleep, and that night he and Eleanor boarded the train for Marion.

The preparation for Laura Copenhaver's funeral seemed endless to Anderson, the ceremony (though it included a short tribute from him) and the burial vulgar. "Christianity is like Communism," he wrote on the twentieth; "it would be all right but for the Christians." Two days later, during the service, he imagined himself playing Laura in a game of croquet. It was another sad holiday, this time not because he remembered the struggles of his family in Clyde; and this time the sadness was not unrelieved. "The woman was so filled with life that she seems to have left the sense of her still alive and no sense of death at all," he wrote his son John. "Just a kind of queer disappointment that she doesn't suddenly walk through the door."

In early January 1941 he and Eleanor were back on the road, she to Chicago, he to New York, and there he saw not only Stanley Young and Ferdinand Schevill and Lewis Galantiere again, but also John Emerson, who had stayed on before returning to California just to see him. When last heard from Emerson had been seriously depressed, but now he seemed recovered — he took Anderson out with "one of his women friends" — at least for the time being. In other gestures to the past, Anderson sent holiday greetings to Trillena White, and he wrote another boyhood friend, Herman Hurd, now a grocer, to help him arrange to have the Clyde library receive copies of any of his books that it didn't already have. He also wrote Henry Wallace, asking him if he might get Eleanor Roosevelt, or some other prominent woman, to talk at a Pan American Woman's Day celebration being held in Tampa — as a favor to his Spanish teacher.

But Anderson himself was not feeling well. He caught the flu, he cursed the cold, he cursed New York. Above all, he missed Eleanor, who did not join him until January 20. A trip to Florida did not help much, but all the while he kept his hand in. In January, the first issue of *Decision: A Review of Free Culture,* published as "a gesture of protest and a gesture of hope," listed Anderson as a member of its Board of Editorial Advisors. That month he worked on a play called *Above Suspicion.* A rough draft of it was among the things he took on his trip with him. The play was his contribution to a series that he and others (including Maxwell Anderson, Archibald MacLeish, and William Saroyan) were writing as an expression of belief in America's fundamental institutions. Each was writing on a basic civil right, or on the subject of freedom generally. Anderson's was on free speech. While he was in Florida, he tried to spend his few days with a Spanish-speaking family in order to work on the language.

Eleanor met him in Marion in mid-February, and on the twenty-third they went back to New York. In the next few days, while he was having a drink with George Jean Nathan at a café called Jack and Charlie's, he ran into Ben Hecht, then a writer for the leftist paper *PM.* Several years had gone by since their last meeting, and Hecht was taken aback to see that Anderson was heavier, that "the too many features of his face included a pelican pouch chin," and to hear something of an imitation of the voice he had remembered so vividly. "It was louder and its water-whistle laughter seemed fakey," Hecht later wrote. "The old superiority singsong was missing." After some banter back and forth about days gone by and who had survived them best, Hecht got up to leave, but Anderson told him to sit down. He was going off to South America, he said. When Hecht asked him for how long, he said, "Maybe a year. Maybe two. Maybe forever." As for Anderson's purpose, Hecht knew him as well as anyone. If Hecht was to do an article on him, Anderson said he could say what he wanted.

Hecht wrote a piece the day Anderson set sail. Its last paragraph went:

> Sherwood Anderson is off to find something that vanished out of the world he knew and wrote about. It disappeared out of the land. It was the America he knew — that moody, whimsical, inarticu-

late hero of the pre-radio, pre-movie hinterlands. Something scotched him. And Sherwood, his great biographer, is off for strange lands, where he can forget his hero is dead.

Anderson's vision was impossible to realize, but Hecht was right: he never stopped trying, and he never lost faith in himself as the hero of his attempts.

Two nights before he and Eleanor sailed, there was a farewell party for about twenty people at Mary Emmett's. The next night they went with James Boyd and Karl to the Galantieres' and then on to Roberto Rondueles's for dinner. On one of those occasions Anderson swallowed a toothpick, and it penetrated his intestine.

At eleven o'clock the morning of February 28, 1941, he and Eleanor boarded the Grace Line's *Santa Lucia.* Among their fellow passengers were Freda Kirchwey, the editor of the *Nation,* and the much younger and more obvious spokesman for the small town, Thornton Wilder, on his way to Colombia on a good-will mission similar to Anderson's. The second day out, the sailing was rough. It was cold and windy; snow was in the air. The morning after that, Anderson was sick. His intestine having been perforated, peritonitis had set in. He was in pain the three days it took to reach the Canal Zone, but his spirits held. He was fairly contemptuous of his illness; at the same time, he joked with Kirchwey about dying in the course of duty, being buried at sea, and earning banner headlines that went, "Noted author dies while carrying out mission of friendship to our southern neighbors." When she said she thought it was a poor idea and that besides he'd get only about a column in the *Nation,* he agreed: it would be better to go on to South America. His condition worsened. In an effort to lighten the atmosphere, she made a joke about his not being able to bear going down the coast with her. True to form he answered, "You expect pretty costly tribute from your admirers, don't you, my girl?" Wilder sent a note to the Andersons' cabin, offering his help and reporting what he had managed to find out about medical facilities in the Canal Zone.

During Anderson's last morning on board ship a barber shaved him, and he sat for a while in the sun. When the pain increased and morphine did no good, Eleanor decided what was to be done. An ambulance met the boat at Cristobal, where it docked on March 4, and took him to the Gorges Hospital at Colón. He died there on March 8.

His body arrived in New York on the twenty-fourth. There Karl, Paul Rosenfeld, Mary Emmett, Stanley Young, and Roberto Rondueles met Eleanor and joined her on the train ride back to Marion. On March 26, a short ceremony was held at Rosemont, the Copenhavers' home. There were readings of the Lord's Prayer and the Twenty-third Psalm; Stanley Young read a tribute from Dreiser, a Reverend Brockhoff read Rosenfeld's. The casket was covered with an American flag, sent on by the War Department because Anderson was a veteran of the Spanish-American War. Afterward, a procession of cars went up to the cemetery on Round Hill, where he and Eleanor had often sat and talked and of which he had once written, "Incidentally, there are few more lovely spots in this world in which to take the long adventure of death than the cemetery at Marion."

He is buried beneath a monument that Wharton Eshrick designed. Its unusual shape, a two-pointed cone, contrasts with all the other stones, most especially with the mausoleum of one of Marion's wealthier families that stands next to it. Even in a cemetery, it seems that Anderson doesn't quite belong.

In the column that Anderson got in the *Nation,* Freda Kirchwey wrote:

> I can think of no other ambassador to Latin America who would have expressed more surely and naturally the characteristics we like to claim for our country — humor and friendliness and courage and a democratic spirit that is bred in the bone.

They make fine last words, and there were times when Anderson would have welcomed them. But at the end of his life, he would have found them overblown. What's more, he had already chosen his epitaph. It was simply: "Life not death is the great adventure."

Notes

Selected Bibliography

Index

NOTES

THE NOTES REFER to letters, journal articles, magazine and news-paper stories, and published books. I have silently corrected Anderson's spelling in his letters. The bibliography gives full references for the sources. Those most frequently referred to are abbreviated thus:

Windy   *Windy McPherson's Son,* rev. ed. (Chicago: University of Chicago Press, 1965)

Winesburg   *Winesburg, Ohio* (New York: Viking Press, 1960)

STS   *A Story Teller's Story* (New York: B. W. Huebsch, 1924)

Tar   *Tar: A Midwest Childhood* (New York: Boni and Liveright, 1926)

Mem./Ros.   Paul Rosenfeld, ed., *Sherwood Anderson's Memoirs* (New York: Harcourt, Brace, 1942)

J/R   Howard Mumford Jones and Walter B. Rideout, eds., *Letters of Sherwood Anderson* (Boston: Little, Brown, 1953)

Mem.   Ray Lewis White, ed., *Sherwood Anderson's Memoirs: A Critical Edition* (Chapel Hill: University of North Carolina Press, 1967)

Anderson/Stein   Ray Lewis White, ed., *Sherwood Anderson/Gertrude Stein* (Chapel Hill: University of North Carolina Press, 1972)

Modlin   Charles E. Modlin, ed., *Sherwood Anderson: Selected Letters* (Knoxville: University of Tennessee Press, 1984)

Bab   William A. Sutton, ed., *Letters to Bab: Sherwood Anderson to Marietta D. Finley, 1916–33* (Urbana: University of Illinois Press, 1985)

Elizabeth   Elizabeth Anderson and Gerald R. Kelly, *Miss Elizabeth* (Boston: Little, Brown, 1969)

Centennial   Hilbert H. Campbell and Charles E. Modlin, eds., *Sherwood Anderson: Centennial Studies* (Troy, N.Y.: Whitson Publishing Company, 1976)

Schevill   James Schevill, *Sherwood Anderson: His Life and Work* (Denver: University of Denver Press, 1951)

Story   *Story* 19 (September–October 1941)

Sutton   William A. Sutton, *The Road to Winesburg* (Metuchen, N.J.: Scarecrow Press, 1972)

Newberry   Sherwood Anderson Papers, Newberry Library

1. "Jobby": 1876–1896

1   His Camden: *Tar,* pp. 6–10.
2   "a strange kind": Ibid., p. 39.
    A diary that she kept: It and Irwin's are discussed in *Tar: A Midwest Childhood,* ed. Ray Lewis White (Cleveland: Press of Case Western Reserve, 1969), pp. 219–30.
3   Anderson's memories of Caledonia: *Mem.,* pp. 34–36.
4   Clyde was a town: See Thaddeus B. Hurd, "Sherwood Anderson's Clyde, Ohio," *Centennial,* pp. 156–61.
6   "small cheaply constructed": *Winesburg,* p. 184.
    Clyde's social calendar: Thaddeus B. Hurd, "Fun in Winesburg," *Midwestern Miscellany* 11 (1983):28–39.
    "were lighted by kerosene": *Tar,* p. 80.
    "a tiny brick house": *Mem.,* p. 33.
7   "in an old rented frame house": *Puzzled America* (New York: Charles Scribner's Sons, 1935), p. 244.
    In older civilizations: Quoted in Sisley Huddleston, *Paris Salons, Cafés, Studios* (New York: Blue Ribbon Books, 1928), p. 80.
    the Hurds: Interview with Thaddeus B. Hurd, December 1985.
8   with his brother Karl: J/R, p. 234.
    "No one had time": *Tar,* p. 39.
    "I was raised": J/R, p. 14.
    "because I am his brother": Modlin, p. 37.
    "Karl is in a strange way": Ibid., p. 83.
    "I think Karl": *Bab,* p. 247.
    Irve who could stand up: *Mem.,* p. 42; *STS,* p. 22.
    he couldn't understand: Sutton, p. 573.
    "He had never before known": *Elizabeth,* pp. 78–79.
9   "characteristic of the American race": Modlin, p. 36.
    "in his own way": *STS,* p. 39.
    In a particularly stunning version: *Tar,* pp. 94–100.
10 "the blustering, pretending": *Windy,* pp. 13, 16, 24.
    "nothing he had ever done": *Winesburg,* p. 44.
    maybe Irwin was not: *Tar,* pp. 33, 286.
11 "He was like this": *Mem.,* p. 79.
    "Don't you worry": Ibid., p. 81.
    only the few books: Karl Anderson "My Brother, Sherwood Anderson," *Saturday Review of Literature* 11 (September 4, 1938):6.

"Well, heavens": "Speech at the Writers' Conference in the Rocky Mountains" (Newberry).

Sherwood discovered it: *Mem.*, pp. 82–85.

12   You could have thrown: *Tar*, p. 334.

involved cabbages: *STS*, p. 50–53.

13   Emma would come: Ibid., p. 6.

"I have seen my own mother": *J/R*, p. 361.

"what you do": *Tar*, p. 162.

a five-year-old: Sutton, pp. 505–7.

"he was in love": *Tar*, p. 161.

"so wonderfully comforting": *STS*, p. 7.

14   "I wanted passionately": *Mem.*, pp. 26–27.

He hawked: Karl Anderson, "My Brother," p. 6.

15   "his pocket jingling": *Windy*, pp. 9–10.

"the one man in town": Karl Anderson, "My Brother," p. 6.

"I still remember": Modlin, p. 218.

16   "If Tar's mother": *Tar*, p. 278.

"He went all to pieces": Quoted in Sutton, pp. 20–21.

"He couldn't have caught a ball": Quoted in John A. Sullivan, "Winesburg Revisited," *Antioch Review* 20 (1960): 217.

"who read *Harper's Young People*": *A Boy's Town* (New York: Harper and Brothers, 1890), pp. 1, 205.

17   Once he cast himself: *STS*, pp. 12–23.

18   "the victim": *Mem.*, pp. 69–71.

"Laura Jean Libbey": *STS*, pp. 155–56.

For John Tichenor, see Sutton, p. 24.

John Telfer: *Windy*, pp. 4–10.

19   "My foolishness": Ibid., p. 59.

his first boyhood friend: *Mem.*, pp. 50–51.

20   "Sometimes when Tar": *Tar*, p. 226.

he first entered: *Mem.*, pp. 85–89.

21   "If it was vile": Ibid., pp. 45–46.

"I had thought": *Mem./Ros.*, pp. 40–44.

"Death in the Woods": Collected in *Death in the Woods and Other Stories* (New York: Liveright, 1933).

22   A long letter from Clyde: *Bab*, pp. 23–26.

24   "A man, if he": *Tar*, p. 166.

"I Want to Know Why": Collected in *The Triumph of the Egg* (New York: B. W. Huebsch, 1921).

As a newsboy: *Tar*, pp. 227–33.

25   "chambermaid in a livery stable": *The Buck Fever Papers*, ed. Welford Dunaway Taylor (Charlottesville: University Press of Virginia, 1971), p. 221.

One night a man: *Mem.*, pp. 110–12.

"The men seemed": *STS*, pp. 199–200.

26   "To most folks": Quoted in Sullivan, "Winesburg Revisited," p. 219.

27   when Anderson was swimming: *Mem.*, pp. 47–48.

Anderson wrote about it: *Tar*, p. 105; *Mem.*, p. 110; *Mem./Ros.*, p. 56.

28 "mystic episodes": *Tar*, p. 73.
"fugue" states: *The Interpersonal Theory of Psychiatry* (New York: W. W. Norton, 1953), pp. 322–23.

29 "the dark evil old woman": *STS*, p. 7.
Part of *that* story: *Mem.*, pp. 135–38.
"I could repay": *Windy*, p. 84.

2. "The Undeveloped Man": 1896–1906

31 By the time Chicago: For Chicago, and for the literary renaissance that took place there in the early part of the century, see Bernard Duffey, *The Chicago Renaissance in American Letters* (East Lansing: Michigan State College Press, 1954), and Dale Kramer, *Chicago Renaissance: The Literary Life in the Midwest: 1900–1930* (New York: Appleton Century, 1966). See also Harold M. Mayer and Richard C. Wade, *Chicago: The Growth of a Metropolis* (Chicago: University of Chicago Press, 1969), and the WPA *Guide* to Illinois (Chicago: A. C. McClurg and Company, 1939).
Chicago went from a mudhole: *Kindergarten Chats* (New York: Wittenborn, Schultz, 1955), p. 109.

32 "An expensive ornament": *Marching Men*, ed. Ray Lewis White (Cleveland: Press of Case Western Reserve, 1972), p. 120.
"All at once": Quoted in the WPA *Guide*, p. 41.
"vacant, sullen materialism": *Kindergarten Chats*, pp. 110–11.
"The city is passing": Quoted in Duffey, *The Chicago Renaissance*, pp. 27–28.

33 "The Upward Movement": Ibid., p. 31.
"the nameless fear": *Poor White* (New York: Viking Press, 1966), p. 31.
"see which fellow": Karl Anderson, "My Brother, Sherwood Anderson," *Saturday Review of Literature* 11 (September 4, 1938):6.

34 "rolling kegs of nails": *STS*, p. 133.
"talked about his dissatisfaction": Quoted in Sutton, p. 57.
"Why should I": *Mem.*, p. 155.
he looked to Clifton Paden: Ibid., pp. 148–56.

35 "always had to be": October 28, 1928 (?) (Newberry).
there were men: *Mem.*, pp. 339–41.

36 Once he followed through: Ibid., pp. 146–48.
"a problem that had": Ibid., pp. 160–66.
Miss Mabel Harper: See Sutton, p. 67.
"Most men": October 1932 (Spear collection).

37 "a shabby trick": *Mem.*, p. 171.

38 "innocent amusements": For the Spanish-American War, see Ray Ginger, *Age of Excess: The United States from 1877 to 1914* (New York: Macmillan, 1965), pp. 192–208.
On the freight train: *STS*, p. 278.
"living part": Gerald F. Linderman, *The Mirror of War: American Society and the Spanish-American War* (Ann Arbor: University of Michigan Press, 1974), p. 66; *STS*, pp. 281–82.

39 a disturbing story: *Mem.*, pp. 188–89.
"physical hardening process": *STS*, p. 279; *Mem.*, p. 186.
40 "Let's get 'em": Ibid., p. 171.
"marching shoulder": *Bab*, p. 64.
"even told to grunt": *STS*, p. 281.
"It is the strength": *Mem.*, p. 185.
In retrospect, the Spanish-American War: *STS*, pp. 277, 279; Modlin, p. 74; *Mem.*, p. 165.
41 "all skin and bones": Karl Anderson, "My Brother," p. 7.
"Why do not you": *Marching Men*, p. 122.
42 "The Oaks": For The Oaks and Mrs. Folger, see William Baker, "Sherwood Anderson in Springfield," *American Literary Realism* 15 (1982):47–61, and *Mem./Ros.*, pp. 259–62.
"a big-legged, big-breasted": *Mem./Ros.*, p. 260.
43 "She was a great woman": Modlin, pp. 227–28.
His first assignment: *Mem.*, p. 200.
sent to convince: *Agricultural Advertising* 11 (August 1904):21–24.
44 "staid and monotonous": George Daugherty, "Anderson, Advertising Man," *Newberry Library Bulletin*, series 2, no. 2 (December 1948):31.
"I'd give my account": "A Mid-Western Ad Man Remembers: Sherwood Anderson, Advertising Man," *Advertising and Selling* 28 (December 1937):35.
45 "The relation of the advertising": *Agricultural Advertising* 12 (April 1905):307.
"Advertising, that's what": Quoted in Stephen Fox, *The Mirror Makers: A History of American Advertising and Its Creators* (New York: William Morrow, 1984), pp. 32–33.
The organization continued: *Mem.*, pp. 211–13.
46 "His charm, interest": Daugherty, "Anderson," p. 31.
"The advertising business": In *A Story Teller's Story*, ed. Ray Lewis White (Cleveland: Press of Case Western Reserve, 1968), pp. 346–47.
47 "A Vacation Story": 11 (May 1904):31–32, and 11 (June 1904):27–29.
"The Solicitor": 11 (August 1904):21–24.
"There was an old fellow": 10 (April 1903):14.
"Chicago Inspirations": Ibid.
48 "Men That Are Wanted": 10 (December 1903):51.
"the Napoleons are dead": 11 (February 1904):19.
"America's greatest": Quoted in Fox, *The Mirror Makers*, p. 63.
"Advertising a Nation": 12 (May 1905):389.
49 every good advertisement: 10 (May 1903):22.
"The Man of Affairs": 11 (March 1904):36–38.
"The Lightweight": 10 (March 1903):18.
50 "The Boyish Man": 11 (October 1904):53.
"The Undeveloped Man": 21 (May 1904):31–32.
51 "Making It Clear": 24 (February 1913):18.
52 "We at home have seen": Letter of May 6, 1904 (Newberry).
"went forth with": 10 (February 1903):14.
"The Traveling Man": 11 (April 1904):39.

53 "good fireplace": Quoted in Sutton, p. 137.
"A Business Man's Reading": 2 (October 1903):503–4.
"The Man and the Book": 3 (December 1903):71–73.
54 "When I first": Quoted in Sutton, p. 129.
55 "very strongly sexed": *Bab*, p. 147.
Once he took a woman: *Mem.*, pp. 230–34.
"Most women simply": *Bab*, p. 147.
56 "When it is over": Ibid., p. 6.

3. Breakdown: 1906–1912

61 "We thought we had": Quoted in Sutton, p. 173.
"a salesman who had got": *Mem.*, p. 238.
"innumerable tales of men": *STS*, p. 213.
"idea of altruism": *Mem./Ros.*, pp. 186–87.
"There would be a great": *STS*, p. 303.
62 "He was an enthusiast": Quoted in Sutton, p. 174.
63 "his *Sister Carrie*": *Mem.*, p. 256.
"an eccentric": Quoted in Sutton, pp. 162–63.
On one memorable: *Mem.*, pp. 246–48; "Speech at the Writers' Conference in the Rocky Mountains."
"never did domesticate": March 1933 (Spear collection).
64 In and with his room: *Mem.*, pp. 249–53.
65 Writing was "curative": Modlin, pp. 20–21.
"It is the only justification": March 1933 (Spear collection).
66 "He began feeling": *Windy*, p. 196.
"Books are not full": Ibid., p. 148.
67 "The home-coming": Ibid., pp. 325–30.
"come to novel writing": J/R, p. 82.
68 "What 'Dreiser'": *Mem.*, p. 257.
"some other and older writer": *No Swank* (Philadelphia: Centaur Press, 1934), pp. 35–46
69 "Those were the days": December 29, 1938 (Newberry).
one man who had suggested: *Mem.*, pp. 278–94.
Anderson brought him: Ibid., pp. 309–11.
70 "You see the woman": *Mem.*, p. 261.
"She had always": *Bab*, pp. 27–28.
71 "Just because I was married": Ibid., p. 45.
One night, tired: *Mem.*, pp. 260–62.
"against money-making": J/R, pp. 81–82.
72 "Losing step": *Marching Men*, ed. Ray Lewis White (Cleveland: Press of Case Western Reserve, 1972), p. 11.
"He knew that he": Ibid., pp. 106–7.
"In all of the time": Ibid., p. 206.
73 "appealed strongly": J/R, p. 16.
"One of the hundreds": *Marching Men*, p. 58.
"in a way the whole": *Bab*, pp. 69–70.

74   it would be *Fascism: Mem.*, pp. 186–87.
     "Ugly crawling things": *Marching Men*, p. 90.
     Anderson tells about a barber: Ibid., pp. 59–70.
75   "shoving imagined people": J/R, p. 448.
     "'form' as form": Ibid., p. 202.
     Anderson introduces a man: *Marching Men*, pp. 114–19.
76   She was "strong": *Bab*, p. 28.
77   "It was quiet": "A New Testament, XI," *Little Review* 7 (July–August 1920):59.
78   a few notes that Anderson dictated: All Elyria documents are among the Anderson papers at the Newberry Library. They are reproduced in Sutton, pp. 552–59.
81   "You are, to my mind": J/R, p. 75.
     "strivings, affects": *The Collected Papers of David Rapaport*, ed. Merton M. Gill (New York: Basic Books, 1967), p. 118.
82   In an example cited: Ibid., p. 388, and David Rapaport, *Emotions and Memory* (Baltimore: Williams and Wilkins, 1942), pp. 201–2.
     "after several days": *Bab*, p. 28.

4. Becoming a Writer: 1912–1915

83   not one to say: Interview with Marion Spear, November 1985.
84   his first story, "The Rabbit-Pen": *Harper's* 129 (July 1914):207–19.
     perhaps the news: "On Being Published," *Colophon* (February 1930):n.p.
85   "dear patient woman": *Bab*, p. 45.
86   Bayard Barton was now: *Mem.*, pp. 328–30.
     "Making It Clear": 24 (February 1913):16.
     The "New Chicago": *The Craftsman* 24 (September 1913):555–65.
87   an artists' colony: See Bernard Duffey, *The Chicago Renaissance in American Letters* (East Lansing: Michigan State College Press, 1954), and Dale Kramer, *Chicago Renaissance: The Literary Life in the Midwest* (New York: Appleton Century, 1966). See also *Mem.*, pp. 336–38.
88   "There is no Middle": *Good-Bye Wisconsin* (New York: Harper and Row, 1928), p. 39.
     "We were in love": *Homecoming* (New York: Farrar and Rinehart, 1933), p. 242.
     "The colonists were": *Mem.*, pp. 335–36.
89   Instead, he crossed: *Mem./Ros.*, pp. 238–39.
90   "with black eyes": Letter to Harry Hansen, 1923 (Newberry).
     "a great human": *Women as World Builders: Studies in Modern Feminism* (Chicago: Forbes and Company, 1913), p. 21.
91   she planned an occasion: Transcript of WBAI radio broadcast, May 26, 1963 (Newberry).
     "the proletarian": *New Republic* 89 (November 25, 1936):103–5.
     "An extremely handsome": "On Being Sherwood Anderson's Literary Father," *Newberry Library Bulletin* 5 (December 1961):315.
     "he looked like": "Laetitia," *Playboy* 10 (July 1963):88, 124.

"in a certain amazement": *My Thirty Year's War* (New York: Covici, Friede, 1930), pp. 38–39.

92   "a great novelist": "A New American Novelist," *Masses* 9 (November 1916):17.

"seen in MS.": "New Novels: A First Glimpse," *Chicago Evening Post,* September 5, 1913, p. 9. Quoted in G. Thomas Tanselle, "Realist or Dreamer: Letters of Sherwood Anderson and Floyd Dell," *Modern Language Review* 58 (October 1963):532.

"a gay happy": *Mem.*, p. 344.

Anderson's "literary father": For the relationship betweeen Dell and Anderson see Dell's "On Being Sherwood Anderson's Literary Father," and Tanselle, "Realist or Dreamer."

94   "a slender delicate": *Homecoming*, p. 237.

95   John remembered: Interview, October 1984.

"I lived in a separate": J/R, pp. 8–9.

thrown it out: Harry Hansen, *Midwest Portraits* (New York: Harcourt, Brace, 1923), p. 122.

96   *Mary Cochran*: Newberry.

97   "I had to undertake": J/R, p. 8.

"He did the right": Quoted in Sutton, p. 236.

a remarkable man: Interview with Marion Spear, November 1985.

98   "Anderson, Ben Hecht": Hansen, *Midwest Portraits,* p. 176.

What private moments: *Mem.*, p. 345.

"Such a wonderful": Ibid.

"just one ecstasy": *My Thirty Years' War,* p. 69.

99   The "new note": *Little Review* 1 (March 1914):23.

"More About": 1 (April 1914):16–17.

he would always credit: James Feibleman, "Literary New Orleans Between World Wars," *Southern Review* 1 (Summer 1965):712; J/R, p. 300; and Sherwood Anderson, "The Works of Gertrude Stein," *Geography and Plays* (Boston: Four Seas, 1922), pp. 5–7.

100   "intellectual recreation": *Gertrude Stein: Writings and Lectures, 1909–1945* (New York: Penguin Books, 1971), p. 142.

"An artist in phrase making": *Centennial,* p. 10.

"Sister": *Little Review* 2 (December 1915):3–4.

"Blackfoot's Masterpiece": *Forum* 55 (June 1916):679–83.

101   "The Story Writers": *Smart Set* 48 (January 1916):243–48.

"The Novelist": *Little Review* 2 (January–February 1916):12–14.

"wholly uncommercial": Letter of Albert Gale (Newberry).

Talbot Whittingham: Newberry.

102   "I understand": *Bab,* p. 51.

Ben Hecht has told: *A Child of the Century* (New York: Simon and Schuster, 1954), pp. 228–30.

"The Man's Story": *Dial* 75 (September 1923):247–64.

103   "the Little Children of the Arts": *Mem.*, pp. 346–48.

"Hands": *Winesburg*, pp. 27–34.

the colony had discovered: *Mem.*, pp. 339–41.

106   "What the devil": *Bab,* p. 37.

naming was all right: *Gertrude Stein,* pp. 125–26.
107 He toned down: William L. Phillips, "How Sherwood Anderson Wrote *Winesburg, Ohio,*" *American Literature* 23 (March 1951):7–30.
"I think the most": J/R, pp. 314–15.
108 "It is there": *Mem.,* pp. 352–53.

5. Emerging Greatness: 1915–1917

109 "like a harp": Quoted in Sutton, p. 428.
"The book is": *Centennial,* pp. 47–48.
110 "see the glimmer": *Bab,* p. xv.
"The Book of the Grotesque": *Winesburg,* pp. 21–25.
The word *grotesque*: See Schevill, p. 102. See also Marilyn Judith Atlas, "Experimentation in the Chicago Little Theatre: Cloyd Head's *Grotesques,*" *Midwestern Miscellany* 7 (1980):7–19, and Kay Kinsella Rout, "Arthur Davison Ficke's 'Ten Grotesques,'" Ibid., pp. 20–27.
111 "who said that": J/R, p. 115.
113 "will suggest the real": Ibid., p. 5.
"a city of the dead": *Bab,* p. 15.
"a leader now": Ibid., p. 61.
"the very blood": Ibid., p. 16.
"A democratic plea": *Harper's* 268 (March 1984):97.
114 "Statements of Belief": 68 (October 1928):204.
"the more compact": Quoted in Schevill, p. 96.
"to develop": J/R, p. 404.
115 "I can accept": Ibid., p. 72.
"It is a form": Quoted in Sutton, p. 434.
"nice little packages": J/R, p. 403.
116 "the theme": Modlin, pp. 153–54.
117 "Sophistication": *Winesburg,* pp. 233–43.
118 "My crowd": *New York Herald Tribune Books,* April 12, 1942, pp. 1–2.
Its prolegomenon: Quoted in James Hoopes, *Van Wyck Brooks: In Search of American Culture* (Amherst: University of Massachusetts Press, 1977), p. 110.
"those personal instincts": *Three Essays on America* (New York: E. P. Dutton, 1934), p. 34.
119 "some prodigious organism": "Young America," *Seven Arts* 1 (December 1916):151.
Edna Kenton was the first: Modlin, p. 252.
"long, gangling script": "Sherwood Anderson: A Personal Note," *Newberry Library Bulletin,* series 2, no. 2 (December 1958):39–43.
"one of the great": "Winesburg, Ohio: After Twenty Years," *Story,* p. 31.
120 "His famous flight": *Days of the Phoenix* (New York: E. P. Dutton, 1957), p. 31.
"what happened to": (New York: Boni and Liveright, 1919), pp. 137, 146.
"the fecund sap": "Sherwood Anderson," pp. 39–41.

her reports: reproduced in Sutton, pp. 581–88.

121 "I have an idea": *Bab,* pp. 8–9.

122 "I am trying": Ibid., p. 30.
"Perhaps no woman": Ibid., p. 281.
"When you are well": Ibid., p. 92.

123 "O my dear friend": Ibid., p. 297.
"a certain litheness": Ibid., pp. 197–200.
"a good adjustment": Ibid., p. 332.
"Why did Sherwood": Ibid., p. xiii.

124 he looks back: Ibid., p. 6.
She had been named: On Tennessee, see her seventy-nine-page autobiographical essay (Newberry).

125 "had a graciousness": Quoted in Sutton, p. 243.
"an Indian": *Bab,* p. 84.
"fatal undertow": Fanny Butcher, *Many Lives — One Love* (New York: Harper and Row, 1972), p. 102.

126 In his, it was she: See "T.M.: The Forgotten Muse," *Centennial,* pp. 175–84.
"subtle and designing": *Across Spoon River* (New York: Farrar and Rinehart, 1936), pp. 301–11.
"There is a blessed": J/R, p. 29.
she introduced him: Irving Howe, *Sherwood Anderson* (New York: William Sloane Associates, 1951), pp. 68, 70.

127 "This lovely camp": Harry Hansen, *Midwest Portraits* (New York: Harcourt, Brace, 1923), p. 174.
several explanations: Sutton, pp. 250–51; Edward Dahlberg, *Alms for Oblivion* (Minneapolis: University of Minnesota Press, 1964), p. 10; August Derleth, *Three Literary Men* (New York: Candlelight Press, 1963), p. 32.

128 But it was she: Howe, *Sherwood Anderson,* p. 82.
her father always: Interview with Marion Spear, November 1985.
they were married: Hansen, *Midwest Portraits,* p. 175; *Bab,* p. 84.
Trigant Burrow: See *A Search for Man's Identity: The Selected Letters of Trigant Burrow, with Biographical Notes* (New York: Oxford University Press, 1958).

129 "Does Burrow think": Trigant Burrow, *Science and Man's Behavior: The Contribution of Phylobiology* (New York: Philosophical Library, 1953), p. 120.
what he had in mind: *A Search,* p. 56.
It was she: *Bab,* pp. 52–53.

130 "timidly, questioning": Ibid., p. 45.
"I do not dare": Ibid., p. 55.

131 "The short story": *Chicago Daily News,* October 4, 1916, p. 1. Quoted in *Bab,* p. 5.
found it repellent: no. 4611 (November 1916):543.
lacked artistry: *Dial* 61 (September 1916):196–97.
"loose and disorderly": "People Who Write," *Bab,* p. 5.
"a new writer": 103 (November 1916):508.

"a freshness": 9 (January 1917):333–34, 336.
Dell recalled: 9 (November 1916):17.
"Emerging Greatness": *Seven Arts* 1 (November 1916):73–78.
132 They were alike: J/R, pp. 6–7.
James Oppenheim's account: "The Story of the Seven Arts," *American Mercury* 20 (June 1930):161.
133 "perhaps given to scribbling": *Bab*, pp. 26–28.
"provincial, middle western": Ibid., p. 66.
"smiling front": Ibid., p. 65.
134 "I want to open": Ibid., p. 66.

6. Unrest: 1917–1919

135 a series of poems — or "chants": See Walter Rideout, "Sherwood Anderson's Mid-American Chants," in *Aspects of American Poetry,* ed. Richard M. Ludwig (Columbus: Ohio State University Press, 1962), pp. 149–70.
136 "submerged in adolescence": J/R, p. 53.
"He man, an eater": "Carl Sandburg," *Bookman* 54 (December 1921): 360–61.
"a suggestion of closed-in": J/R, p. 12.
137 "I would publish": Ibid., p. 17.
"See the corn": Ibid.
"From Chicago": *Seven Arts* 2 (May 1917):41–59.
"There will be woods": J/R, p. 10.
138 "a streak of barely": *Bab*, p. 84.
"to come close": Ibid., p. 85.
"to be molded": J/R, p. 15.
139 "There was a Doctor": *Little Review* 5 (July 1918):24–31.
141 "An Apology for Crudity," *Dial* 63 (November 8, 1977):437–38.
"gone insane": J/R, p. 27.
142 "poetic rather": October 29, 1917 (Newberry).
"It don't matter": J/R, p. 24.
143 "the bourjoices": *Mem.,* pp. 356–58.
"the emperor of the intellectual": *The Autobiography of Emanuel Carnevali* (New York: Horizon Press, 1967), p. 168.
Anderson is Warren Lockwood: (Chicago: The University of Chicago Press, 1963), pp. 215–39.
144 trying to write a play: (New York: Simon and Schuster, 1954), p. 227.
"If we are not careful": Quoted in Bernard Duffey, *The Chicago Renaissance in American Letters* (East Lansing: Michigan State College Press, 1954), p. 250.
"As you must know": J/R, p. 20.
145 "I should be": n.d. (Newberry).
he actually mapped: 1919(?) (Newberry).
"Just like brothers": September 1919 (?) (Newberry).
"The struggle is hard": *Mem.,* p. 449.

146   "People I had long": J/R, p. 21.
       "What matter": Ibid., p. 27.
       "His is to me": *Bab*, p. 101.
       "the scholar with": Quoted in Sutton, p. 281.
       "As for Brooks": J/R, p. 35.
       calling *Winesburg, Ohio:* August 15, 1920 (?) (Newberry).
       too much the "just judge": J/R, p. 104.
       "fresh healthy mind": Preface to "Letters to Van Wyck Brooks, *Story*, p.
       42; *Days of the Phoenix* (New York: E. P. Dutton, 1957), pp. 12–13.
147   "I wish you": J/R, p. 60.
       "both you and Brooks": Ibid., p. 35.
       wrote about his trips: *A Story Teller's Story*, ed. Ray Lewis White (Cleve-
       land: Press of Case Western Reserve, 1968), pp. 277–86.
       "the most vivid": Modlin, p. 252.
148   "Dear Barton": "Letters to Van Wyck Brooks," *Story*, p. 50.
       she was a fool: *Bab*, p. 91.
149   Tennessee's trenchant: Fanny Butcher, *Many Lives — One Love* (New York:
       Harper and Row, 1972), p. 102.
       "at the edge": *Bab*, p. 66.
       "Take long walks": Letter of Karen Hollis to Harry Hansen, March 21,
       1941 (Newberry).
       "the provocative trash": *A Girl Like I* (New York: Viking Press, 1966),
       pp. 220, 228.
150   "There is a certain": *Bab*, p. 96.
152   "And all over": *Poor White* (New York: Viking Press, 1966), pp. 61–62.
153   "those who are kindly": Ibid., p. 153.
       "One should be able": Ibid., p. 169.
154   "The American man": *The Education of Henry Adams* (Boston: Houghton
       Mifflin, 1973), pp. 442–45.
155   "The same light": *Poor White*, p. 358.
       "rather better in the Middle West": J/R, pp. 43–44.
156   "too gloomy": William L. Phillips, "How Sherwood Anderson Wrote
       Winesburg, Ohio," *American Literature* 23 (March 1951):30.
157   "I wrote Ben": Modlin, p. 12.
       even *The Boston Transcript:* June 11, 1919, p. 6; William Lyon Phelps,
       New York Times Book Review, June 29, 1919, p. 353.
       "Into the soul": *Chicago Tribune,* June 7, 1919, p.13.
       "Here is the goal": *Smart Set* 59 (August 1919):140, 142.
       "the entire paraphernalia": *Pagan* 4 (September 1919):60–61.
       "two or three weeks'": J/R, p. 45.
       "too dreadfully": Ibid., p. 44.
       "The Triumph of the Egg": *Dial* 68 (March 1920):295–304, and, as
       "The Egg" in *The Triumph of the Egg* (New York: B. W. Huebsch,
       1921).
158   "I want constantly": J/R, p. 46.
       "achieved by the autobiography": Ibid., p. 50.
       asked Huebsch: Modlin, p. 13.
       "These days out": *Bab*, p. 108.

159 "Tennessee has genius": Modlin, p. 14.

"gulped the mess": *Bab,* p. 110.

"constantly more like eating": "Letters to Van Wyck Brooks," *Story,* p. 53.

"an odd kind": *Bab,* pp. 108–10.

160 a series of letters: Ibid., pp. 111–16.

"a madhouse": Modlin, p. 15.

"I know nothing": J/R, p. 51.

"breaking under": Modlin, pp. 14–15.

161 "I turn to women": *Bab,* p. 113.

"a striking story": Ibid., p. 117.

7. Alabama and Paris: 1920–1921

162 "new door of the house": *Bab,* p. 121.

In Mobile: *Mem.,* pp. 353–56.

163 The town had been settled: For Anderson's time in Fairhope, see *Mem.,* pp. 365–66; *Bab,* pp. 118–24; Modlin, pp. 19–20; and *France and Sherwood Anderson: Paris Notebook, 1921,* ed. Michael Fanning (Baton Rouge: Louisiana State University Press, 1976), pp. 59–61.

165 one painting class: J/R, p. 57.

"lay into them": Modlin, p. 54.

reportedly liked his work: Letter from Paul Rosenfeld to Anderson, July 1920 (Newberry).

"There are certain images": *Little Review* 7 (January–March 1921):64.

166 "own kind of poetry": J/R, p. 55.

"the Hebrew poets": Ibid., p. 77.

"A Poet": *A New Testament* (New York: Boni and Liveright, 1927), p. 59.

167 "experiments in rhythm": Modlin, p. 50.

"something looser": J/R, pp. 55, 58.

"for a Chicago friend of hers": Ibid., p. 57.

"be utterly reckless": Ibid., p. 54.

"the golden days": Ibid., p. 57.

168 "O, for a world": Ibid., p. 55.

"there came that moment": Introduction to *Poor White* (New York: Modern Library Edition, 1926), p. x.

"The Man in the Brown Coat": *Little Review* 7 (January–March 1921):18–21.

169 "Can it be true": J/R, p. 103.

"Honest to God tales": Ibid., p. 69.

"to mend the broken": Ibid., p. 57.

170 "the realization of life": *Bab,* p. 127.

But one incident: *Mem.,* pp. 366–69.

"only a box": J/R p. 63; *Bab,* p. 132.

171 "to sit under a fig": J/R, pp. 63–64.

"among the finest": Quoted in Schevill, p. 126.

Mencken praised: *Smart Set* 63 (December 1920):138–39.
"well thought out": *Bab*, p. 136.
Francis Hackett complained: *New Republic* 24 (November 1920):330.
"large, loose sense": J/R, p. 72.
"spiritually tired": *Bab*, p. 137.
probably sold more: J/R, p. 70.
he wrote Huebsch: Quoted in Sutton, p. 450.

172 They called their place: For "The Domicile" and Anderson's meetings with Hemingway, see Charles A. Fenton, *The Apprenticeship of Ernest Hemingway* (New York: Farrar, Straus and Young, 1954), pp. 98–110, and Michael Reynolds, *The Young Hemingway* (New York: Basil Blackwell, 1986), pp.. 158–59, 178–88.

173 "Sherwood was like a jolly": *Ernest Hemingway: Selected Letters*, ed. Carlos Baker (New York: Charles Scribner's Sons, 1981), p. 862.

174 "sucked dry": *Bab*, p. 143.
"a rotten winter": J/R, p. 71.
"an amazing force": *Story*, p. 6.
Rosenfeld had come by: For Rosenfeld, see Sherman Paul, "Paul Rosenfeld," in Rosenfeld's *Port of New York* (Urbana: University of Illinois Press, 1961), pp. vii–lvi.

175 "stupid," "slow": J/R, pp. 77–80.
"walking a tight-rope": *Bab*, p. 157.
"flighty, feminine": Edward Dahlberg, *Alms for Oblivion* (Minneapolis: University of Minnesota Press, 1964), p. 6.
"old scars": *Bab*, p. 166.

176 "a great companion": J/R, p. 73.
"raw-boned prairie": "Paul Rosenfeld: Three Phases," in *Paul Rosenfeld: Voyager in the Arts*, ed. James Mellquist and Lucie Wiese (New York: Creative Age Press, 1948), p. 5.
"frankly an old-fashioned": Letter to Anderson, November 5. 1923 (Newberry).
While he was there: For Anderson's trip, see Fanning, *France and Sherwood Anderson*.
"upper middle class": *Bab*, p. 159.

177 "no such luck": Ibid., p. 164.
"These men love": Fanning, *France and Sherwood Anderson*, p. 42.
The day he and Rosenfeld: *STS*, pp. 398–410.

179 "like a light": Fanning, *France and Sherwood Anderson*, pp. 27–28.
"an empty man": Ibid., p. 12.
Marguerite Gay . . . Sylvia Beach . . . Adrienne Monnier: Fanning, *France and Sherwood Anderson*, pp. 13, 16, 18–19.

180 "great kitchen": 32 (October 11, 1922):171–73.
"really the only": *Anderson/Stein*, p. 10.
"I have never": Ibid., p. 12.
"Yes, undoubtedly": *Story*, p. 63.
Faulkner in the University, ed. Frederick L. Gwinn and Joseph L. Blotner (Charlottesville: University Press of Virginia, 1959), p. 230.
"with an American": Fanning, *France and Sherwood Anderson*, p. 51.

181 "It became the period": *The Autobiography of Alice B. Toklas* (New York: Modern Library Edition, 1933), p. 212.

"never . . . off": *Anderson/Stein*, p. 18.

"his great, beautiful": *A Moveable Feast* (New York: Charles Scribner's Sons, 1964), pp. 27–28.

"passionately interested": *Autobiography*, pp. 212, 217.

"very handsome": Linda Simon, *The Biography of Alice B. Toklas* (Garden City, N.Y.: Doubleday, 1977), p. 114.

the "Americans": *The Ferment of Realism: American Literature, 1884–1919* (New York: Free Press, 1965), pp. 297–98.

182 a short piece on Dreiser: 3 (April 1916):5.

"When he grew": *Tar*, p. 166.

"with that America": *STS*, p. 410.

183 "the director of": *Bab*, p. 164.

"Hello Yank": 132 (August 6, 1921):172–74.

8. Another Flight: 1921–1922

184 "with fire and feeling": *Bab*, p. 167.

"the country's most": *Freeman* 4 (November 30, 1921):282.

"one of the most": *New Statesman* 19 (July 22, 1922):444.

"If the *Dial*'s": Quoted in Schevill, p. 152.

185 he went to hear: *Bab*, pp. 171–72.

"Celebrity": Ibid., p. 167.

"a distinct flavor": Modlin, p. 27.

"by shoveling mud": *Bab*, p. 167.

"The figures of the fancy": *Ibid.*, pp. 168–69.

186 he sounded like: Harry Hansen, *Midwest Portraits* (New York: Harcourt, Brace, 1923), p. 171.

On a late January day: Modlin, pp. 29–30.

when it came out: Ibid., p. 29.

"She gives me": *Bab*, p. 176.

187 an intelligent appreciation: 2 (July 1921):42–45.

"Sherwood Anderson and Our": N. Bryllion Fagin, 7 (January–February 1925):246–55.

"New Orleans, the Double": 3 (March 1922):119–26.

"itinerant literary": *Philosophers Lead Sheltered Lives* (London: George Allen and Unwin, 1952), p. 24.

they seemed just overprivileged: Modlin, p. 31.

188 "the whole expression": *Bab*, p. 179.

"like a man": *Anderson/Stein*, p. 14.

written fifty thousand: Modlin, p. 32.

"to get a quick nervous": Ibid., p. 33.

"The Contract": 1 (December 1921):148–53.

189 no, it didn't seem: Modlin, p. 28.

"One might think": *Many Marriages* (New York: B. W. Huebsch, 1923), p. 42.

"If one kept": Ibid., pp. 190–91.
190   Balthus admired: *Anderson/Stein*, p. 112.
"After it is all": *Beyond Desire* (New York: Liveright, 1932), p. 171.
191   "You do a little": *Anderson/Stein*, p. 27.
"the fullblown flower": "Sherwood Anderson on the Marriage Question," *New York Herald,* March 4, 1923, sec. 9, p. 5.
"a haunting book": *The Letters of F. Scott Fitzgerald,* ed. Andrew Turnbull (New York: Charles Scribner's Sons, 1963), p. 476.
"There should be": *Anderson/Stein*, p. 27.
"a god-forsaken time": Modlin, p. 34.
"Am I not": Ibid.
"Have run away": *Anderson/Stein*, p. 20.
192   "his roaming years": *Days of the Phoenix,* (New York: E. P. Dutton, 1957), p. 11.
"a half diseased desire": *Bab,* p. 182.
"I have thought": Modlin, p. 39.
"with wine and song": *Bab,* p. 184.
He came to dinner: For Anderson's stopover in Cleveland, see John Unterecker, *Voyager: A Life of Hart Crane* (New York: Farrar, Straus and Giroux, 1969), pp. 249–51.
193   "like a crazy man": J/R, p. 186.
"Ohio: I'll Say": August 9, 1922, pp. 146–48.
"Any sign of patronage": J/R, p. 89.
"As the flapper": *Bab,* p. 178.
"five short stories": J/R, p. 89.
194   "A Man's Story": *Dial* 75 (September 1923):247–64.
195   "The Sad Horn Blowers": *Harper's* 146 (February 1923): 273–89.
"The Man Who Became a Woman": Collected in *Horses and Men* (New York: B. W. Huebsch, 1923).
197   Now Anderson was so: *Elizabeth,* pp. 49–50.
198   "the most male": *The Portable Sherwood Anderson,* ed. Horace Gregory (New York: Viking Penguin, 1972), p. 462.
they invited Anderson: For the occasion, see Townsend Luddington, *John Dos Passos: A Twentieth Century Odyssey* (New York: E. P. Dutton, 1980), p. 221.
"There's nobody": Letter of January 7, 1922 (Newberry).
199   the Stettheimer sisters: See Schevill, p. 174.
"some warm exotic": *Sherwood Anderson's Notebook* (New York: Boni and Liveright, 1926), pp. 167–68.
"Wriggling" in response: Letter of June 4, 1926 (Newberry).
200   "the old lesson": J/R, p. 51.
"Strength and Beauty": Letter of October 11, 1923 (Newberry).
201   "receives the *World*": Quoted in Dorothy Norman, *Alfred Stieglitz: An American Seer* (New York: Random House, 1973), pp. 136–38.
"That's all we": Quoted in Sarah Greenough and Juan Hamilton, *Alfred Stieglitz: Photographs and Writings* (Washington, D.C.: National Gallery of Art, 1983), p. 206.
"You seemed to stand": Letter of October 11, 1923 (Newberry).

"the turgid head": J/R, p. 97.

"Impressions": October 11, 1922, pp. 171–73; October 25, 1922, pp. 215–17.

9. Tutoring Faulkner and Hemingway: 1922–1926

203 Elizabeth Prall: For Elizabeth Prall in New York, see *Elizabeth,* pp. 39–55.

"Very elegant": Ibid., p. 40.

204 "I ran into the road": *A New Testament* (New York: Boni and Liveright, 1927), pp. 112–13.

205 "Like a teenager": *Elizabeth,* p. 55.

"New York and the neurotics": J/R, p. 94.

"a sort of process": Modlin, p. 46.

Reno was a quiet: For Reno, see Richard G. Lillard, *Desert Challenge: An Interpretation of Nevada* (New York: Alfred A. Knopf, 1949), pp. 307–75.

206 "rather a gentleman": Modlin, p. 49.

heard of Carl Sandburg: In *Paul Rosenfeld: Voyages in the Arts,* ed. James Mellquist and Lucie Wiese (New York: Creative Age Press, 1948), p. 221.

Men, Women: (New York: G. P. Putnam's Sons, 1931).

"noisy brutal children": Modlin, p. 51.

One day Anderson drove out: J/R, pp. 113–14.

207 "a few people in whom": *Paul Rosenfeld,* p. 214.

What she determined: *Elizabeth,* p. 65.

"partly as a substitute": *Centennial,* p. 81.

he named Stein: J/R, p. 95.

he added Jean Toomer: Ibid., p. 118.

"bogged and mired": 75 (September 1923):246.

208 Brooks explained: Letter of September 1923 (Newberry).

"isn't there at least": J/R, p. 109.

"disintegrated, gone": Ibid., p. 97.

"the autobiography": Ibid., p. 50.

"unload it, as it were": *Anderson/Stein,* p. 35.

209 "essential intelligence": Ibid., p. 45.

"gorgeous book": *The "Writer's Book" by Sherwood Anderson,* ed. Martha Mulroy Curry (Metuchen, N. J.: Scarecrow Press, 1975), p. 38.

"the most masculine and manly": *The Portable Sherwood Anderson,* ed. Horace Gregory (New York: Viking Penguin, 1972), p. 462.

"adventures with men": J/R, p. 106.

"Father Abraham": *The Sherwood Anderson Reader,* ed. Paul Rosenfeld (Boston: Houghton Mifflin, 1947), pp. 530–602.

"no presumptuousness": J/R, p. 35.

210 "When I Left Business": *Century* 108 (August 1924):489–96.

"come that far": *STS,* p. 398.

Saturday Review of Literature 2 (August 1, 1925):1–3.

211   wrote with a "gaiety": Modlin, p. 203.
      "the mercy of her whim": The *"Writer's Book,"* p. 254.
      "those great romanticists": Letter to Bernadine Szold, September 4, 1926
      (Newberry).
      "The most amusing thing": Ibid., 1926.
      They were met: Interview with Rhea Radin, March 1987.
212   "a violent case": *Centennial*, p. 9.
      "shockingly intellectual": Radin interview.
      "I spit out": J/R, 124.
      "little philosopher": *Bab*, p. 204.
      "had very little formal": *Elizabeth*, p. 75.
213   "he was something special": James Feibleman, "Literary New Orleans
      Between World Wars," *Southern Review* 1 (Summer 1965):702–19, and
      "Memories of Sherwood Anderson, *Shenandoah* 13 (Spring 1962):32–45.
214   "our Royal Personage": Joseph Blotner, *Faulkner*, vol. 1 (New York: Ran-
      dom House, 1974), p. 393.
      "I was rich": Modlin, p. 55.
215   "starved for affection": *Bab*, pp. 215–16.
      "a desert trail": STS, p. 387.
      "lecture, spit over": *Anderson/Stein*, p. 43.
      "When the Writer Talks": April 18, 1925, pp. 1–2.
216   "sound and honest": Quoted in *Bab*, p. 238.
      his idol looked "soft": "His Collaborators," *Story*, p. 76, and *Here Comes,
      There Goes, You Know Who* (New York: Simon and Schuster, 1961), p.
      16.
      "a referee at a snake": Louis Kronenberger, "Gambler in Publishing: Hor-
      ace Liveright," *Atlantic* 215 (January 1965):95.
      "an eager rather corrupt": *Bab*, p. 222.
      "felt like a dog": J/R, p. 132.
      "honest, fussy": *Bab*, p. 222.
217   yet to find a copy: J/R, p. 132.
      "A man can't stay": Modlin, p. 69.
      "very much the intellectual": *Bab*, pp. 249, 253–54.
      "the best short story": *Dallas Morning News*, April 26, 1925, part 3,
      p. 7.
218   his conversation with Anderson: For their relationship, see William
      Faulkner, "Sherwood Anderson: An Appreciation," *Atlantic* 191 (June
      1953):27–29.
      "visiting Sherwood Anderson": Blotner, *Faulkner*, vol. 1, p. 411.
      "an uproarious week": *Elizabeth*, pp. 84–85.
      mostly half-gallon jars: "They Come Bearing Gifts," *American Mercury* 21
      (October 1930):129–37.
      "A Meeting South," *Dial* 78 (April 1925):269–79.
219   sketches in the *Times-Picayune:* Collected in *New Orleans Sketches*, ed. Car-
      vel Collins (New Brunswick, N.J.: Rutgers University Press, 1958).
220   "could have shared": Robert Coughlan, *The Private World of William
      Faulkner* (New York: Harper and Row, 1954), p. 60.
      "the one writer of promise": Modlin, pp. 69–70.

221 "the man personally": J/R, p. 155.
A review of Anderson's work: Reprinted in *The Princeton University Library Chronicle* 18 (Spring 1957):89–94.
Sherwood Anderson and Other Creoles: (New Orleans: Pelican Bookshop, 1926).

222 *Times-Picayune* put it: January 2, 1927, p. 4.

223 "a deceptively sedate": *Mosquitoes* (New York: Liveright, 1927), pp. 80, 248–49.
"the whole thing": J/R, pp. 141–42.
"a fantasy": Ibid., p. 130.
"the neuroticism": Ibid., p. 142.

224 "the sense of a dancing": Ibid., p. 147.

225 "starting place for the prose": Ibid., 148.
Lawrence's neurotic dreams: J/R, p. 144.
representing "Kingship": "A Man's Mind," *New Republic* 63 (May 21, 1930):22–23, and "Lawrence Again," in *No Swank* (Philadelphia: Centaur Press, 1934), pp. 95–103.
"That Lawrence": *Bab,* p. 201.
hoped Anderson would try: 2 (July 1921):44.
"of the Negro": Modlin, p. 42.
"There was less": Ibid., p. 54.
"nervous distraught": Ibid., p. 53.

226 "a bit too Negro": Ibid., p. 43.
could not have matured: Letter of December 18, 1922 (Newberry).
"To Sherwood Anderson": *Centennial,* p. 138.
"America's Most Distinctive": 27 (December 1926):88.

227 *"one of the very best":* The Letters of F. Scott Fitzgerald, ed. Andrew Turnbull (New York: Charles Scribner's Sons, 1963), p. 187.
just *"lousy":* Ibid., p. 192.
scornfully of the press's: Ibid., p. 194.

228 "lots of things": *Ernest Hemingway: Selected Letters,* ed. Carlos Baker (New York: Charles Scribner's Sons, 1981), p. 62.
Hemingway said no: Edmund Wilson, *The Shores of Light* (New York: Farrar, Straus and Young, 1952), p. 117.

229 hoarse reading it to friends: Hemingway, *Letters,* p. 176; Szold, quoted in Dale Kramer, *Chicago Renaissance: The Literary Life in the Midwest: 1900–1930* (New York: Appleton Century, 1966), p. 338; Mitchell in letter to Szold (Newberry); Murphys in Calvin Tomkins, *Living Well Is the Best Revenge* (New York: Viking Press, 1971), p. 27; others in Carlos Baker, *Ernest Hemingway* (New York: Charles Scribner's Sons, 1969), pp. 159–60.
Looking up at Anderson's: Noel Riley Fitch, *Sylvia Beach and the Lost Generation* (New York: W. W. Norton, 1983), p. 116.
"about the best comic": *Correspondence of F. Scott Fitzgerald,* ed. Matthew J. Bruccoli and Margaret M. Duggan (New York: Random House, 1980), p. 183.
"Why shouldn't a man": (New York: Charles Scribner's Sons, 1972), p. 23.

230 "A man was": Ibid., pp. 12–13.
     "Tears came into": Ibid., p. 33.
231 "somebody starts to slop": *Letters,* ed. Baker, pp. 205–6.
     "You always do speak": Modlin, p. 80.
     "almost a vicious parody": *Letters,* ed. Turnbull, p. 195.
     "Today, for example": *The Portable Sherwood Anderson,* ed. Horace Gregory
     (New York: Viking Penguin, 1972), 480.
     "Sherwood, what the hell": *Mem.,* p. 466.
232 "an inner sympathy": J/R, pp. 392–93.
     "Ernest is such": Ben Hecht, *Letters from Bohemia* (Garden City, N.Y.:
     Doubleday, 1964), p. 98.
     Hemingway's "glums": J/R, p. 205.
     "Come out of it": Modlin, p. 80.
     "fill of hitting": *Bab,* p. 265.
     "vitality — the ability": Modlin, p. 81.
     "this side of bughouse": *Letters,* ed. Baker, p. 218.
     "Aren't there any": Modlin, p. 86.

10. Withdrawal: 1926–1929

233 "childhood dramatized": *Bab,* p. 231.
     "gentle and whimsical": J/R, p. 141.
     "Tar lay, listening": p. 116.
234 "a means of self-affirmation": "A Memoir of Sherwood Anderson," *Per-
     spective* 7 (Summer 1954):84–85.
     any place in the mountains: Modlin, p. 71.
     a family named Greear: For the Andersons' stay with the Greears, see
     Caroline Greear, "Sherwood Anderson as a Mountain Family Knew Him"
     (Newberry); *Mem.,* pp. 485–86; and *Bab,* pp. 227–28.
236 "a little house": *Bab,* p. 229.
     "It does so beat": J/R, p. 145.
     one woman confronted: *Mem.,* p.. 501, and *Bab,* pp. 264–65.
     "to put it": "These Mountaineers," *Vanity Fair* 33 (January 1930):94.
     another by Ripshin: *Mem.,* pp. 488–90.
     a down payment of $50: *The "Writer's Book" by Sherwood Anderson,* ed.
     Martha Mulroy Curry (Metuchen, N. J.: Scarecrow Press, 1975), p. 142.
     a puritan would probably: *Bab,* p. 263.
237 Marion Ball: For Marion Ball, see *Mem.,* pp. 495–97; *Elizabeth,* pp.
     145–51; and Modlin, p. 77.
     earned eight thousand dollars: *The "Writer's Book,"* p. 141.
     "got me a dog": *Bab,* p. 266.
     "being shepherds": Modlin, p. 93.
238 "a small silent fellow": *STS,* p. 8.
     "If I was silent": Quoted in *Bab,* p. 248.
     "the most beautiful": Ibid., p. 273.
     the brother to whom: Modlin, pp. 81–82.
     "Men think": J/R, p. 159.

239 "gone back on him": *Bab,* p. 254.
"arrogant and terrible": Modlin, p. 130.
"in a strange way": Ibid., p. 83.
he'd often been unfair: Ibid., pp. 83–84.
"I don't believe": Letter of April 2, 1929 (Newberry).
long, unpublished: *One Was a Celibate* (Newberry).
240 "creeping to Elizabeth": J/R, p. 160.
"rather to pieces": Modlin, p. 83.
"Another Wife": *Scribner's Magazine* 80 (December 1926):587–94.
241 "This year, I": J/R, p. 160.
"very humble": *Bab,* p. 283.
"cheap romancing": *Mem.,* p. 438.
In Paris: For the Andersons in Paris, see *Elizabeth,* pp. 154–70.
242 "not at all sore": *Ernest Hemingway: Selected Letters,* ed. Carlos Baker (New York: Charles Scribner's Sons, 1981), p. 241.
"Here's how": *Mem.,* pp. 464–65.
"Sherwood Anderson": J/R, pp. 168–69.
"a dead, blank time": Ibid., p. 166.
"a dumb summer": *Anderson/Stein,* p. 63.
243 recalled one incident: *Elizabeth,* pp. 166–67.
"Lots of times": *Bab,* p. 305.
"He simply could not": *Elizabeth,* p. 166.
"Sherwood Anderson: Sick": Lawrence S. Morris, *New Republic* 51 (August 3, 1927):277–79.
"We are all": Modlin, p. 95.
"I want a new youth": *Bab,* p. 306.
by Cleveland Chase: *Sherwood Anderson* (New York: Robert M. McBride, 1927).
244 "I have decided": J/R, pp. 174–75.
"too old a bird": Ibid., p. 165.
"It takes an awful": *Absalom, Absalom!* (New York: Random House, Vintage Books, 1972), p. 350.
For Anderson's newspaper work, see *The Buck Fever Papers,* ed. Welford Dunaway Taylor (Charlottesville: University Press of Virginia, 1971); *Return to Winesburg: Selections from Four Years of Writing for a Country Newspaper,* ed. Ray Lewis White (Chapel Hill: University of North Carolina Press, 1967); and his own *Nearer the Grass Roots and Elizabethton* (San Francisco: Westgate Press, 1929).
245 "insure" him for: Modlin, p. 89.
"Suppose you do not": *Centennial,* p. 13.
with two notes: Ibid., pp. 18–19.
"the most fun": *Nearer the Grass Roots,* p. 16.
"He crowded himself": J/R, p. 179.
246 telling Emmett: *Centennial,* p. 20.
"having something": Ibid., pp. 14–15.
"being very busy": J/R, p. 181.
247 "up out of the sea": *Return to Winesburg,* p. 141.
248 "It is education": Ibid., p. 122.

"An editor's thoughts": (New York: Horace Liveright, 1929), pp. 24–25.

249 "wild purchasing": Modlin, p. 103.
she received what: *Elizabeth,* p. 189.

250 "I really loved": Letter to Hans Poppe, September 15, 1947 (Newberry).
"Poor E.": Modlin, p. 103.
"This sheer loneliness": Ibid.
"least of all from any woman": *Bab,* p. 321.
"You have, my dear": Ibid., p. 318.
"at the end of *things*": Ibid., p. 320.
"As to me": Ibid., p. 319.

251 "a bad year": Modlin, p. 106.
"Let's Go": *Outlook* 151 (February 13, 1929):247, 278, 280.
"But you do not love": Modlin, p. 108.

252 "another ex-wife": Letter of December 5, 1929 (Newberry).
"a certain crudeness": Modlin, p. 109.
"Women do get me": Quoted in Sutton, p. 255.
"Perhaps the bare": J/R, p. 115.
"I could wreck myself": Modlin, p. 109.
"had so many fine": Letter to Marion Spear, December 1929 (Spear collection).

11. The Political Years: 1929–1933

253 "funeral oration": Modlin, p. 104.
"Hello, readers": Geoffrey Hellman, "Hello Sherwood," *New Republic* 58 (May 15, 1929):365.
"only decent thing": J/R, p. 193.
"No Love": Newberry.
"to live first": Modlin, p. 104.

254 "on the road of feeling": J/R, p. 195.
"middle-class people": Ibid., p. 202.
"the story of sex": Ibid., p. 206.
"dreadful kind of slack": Modlin, p. 111.
"By God, man": J/R, p. 203.

255 "As regards my work": *Bab,* p. 326.
"the great big story": J/R, p. 206.
his initiation: See his "Elizabethton," in *Nearer the Grass Roots and Elizabethton* (San Francisco: Westgate Press, 1929), pp. 21–35.

257 in factories for years: J/R, p. 210.
"a little dark-eyed": Ibid., p. 220.
the Copenhaver he seemed: Interview with Eleanor Copenhaver Anderson, September 1984.

258 "a bearer of poison": "The Artist and His Children," *The New Generation,* ed. V. F. Calverton and Samuel D. Schmalhausen (New York: Macaulay, 1930), pp. 357–64.
"They are such": Modlin, p. 129.

"It was a woman": *Perhaps Women* (New York: Horace Liveright, 1931), p. 111.
259 "Stay looking": Ibid., p. 116.
"baubles" with "antique": Modlin, p. 111.
260 "the defeated people": J/R, p. 204.
If Emmett sent him: *Centennial*, p. 22.
"Me with my full belly": Ibid., p. 12.
"It is perhaps only": J/R, p. 206.
There were so many: Ibid., p. 211.
261 "to tackle the inside": Ibid., p. 209.
enlisted Emmett's: Modlin, pp. 124–25.
"Perhaps I have got": J/R, p. 228.
262 "The original revolving": "The First Reader," *New York World Telegram* April 9, 1942.
"We inside us": *Gertrude Stein: Writings and Lectures, 1909–1945* (New York: Penguin Books, 1971), pp. 101, 117.
"concentrate on pure": J/R, p. 226.
263 "the work of a metaphysician": *Mem.*, p. 550.
the makings of an opera: J/R, p. 280.
264 "Little red blotches": *No Swank* (Philadelphia: Centaur Press, 1934), p. 94.
"Touch this key": *Perhaps Women*, p. 16.
265 "a change of heart": J/R, p. 207.
"rather nice": *Perhaps Women*, p. 68.
267 "The better living": J/R, pp. 226–28.
literally a moderator: Ibid., p. 227. For the speech, see Newberry.
"Cotton Mill": 88 (July 1930):1–11.
"laying for that bird": J/R, p. 208.
268 *Cheap and Contented Labor:* (New York: United Feature Syndicate, 1929).
269 addressed a meeting: See his "Danville, Virginia," *New Republic* 65 (January 21, 1931):266–68.
270 *The Hosiery Worker:* Clippings with Danville speech (Newberry).
271 "real knowledge of poverty": *Money Writes!* (New York: Albert and Charles Boni, 1927), p. 119.
"socialists, or conservatives": Modlin, pp. 5–6.
"the politics of poetry": J/R, p. 23.
"With war": *Bab,* p. 89.
"no political turn of mind": J/R, p. 156.
"Nothing in the world": 27 (November 1926):51–52.
"I seem to be getting": J/R, p. 227.
"I Want to Be Counted": Theodore Dreiser et al., *Harlan Miners Speak: Report on Terrorism in the Kentucky Coal Fields* (New York: Harcourt, Brace, 1932), pp. 298–312.
272 "what is the difference": J/R, p. 231.
"becoming more and more": Modlin, p. 143.
273 "the right thing": Ibid., p. 144.
"their goddam childish": J/R, p. 255.
"something to check": *Centennial*, p. 27.

"I guess": *Harlan Miners,* p. 310.

"when the rub comes": Modlin, p. 146.

J'Accuse: J/R, p. 258.

"a temporary dictatorship": For the manifestoes and Anderson's role, see Daniel Aaron, *Writers on the Left: Episodes in American Literary Communism* (New York: Harcourt, Brace and World, 1961), pp. 190–98, and Harvey Klehr, *The Heyday of American Communism* (New York: Basic Books, 1984), pp. 77–81.

274   "an attempt on the part": Modlin, p. 148.

"There is a gentleness": Ibid., pp. 147–48.

"marching thousands": "At Amsterdam," *New Masses* 8 (November 1932):11.

"How I Came to Communism": 8 (September 1932):8–9.

275   "He should perhaps keep": 6 (Summer 1932):12.

"a bad actor": *Mem.,* pp. 542–45.

The "Army" or "Bonus": For the "Bonus Army," see Irving Bernstein, *A History of the American Worker, 1920–1933: The Lean Years* (Boston: Houghton Mifflin, 1960), pp. 437–455.

276   Hoover's office the first: *Return to Winesburg: Selections from Four Years of Writing for a Country Newspaper,* ed. Ray Lewis White (Chapel Hill: University of North Carolina Press, 1967), pp. 60–68.

277   write Hoover a letter: J/R, p. 261.

"Men like me don't": 135 (August 31, 1932): 191–93.

"Delegation": 9 (December 9, 1933):36, 38.

278   a public debate with Bertrand: For his speech, see Charles E. Modlin, "Sherwood Anderson's Debate with Bertrand Russell," *The Winesburg Eagle* 12 (November 1986):4–11.

Beyond Desire: (New York: Liveright, 1932).

279   "disturbing," "too close": J/R, p. 264; Modlin, p. 164.

280   Reinhold Niebuhr: "Still on Probation," *World Tomorrow* 15 (November 30, 1932):525–26.

New Masses applauded: 7 (June 1932):9.

Granville Hicks said: "Red Pilgrimage," *New Republic* 73 (December 21, 1932):168–69.

"confused political": p. 286.

"so-called communist": *American Writers' Congress,* ed. Henry Hart (New York: International Publishers, 1935), p. 60.

"I-Am-Dumb school": Ibid., p. 108.

281   a long letter: J/R, pp. 291-94.

Scribner's piece: "The Authors and Politics," *Scribner's* 93 (May 1933):318–20.

something had gone: J/R, pp. 291–94.

"one of the finest": Ibid., p. 278.

283   "the American dramatist": *Mem./Ros.,* p. 303.

"passionately to write": *Bab,* p. 210.

284   "I have a hunch": J/R, p. 313.

"but different": Ibid., p. 318.

"pure horrible": Ibid., p. 285.

Anderson went to see him: *Mem.*, pp. 517–19.
met with Paul Muni: J/R, pp. 288–89.
285 "Tell me something": Modlin, p. 168.
a long, empathic: J/R, pp. 286–88.
"the real story": Modlin, pp. 169–70.
286 Barton got me: Ibid., p. 171.
"rather a chump": Ibid., p. 175.

12. Finally at Ease: 1933–1940

287 Older men like: p. 165.
"I am trying": Modlin, p. 139.
288 "a certain determined": *Centennial,* p. 30.
"little ham actors, prize": Modlin, p. 164.
work he did for her: See his "Kansas City Notes" (Newberry).
289 "When a world": *Centennial,* p. 30.
"As regards E.": Modlin, p. 195.
she had "chucked": Ibid., p. 198.
"I should have two": Ibid., p. 222.
"afraid of marriage": Ibid., p. 167.
"I am sorry": J/R, p. 290.
290 "Poor as I am": Spear collection.
In Deeter's hands: See John C. Wentz, "Anderson's *Winesburg* and the Hedgerow Theatre," *Modern Drama* 3 (May 1960):42–51.
291 "In his patient": For Anderson on Deeter and the Hedgerow Theatre, see his "Jasper Deeter: A Dedication," *Plays: Winesburg and Others* (New York: Charles Scribner's Sons, 1937), pp. xi–xxii.
a lecture Anderson gave: See "Finds Quality of Loneliness Americans' Distinctive Mark," *Baltimore Sun,* January 18, 1936.
The players were: Modlin, p. 196.
292 "The Nationalist": 2 (December 1933):1.
293 his first contribution: "To Remember," 1 (May 1933):1.
"Sherwood Anderson to": 1 (June 1933):1.
a little squib: 2 (February 1934):1.
"ever added anything": *Mem.,* p. 537.
"an American political": Quoted in Schevill, p. 309.
"You see this Henry": "No Swank," *Today* 1 (November 11, 1933):4–5, 23–24.
"Some new workers": *Centennial,* p. 33.
294 on Roosevelt himself: "Explain! Explain! Again Explain!" 1 (December 2, 1933):3.
"a town in which": "Nobody's Home," 3 (March 30, 1935):6–7, 20–21.
295 "We have been": *Puzzled America* (New York: Charles Scribner's Sons, 1935), p. 20.
"the hidden injuries": Richard Sennett and Jonathan Cobb, *The Hidden Injuries of Class* (New York: Alfred A. Knopf, 1972).
"a hunger for belief": *Puzzled,* pp. xv–xvi.

296   "Of course": Quoted in Schevill, p. 311.
      "beaten, ignorant": J/R, p. 310.
      "New Tyrants of the Land": *Today* 1 (May 26, 1934):10–11, 20.
      "there was a good deal": *Puzzled,* pp. xii–xiii.
      "Tough Babes in the Woods": *Today,* 1 (February 10, 1934):6–7, 22.
297   "Yes he undoubtedly' *Anderson/Stein,* pp. 96–97.
      "Of all the writers": "Ubiquitous Critics and the Author," *Newberry Library Bulletin* 5 (December 1958):10.
      an essay by Lionel Trilling: "Sherwood Anderson," *Kenyon Review* 3 (Summer 1941):293–302.
298   "one of the few books": *Sherwood Anderson* (New York: William Sloane Associates, 1951), p. 228.
      "there was no one": *The Last of the Provincials* (Boston: Houghton Mifflin, 1947), pp. 278–79.
      "a kind of intellectual": J/R, pp. 294–95.
      making $536: Ibid., p. 329.
      Kit Brandon: (New York: Charles Scribner's Sons, 1936).
299   "to get a bit more": J/R, p. 335.
      "much more objective": Modlin, p. 203.
      Mamie Palmer: *Return to Winesburg: Selections from Four Years of Writing for a Country Newspaper,* ed. Ray Lewis White (Chapel Hill: University of North Carolina Press, 1967), p. 117.
      "City Gangs Enslave": 12 (November 2, 1935):12–13.
300   "She was neatly": *Kit Brandon,* p. 207.
      "I'm only half": Ibid., pp. 372–73.
301   "a pretty good chance": Modlin, p. 203.
      fewer than 6,500 copies: A. Scott Berg, *Editor of Genius* (New York: E. P. Dutton, 1978), p. 381.
      "a rotten play": *The Sherwood Anderson Diaries, 1936–1941,* ed. Hilbert H. Campbell (Athens: University of Georgia Press, 1987), entry of January 16, 1936.
      "Sherwood Anderson Says": Herbert Little, *Washington Daily News,* May 1, 1937, p. 16.
      "They become silent": Modlin, p. 192.
302   "writers may be made": *Diaries,* July 27, 1937.
      "Though only sixty": Martha Monigle, "Sherwood Anderson in Boulder," *Michigan Quarterly Review* 9 (1970):55–56.
      by his own admission: Modlin, p. 232.
      "Bill, I simply": William Spratling, *Spratling on File* (Boston: Little, Brown, 1967), p. 123.
303   "a feeling of something": Modlin, p. 187.
      "I think she a little": *Diaries,* June 25, 1937.
      "doctor's orders": Modlin, p. 205.
      "Too much ringing": J/R, p. 394.
      "our amazing Mary": *Centennial,* p. 37.
      "He is a passionate": ed. Alfred Kreymborg, Lewis Mumford, Paul Rosenfeld (New York: W. W. Norton, 1936), p. 654.

304   "where Eleanor has to": Modlin, p. 199.
      "Now what I have been": *The Portable Sherwood Anderson,* ed. Horace
      Gregory (New York: Viking Penguin, 1972), pp. 476–81.
305   "as solitary as": *From the Shadow of the Mountain* (New York: E. P. Dutton,
      1961), p. 38.
      "some sort of communication": Modlin, pp. 196–97.
      "He needs his fellow": J/R, pp. 313–14.
      "For a long time": Modlin, p. 87.
      "to push themselves": *The Portable Sherwood Anderson,* p. 479.
306   "an attempt at expression": J/R, p. 334.
      "What is really": Ibid., pp. 322–28.
307   "The present way": *Diaries* August 6, 1936.
      "Evening with Funk": Ibid., January 15, 1936.
308   "so much suggestion": J/R pp. 358–61.
      White Top Folk Festival: For the festival, see David E. Whisnat, *All
      That Is Native and Fine* (Chapel Hill: University of North Carolina Press,
      1983), pp. 181–252.
      "Young men from New": *The Portable Sherwood Anderson,* p. 492.
      "Folksong and Cultural Politics": *Modern Music* 17 (November–Decem-
      ber, 1939):23. Quoted in Whisnat, *All That Is Native,* p. 246.
      "The Third": *Bab,* p. 185.
309   "It seems I've become": Modlin, p. 237.
      "a gorgeous achievement": Ibid., p. 182.
      "in a voice heard": J/R, p. 368.
      "The man is a flood": Ibid., p. 386.
      "Every man of force": Modlin, pp. 211–12.
      a flip remark: "An Interview with Eleanor Copenhaver," *Centennial,* pp.
      75–76.
      "woman-ridden": J/R, p. 402.
      Anderson was inclined: See Wolfe's letter to Anderson, December 29,
      1937 (Newberry).
      "God, the poor man": J/R, p. 402.
310   "the most important": "Dreiser," *Saturday Review of Literature* 2 (January
      9, 1926):475.
      clearly lifted: See W. A. Swanberg, *Dreiser* (New York: Charles Scribner's
      Sons, 1965), pp. 313–14.
      Dreiser was too great: Quoted in *The "Writer's Book" by Sherwood Anderson,*
      ed. Martha Mulroy Curry (Metuchen, N.J.: Scarecrow Press, 1975), p.
      189.
      "You are a provoking": *Letters of Theodore Dreiser,* vol. 3 (Philadelphia:
      University of Pennsylvania Press, 1959), ed. Robert H. Elias, p. 763.
      "kindly and beautiful": Ibid., vol. 2, p. 754.
      "a comforting figure": p. 4.
311   "the turning aside": Modlin, p. 186.
      "the People's this and that": J/R, p. 393.
      "Why Men Write": *Story* 8 (January 1936):4, 103, 105.
      "The Story Teller's Job": *Book Buyer* 2, ser. 4 (December 1936):8.

"Why I Write": *Writer* 49 (December 1936):363–64.

"So You Want to Be a Writer?": *Saturday Review of Literature* 21 (December 9, 1939):13–14.

312 "You must begin": *American Magazine* 128 (October 1938):58.

"His Chest of Drawers": *Household Magazine* 39 (August 1939):4–5.

"Two Lovers": *Story* 14 (January–February 1939): 16–25.

"Nice Girl": *New Yorker* 12 (July 25, 1936): 15–17.

"Not Sixteen": *Tomorrow* 5 (March 1946):28–32.

"Daughters": *The Sherwood Anderson Reader,* ed. Paul Rosenfeld (Boston: Houghton Mifflin, 1947), p. 522–50.

"A Moonlight Walk": 70 (December 1937):43–45, 100–4. See Hilbert H. Campbell, "Sherwood Anderson and His 'Editor': The Case of 'A Moonlight Walk,'" *Papers of the Bibliographical Society of America* 79 (1985):227–32.

313 "The Corn-Planting": *American Magazine* 118 (November 1934):47, 149–50.

314 "I'm trying again": Modlin, p. 233.

a long list of "shots": Ibid., pp. 244–45.

a draft of his essay: *Reader,* pp. 740–810.

"One of the most": January 1941.

315 "If we could only": Modlin, p. 239.

"a high-grade child": Ibid., p. 248.

on whom he wrote: "Maury Maverick in San Antonio," *New Republic* 102 (March 25, 1940):398–400.

"a good man to do": J/R, p. 456.

13. Starting Out Again: 1941

316 "to be able to": *The Sherwood Anderson Diaries, 1936–1941,* ed. Hilbert H. Campbell (Athens: University of Georgia Press, 1987), entry of January 9, 1936.

317 "much as I have": J/R, p. 465.

318 "ordinary North Americans": Ibid., p. 462.

"I put the records": *The Portable Sherwood Anderson,* ed. Horace Gregory (New York: Viking Penguin, 1972), p. 497.

"a bum revolutionist": J/R, p. 378.

"live a little in others": Ibid., p. 287.

a defense of enthanasia: "The Right to Die: Dinner in Thessaly," *Forum* 95 (January 1936):40–41.

"The hell is to know": J/R, p. 429.

319 "not carry on": *Mem.,* p. 26.

"seminude and flabby": William Spratling, *Spratling on File* (Boston: Little, Brown, 1967), p. 122.

"looking lovely": *Diaries,* October 27, 1940.

"It will be a great sickness": Ibid., September 1, 1939.

320 "a fine offer": Ibid., November 18, 1940.

"a good deal": Modlin, p. 251.

"Christianity is like": *Diaries,* December 20, 1940.

"The woman was": Modlin, p. 254.

"one of his women": *Diaries,* January 4, 1941.

to help him arrange: Modlin, p. 255.

Wallace, asking him: Letter of February 27, 1941 (Newberry).

Above Suspicion: In *The Free Company Presents: A Collection of Plays About the Meaning of America* (New York: Dodd, Mead, 1941), pp. 269–301. It was completed by "The Free Company," probably by James Boyd, and performed by it on CBS after Anderson died.

321 ran into Ben Hecht: For the meeting and Hecht's tribute, see Hecht's "Adios," in *Letters from Bohemia* (Garden City, N.Y.: Doubleday, 1964), pp. 98–99.

322 Freda Kirchwey, the editor: For her account and tribute, see *Nation* 152 (March 23, 1941):313–14.

offering his help: Newberry.

a short ceremony: *Marion Democrat,* April 1, 1941.

323 "Incidentally, there are": *Return to Winesburg: Selections from Four Years of Writing for a Country Newspaper,* ed. Ray Lewis White (Chapel Hill: University of North Carolina Press, 1967), p. 158.

SELECTED BIBLIOGRAPHY

Primary Sources

Windy McPherson's Son. New York: John Lane, 1916; rev. ed., 1922; Chicago: University of Chicago Press, 1965.

Marching Men. Critical ed., edited by Ray Lewis White. New York: John Lane Company, 1917; Cleveland: Press of Case Western Reserve, 1972.

Mid-American Chants. New York: John Lane, 1918.

Winesburg, Ohio. New York: B. W. Huebsch, 1919; New York: Viking Press, 1960.

Poor White. New York: B. W. Huebsch, 1920; New York: Viking Press, 1966.

The Triumph of the Egg. New York: B. W. Huebsch, 1921.

Many Marriages. Critical ed., edited by Douglas D. Rogers. New York: B. W. Huebsch, 1923; Metuchen, N.J.: Scarecrow Press, 1978.

Horses and Men. New York: B. W. Huebsch, 1923.

A Story Teller's Story. New York: B. W. Huebsch, 1924.

Dark Laughter. New York: Boni and Liveright, 1925.

Sherwood Anderson's Notebook. New York: Boni and Liveright, 1926.

Tar: A Midwest Childhood. New York: Boni and Liveright, 1926.

A New Testament. New York: Boni and Liveright, 1927.

Hello Towns! New York: Horace Liveright, 1929.

Nearer the Grass Roots and Elizabethton. San Francisco: Westgate Press, 1929.

Perhaps Women. New York: Horace Liveright, 1931.

Beyond Desire. New York: Liveright, 1932.

Death in the Woods and Other Stories. New York: Liveright, 1933.

No Swank. Philadelphia: Centaur Press, 1934.

Puzzled America. New York: Charles Scribner's Sons, 1935.

Kit Brandon. New York: Charles Scribner's Sons, 1936.

Plays: Winesburg and Others. New York: Charles Scribner's Sons, 1937.

Home Town. New York: Alliance Book Corp., 1940.

Sherwood Anderson's Memoirs. Edited by Paul Rosenfeld. New York: Harcourt, Brace, 1942.
The Sherwood Anderson Reader. Edited by Paul Rosenfeld. Boston: Houghton Mifflin, 1947.
The Portable Sherwood Anderson. Edited by Horace Gregory. 1949; rev. ed., New York: Viking Penguin, 1972.
Letters of Sherwood Anderson. Edited by Howard Mumford Jones and Walter B. Rideout. Boston: Little, Brown, 1953.
Return to Winesburg: Selections from Four Years of Writing for a Country Newspaper. Edited by Ray Lewis White. Chapel Hill: University of North Carolina Press, 1967.
Sherwood Anderson's Memoirs: A Critical Edition. Edited by Ray Lewis White. Chapel Hill: University of North Carolina Press, 1969.
The Buck Fever Papers. Edited by Welford Dunaway Taylor. Charlottesville: University Press of Virginia, 1971.
Sherwood Anderson/Gertrude Stein. Edited by Ray Lewis White. Chapel Hill: University of North Carolina Press, 1972.
The "Writer's Book" by Sherwood Anderson. Critical ed., edited by Martha Mulroy Curry. Metuchen, N.J.: Scarecrow Press, 1975.
France and Sherwood Anderson: Paris Notebook, 1921. Edited by Michael Fanning. Baton Rouge: Louisiana State University Press, 1976.
Sherwood Anderson: Selected Letters. Edited by Charles E. Modlin. Knoxville: University of Tennessee Press, 1984.
Letters to Bab: Sherwood Anderson to Marietta D. Finley, 1916–33. Edited by William A. Sutton. Urbana: University of Illinois Press, 1985.
The Sherwood Anderson Diaries, 1936–1941. Edited by Hilbert H. Campbell. Athens: University of Georgia Press, 1987.

Secondary Sources

Anderson, Elizabeth, and Gerald R. Kelly. *Miss Elizabeth.* Boston: Little, Brown, 1969.
Campbell, Hilbert H., and Charles E. Modlin, eds. *Sherwood Anderson: Centennial Studies.* Troy, N.Y.: Whitson Publishing Company, 1976.
Howe, Irving. *Sherwood Anderson.* New York: William Sloane Associates, 1951.
Schevill, James. *Sherwood Anderson: His Life and Work.* Denver: University of Denver Press, 1951.
Sheehy, Eugene P., and Kenneth A. Lohf. *Sherwood Anderson: A Bibliography.* Los Gatos, Calif.: Talisman Press, 1960.
Story 19 (September–October, 1941). (The Anderson commemorative issue.)
Sutton, William A. *The Road to Winesburg.* Metuchen, N.J.: Scarecrow Press, 1972.
White, Ray Lewis, ed. *Sherwood Anderson: A Reference Guide.* Boston: G. K. Hall, 1977.

INDEX

Aaron, Daniel, 280
Above Suspicion (SA), 321
Across Spoon River (Masters), 126
Art of the Vieux Colombier (Frank), 156
Adams, Henry, 154, 155, 263, 265
Addams, Jane, 90
Ade, George, 143
"Adventure" (SA), 112
Agricultural Advertising: SA's writings for, 47–51, 52–53, 65, 76, 86, 91, 116, 136
Alabama: SA in, 162–69
Allen, Margaret, 98
All God's Chillun Got Wings (O'Neill), 226
Altgeld, Peter, 37–38
"America: A Storehouse of Vitality" (SA), 215
American Caravan, 303
"American Fiction" (Woolf), 210
American Merchants Company, 60–83, 84
American Mercury, 292
American Spectator, 292
American Writers' Conference, First, 280
America's Coming of Age (Brooks), 118, 120, 132
Anderson, Earl, 3, 55, 70, 130; influence on SA's writings, 69–70; reunion with SA, 238–39, 240; death of, 241
Anderson, Emma Smith: courtship and marriage of, 2–3; SA's relations with, 12–14; death of, 13, 28–29
Anderson, Fern, 3, 122, 287
Anderson, Irwin, Jr. (Irve), 3, 8, 17–18, 29, 41, 239

Anderson, Irwin McLain: career of, 2, 4; courtship and marriage of, 2–3, 310–11; relations with SA, 9–12, 29–30, 55; after death of Emma, 29–30; death of, 30; in SA's writings, 210
Anderson, John Sherwood, 62, 64, 95, 209, 241, 242, 254; relations with father, 215, 259; 307; education of, 238
Anderson, Karl, 21, 28, 33, 34, 41, 42, 52, 88, 89, 92, 100, 144, 150, 156, 164–65, 185, 186, 193, 237, 240, 258, 273, 319, 323; birth of, 3; relations with SA, 7–8; education of, 15; relations with brothers, 238, 239; painting of SA and brothers, 239
Anderson, Margaret, 88, 98; on SA, 91–92
Anderson, Marion (Mimi), 62, 64, 214, 241, 251, 252, 259, 289, 290, 307
Anderson, Mary, 307
Anderson, Maxwell, 321
Anderson, Ray, 3, 41
Anderson, Robert Lane: birth of, 60, 62, 64; and SA's breakdown, 78, 79, 80; relations with father, 215, 259, 307; education of, 238; helps SA with newspaper business, 251
Anderson, Sherwood: birth of, 1, 3; re-creation of Camden, 1–2, 294; in Clyde, 4, 6–30, 38, 41; early sibling relations, 7–9; relations with father, 9–12, 29–30, 55; early work in Clyde, 14–15, 24–26; education of, 15, 36–

37, 41–43; in National Guard, 16, 37, 38, 39–41; youthful self-consciousness, 16–17; role-playing, 17–18, 26–27, 49–50, 64; early sexuality, 19–28; "fugue" states, 27–28, 81–82, 84–85; in Chicago, 30–33, 43–46, 52–56, 83–84, 86–108; early work in Chicago, 33–34; in Spanish-American War, 37–41; and male bonding in army, 39–40; in Cuba, 39–41; at "The Oaks," 42–43; advertising career, 43–46, 48–49, 50–51, 52–53, 55–57, 83, 86, 87, 94, 98, 101, 103, 105–6, 109, 114, 122, 133, 134, 148, 159, 171–72, 192, 260; earliest writings, 46–51, 52–53; writings for *Agricultural Advertising*, 47–51, 52–53, 65, 76, 86, 91, 116, 136; courtship and marriage to Cornelia Lane, 51–52; readings, 53–54, 65, 68, 92; marital relations with Cornelia, 53–57, 63, 70–71, 78–79, 86, 87, 94–95, 97–98, 109, 124, 189, 203, 207; in Cleveland, 56–60; at United Factories Company, 58–60; birth of children, 60, 62, 64; in Elyria, Ohio, 60–83; and American Merchants Company, 60–83; golf playing, 62–63; drinking habits, 63, 319; writing retreat in Elyria, 63–65, 71–72; writing in Elyria, 65–81; early literary influences on, 68–69; breakdown, 70–83; form and content in writing, 75; at Taylor-Critchfield, 83, 86–87, 94, 98, 101, 103, 106, 109, 114, 122, 148, 159, 172, 192, 260; separation from Cornelia, 84, 97–98, 102, 103; self-portrait in "The Rabbit-Pen," 85; relations with Dell and Currey, 88–90; and the colonists, 88–92, 98, 203–4; appearance, 91, 213, 302; Dell's influence on, 92–94; and "curative" writing, 94; self-portrait in *Mary Cochran*, 96; on writing craft, 99–101; self-portrait in *Talbot Wittingham*, 101–3, 107; at Cass Street, 103–4, 106, 109–10; defense of characters in *Winesburg, Ohio*, 109–10; on "grotesques," 110–11; and *Seven Arts*, 118, 119–20, 132–34, 145–48; correspondence with Bab Finley, 120–24, 129–30, 131, 133, 134, 149–50, 159–60, 161, 183, 186, 197, 217, 232, 238, 239, 243, 250, 255; relations with Bab Finley, 120–24,

129–30, 259, 288; marriage and relations with Tennessee Mitchell, 123, 127–28, 130–31, 137–38, 145, 149, 159, 160–61, 167, 168–71, 174, 185, 186, 191; at Camp Owlyout, 127–30, 132; divorce from Cornelia Lane, 128; relations with Waldo Frank, 132, 137–39, 141–42, 145–46, 147, 148, 155–56, 159, 209, 310; in New York (1917), 132–34; poetry writing, 135–37, 144–45, 150, 156, 157; literary criticism by, 141, 144, 146; self-creation as artist, 142; relations with Chicago journalists, 142–43; in Hecht's writings, 143–44; relations with Van Wyck Brooks, 146–47, 148, 155–56, 158, 159, 168, 185, 207–8, 305, 310; in New York (1918), 149–55; on industrialism and mechanization, 150–55; on "craft love," 152; returns to Chicago, 155–61; nomadic life, 156; crisis over lifestyle (1919), 159–61; in Alabama, 162–69; interest in blacks, 164, 165, 166–67, 224–26; experiments with painting, 164–67, 172, 206; in Palos Park, 170–74; relations with Hemingway, 172–74, 181, 228, 242, 309; relations with Faulkner, 173, 180, 217–23, 227, 231–32; travels to Europe, 174–83, 241–43; in London, 176–77, 183; in Paris, 176–82; and James Joyce, 178–79, 181, 241–42; critical reception in Europe, 178–83; relations with Gertrude Stein, 179–81, 188, 191, 198, 199, 201, 202, 207, 208, 215, 241, 242, 249, 310; and generational differences among American writers, 181–82; categorized with "younger American writers," 184; *Dial* award to, 184, 185–86; increasing fame of, 184–85, 199–200; in New Orleans, 186–91; relations with Hart Crane, 192–93; on satire, 193; relations with Dreiser, 197–98, 207, 304, 305, 306, 310; relations with Fitzgerald, 198–99; reputation in early 1920s, 199–200; relations with Stieglitz, 200–202, 206, 207, 212, 236, 245, 310; divorce from Tennessee Mitchell, 205, 211; in Reno, Nev., 205–11; network of friends, 207–8; autobiographical elements of *Story Teller's Story*, 208–11; marriage to Elizabeth Prall, 211–12; relations with

Anderson, Sherwood (*cont.*)
Pralls and Radins, 211–12; in
California, 211–13; international
reputation, 213; social circle in New
Orleans, 213–14; income from writing
and book sales, 214, 215–17, 237,
240; relations with children, 214–15;
lecture tours, 215–16, 218, 278, 301–
2; publishes with Liveright, 216–17;
Faulkner's assessment of, 220–22; and
D. H. Lawrence, 225, 263–64; loss of
reputation from *Dark Laughter,* 227;
parodied by Hemingway, 227–32;
retreat from writing after *Tar,* 234,
240–44; in Troutdale, Va., 234–36;
marital relations with Elizabeth Prall,
235, 237, 242–43, 246, 249–50; and
Ripshin, 236–38, 239, 240, 246, 249,
250, 259–60; visitors and family at
Ripshin, 237–39; and education of
children, 238; relations with brothers,
238–39, 240, 241; painted with
brothers, 239; depression, 240–43; and
newspaper business, 244–48, 250–51,
260; sale of manuscripts to Burton
Emmett, 245; in Marion, Va., 246–49;
separation and divorce from Elizabeth
Prall, 249–50; in Saint Petersburg,
Fla., 251, 254–55, 259, 261; in
Elizabethon, Tenn., 255–56; 259; and
labor movement, 255–57, 259–60,
263–65, 267–82; relations with
Eleanor Copenhaver, 255–59, 261,
265, 280–81, 285–86, 287–90; speech
at "Industrialism vs. Agrarianism"
debate, 267; and Sinclair Lewis's Nobel
award, 267–68; at Danville, Va., 269–
70, 271, 295, 296; political
commitment, 271–83; and Communist
Party, 272–79, 297; and Bonus Army,
275–77; playwrighting, 283–84, 290–
91, 301; collaboration with Arthur
Barton, 284, 285–86; marriage to
Eleanor Copenhaver, 287, 290;
enthusiasm for FDR's New Deal, 292–
97; marital relations with Eleanor
Copenhaver, 293–94, 302–4, 310,
319, 322; moves to Scribner's, 298,
299, 301; loss of readership and
celebrity, 301; as writer-in-residence,
301–2; appearance at sixty, 302; travels
to overcome depression, 302–4, 310;
solace of friendships, 304–8, 310, 316;
on male friendship, 306–7; relations
with Thomas Wolfe, 309–10; requests
photographs from friends, 310;
unfulfilled writing projects, 311;
periodical writing, 311; essays on
"writing and writers," 311–12; late
short stories, 312–13; last writings,
314–15; trip to South America, 315,
317–22; self-renewal, 316–17; Spanish
lessons, 318, 322; on euthanasia, 318;
moves to Harcourt, Brace, 320, 322,
323; peritonitis and death, 322–23;
burial site, 323
Anderson, Stella, 3, 15, 41, 84, 122;
housekeeping by, 28–29
Anderson Manufacturing Company, 60–
83
"Another Man's House" (SA), 240, 241,
242
"Another Wife" (SA), 240, 242
Antioch College, 302
Antony family, 222, 307
"Apology for Crudity, An" (SA), 141,
144, 146, 233, 256
Armour, Morris, and Swift, 59
Arnold, Matthew, 273
"artist class": SA on role of, 272
"artist man" theme, 209
Atheneum: reviews SA, 131
Athenian Literary Society, 41, 43
Atlantic, 220, 319
"Authors and Politics, The" (Rosenfeld),
281, 282
"Awakening, An" (SA), 116–17

Baker, Martha, 87
Ball, Marion, 237
Ballard, Wallace, 41
Balthus, 190
Baraka, Amiri, 263
Barney, Natalie, 242
Barr, Stringfellow, 267
Bartlett, Judge George, 206
Barton, Arthur: collaboration with SA,
284, 285–86
Barton, Bayard, 86, 98, 148
Barton, Bruce, 48
Basso, Hamilton, 213, 214, 222, 308–9
Baxter, Edwin, 77–78
Bazalgette, Leon, 178
Beach, Sylvia, 179
Bennett, Arnold, 62, 68, 183, 241
Bentley, Alys, 127, 128, 129, 132, 260
Benton, Thomas Hart, 153
Berkeley, Calif.: SA in, 212–13

Berthoff, Werner, 181
Best Short Stories of 1920, 171
Best Short Stories of 1923, 228
Beyond Desire (SA), 253, 278–81, 283, 297, 311; theme of, 278–79
Bishop, John Peale, 184, 302
"Blackfoot's Masterpiece" (SA), 100–101
blacks: SA's interest in, 164, 165, 166–67, 224–26, 317; as theme in 1920s literature, 226
Blake, William, 113
Blakelock, Ralph, 100–101
Blum, Jerome, 170–71, 174, 185
Blum, Lucille, 170–71, 174, 185
Bockler, Charles, 251, 254, 261, 262, 267, 271, 273, 291, 298
Bodenheim, Maxwell, 143, 204, 246
Bolm, Adolph, 199
Bonus Army, 275–77
Bookman's, The, 114, 200
"Book of the Grotesque, The" (SA), 110, 111, 118, 176
Borrow, George, 68, 173
Boston Transcript, 157
Bottger, George, 59, 70
Bourne, Randolph, 147–48
Boyd, Ernest, 198
Boyd, James, 309, 322
"Boyish Man, The" (SA), 50
Boyle, Kay, 181
Boy's Town, A (Howells), 17
"Broken" (SA), 195
Brooks, Van Wyck, 118–19, 120, 132, 136, 156, 169, 173, 175, 192, 281; relations with SA, 146–47, 148, 155–56, 158, 159, 168, 185, 207–8, 305, 310
Broom, 188
"Brother Death" (SA), 281–82
"Brothers" (SA), 168–69
Browne, Maurice, 120
Browning, Robert, 53, 96
"Buck Fever" character, 246, 248, 311
Burnham, Daniel, 33
Burnham and Root, 32
Burrow, Trigant, 128–29, 138–39, 140, 159, 298
"Business Man's Reading, A" (SA), 53
"Business Types" (SA), 47

Cabell, James Branch, 228
Caledonia, Ohio: SA in, 3–4
California: SA in, 211–13, 302

Calverton, V. F., 275
Camden, Ohio: re-creation by SA, 1–2, 294
Camp Owlyout: SA at, 127–30, 132, 137
Canadian Forum, 311
Cane (Toomer), 225, 226
Carlyle, Thomas, 53, 54, 64
Carr, Michael Carmichael, 87, 94, 98
Carswell, Catherine, 264
Cary, Lucian, 87
Cather, Willa, 200
Cellini, Benvenuto, 283
Centaur Press, 298
Cézanne, Paul, 229
Chartres Cathedral: impression on SA, 177–78, 210, 265
Chase, Cleveland, 243
Chateaugay, Lake: artists' colony at, 127–30, 132; SA at, 128–30, 132, 137–38, 145
Cheap and Contented Labor (Lewis), 268, 269
"Cheest" (Faulkner), 219
Chekhov, Anton, 131, 157, 194
Chicago: growth and character of, 31–33; architecture of, 32; cultural life, 32–33; Columbian Exposition of 1893, 32, 87; Art Institute of, 32, 88, 170; SA in, 30–33, 43–46, 52–56, 83–84, 86–108, 142–43, 155–61, 191; character of, 86–87; Armory Show, 88, 165; race riots (1919), 159
Chicago Civic Federation, 33
Chicago Daily News, 131, 142
Chicago Evening Post, 87, 92
"Chicago Hamlet, A" (SA), 195
"Chicago Inspirations" (SA), 47–48
Chicago Poems (Sandburg), 136
Chicago Tribune, 157, 297
Child of the Century, A (Hecht), 144
Christ, 101–2
Church, Ralph, 242–43, 244, 246
City Club, Chicago, 86
Civilian Conservation Corps (CCC), 296
Cleveland: SA in, 56–60
Clyde, Ohio: SA in, 4, 6–30, 72; growth of, 4–7
Clyde Cutlery Company, 5
Clyde Natural Gas Company, 5
Coal Operators Association, 271
"Cobbler, The" (Faulkner), 219
colonists (artists' colony), 87–92, 93, 98, 103–4, 105, 145

Colorado, Univ. of, Writer's Conference (1937), 301–2
Colum, Mary, 184
Columbian Exposition of 1983, Chicago, 32, 87
Columbia Steel Works, 60
Columbus, Ohio, 4
"Commercial Democracy," 60–61, 62
Communist Party: SA and, 272–79, 297
Confessions of a Young Man (Moore), 88
Connick, Charles, 248
Conrad, Joseph, 111, 115
"Contract, The" (SA), 188–90, 191
Cook, George Cram, 87, 92
Cooper, James Fenimore, 208
Co-Operative Society of America, 172
Copeau, Jacques, 142, 176, 283, 284
Copenhaver, Bascom E., 248, 289–90
Copenhaver, Eleanor, 248, 255–59, 261–309; friendship with SA, 255–59, 261, 265, 280–81, 285–86, 287–90; marriage to SA, 287, 290; and YWCA, 289, 303; marital relations with SA, 293–94, 302–4, 310, 319, 322; trip to South America with SA, 322
Copenhaver, Laura, 248, 249, 257, 259, 273, 287, 288, 289, 307, 311, 320
"Corn-Planting, The" (SA), 313
Corpus Christi, Tex.: SA in, 302
"Cotton Mill" (SA), 267, 268
Country of the Pointed Firs, The, (Jewett), 115
Cournos, John, 183
Cowley, Malcolm, 280
Cram, Edith, 274
Crane, Hart, 46, 157, 187, 189, 212, 225, 226, 304, 309; relations with SA, 192–93
Cray, Edward, 59
Crockett, Davy, 48
Croly, Herbert, 238
Crowell Publishing Company, 41, 42, 43
"Cry in the Night, The" (SA), 262, 266
Cuban revolution, 37–38
Cubists, 165
Culture and Crisis, 274
Currey, Margaret, 87, 88, 89, 90, 92, 94, 98, 125, 130, 178
Curtis, Cyrus H. K., 45
Curtis Company, 45

Dahlberg, Edward, 175
Dallas Morning News, 221, 223
Danville, Va.: SA at, 269–70, 271, 295, 296

Dark Laughter (SA), 223–27, 229, 234, 237, 278, 279, 284; success of, 223, 226–27
Dark Mother (Frank), 145, 193
Darrow, Clarence, 127, 147, 207
Daugherty, George, 42, 43, 46, 214
"Daughters" (SA), 312
Davidson, Donald, 216
Davila, Carlos, 320
"Death in the Woods" (SA), 22, 233
Death in the Woods and Other Stories (SA), 281–83
Debs, Eugene, 193
Decision: A Review of Free Culture, 321
Deeter, Jasper, 290–91, 292, 301, 305
"Delegation" (SA), 277
Dell, Floyd, 87, 88, 89–90, 91–92, 105, 130, 138, 142, 145, 178, 203, 204; on SA, 91; influence on SA, 92–94; on Winesburg, Ohio (SA), 114; publishes SA in Masses, 118; reviews SA, 131
Depression, 254, 269, 271, 273, 292, 294
Derleth, Auguste, 315
Dial, 32, 141, 157, 187, 207, 219; award to SA, 184, 185–86; serially publishing Many Marriages (SA), 200
Different (O'Neill), 283
Dill Pickle Club, Chicago, 142, 143, 163
Discussion Guild, 278
"Door of the Trap" (SA), 168, 171
Dos Passos, John, 181, 198–99, 217, 229, 273
Dostoevsky, Fyodor, 131, 157, 260
Double Dealer, 172, 187, 213, 219, 222, 225
Dreiser, Theodore, 32, 63, 93, 120, 131, 147, 182, 231, 267, 268, 271, 290, 292, 298, 299, 301, 323; relations with SA, 197–98, 207, 304, 305, 306, 310; charge of criminal syndicalism, 272
Dubliners (Joyce), 115
Duchamp, Marcel, 199
Duncan, Isadora, 125
Dunne, Finley Peter, 143, 247
Dynamo (O'Neill), 265

Eastman, Crystal, 203, 319
Eastman, Max, 203, 319
East Saint Louis, Mo.: SA on, 294–95
Editors' Press Service, 320
Education of Henry Adams (Adams), 154, 155
"Egg, The" (SA), 157, 167, 171

Eisenhower, Maj. Dwight D., 276
Eliot, T. S., 46, 99, 181, 184
Elizabethon, Tenn.: labor movement in, 255–57, 259, 266, 281
Elyria, Ohio: growth and character of, 60–61; SA in, 60–83
Elyria Business College, 60
Elyria Country Club, 62, 63, 88
Elyria Evening Telegram, 83
Elyria Iron and Steel Company, 60
Emerson, John (Clifton Paden), 7, 34–35, 36, 61, 132, 138, 149–50, 159, 310, 320
Emerson, Ralph Waldo, 53, 110–11, 132, 263
Emmett, Burton, 245, 246, 247, 254, 260, 261, 285, 298, 302, 305, 310, 318
Emmett, Mary: relations with SA and Eleanor, 302–3, 310, 323
Emperor Jones (O'Neill), 311
Ephraim, Wis.: SA at, 158–59
Erik Dorn (Hecht), 143–44, 223
Eshrick, Wharton, 163, 248, 290, 291, 323
Europe: SA's critical reception in, 178–83
Evans, Ernestine, 90–91, 176
Evans, Walker, 268
"Experience" (Emerson), 111

"Factory Town" (SA), 262
Fairhope, Ala.: SA in, 163–67
Farm Security Administration, 314
Farrell, James T., 234, 280
Fascism, 74
Faulkner, William: 187, 201, 204, 231, 232, 244, 268, 292; relations with SA, 173, 180, 217–23, 227, 231–32; on SA, 220–22, 227; reviews SA, 221, 223
Fauvists, 165
Faxon, Starr, 62
Fay Stocking Company, 60
Federal Manufacturing Company, 60
Feibleman, James, 187, 213
Ficke, Arthur Davison, 87, 92, 110
Fielding, Henry, 51, 230
Fifty-seventh Street (Chicago) colonists, 87–92, 93, 98, 103–4, 105, 145
Finley, Marietta "Bab": relations with SA, 120–24, 129–30, 259, 288; correspondence with SA, 121–24, 129–30, 131, 133, 134, 148–50, 159–60, 161, 183, 186, 192, 217, 232, 238, 239, 243, 250, 255

Fitzgerald, F. Scott, 147, 171, 181, 191, 198–99, 229, 231; relations with SA, 198–99; on SA's writing, 227
Fitzgerald, H. R., 269, 270
Fitzgerald, Zelda, 198, 199
Foley, Edith, 172
Folger, Louisa, 42
Ford, Ford Madox, 183, 302
"Four Impressions" (SA), 268
Four Saints in Three Acts (Stein/Thompson), 199
Fox, John, Jr., 301
Fox Furnace Company, 60
France: SA's impressions of, 176–78
Frank, Waldo, 118, 119, 167, 173, 175, 193, 226, 273, 276, 277; on SA, 119, 120; reviews SA, 131, 132; meets SA, 132; relations with SA, 132, 137–39, 141–42, 145–46, 147, 148, 155–56, 159, 209, 310
Frank B. White Advertising Agency, 44
Franklin, Benjamin, 247
Freer Gallery, Washington, D.C., 276, 277
Freewoman, The, 90
Freud, Sigmund, 92, 105, 128, 129
"Friday Literary Review," 87, 90, 142
Friend, Julius, 187, 213
Friends of American Authors, 304
"From Chicago" (SA), 120, 137, 233
Frost, Robert, 118
Fuller, Henry, 33, 68
Funk, Charles "Andy," 248, 307

Galantiere, Lewis, 178, 179, 181, 191, 307, 309, 319
Garland, Hamlin, 33, 86
Gastonia, N.C., strike (1929), 268, 269, 278, 319
Gauguin, Paul, 161, 164, 165, 248
Gay, Marguerite, 179, 228
Geismar, Maxwell, 298
Gentlemen Prefer Blondes (Loos), 217
Geography and Plays (Stein), 180
George, Henry, 163
"Ghosts" (SA), 265
Gibran, Kahlil, 118
Gilman, Charlotte Perkins, 90, 318
Ginn, Hal, 15
Gladstone, William, 48
Glaspell, Susan, 87, 92, 203
"Godliness" (SA), 150, 151
Gorky, Maxim, 131
Gould, Jay, 53, 61
Grant, Ulysses S., 61, 241

"Great Factory, A" (SA), 271
Greear, Caroline, 235
Greear, John, 237
Greear family, 234–35, 236
Green, Paul, 309, 315
Greer, Mary, 251, 258
Gregory, Alyse, 207–8
Grotesque: A Decoration in Black and White
    (Head), 110
Gruenberg, Louis, 311

Hackett, Francis, 131, 156, 171, 185,
    319
Hahn, E. Vernon, 123, 250
Hamer, William, 5
Hamlet (Shakespeare), 80–81
"Hands" (SA), 104–8, 109, 110, 111,
    116, 118, 181, 194, 311
Hansen, Harry, 142, 262
Harcourt, Alfred, 93
Harcourt, Brace: as SA's publisher, 320,
    322, 323
Harding, Warren, 221
Hardy, Thomas, 68
Harlan County, Kty., strike, 271
Harper, Mabel, 36
Harper's, 85
Harris, Joel Chandler, 234
Harris, Julia, 234
Harris, Julian, 234
Haywood, "Big Bill," 193
Head, Lloyd, 98, 110
Hecht, Ben, 87, 89, 91, 92, 98, 102,
    142, 283; on SA, 91, 223, 321–22;
    relations with SA, 143–44, 207, 232,
    321–22
Hedgerow Theatre, Philadelphia, 290,
    305
Hello Towns! (SA), 251, 253
"Hello Yank" (SA), 183
Hemingway, Ernest, 9, 179, 181, 187,
    211, 241, 268, 300; SA meets, 172;
    relations with SA, 172–74, 181, 228,
    242, 309; parodies SA, 227–32, 242
Hemingway, Hadley, 227, 229
Henry Holt and Company, 93
Herbst, Josephine, 297
Herrick, Robert, 33
Heyward, DuBose, 226
Hicks, Granville, 280
"His Chest of Drawers" (SA), 312
Hochdoerfer, Karl, 42
Holiday (Frank), 226
Home Town (SA), 314–15

homosexuality theme, 19–20, 35–36,
    104–8, 111, 195–96, 209, 306
Hooker Settlement, 94–95, 97, 98
Hoover, Herbert, 246, 275–76, 277,
    281, 294
Horne, Bill, 172
Horses and Men (SA), 115, 193, 195, 197,
    212, 214, 221
Hosiery Worker, The, 270
"How I Came to Communism" (SA),
    274–75
Howe, Edgar W., 39, 113
Howe, Irving, 298
Howells, William Dean, 6, 17, 68, 85,
    100, 141, 209
Huebsch, Ben: as SA's publisher, 156,
    157, 158, 160, 171, 188, 191, 193,
    216–17
Hurd, Herman, 7, 28, 320
Hurd family, 7, 11, 18, 41
Huxley, Aldous, 222
Huysmans, J. K., 177

Ibsen, Henrik, 96
I Build My House (SA), 298
"I Lead a Dozen Lives" (SA), 312
Illinois Athletic Club, 86
"I'm a Fool" (SA), 217, 219
Immaturity (SA), 141–42, 150, 208
"Impressions" (SA), 201–202
Industrial Vistas (SA), 158
industrialism: SA criticism of, 150–55,
    193, 255–57, 259–61, 263–65, 267–
    82, 317
Ingersoll, Robert, 124
In Our Time (Hemingway), 228
Intent of the Artist, The, 302
International Committee for Political
    Prisoners, 271
International Harvester, 59
Is Marriage Necessary? (Bartlett), 206
"It's a Woman's Age" (SA), 262
"I Want to Be Counted" (SA), 271–72
"I Want to Know Why" (SA), 24, 157,
    167, 171

James, Henry, 141, 169
James, William, 262
"Jazz Age," 198
"Jealousy" (Faulkner), 219
Jewett, Sarah Orne, 115
John Emerson–Anita Loos Productions,
    149–50

John Lane Company: as SA's publisher, 93, 142, 156
Johns Hopkins University, 291
Jones, Jack, 142, 143, 163, 170
Jones, Llewellyn, 87
Josephson, Matthew, 273
Joyce, James, 99, 115, 156, 225; SA and, 178–79, 181, 241–42

Kaun, Alexander, 98
Kenton, Edna, 118, 119
Kirchwey, Freda, 322, 323
Kit Brandon (SA), 298–301, 309, 311
La Cathédrale (Huysmans), 177
labor movement: SA and, 255–57, 259–61, 263–65, 267–82

Ladies' Home Journal, 45
Lane, Cornelia: courtship and marriage to SA, 51–52; marital relations with SA, 53–57, 63, 70–71, 78–79, 86, 87, 94–95, 97–98, 109, 124, 189, 203, 207; birth of children, 60, 62, 64; and SA's breakdown, 78, 79, 80, 81, 82; separation from SA, 84, 97–98, 102, 103, 194; divorce from SA, 128, 211
Lane, John, 142, 156
Lane, Margaret, 52, 203, 204
Lane family, 83
Lankes, J. J., 298, 302
Lardner, Ring, 143, 173, 199, 201, 217, 228
Lasker, Albert, 48
Last of the Mohicans, The (Cooper), 17
Last of the Provincials (Geismar), 298
Lavengro (Borrow), 68
Lawrence, D. H., 156, 208, 225, 299; SA's admiration of, 263–64
League of Professional Groups for Foster and Ford, 274
Leaves of Grass (Whitman), 132
Lee, Robert E., 209
Leigh Lecture Bureau, 215
"Let's Go Somewhere" (SA), 251
Lewis, Sinclair, 113, 171, 201, 275; receives Nobel Prize, 267–68; and labor movement, 268, 269
Lewis Institute (Illinois Institute of Technology), 36
"Liar, The" (Faulkner), 219
Liberator, 203
Liberty, 299
"Lightweight, The" (SA), 49, 50
Lincoln, Abraham, 48, 61, 151, 209

Lindbergh, Charles, 265
Lindsay, Vachel, 98, 304
Lippincott, 320
Little Review, 88, 98–99, 103, 110, 122, 130, 152, 157, 158, 166, 182, 187, 197, 227, 312
"Little Room, The," 33
Liveright, Horace, 221, 228, 231, 254, 260, 284; as SA's publisher, 216–17, 233, 283; publishes Faulkner, 220; bankruptcy and death of, 298
London: SA in, 176–77, 183, 241
"Loneliness" (SA), 69–70, 119, 130
Long, Maurice, 251, 254, 298
Long-Critchfield Agency: SA at, 44–45, 46–47, 55–56, 59
Long-Critchfield Corporation Dinner: SA's speech at, 44, 49
"Loom Dance" (SA), 262
Loos, Anita, 35, 149–50, 217, 310, 318
Lovett, Robert Morss, 91
Lowell, James Russell, 247
Luhan, Mabel Dodge, 206, 264

MacArthur, Gen. Douglas, 276
Macaulay, Thomas, 54
MacDonald, Dwight, 253
"Machine Song" (SA), 262, 264, 265
MacLeish, Archibald, 321
Madrigal, Margarita, 318
Mailer, Norman, 263
Main Street (Lewis), 113, 171, 268
Maine (ship), 37
"Making Good" (SA), 44, 49
"Making It Clear" (SA), 51, 86
male friendship: SA on, 306–7
"Man and His Imagination" (SA), 302
"Man and the Book, The" (SA), 53
Man Bites Dog (Barton), 284
manhood theme, 155, 195–97, 198, 202, 223, 263–64
"Man in the Brown Coat, The" (SA), 168
"Man of Affairs, The" (SA), 49, 50
"Man's Story, The" (SA), 102–3, 194–95, 214, 215
"Man Who Became a Woman, The" (SA), 195–97
Many Marriages (SA), 167, 168, 170, 187–91, 216, 221, 223, 227, 229, 254; theme of, 187–88, 189; reception of, 191; publication and sales of, 200, 204
Marble Faun, The (Faulkner), 218
Marching Men (SA), 41–42, 71–76, 96,

Marching Men (cont.)
  129, 137, 150, 229, 284; publication
  and reviews of, 142, 144
Marcus, Lillian, 222
Marion, Virginia: SA in, 246–49, 260
Marion Democrat, 244, 245
Marion Publishing Company, 251
marriage theme, 96–97, 168–69, 188–
  92, 194–95, 223
Martí, José, 37
Mary Cochran (SA), 96–97, 126, 167,
  168
Masefield, John, 183
Masses, 92, 93, 118, 131, 145, 203;
  publishes SA, 118
Masters, Edgar Lee, 87, 110, 113, 125–
  26, 127–28, 140, 147, 157, 305
Maugham, Somerset, 161, 164, 319
Maverick, Maury, 315
McPherson, Gen. James Birdseye, 6
McPherson, William, 4
mechanization: SA's criticism of, 150–55
"Meeting South, A" (SA), 218, 282
Memoirs (SA), 12, 13, 14, 19, 22, 27, 36,
  69, 92, 104, 262, 298, 308, 318,
  319–20
Mencken, H. L., 93, 145, 157, 184,
  198, 227, 229, 310
"Men That Are Wanted" (SA), 48
Mexico: SA in, 302, 303
Mid-American Chants (SA), 135–37, 144–
  45, 150, 156, 157, 188, 316
"Mid-American Writing" (SA), 215
Millay, Edna St. Vincent, 203
"Mill Girls" (SA), 279
Mitchell, Ann, 163, 170
Mitchell, Tennessee, 87, 98, 123, 124–
  28, 203, 204, 214, 229; marriage and
  relationship with SA, 123, 127–28,
  130–31, 137–38, 145, 149, 150, 159,
  160–61, 167, 168–71, 174, 185, 186,
  191, 207, 259, 288; in Alabama, 167–
  69; work in clay, 168, 171, 211; in
  Paris, 175–76, 179; divorce from SA,
  205, 211; death of, 251–52
Mobile, Ala., 162, 213
modernism: SA and, 88–90, 212, 213
Modern Library, 217
Modern Quarterly, 275
"Modern Writer, The" (SA), 213, 215
Moley, Raymond, 293, 294, 296
Monnier, Adrienne, 179
Monroe, Harriet, 32
Montgomery Ward, 31

Moon and Sixpence, The (Maugham), 161,
  164
Mooney, Tom, 275
"Moonlight Walk, A" (SA), 312–13
Moore, George, 88
Morgenthau, Henry, 299
Morris, William, 118, 291
Morrow, Marco, 42–43, 44, 47, 50, 52,
  59
Mosquitoes (Faulkner), 218, 222
"Mother" (SA), 119, 301
Mountain Mission Associates, 260
Mumford, Lewis, 273
Muni, Paul, 284–85
Munson, Gorham, 192–93
Murphy, Gerald, 229
Murphy, Sara, 229
Murry, John Middleton, 264
Mussolini, Benito, 274
M. W. Savage Company, 101
"My Old Man" (Hemingway), 228

Nathan, George Jean, 321
Nation, 193, 277, 322, 323; on SA, 131,
  184
National Committee for the Defense of
  Political Prisoners, 271
National Packing Company, 59
National Recovery Administration, 295
Newberry Library, Chicago, 32
"New Chicago," 86–87, 91
New Deal: SA and, 292–97
New Masses, 273, 274, 280
"New Note" (SA), 99, 152
New Orleans: SA in, 186–91, 213–32,
  302, 304
"New Orleans, the Double Dealer and the
  Modern Movement" (SA), 187
New Orleans Times-Picayune, 213, 215,
  218, 219
New Republic, 149, 180, 201, 203, 238,
  243, 246, 253, 260, 264, 270, 315
New Testament, A (SA), 158, 166–67,
  188, 243
"New Testaments" (SA), 187, 204, 316
New University Club, Chicago, 86
New York: SA in, 193–202
New Yorker, 277
New York Evening Post Literary Review, 216
New York Herald, 191
New York Post, 319
New York Sun, 157
New York Times, 246

"Nice Girl," 312
Niebuhr, Reinhold, 280
Nietzsche, Friedrich, 92
Nigger Heaven (Van Vechten), 226
Nigger of the Narcissus, The (Conrad), 115
"Night in a Mill Town" (SA), 262
"Nobody Knows" (SA), 23, 116–17
"No Love" (SA), 253–54
No Swank (SA), 298
Norfeldt, Bior, 87
Norris, Frank, 68
"Not Sixteen" (SA), 312
"Novelist, The" (SA), 101, 118, 122, 137

"Oaks, The," 42–43
O'Brien, Edward J, 171, 183, 228
Of Time and the River (Wolfe), 309
"Ohio: I'll Say We've Done Well" (SA), 193
Ohio National Guard: SA in, 16, 37, 38, 39–41
Ohio Pagans (SA), 170, 187–88
O'Keeffe, Georgia, 165, 200, 201, 206, 245, 310
Olivet College, 302
O'Neill, Eugene, 226, 265, 283, 305, 311; relations with SA, 305
Oppenheim, James, 118, 132, 133
"Other Woman, The" (SA), 312, 168, 171, 312
Our America (Frank), 120
Our Town (Wilder), 290
Outlook, 251
"Out of Nowhere into Nothing" (SA), 168
Owensboro Grader and Ditcher Company, 101

Paden, Clifton (John Emerson), 7, 34–35, 36, 61, 132, 138, 149–50, 159, 310, 320
Paden family, 33
Palmer, Mamie, 299
Palos Park, Ill.: SA in, 170–74
Panama Canal, 317
"Paper Pills" (SA), 113–14
Paris: SA in, 176–82, 241
Parody Outline of History (Stewart), 228
Pater, Walter, 92, 98
Patton, George, 276
Perhaps Women (SA), 258–59, 262–68, 278, 279, 280, 283, 311; theme of, 263

Perkins, Maxwell, 227, 231, 242, 309, 320; and SA's move to Scribner's, 298, 299, 301
Peters, Rollo, 283
Pfeiffer, Pauline, 229
Phantasmus, 214
Phelps, William Lyon, 131, 157
Picasso, Pablo, 177, 229
Pilgrim's Progress, The (Bunyan), 11
Plays (SA), 301
PM, 321
Poe, Edgar Allan, 102, 110, 194
Poetry, 98–99, 103, 137
Point Counter Point (Huxley), 222
Poor White (SA), 33, 49, 177, 183, 188, 256, 266, 284, 297, 299, 301, 311, 316; writing of, 150, 156, 157, 160, 164, 167, 168; theme of, 150–55, 167; publication and reviews of, 171, 183; Modern Library edition, 217
post-Impressionists, 165
Pound, Ezra, 99, 179, 181, 184
Powys, Llewellyn, 198
Prall, David, 207, 211, 212
Prall, Elizabeth: and Faulkner, 203, 217, 220; lifestyle in New York, 203–4; meets SA, 204; in Reno, 207; marriage to SA, 211–12; marital relations with SA, 235, 237, 242–43, 246, 249–50, 259, 319; at Ripshin, 237; and Joyce, 241–42; travels to Europe with SA, 241–43; separation and divorce from SA, 249–50, 302
Princeton University, 302
Prisoner's Relief Fund, 273
Progress and Poverty (George), 163
Prohibition, 198
Purcell, Waldo, 83–84
Puzzled America (SA), 295, 297, 298, 301

"Rabbit-Pen, The" (SA), 84–85, 89
Radin, Dorothea Prall, 211
Radin, Max, 211, 246
Radin, Rhea, 211, 212
Ramsey, Fedya, 98
Rankin, Annette, 147
Ransom, John Crowe, 187, 267, 302
Rascoe, Burton, 157, 198
Reader, The: SA's writings for, 53, 65
Reader's Digest, 317
Redbook, 312
Rendueles, Roberto, 320, 322
Reno, Nev.: SA in, 205–11
Renoir, Pierre Auguste, 229, 248

"Return, The" (SA), 282–83
R. H. Lane and Company, 51
Richardson, Samuel, 32
Ripshin, 236–38, 239, 240, 246, 249,
    250, 259–60, 284, 285, 289, 303,
    307, 308, 309, 310; building of, 236–
    38, 239, 240, 249
Robinson Crusoe (Defoe), 11, 18
Rodin, Auguste, 176, 229
Rolland, Romain, 118
Romany Rye, The (Borrow), 68
"Roof-Fix," 60, 61, 84
Roosevelt, Eleanor, 321
Roosevelt, Franklin D., 281, 319; SA's
    enthusiasm for, 292–97
Roosevelt, Theodore, 48
Rorty, James, 273
Rosenfeld, Paul, 118, 148, 165, 193,
    199, 201, 202, 210, 223, 281, 282;
    character of, 174–75; relations with
    SA, 174–75, 185, 192, 206, 207,
    208, 244, 281–83, 291, 307, 308,
    310, 319, 323; travels to Europe with
    SA, 174–83; collects and publishes SA's
    Memoirs, 308
"Rot and Reason" (SA), 47
Round Table Club, 62, 68, 90, 94, 142,
    189
Ruskin, John, 291
Russell, Bertrand, 278

"Sad Horn Blowers, The" (SA), 195
Saint Petersburg, Fla.: SA in, 251, 254–
    55, 259, 261
Sandburg, Carl, 38, 87, 136–37, 147,
    206
Saroyan, William, 321; on SA, 216
Sartor Resartus (Carlyle), 64
Saturday Evening Post, 45
Saturday Review (British), 183
Saturday Review of Literature, 311
Schevill, Ferdinand, 252, 254, 281, 307,
    310, 319, 320
Schreiner, Olive, 90
Schuster, Max, 320
Scribner's, 240, 242, 267; as SA's
    publisher, 298, 299, 301
Sears, 31
Secession, 192
"Seeds" (SA), 139–40, 167
Sell, Harry Blackman, 142
Sergel, Roger, 207, 240, 241, 254, 284,
    286, 289, 306, 307, 310, 314, 315,
    318

Seven Arts, 174–75, 206, 209, 227; SA
    and, 118, 119, 132–34, 135, 145–48;
    publishes SA, 119–20; reviews SA,
    131–32
sexuality theme, 20–28, 35–36, 55–56,
    72, 73, 105–6, 139–40, 153–54, 194–
    95, 263
Shakespeare and Company, Paris, 179
Sharpe, Willy Carter, 299
Shaw, Bernard, 54
Sherwood Anderson and Other Creoles
    (Faulkner), 221–22
Sherwood Anderson Reader (ed. Rosenfeld),
    308
Sherwood Anderson's Notebook, 199, 233
"Sherwood Anderson to Theodore Dreiser"
    (SA), 293
Shute, Frances, 76–77, 82, 89
"Silent Men" (SA), 48
Simmons, Harry, 42, 43
"Single Taxers," 163
"Sister" (SA), 100, 118
Sister Carrie (Dreiser), 63, 299
Skinner, B. F., 298
Slave Cabin Jubilee Singers, 6
"Small Boy Looks at His World, A" (SA),
    233
Smart Set, 137, 157
Smith, Doodles, 172
Smith, Katy, 172
Smith, Y. K. (Kenley), 172, 173, 307
Smyth County News, 244
socialism: SA and, 267, 271, 273
Soldier's Pay (Faulkner), 220
"Solicitor, The" (SA), 47
Songs and Sonnets (Masters), 126
Sons and Lovers (Lawrence), 225, 299
"Sophistication" (SA), 117, 244
South America: SA travels to, 315, 317–
    22
Spanish-American War, 10, 73; SA in,
    37–41, 323
Spear, Russell, 307
Spirit of Modern French Letters, The (Frank),
    132
Spoon River Anthology (Masters), 12, 110,
    113, 157
Sportsman's Sketches (Turgenev), 115
Spratling, William, 218, 222, 236–37,
    250, 302, 319
Springfield, Ohio: SA in, 41–43
"Statement of Belief: The 'Credos' of
    America's Leading Authors" (*The
    Bookman's*), 114

Steichen, Edward: photographs SA, 227
Stein, Gertrude, 198, 199, 201, 202, 228, 229, 262, 298, 318; influence on SA, 50, 92, 99–100, 279; relations with SA, 179–81, 188, 191, 198, 199, 201, 202, 207, 208, 215, 241, 242, 249, 310; on SA's *Puzzled America*, 297; American tour, 302
Steinbeck, John, 309
Steiner, Edward, 42
Stettenheimer family, 319
Stevens, Wallace, 46
Stevenson, Robert Louis, 54
Stewart, Donald Ogden, 228
Stieglitz, Alfred, 175, 248, 254; relations with SA, 200–202, 206, 207, 212, 236, 245, 310; photographs of SA, 208
Stone, Phil, 217, 218
Story, 311
Story of a Country Town, The (Howe), 39, 113
Story Teller's Story, A (SA), 34, 116, 178, 182, 208–11, 214, 215, 217, 220, 221, 238, 298, 310
"Story Writers, The" (SA), 101, 118
"Strength of God, The" (SA), 118
Strettheimer, Ettie, 199
Strettheimer, Florine, 199
Stryker, Roy, 314, 315
Studies in Classic American Literature (Lawrence), 225
Studs Lonigan (Farrell), 234
Sullivan, Henry Stack, 28
Sullivan, Louis, 31, 32
Sunwise Turn, The, New York: SA's painting exhibit at, 165
Swift, Jonathan, 51
Swinnerton, Frank, 241
Szold, Bernadine, 229, 252

Talbot Whittingham (SA), 29, 101–3, 107, 194
"Tandy" (SA), 310
Tar: A Midwest Childhood (SA), 6, 12, 15, 20, 24, 233, 234, 235, 240, 287
"Tar's Wonderful Sunday" (SA), 233
Tate, Allen, 187
Taylor-Critchfield: SA at, 83, 86–87, 94, 98, 101, 103, 106, 109, 114, 122, 148, 159, 172, 192, 260
"Ten Grotesques" (Ficke), 110
Tender Buttons (Stein), 100
Tennessee Valley Authority (TVA), 296
Tennyson, Alfred, Lord, 11, 53

Thackeray, William, 96
"That Sophistication" (SA), 283
"There She Is — She Is Taking Her Bath" (SA), 283
"They Come Bearing Gifts" (SA), 221
"They Married Later" (SA), 301
They Shall Be Free (SA), 284
This Side of Paradise (Fitzgerald), 171
Thomas, Norman, 281
Thompson, Virgil, 199
Three Soldiers (Dos Passos), 198
Three Stories and Ten Poems (Hemingway), 228
Thurber, James, 266
Tichenor, John, 18
Tietjens, Eunice, 88, 98
Titus, Robert, 98
Today, 293–95
Toklas, Alice B., 179, 181, 242, 249, 302
Toledo, Ohio, 4
Tolstoy, Leo, 96, 131, 157
Toomer, Jean, 187, 207, 225–26
Torrents of Spring (Hemingway), 227–32, 242
Trade Union News, 270
Trilling, Lionel, 297
"Triumph of a Modern, The" (SA), 193
Triumph of the Egg, The (SA), 115–16, 139, 167, 168, 188, 210, 226, 312–13; publication and reviews of, 184; sales of, 186; dramatization of, 283, 301
Tucson, Ariz.: SA in, 302
Turgenev, Ivan, 115, 131, 173, 228, 311
Twain, Mark, 131, 141, 146, 177, 209
"Two Lovers" (SA), 312
"291" gallery, 175

Ulysses (Joyce), 179, 225, 241
"Undeveloped Man, The" (SA), 50–51, 58
Union Pier, Ill.: SA at, 97, 98, 103
United Factories Company: SA and, 58–60
University of Chicago, 32, 87
"Untold Lie, The" (SA), 114, 119, 312
Unwelcome Man, The (Frank), 132, 145
Updike, John, 113
"Up in Michigan" (Hemingway), 228

"Vacation Story, A" (SA), 47
Van Gogh, Vincent, 248, 267
Van Vechten, Carl, 198, 199, 226

Vanderbilt, Cornelius, 61
Vanity Fair, 172, 226–27, 271; SA
    contracts for articles with, 240, 283
Veblen, Thorstein, 87
Vorse, Mary Heaton, 319

Walden Book Store, Chicago: SA's
    painting exhibit at, 165
Wallace, Henry, 293–94, 320–21
Wallace's Farmer, 293
Washington Daily News: interviews SA,
    301
Weeks, Edward, 319
Weller Manufacturing Company, 60
Wells, H. G., 61, 96
Wells College, 302
Wertel, Frank, 41
West, Rebecca, 184
Westcott, Glenway, 88
Western Automatic Machine Screw
    Company, 60
"When the Writer Talks" (SA), 215–16
White, Trillena, 42–43, 53, 68–69, 85,
    122, 320
White, William Allen, 200, 314
White Top Folk Festival, 308
Whitman, Walt, 19, 92, 96, 101, 118,
    131–32, 137, 141, 166, 178, 217,
    262
Why I Am a Socialist (SA), 61
Wilder, Thornton, 290, 322
Williams, William Carlos, 46, 184
Wilson, Edmund, 176, 217, 228, 273
Winchell, Walter, 284
Windy McPherson's Son (SA), 10, 14–15,
    19–20, 29, 66–68, 71, 75, 76, 91,
    92, 93, 96, 97, 131–32, 141, 142,
    150, 169, 271, 297, 310; publication
    and reviews of, 131
Wine of the Puritans, The (Brooks), 132
Winesburg, Ohio (SA), 10, 30, 42–43,
    109–22, 127, 130, 132–33, 140, 141,
    171, 173, 188, 221, 226, 227, 232,
    243, 253, 256, 275, 297, 310, 316;
    dedicated to SA's mother, 13; "Nobody
    Knows," 23, 116–17; "Loneliness,"
    69–70; "Hands," 104–8, 109, 110,
    111, 116, 118; literary form of, 111–
    12, 114–15; "Adventure," 112; "Paper
    Pills," 113–14; "The Untold Lie," 114;
    theme of, 116–17; "An Awakening,"
    116–117; "Sophistication," 117;
    publication and reviews of, 118, 156–
    57, 216; "Godliness," 150, 151;
    French translation of, 179; sales of,
    186; Modern Library edition, 217;
    dramatization of, 283–84, 290–91,
    298
Wittenberg Academy, Springfield, Ohio:
    SA at, 41–43, 51, 72
Wolfe, Thomas, 231, 232; relations with
    SA, 309–10
womanhood theme, 139–40, 153–54,
    197, 224–25, 263–66
Woman's Home Companion, 42, 43, 172,
    233
Women as World Builders: Studies in Modern
    Feminism (Dell), 90, 96
women's movement, 90, 124, 126
Woodhull and Claflin's Weekly, 124
Woolf, Virginia: on SA, 210, 243
World Congress Against Imperialist War,
    274
World Congress Against War, 274
World War I, 159, 276; SA and, 40
World War II, 319
Worthington Manufacturing Company, 60
Wright, Don, 44–45, 172
Wright, Frank Lloyd, 98
Writers on the Left (Aaron), 280

Yale Literary Review, 253
Yerkes, Charles Tyson, 33
Young, Stanley, 320, 323
Young, Stark, 203, 237